Accounting
for Librarians

and Other Not-for-Profit Managers

Accounting for Librarians

and Other Not-for-Profit Managers

G. Stevenson Smith

American Library Association
Chicago 1983

Designed by Ellen Pettengell.
Composed by Automated Office Systems, Inc.
  in Times Roman on a Text Ed/VIP
  phototypesetting system.
Printed on 50-pound Glatfelter, a pH-
  neutral stock, and bound in
C-grade Holliston cloth
  by Braun-Brumfield, Inc.

Library of Congress Cataloging in Publication Data

Smith, G. Stevenson.
  Accounting for librarians and other not-for-profit managers.

  Includes index.
  1. Library finance.   2. Corporations, Nonprofit—
Accounting.   3. Fund accounting.   I. Title.
Z683.S6   1983   025.1′1   83-11896
ISBN 0-8389-0385-1

This book is dedicated to my mother, who
told me "be an accountant," and to my wife,
Carol, who has to live with one.

Contents

Part 2. Accounting for the Three Major Funds

Chapter 11. Combined Financial Statements and Review of Accounting Cycle   305

Part 3. An Evaluation of Financial Results

Chapter 12. Ratio Analysis   353

Chapter 13. Exercising Accounting Control   381

Appendix: Answers to Exercises

Part 1.

The Foundations of Fund Accounting

The chapters in part 1 introduce the basics of a fund accounting system in a not-for-profit organization and provide the foundation for later chapters.

1.

Where Are We Headed?

Because serious organizational consequences can result from mis-
understanding accounting reports, this book intends to eliminate
misunderstandings associated with not-for-profit (NFP) accounting.
Specifically, it explains the use of accounting systems in medium-
size public libraries. It also provides guidelines for other similar-size
organizations such as civic art centers, museums, and zoological or
botanical societies. Although the objectives of such organizations
differ, accounting transactions among them involve similar results.
Users' fees, donations, acquisitions of buildings and equipment, and
payroll accounting involve examples of similar accounting transactions. All these organizations deal with these transactions on a continual basis. Therefore, little difference exists in accounting for donations to an art center or to a library.

What Is Fund Accounting?

Accounting based on funds is the common method of accounting in
NFP organizations. Fund accounting establishes a system of accounts
within one NFP organization that exists in a group that is more or less
independent of one another. On a personal level, a family that uses a

3

fund accounting system would establish a separate checking account for each member of the family. Each checking account acts as a separately balanced account, even though each member of the family forms one unit. It is assumed that the objectives of the money in each checking account are slightly different: dad's checking account is used to support the family, and junior's account is used more for purchasing records. In this way, each family member has his or her own fund (i.e., checking account) with slightly different objectives. Organizational application of this concept results in a fund accounting system.

A fund accounting system exists when the books of an NFP organization contain several sets of separate, self-balancing account groups within the organization. Each of these separate, self-balancing account groups has a different objective and the monies in these funds are used to meet those different objectives.

At this point, a distinction should be made between the terms "fund" and "funds." A fund is a self-balancing set of accounts, and two sets of self-balancing accounts are considered to be two *funds*. In some cases, funds are a synonym for "monies." In this book, "funds" is not used to mean money. Any reference to a "fund" or "funds" will refer to a self-balancing set of accounts in an NFP organization.

Who Should Use This Book?

Although the accounting applications in this book relate to all NFP organizations, the book directs its main emphasis toward libraries. Within libraries, the book is directed at individuals *without* an extensive accounting background who work (in some manner) with an accounting system. It is not directed at the professional accountant. The director of an art center, museum, or library who is concerned about understanding the production of accounting records for decision-making purposes, as well as preparation of financial reports for the public, would also find this book very useful.

The examples in the book review the "nuts and bolts" of a fund accounting system at a very practical level. For the person who is responsible for the accounting system, it provides illustrations of "how do I do this?" For the administrator, professionally trained as a librarian or curator, it explains the basics of the fund accounting system. Also, it provides insights into financial decision making.

In summary, a person with little background in accounting will find this book useful.

What's in the Book?

This book assumes minimum knowledge of accounting and begins with the foundations of accounting: debits and credits. Readers familiar with the basic debiting and crediting of various accounts, including the budgetary accounts, can omit chapters 2 and 4. The subsequent chapters build upon the introduction of debits and credits in chapter 2; therefore, it is important to be familiar with debit and credit procedures before proceeding to subsequent chapters. A reader who is unconcerned with the mechanics of an NFP accounting system, but only with the results, can turn to the final chapters, which deal with production of the combined financial statements (chapter 11) and their interpretations (chapter 12). Chapter 13 should be of interest to this reader, as it is concerned with financial controls for internal decision making.

Completion of chapters 2 and 3, which deal with the explanation of debiting and crediting procedures and the foundations of fund accounting, respectively, leads into the use of the budgetary accounts in chapter 4. Chapter 5 explains the year-end accounting procedures which affect certain accounts. Chapters 6 through 11 deal with specific funds, their financial statements, and the typical entries in these funds. These six chapters deal with the "Harold Know Fines Library," a hypothetical case, and its accounting transactions. Chapters 12 and 13 deal with analysis of financial statements and preparation of reports for internal decision making, respectively.

Why Set Accounting Standards?

When the same accounting events are recorded differently, it creates difficulties for those who try to interpret the summarized financial results. Rules are needed to establish accepted accounting procedures. It is necessary to follow certain prescribed rules in the recording of transactions in order to understand the summarized results. For example, it would be difficult to make comparisons between baseball leagues if one league counted three strikes before a batter was struck out and another counted four strikes. The same problem arises, with more complexity, between organizations that use different methods to record the same accounting transaction.

Therefore, NFP organizations need to follow established accounting standards for correct analysis of the summarized results. In addition, certain basic principles exist in accounting, and the accounting methods used by an NFP organization should be guided by these accepted standards. This book follows the standards currently recommended for NFP organizations by the official bodies that set accounting standards in the NFP area.

Who Sets Accounting Standards for NFP Organizations?

Accounting standards in the United States are set by the Financial Accounting Standards Board (FASB), which consists of seven full-time members, supported by a staff structure. The objective of the FASB is to solve accounting problems through the establishment of accounting standards to be followed by the profession. These standards are issued through series of "Statements" by the FASB, and they represent enforceable accounting practices.

In addition to the FASB, the American Institute of Certified Public Accountants (AICPA) issues accounting guidelines to be followed through its "Statement of Position " (SOP). SOPs are not binding, like Statements issued by the FASB, but they are considered representative of the best accounting practices. The accounting for NFP organizations has been affected by SOPs.

Accounting attention has recently focused on the area described by the accounting profession as "nonprofit organizations."[1] One AICPA publication, *Accounting Principles and Reporting Practices for Certain Nonprofit Organizations,* describes the suggested methods of accounting to be followed by these NFP organizations:

Cemetery Organizations	Private Elementary
Civic Organizations	and Secondary Schools
Fraternal Organizations	Professional Associations
Labor Unions	Public Broadcasting
Libraries	Stations
Museums	Religious Organizations
Other Cultural Institutions	Research and Scientific
Performing Arts	Organizations
Organizations	Social and Country Clubs

---

1. A number of different terms have been used to describe NFP organizations. The American Institute of Certified Public Accountants has used the term "nonprofit." The Financial Accounting Standards Board, the major standard-setting body in the United States, has used the term "nonbusiness." In this book, the term "not-for-profit" is used. Regardless of which of the three terms is used, they are all considered synonyms.

Political Parties
Private and Community
Foundations

Trade Associations
Zoological and Botanical
Societies.[2]

The publication also provides examples and guidelines for the formulation of the typical financial statements used by NFP organizations. Again, it should be noted that these are *suggested* guidelines.

Many NFP organizations are required to have an audit, and audits of NFP organizations also have been affected by AICPA publications. An audit is an annual review of an NFP organization's financial records by an independent accountant to determine whether accepted accounting standards are being followed. In conjunction with the audit, an opinion is issued on the results of the audit. Audits are more fully described in chapter 3, but it should be pointed out that the AICPA has affected the performance of an audit at NFP organizations through its audit guide, *The Audits of Certain Nonprofit Organizations*.[3]

An audit guide is issued for the benefit of the independent accountant who performs an audit of the financial records of an organization. Any departures from an audit guide's procedures place the accountant in the position of being required to justify such departures. As this can be professionally embarrassing for the accountant, audit guide procedures are likely to be followed. This can affect the way accounting functions are performed at an NFP organization because of the changes suggested by the accountant to meet the audit guide's standards. The audit guide issued by the AICPA affects all organizations previously listed.

2. American Institute of Certified Public Accountants, Statement of Position 78–10, *Accounting Principles and Reporting Practices for Certain Nonprofit Organizations* (New York: AICPA, 1979), p. 18. Although most of the guidelines in the NFP area have been established by the AICPA, the Financial Accounting Standards Board (FASB) has been active too. The FASB has issued Statement of Financial Accounting Concepts No. 4, *Objectives of Financial Reporting by Nonbusiness Organizations* (Stamford, Conn.: FASB, 1980). This publication establishes a general foundation for nonprofit accounting. As such, it describes a generalized type of accounting environment for the NFP area. Outside the NFP area but closely related to fund accounting, the National Council on Governmental Accounting (NCGA) has issued the most recent edition of *Governmental Accounting, Auditing, and Financial Reporting* (Chicago: Municipal Finance Officers Association, 1980). This book describes recommended accounting procedures for state and local governments.

3. American Institute of Certified Public Accountants, *Audits of Certain Nonprofit Organizations* (New York: AICPA, 1981).

2.

Those Pesky Debits and Credits

The beginning of fund accounting starts with analysis of transactions that affect the organization. A transaction is an event, occurring inside or outside the organization, which requires a change in the accounting records. A simple example is the receipt of cash by the organization. This process of analyzing and recording transactions, referred to as "transaction analysis," involves analysis of a transaction for its accounting effect on the organization. Analysis begins with the concept of debits and credits, but before this consideration, several preliminary terms and concepts must be explained. In addition, the fund accounting cycle is described.

An account summarizes all the dollar changes that affect a specific accounting category. It provides an easy way to determine the total dollar amount in an account classification. For example, it summarizes all the debits and credits affecting "Cash." It refers to a specific summarization, such as the "Cash *account,*" or to a more generalized summarization, such as the "Asset *accounts.*" Through the use of an account, we know the total dollar amount in the Cash account, or "how much cash we have left."

Next, an explanation is provided for the term "entity" in an accounting sense. The term describes several relationships in a fund accounting system. Basically, it defines the territorial separation of one accounting system from another accounting system. For example, John Smith's personal accounting system is a separate entity from Tom Brown's. If John Smith owns a business, the business accounting system is separate from his personal records. Therefore, when John Smith buys Mrs. Smith a mink coat, this transaction does not appear on the books of his business.

In a fund accounting system, the entity concept applies to separate NFP organizations (i.e., a city library and an art center). In addition to this type of external division, the entity concept has applications within one specific NFP organization. This situation occurs within the NFP organization because there are a number of separate funds, that is, self-balancing account groups. These funds represent separate accounting systems for different types of activities, almost in the same sense as separate organizational entities. One fund may represent the activities of the general operations or unrestricted resources of the organization, and this fund is accounted for separately from a fund established to account for restricted resources. Therefore, the entity concept also applies on an individual fund basis.

At this point, one more important consideration remains: the fund accounting *cycle,* which outlines the sequence of accounting procedures in the order they should be performed in a fund accounting system. Performance of these accounting steps in this sequence ensures the proper functioning of any fund accounting system. They are outlined here to provide a guide to the direction of subsequent material, and will be expanded upon and defined more extensively in subsequent chapters.

1. *Analyzing Transactions.* This process involves an analysis of source documents, such as invoices and purchase orders, to determine the proper accounts to debit and credit. This procedure also involves the accounting analysis of budgets established by the governing board which has fiscal responsibility over the NFP organization.

2. *Journalizing Transactions.* These procedures involve the recording of debits and credits in the general journal and the special journals. Journalizing transactions occur after the source documents have been analyzed. The "journalization" of a transaction is its entry point into the accounting system.

3. *Posting.* The posting process involves transferring entries from the journals to the accounts in the ledgers. The ledgers are a listing of all the accounts with their balances.

This procedure may occur less frequently than the journalizing process.

4. *Adjusting Entries and Posting.* There are certain types of accounting activities that are recorded as adjustments at the end of the fiscal year. These adjustments can be "catchup" adjustments or they can be adjustments that are necessary to correct for missing or inaccurately recorded journal entries.

5. *Preparing the Trial Balance.* The trial balance is a summation of all the balances in the accounts contained in the ledger to ensure that the debits are equal to the credits. The trial balance must be prepared prior to the preparation of the financial statements to make cetrtain that the accounts are in balance.

6. *Preparing the Financial Statements.* The monthly schedules and year-end financial statements that are prepared provide the governing board and the management of the NFP organization with an indication of performance levels during the time period under consideration. These reports are important for decision making.

7. *Journalizing and Posting the Closing Entries.* The balances in certain accounts need to be closed at the end of the fiscal year because they are temporary accounts that only relate to a specific time period. These accounts are the expense, revenue, and budgetary accounts.

8. *Preparing a Final Closing Trial Balance.* This is a year-end trial balance that is the final step in the fund accounting cycle, and it is prepared after the final closing entries have been posted to the ledger accounts. The purpose of this trial balance is to ascertain that the debits and credits in the accounts that have not been closed are in balance.

The eight-point fund accounting cycle is the sequence that should be followed periodically in any fund accounting system. The cycle is illustrated here to show the procedures that will be covered in later chapters. There are a number of new terms in the cycle, but unfamiliarity with these terms should not be a concern as they will be explained in later chapters. For now, it should be indicated that performance of the first two steps occurs more frequently than the other procedures, and the beginning chapters will concentrate on these beginning steps. The time sequence of these events is recorded in figure 2–1, where it can be seen that, after the analyzing and journal-

Steps in the Fund Accounting Cycle	7/31	8/31	9/30	10/31	11/30	12/31	1/31	2/28	3/31	4/30	5/31	6/30
Analyzing Transactions				Continual Process								
Journalizing Transactions				Continual Process								
Posting to Ledger (End of Month)	X	X	X	X	X	X	X	X	X	X	X	X
Preparing a Trial Balance	X	X	X	X	X	X	X	X	X	X	X	X
Journalizing Adjusting Entries												X
Preparing the Financial Statements												X
Journalizing the Closing Entries												X
Preparing a Final Closing Trial Balance												X

FIG. 2–1. Timetable for Executing Eight-Point Fund Accounting Cycle in an NFP Organization with a Fiscal Year Ending June 30

izing transactions, the most commonly performed accounting activities are posting and the preparing of trial balances. Although the financial statements may be prepared on a quarterly basis in a summarized form, the year-end financial statements are the major financial documents prepared for public distribution by the NFP organization. In addition, at the year-end certain closing journal entries and a final trial balance are prepared.

What's an Asset?

The fund accounting cycle lists the fundamental procedures in an accounting system, but basic to the cycle is the analysis of debits and credits. Therefore, the major portion of this chapter is devoted to analyzing the changes that occur in the accounts from debit and credit entries.

In analyzing the various types of accounts to determine how debits and credits affect them, the first step is to classify these accounts into assets, liabilities, or parts of the "Fund Balance." Assets, liabilities, and the Fund Balance represent part of the major classifications for categorizing an account. To understand the effect of debits and credits upon an account, the reader must develop the ability to classify a specific account as an asset, liability, or part of the Fund Balance.

As a first step in separating an asset, a liability, and the Fund Balance from each other, it is necessary to define the various account classifications and to provide examples of each type of account, and the analysis begins with "assets." An asset describes anything that provides a benefit to the entity. This benefit occurs in the future. For example, Cash is an asset, and its future benefit arises when the entity pays cash to reduce amounts owed to others or to make purchases. Another example of an asset is a truck or a car. Both of these vehicles provide a future benefit to the organization. The future benefit becomes available through the use of the car or truck.

Yet there has to be another stipulation with regard to assets beyond the provision of a future benefit. Specifically, the organization must legally own the asset. For example, your personal car is your asset, but your neighbor's car is not your asset, even if you have a right to use it whenever you want it. Therefore, two criteria exist for classifying an account as an asset: (1) it has to provide a future benefit to the organization and (2) legal ownership must exist.

Common examples of assets normally encountered in the NFP organization are the following:

Cash	Equipment
Accounts Receivable	Grants Receivable
Pledges Receivable	Prepaid Assets
Inventories	Due from Employees
Investments	Due from Other Governments
Land	Petty Cash
Buildings	

Not all these asset accounts occur in every NFP organization. All well-constructed accounting systems would have the more common accounts, such as Cash, Inventories, Land, Buildings, and Equipment. Along with the more common assets, some type of receivable would likely appear in a well-constructed accounting system. In the list of asset accounts are four types of receivables, each of which will be explained.

A "receivable" represents a sum of money that is due to the entity. The reason for the sum being owed to the entity can vary. With an Accounts Receivable, the sum is owed because the entity provided some type of service or transferred goods to another entity, and instead of receiving cash a claim was received. With Pledges Receivable, a money commitment, as yet uncollected, has been made to the entity by an outside party. In such a case, the outside party asks for nothing tangible in return. (Churches commonly have this account on their books.) Recognition of a Grants Receivable account indicates that grants from another organization have been awarded to the entity but not received. Usually a "grant" represents a definite dollar amount, and requires that these monies be spent in a specific manner. An example of a grant is monies awarded (but as yet uncollected from, say, the federal government) to a library to start a program for handicapped persons.

Another type of receivable is represented by the accounts Due from Employees and Due from Other Governments. As an example of the use of a Due from Other Governments account, assume that the town of Morgan lends the Morgan City Library $5,000. When the town transfers the monies to the library, two accounts are affected. The town recognizes a reduction of its cash account and, at the same time, a receivable is recognized on the town's books. The receivable is called "Due from Morgan City Library," and is an example of the use of the Due from Other Governments account. This type of account represents a very common example of a receivable. An account such as Due from Employees might be needed in an organization where employees make personal purchases through the organization's purchasing officer. In such a situation, the employee owes the organization the purchase price, and that purchase price is considered a receivable.

Prepaid Assets are an account classification that may not occur as often in an NFP organization. A prepaid asset is an expense that has been paid for before the organization uses it, and a common example is the prepayment of rent. As time passes, the prepaid rent becomes an expense and the asset is reduced.

The final asset account listed is Petty Cash, which is a subdivision of cash. Although Petty Cash acts as a subdivision of the Cash account, it is maintained separately from the Cash account. Its purpose is to pay for small, miscellaneous types of payments, such as C.O.D. deliveries. The accounting procedures for using this account are explained in chapter 7.

What's a Liability?

The next major classification of accounts relates to "liabilities." Very simply defined, liabilities are the amounts owed to others outside the specific organization or specific fund. Liabilities exist as legitimate claims against the assets of an entity, and can exist between a specific NFP organization and an external organization. In addition, a liability can exist between funds in the same NFP organization when one fund owes monies to another fund. The reason for liabilities within the funds of a specific NFP organization relates to the entity concept; that is, each fund is a separate accounting entity.

Liabilities occur in our personal finances as claims of others against us. For example, on a personal level a bank can have a claim on our assets in terms of the amount we owe on a home mortgage. An NFP organization also can owe monies to others outside the organization, but in addition the funds within an NFP organization can have liabilities between themselves. For example, assume there are two funds, Fund A and Fund B, in the same NFP organization. On May 1, Fund A borrows $100 from Fund B. As of that date, Fund A recognizes a liability on its books, and Fund B has a claim on the assets of Fund A. This $100 liability remains on A's books until a $100 repayment is made to Fund B.

Typical examples of the types of liabilities that might be found in an NFP organization are the following:

Accounts Payable
Loans Payable

Deferred Restricted Contributions
Due to Other Funds
Taxes Payable.

Remember, not all the listed accounts occur in every NFP accounting system. Whether these types of liabilities occur in a fund accounting system depends on basic decisions as to the type of system in use. (These decisions will have to await discussion in chapter 3.)

The most commonly encountered liability account is Accounts Payable, owed to those outside the organization from whom purchases of supplies, books, inventories, or services have been made. Normally, Accounts Payable are repaid within one year. Loans Payable, which act as a form of temporary financing, are also repayable within a year. Lending institutions, such as commercial banks, usually have made short-term monies available to the NFP organization if the Loan Payable account appears on the NFP's books. Another form of financing is Long-Term Debt, but usually only large NFP organizations have a Long-Term Debt account.[1] Long-Term Debt's distinguishing characteristic is the longer period available for repayment, compared with other payables.

The liability account Deferred Restricted Contributions occurs when monies are advanced to an organization in anticipation of some service the organization will perform. The organization accepts the monies with the knowledge that it must perform the service or request, but the performance itself has been delayed or "deferred." Once the monies have been accepted, the organization has an obligation to provide the service or request, and that obligation for performance is a liability. Upon completion of the service or accomplishment of the request, the liability is removed from the books.

As an example of this type of deferred liability, assume money is received by the Brooks City Library from Colonel Chesty Hammer, U.S. Army, ret., for the purchase of books on military history *only*. Once the monies are accepted by the library, it has an obligation to purchase books on military history *only*. This obligation is a liability that requires recognition on the books. Utilization of the monies

---

1. Most small to medium NFP organizations do not have the ability to raise long-term debt financing as they do not have a revenue base or the backing, in the form of a guarantee, of an organization which *does* have a revenue base. In addition, they may not have any legal authority to raise this type of monetary inflow. Therefore, long-term debt is not commonly found on their financial statements as a liability. If an asset should be used as a pledge on a loan, whether it is a short-term or long-term loan, this needs to be disclosed in the financial statements.

received for purposes *other* than the purchase of military history books can result in Col. Hammer's requesting the return of his money. Usually a legal right exists for this type of action. The Brooks City Library has not fulfilled its obligation until it has purchased books on military history up to the full extent of the monies made available by the colonel.

Another type of account in the list of liabilities is called Due to Other Funds. This liability, previously discussed with the example of Fund A and Fund B, occurs between separate funds within a specific NFP organization. Continuing the example of Funds A and B, we assume the $100 that Fund A borrowed from Fund B is recognized on Fund A's books. In such a case, a liability account, called "Due to Fund B," appears in Fund A's accounts, showing that Fund A owes Fund B $100. Monetary transfers between funds can be fairly common.

The final liability account in the list is Taxes Payable. Actually, this account represents a number of different types of taxes that are payable to the state or federal government. This group of accounts includes Federal Income Taxes Payable and Employer's FICA Taxes Payable. The latter liability is more commonly known as "social security taxes." In chapter 7, the material on payroll accounting includes explanations on how to account for these taxes.

What's the Fund Balance?

Of the three major account classifications now under consideration, the last one is the Fund Balance. A residual account, it develops because of the difference between assets and liabilities. The Fund Balance functions as both a residual between the assets and liabilities and the account where the summarization of each year's difference between the inflows of resources[2] and expenses occurs.[3] For the moment, expenses can be considered as the outflow of resources.

If any monies are available in the Fund Balance, the organization can usually use some of it for its operational expenses.[4] When expenses during a year are higher than resource inflows, a decrease in the Fund Balance occurs. Conversely, resource inflows that are larger than

2. For the moment, consider the inflow of resources to be revenues.

3. Those familiar with the workings of a fund accounting system will recognize that other factors besides the differences between expenses and revenues can cause changes in the Fund Balance account. One such factor is the difference between estimated revenues and appropriations.

4. It should be noted that there may be restrictions on the amount of the Fund Balance that can be used for current operations. These restrictions are discussed in a later chapter.

expenses (during a year) cause an increase to occur. In effect, the Fund Balance provides a place for recording the difference between resource inflows and expenses. The concept of the Fund Balance as a residual account is further developed in the following section.[5]

The Bookkeeping Equation

Although the relationship between assets, liabilities, and the Fund Balance has been hinted at in the previous explanations, the "bookkeeping equation" explicitly sets forth that relationship. The equation is presented in figure 2–2, and, as illustrated, it can be used in several forms.

(A) Assets	=	Liabilities	+	Fund Balance
(B) Fund Balance	=	Assets	−	Liabilities
(C) Liabilities	=	Assets	−	Fund Balance

FIG. 2–2. The Three Forms of the Bookkeeping Equation

The equation usually appears as shown in A. The form of equation B illustrates the meaning attached to considering the Fund Balance as a residual between the assets and liabilities. In equation B, if the liabilities are larger than the assets, the Fund Balance would have a negative balance; that is, it would be "in the hole."

The equations illustrate the importance of reaching a correct balance in the account classification and the problems that arise from an "out-of-balance" account. Asset totals have to equal the total of liabilities and the Fund Balance for the books to be in balance. For example, if the assets are equal to $100,000 and the Fund Balance is equal to $25,000, the liabilities should be equal to $75,000.[6] The

5. In a commercial enterprise, the Fund Balance is called the "equity," and it is considered to be the amount of monies available to the stockholders. Therefore, the owners of the business consider increases in the equity to be a good sign. In an NFP organization, no such meaning attaches to the Fund Balance. The reason for the different connotation arises because of the differences in the goals of the two organizations, i.e., profits versus service objectives. Of course year-after-year deficits for an NFP organization could signify problems if no new sources of monies are located. This situation is represented by a Fund Balance having a debit balance, i.e., being "in the hole."

6. This equation assumes the use of an accrual accounting system (see chapter 3.) Otherwise, under a cash system, no liabilities are recognized, and the bookkeeping equation becomes: Assets = Fund Balance.

problems in exercise 2–1 continue this example (working these problems will facilitate familiarity with the bookkeeping equation).

Exercise 2–1. The bookkeeping equation
          (Answers are in appendix at the end of the book.)

1. The Sweetwater Library has liabilities of $35,000 and a current Fund Balance equal to $40,000. How much does it have in assets?

2. The Henry County Art Center wants to know how much is available in its fund balance. It has assets of $45,000 and liabilities of $45,000. Determine the amount in the Fund Balance.

3. The Maryland Tulip Society has assets of $55,000 and a Fund Balance equal to $15,000. Determine the amount of liabilities.

4. The Fayetteville Cultural Center has assets of $15,000 and liabilities of $17,500. What is the amount in the Fund Balance? What does this balance mean?

5. Assume that the assets and liabilities of the Sexton City Library have been certified to be $25,000 and $15,000 respectively. Further assume the bookkeeper is unsure of the amount that is supposed to be in the Fund Balance. The records show the Fund Balance is equal to $8,000. Is this the correct balance?

Another use of the bookkeeping equation is to introduce the concept of debits and credits and the manner in which they affect the assets, liabilities, and the Fund Balance. It is very important to understand how to debit and credit accounts, before additional accounting procedures can be appreciated.

Analyzing Debit and Credit Changes in Assets and Liabilities

There is a story about an accounting instructor who, in exasperation from trying to explain debits and credits to his class, finally told them that debits appear on the left side of the classroom, by the door, and credits appear on the right side, by the windows. In the following explanation of debits and credits, the bookkeeping equation and "T accounts" will serve in place of windows and doors.

The T account is used for illustrative purposes, to represent an account. It receives its name from the form it takes, the shape of a T.

The debits, abbreviated "Dr.," appear under the left part of the T, and the credits, abbreviated "Cr.," on the right side. The name of the account appears across the top of the T. Figure 2–3 is an illustration of a T account for Cash.

Cash
Dr. | Cr.

Fɪɢ. 2–3. The "T" Account

Before we use the T account, the term "balance" needs to be defined, and "balance of an account" summarizes it. The balance is found by subtracting the sum of one side from the sum of the other. If the account is an asset, as in figure 2–3, a debit increases the balance in the account and a credit decreases the balance. With the Fund Balance or a liability, a debit decreases the balance and a credit increases it. This relationship is illustrated in figure 2–4.

Effect of:	Assets	=	Liabilities	+	Fund Balance
Debits	+*		−		−
Credits	−		+*		+*

* "Normal" balance

Fɪɢ. 2–4. Summary of Effect of Debits and Credits on Assets, Liabilities, and Fund Balance

In work with account balances, it is common practice to refer to the "normal balance," which refers to the type of balance commonly found in an asset, liability, or the Fund Balance. (The normal balances have been marked with an asterisk in figure 2–4.) In figure 2–4 the normal balance for assets is a debit balance, whereas the normal balances for liabilities and the Fund Balance are credit balances.

The relationship in figure 2–4 is not difficult to remember. If the effect of debits and credits on assets is kept in mind, the effect on liabilities and the Fund Balance occurs in the opposite order. The more difficult part of this analysis relates to understanding the effect of transactions on the accounting system. (As previously stated, this is described as "transaction analysis.")

Using Transaction Analysis with Assets and Liabilities

Two transactions will be analyzed to determine the effect of debits and credits upon assets and liabilities, involving the inflow and outflow of cash. After the transactions have been analyzed, review exercises provide readers a chance to test their understanding.

TRANSACTION 1

In this transaction, Overdrew City Library receives cash deposits from patrons who check out video equipment and cassettes for home use. These deposits are returned to the patrons when the video equipment and cassettes are brought back into the library (the receipt and repayment of deposits is a continual process during the year). For illustrative purposes, assume the library collects and repays a $50 deposit. The following transaction analyzes the collection and repayment of this deposit. If, in an actual accounting system, these types of deposits are a fairly common occurrence, they are recorded in total on a daily basis in the books.[7]

(It is unlikely that one deposit would be recorded, as shown here. Also, it is important to know the organizational viewpoint from which the transaction is analyzed. In other words, is the viewpoint from Overdrew City Library or the depositor's accounting system? In this case it is obvious that attention is focused on the library's accounting system, but in other instances the distinction is not as clear.)

The process of transaction analysis begins with a series of questions, the answers to which provide the proper debits and credits to a transaction. The procedure is followed with each transaction in the remaining portions of this chapter.

The following analysis is useful for anyone who is beginning to classify debits and credits.

Questions	*Answers*
1. What is the library receiving or giving up?	1. The library is receiving Cash.
2. Is Cash an asset, liability, or part of the Fund Balance?	2. Cash is an asset.

---

7. A record separate from the accounting records is kept regarding the deposit and the patron who made it.

3. Is Cash increasing or decreasing?   3. Increasing.

4. What registers an increase in an asset?   4. A debit.

5. Is another asset affected?   5. No.

6. Is a liability affected?   6. Yes. (See following explanation.)

7. Is the Fund Balance affected?   7. No.

8. Is a liability increasing or decreasing?   8. Increasing.

9. What registers an increase in a liability?   9. A credit.

Transaction analysis is a step-by-step procedure that allows the investigator to determine which accounts are affected and how they are affected. Notice that in question 6 it was determined that the amount to be repaid to the depositors was a liability, but in question 7 the effect on the Fund Balance was still investigated. This is an important question because more than one debit or credit may occur in a single transaction. Assets must equal liabilities and the Fund Balance, but this does not mean that only one credit or debit change occurs in every transaction. *More* than one debit or credit change can occur.

Through transaction analysis it is determined that the Cash account[8] is debited and a liability account (as yet unnamed) is credited. Although it is obvious that the deposit affects the Cash account, the question may arise as to why a liability account is affected. To understand this, it must be remembered that the $50 deposit must be repaid when the patron brings the video equipment and cassettes back to the library, which has a legal obligation to return the deposit. Therefore, the deposit is a liability the library owes the patron upon receipt of the undamaged equipment and cassettes. This type of liability could simply be called "Video Room Deposits" or "Deposits Payable."

From a learning viewpoint, it is important to understand the effect of debits and credits on the bookkeeping equation. For this purpose, the bookkeeping equation is reviewed after each transaction to ascer-

---

8. The deposits can be maintained in an account separate from the Cash account, for example, Cash—Deposits.

tain that it remains in balance and to investigate the changes that have occurred in the accounts. (This is not the normal operating procedure in an actual accounting system.)

Figure 2–5 contains the changes in the bookkeeping equation for the transaction just reviewed. Assume that the library had only a Cash asset of $10,000 before the $50 deposit was left with the library. In such a case, the bookkeeping equation would appear as shown in figure 2–5, equation 1.

1. Assets	=	Liabilities	+	Fund Balance
$10,000		$0		$10,000

2. Assets	=	Liabilities	+	Fund Balance
$10,050		$50		$10,000

FIG. 2–5. Bookkeeping Equation after Deposit Is Recorded

After the library receives the deposit, its Cash balance increases by $50, and at the same time the liability balance also increases by $50. This is apparent in figure 2–5, equation 2. The bookkeeping equation is in balance both before and after the transaction. As previously stated, checking the bookkeeping equation after each transaction is not practical, but periodically, in all accounting systems, the debits and credits must be balanced against one another to determine if they are equal. This is done through use of a "trial balance" (which is explained later).

This analysis also can be shown through T accounts, which show how the balances in the asset and liability accounts change through the entry of debits and credits to those accounts. The first set of T accounts (figure 2–6) represents the situation prior to receipt of the deposit. The second set of T accounts shows the balances after the deposit has been received. When T accounts are used for the analysis, an asset and liability account needs to be specified for recording the debit and credit entry. In this case, the asset account Cash and the liability account Deposits Payable are used.

The $50 deposit appears in the Cash account as a debit of $50, which increases the Cash balance to $10,050. The liability account, Deposits Payable, also increases as a result of the credit entry to $50. Yet, as the bookkeeping equation showed, the debits and credits are equal.

Before Receipt of Deposit

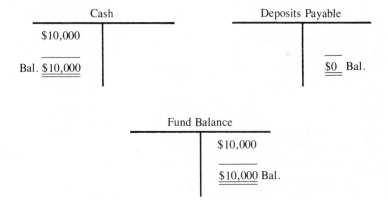

After Receipt of Deposit

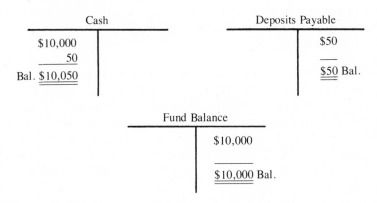

FIG. 2–6. T Account Analysis of Receipt of Deposit

TRANSACTION 2

In this transaction, assume that the patron returns the undamaged equipment and cassettes to Overdrew City Library within the loan period. At that time, the library must return the deposit to the patron. Another transaction has occurred, and is analyzed through transaction analysis.

Questions	*Answers*
1. What is the library receiving or giving up?	1. The library is giving up Cash.
2. Is Cash an asset, liability, or part of the Fund Balance?	2. Cash is an asset.
3. Is Cash increasing or decreasing?	3. Decreasing.
4. What registers a decrease in an asset?	4. A credit.
5. Is another asset affected?	5. No.
6. Is a liability affected?	6. Yes.
7. Is the Fund Balance affected?	7. No.
8. Is a liability increasing or decreasing?	8. Decreasing.
9. What registers a decrease in a liability?	9. A debit.

Through the transaction analysis procedure, a determination is made that a liability account, in this case Deposits Payable, is debited and the asset account, Cash, is credited. The next step is to review the changes in the bookkeeping equation.

After transaction 1, the bookkeeping equation appears as shown in equation 2 in figure 2–7. The changes from the debiting and crediting entries in transaction 2 cause Cash to decrease and the repayment of an obligation through decrease in the liability account, Deposits Payable, to occur. After these changes are reflected in the bookkeeping equation, the equation appears as equation 3 in figure 2–7. Overdrew City Library's accounts have returned to their original balances, prior to receipt of the deposit.

2. Assets	=	Liabilities	+	Fund Balance
$10,050		$50		$10,000
3. Assets	=	Liabilities	+	Fund Balance
$10,000		$0		$10,000

FIG. 2–7. Bookkeeping equation before and after Return of $50 Deposit

The T accounts, with the transactions recorded in them, appear in figure 2–8. These T accounts provide a summary of all transactions from receipt of the deposit to its return.

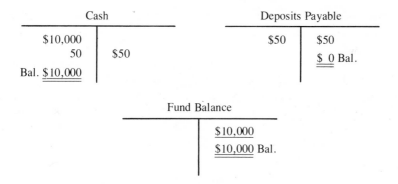

FIG. 2– 8. T Account Analysis of Return of Deposit

Exercise 2–2. Debiting and Crediting Assets and Liabilities

1. Green County Library purchases book shelving for $1,200 in cash. Determine the account classification(s) to debit and credit. What are the names of these accounts?

2. Macomb City Library also purchased $1,200 worth of book shelving, but this shelving was purchased on 30-day credit terms. Determine the account classification(s) to debit and credit. What are the names of these accounts?

3. Took City Library received $2,500 from a patron's estate. The money is to be used specifically for programs for senior citizens. Determine the account classification(s) to debit and credit. What are the names of these accounts?

4. Carter Art Center recently lost a large share of its funding. To continue to operate in the current year, it has received a $17,000 loan from an affiliation of local businesses. It is anticipated that the loan will be repaid when funding is restored. Determine the account classification(s) to debit and credit. What are the names of these accounts?

What Are Revenues and Expenses?

Up to this point, the illustrated transactions have not affected the Fund Balance. As previously stated, the Fund Balance acts as a residual between assets and liabilities. In addition, any increases or decreases in the Fund Balance from one year to the next are attributed to two other account classifications: revenues and expenses. The relationship between the Fund Balance and all these accounts is illustrated in figure 2–9. The Fund Balance is shown as a residual between assets and liabilities. At the same time, the current increase in the Fund Balance occurs because the revenues are more than the expenses. Therefore, the Fund Balance acts as a connecting point between assets, liabilities, revenues, and expenses. (The accounts that create a yearly increase or decrease in the Fund Balance are considered next.)

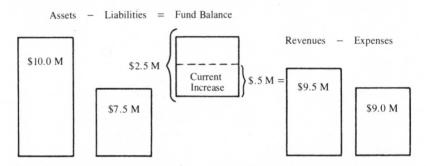

Fɪɢ. 2–9. The Fund Balance is equal to the portion of assets that exceed liabilities. At the same time, current increase in the Fund Balance is due to excess of revenues over expenses.

Basically, "revenues" are considered inflows of resources to the organization that increase the Fund Balance; whereas "expenses" cause reductions in resources and reduce the Fund Balance. Expenses also provide a benefit to the current fiscal period. Expenses are recorded in the accounts at the time a legal obligation is incurred for payment. This may not occur at the same time that the expense is paid for with cash; that is, the legal obligation may be incurred before the cash flows out of the organization.

Before we explore the characteristics of revenues, it is necessary to recognize a distinction between the terms "expenditures" and "expenses." A fundamental difference exists between the two terms, and they should not be confused. Expenditures cause a reduction in resources and decreases in the Fund Balance to occur, but they include a broader classification of transactions than those included under an expense classification. In addition, expenses are considered to be those reductions of resources that benefit the current reporting period only. The range of resource reductions that occur under the expenditure concept benefits the current period as well as future periods. Therefore, the term "expenditure" includes all expense classifications.

The basic question that surrounds expenses and expenditures is when will the decrease in the Fund Balance occur? One fundamental difference that illustrates this question of timing between the two methods relates to the manner in which the purchase of assets is handled. For example, under the expense concept the purchasing of an automobile increases an asset account called Vehicles and decreases an asset account called Cash. It is assumed that some sort of benefit will be received from the new car as it is used by the organization. As those benefits are received—that is, its use—there are periodic changes called expenses made against the Fund Balance over the life of the car. Therefore, the charges against the Fund Balance are made as the car's benefits are provided to and used by the organization. Those readers more familiar with this accounting technique will recognize it as depreciation. Depreciation will be explained on pages 238–41.

When the expenditure concept is adopted and an automobile is purchased, an expenditure account is increased for the entire purchase price of the car at the time it is purchased, and the Cash account is decreased by an equal amount. The expenditure approach charges the entire purchase cost of the automobile against the Fund Balance during the fiscal year the car is purchased, and it does not allocate expenses to the Fund Balance as the benefits are received from the use of the car. In this book, the expense concept is used with all its implications rather than the expenditure concept.

Expenses are classified in an NFP organization on either a functional or an object basis. Typical examples of the types of expense classifications under these two methods are shown in figure 2–10.

Object Classification	Functional Classification
Maintenance	A. Libraries:
Supplies	Circulating Library
Personnel Services	Audio-Visual Library
Books and Standing Orders	Children's Library
Publicity	Regional History Library
Miscellaneous Expenses	Community Services
Professional Fees	
Telephone	B. Art Center or Museum:
	Publicity
	Exhibits
	Fellowships
	Crafts Education

FIG. 2–10. These classifications separate expenses according to the expense of the object or function.

The types of expense accounts used depend on the decision-making needs of the administrators in the entity as well as the needs of outside monitoring agencies. For example, an agency that provides a grant could act as a monitoring agency and require the filing of certain types of expense classifications relating to the grant.

As stated, revenues are generally considered an inflow of resources to the NFP organization, but revenues can be recognized without an actual inflow of revenue dollars. In addition to being an inflow of resources, revenue is not a refund of any type from previous expenses. Also, they are an inflow that occurs without creation of any form of obligation through a liability. If they are refunds or create a liability, they are *not* revenues. Revenues are recorded when resources are transferred to the NFP organization or if it is clear that the organization will receive these funds because they have been earned.[9] In the latter case, revenues are recognized although the inflow has not occurred.

Examples of typical revenue accounts vary with types of organization activities, but some common types of revenue accounts are presented in figure 2–11.

A. Library:
  User's Fees
  Book Fines
B. Art Center:
  Admission Fees
  Tuition Fees

C. Botanical Society:
  Admission Charge
  Membership Dues
D. General Revenue Sources:
  Investment Revenue
  Dividend Income

FIG. 2–11. Accounts represent types of revenue in various NFP organizations.

Exercise 2–3. Revenues and Expenditures

1. Waterford Library received cash from the following sources last month. Determine which sources are revenues.

    a) Borrowed $750 from First National Bank.
    b) Sold an old typewriter for $75 cash.
    c) Charged patrons a $2 user's fee; collected $450.
    d) Received $1,200 in interest from investments owned by the library.

9. The inflow of resources is described here as revenues. In later chapters a distinction is made between revenues and support. Revenues are earned inflows and support is recognized as those inflows that are given to the NFP organization without anything given up to receive the support. Examples of support are gifts or grants.

2. Cabell County Library completed the following transactions during the past month. Determine which involve expenditures and expenses.

    a) Paid $100 for repair work on the roof.
    b) Paid $1,200 for new duplicating machine.
    c) Brought $1,500 worth of new books.
    d) Paid $97 for cleaning supplies.

Analyzing Debit and Credit Changes in Revenue and Expense Accounts

To understand the function of revenue and expense accounts, it is necessary to understand the effect of debits and credits on them. Transaction analysis will be used to investigate the changes that occur in revenue and expense accounts.

Previously, equation A set forth the relationship between assets, liabilities, and the Fund Balance. When the effect of expenses and revenues is taken into consideration, equation A requires adjustment, and equation D incorporates that adjustment:

$$(D)\quad \text{Assets} = \text{Liabilities} + \text{Fund Balance} + \text{Revenues} - \text{Expenses}$$

A factor in this relationship that is important to recognize is shown in equation E, where the change in the Fund Balance is attributed to the difference between revenues and expenses. This change is computed on a periodic basis, usually yearly.

$$(E)\quad \text{Change in the Fund Balance} = \text{Revenues} - \text{Expenses}$$

To understand how revenues and expenses function in an accounting system, it is necessary to know the effects of debits and credits on them. A method that is useful in remembering the relationship is illustrated in figure 2–12, where expenses are shown as debits and revenues as credits. The Fund Balance account normally has a credit balance, and the effect of expenses on it is to decrease the "normal" balance, whereas the effect of revenues is to increase the "normal" balance. For this relationship to exist, expenses must normally have a debit balance. Figure 2–12 helps us remember that expenses (on the debit side of the Fund Balance) normally have a debit balance and revenues (on the credit side of the Fund Balance) normally have a credit balance. Although expenses may occasionally be credited and revenues debited, the "normal" entries for these accounts result in a debit to an expense account and a credit to a revenue account.

Fund Balance

Expenses (Dr.)	Revenues (Cr.)
−	+

FIG. 2–12. Expenses cause decreases in Fund Balance and are shown as debits; whereas revenues cause increases and are shown as credits.

These relationships are summarized in figure 2–13, where the effects of debits and credits on expenses and revenues are shown. The Fund Balance is included in the illustration so that the effects of debits and credits on the three account classifications are comparable. A comparison shows that debits and credits affect the Fund Balance account and revenues in the same manner.

Effect of:	Fund Balance	Revenue	Expenses
Debits	−	−	+*
Credits	+*	+*	−

* "Normal" balance in account

FIG. 2–13. Effects of debits and credits on Fund Balance, revenues, and expenses

Using Transaction Analysis with Revenues and Expenses

The following two transactions use the information in figure 2–13 in more detail.

TRANSACTION 3

Assume that Howl Creek Library charges an annual user's fee of $2 for each patron. The fees are charged for identification cards, which are necessary to use the library, and the library receives a total of $2,000 in user fees during the year. The technique of transaction analysis is again used to determine the proper accounts to debit and credit.

Questions	*Answers*
1. What is the library receiving or giving up?	1. Cash is received.
2. Is Cash an asset, liability, part of the Fund Balance, an expense, a revenue item?	2. Cash is an asset.
3. Is Cash increasing or decreasing?	3. Increasing.
4. What registers an increase in an asset?	4. A debit.
5. Is another asset affected?	5. No.
6. Is a liability affected?	6. No.
7. Is the Fund Balance affected?	7. Not immediately.
8. Is an expense made?	8. No.
9. Are revenues received?	9. Yes.
10. Are revenues increasing or decreasing?	10. Increasing.
11. What registers an increase in a revenue item?	11. A credit.

Transaction analysis determines that the cash received is a revenue item. The necessary entry is a debit to Cash and a credit to a revenue account, such as ''User's Fee Revenues.'' Figure 2–14 shows the effect of receipt of the $2,000 cash on the bookkeeping equation. After transaction 2, the bookkeeping equation appeared as shown in figure 2–14, equation 3. Once the effect of transaction 3 is recorded, the bookkeeping equation appears as shown in equation 4.

3. Assets	=	Liabilities	+	Fund Balance
$10,000		$0		$10,000

4. Assets	=	Liabilities	+	Fund Balance
$12,000		$0		$10,000
				+ 2,000 Rev.

FIG. 2–14. Bookkeeping Equation before and after Receipt of $2,000 Revenues from User's Fees

Although the effect of the revenues is shown as an increase in the Fund Balance account, this change does not immediately occur. This change is only transferred to the Fund Balance at the end of the year—for example, on June 30. The effect of expenses and revenues is not reflected in the Fund Balance immediately as each transaction occurs. In equation 4, this effect is recorded immediately in the Fund Balance to illustrate the relationship of revenues and expenses on the Fund Balance.

All expense and revenue accounts are considered "temporary" accounts because their balances are cleared to the Fund Balance at the end of the yearly financial period. The reason for this clearing is that the focus of expenses and revenues is related to a short period. More importantly, it makes no sense to keep totaling each year's revenues and expenses. Without a clearing of these accounts, an NFP organization's revenues and expenses are a function of how long they have been in existence. To avoid a confusing situation, each financial year's difference between all revenues and expenses is transferred into the Fund Balance. As a result, each year's revenues and expenses are viewed independently of every other year.

The assets, liabilities, and the Fund Balance are considered "permanent" because the balances in these accounts are carried on from one year to the next. The procedures for transferring the temporary account balances to the Fund Balance are explained in chapter 5, but equation 4 illustrates the effect.

T accounts summarize the effect of transaction 3 in figure 2–15. The Cash account contains the effects of transactions 1 and 2 as well as transaction 3. With the bookkeeping equation, the effect of the revenues was contained in the Fund Balance, but under T account analysis

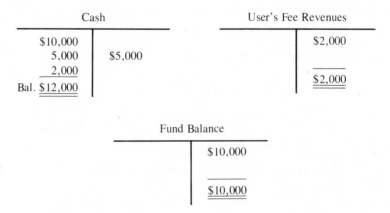

FIG. 2–15. T Account Analysis of Receipt of Revenues

a separate revenue account, User's Fee Revenue, is established. All cash received as user's fees is recorded in this account. At financial year-end, the total balance in the account is transferred into the Fund Balance account as a credit. Prior to the transfer, the bookkeeping equation, as illustrated in equation A or equation 4, will not balance.

At this point, it may appear possible to place revenues under the Fund Balance account only and avoid the complications of maintaining a separate revenue account. Although this would be possible, in the sense that debits and credits would balance, under such a system the information available about specific revenues is difficult to obtain. For this reason, it is important to maintain separate revenue accounts.

TRANSACTION 4

The only major account classification remaining to be analyzed is "expense" accounts, and they are the next consideration. In this transaction, assume the Howl Creek Library is paying $1,500 for roof repairs with a check. Transaction analysis is again used to develop the correct questions and answers about the types of accounts to debit and credit.

Questions	*Answers*
1. What is Howl Creek Library receiving or giving up?	1. Cash.
2. Is Cash an asset, liability, part of the Fund Balance, an expense or revenue item?	2. Cash is an asset.
3. Is Cash increasing or decreasing?	3. Decreasing.
4. What registers a decrease in an asset?	4. A credit.
5. Is another asset affected?	5. No.
6. Is a liability affected?	6. No.
7. Is the Fund Balance affected?	7. Not immediately.
8. Is an expense made?	8. Yes.
9. Are revenues received?	9. No.
10. Are expenses increasing or decreasing?	10. Increasing.
11. What registers an increase in an expense?	11. A debit.

The payment for the roof repairs is recorded as an expense. This transaction results in a debit to an expense, like Repairs Expense, and a credit to the Cash account. The effect on the bookkeeping equation is presented in figure 2–16. Equation 4 illustrates the bookkeeping equation prior to the payment for roof repairs, and equation 5 shows the changes after payment is made. In the equation, assets are reduced by the payment of cash. Furthermore, the expense reduces the Fund Balance account by $1,500. Yet equation 5 is in balance. The assets and the Fund Balance are both equal to $10,500. Again it should be noted that this summarization of expenses and revenues in the Fund Balance only occurs at year-end. It is presented in this manner to illustrate the effect of expenses and revenues on the Fund Balance.

4. Assets	=	Liabilities	+	Fund Balance
$12,000		$0		$10,000
				+ 2,000 Rev.

5. Assets	=	Liabilities	+	Fund Balance
$10,500		$0		$10,000
				+ 2,000 Rev.
				− 1,500 Exp.

Fig. 2– 16. Bookkeeping Equation before and after Payment of $1,500 for Roof Repairs

When this transaction is recorded in the T accounts, it is recorded in a specific account and not in a general classification, such as "assets" or "expenses." The T account analysis in figure 2–17

Cash		Repair Expense	
$10,000		$1,500	
5,000	$5,000		
2,000	1,500		
		Bal. $1,500	
Bal. $10,500			

User's Fee Revenues		Fund Balance	
	$2,000		$10,000
	$2,000 Bal.		$10,000 Bal.

Fig. 2– 17. T Account Analysis of Payment of Roof Repairs

provides the needed accounts; they are Repair Expense and Cash. Note that the Cash account carries forward all the debits and credits of previous transactions. This illustrates the summarization process that occurs in a T account. In addition, the User's Fee Revenue account is included as part of figure 2–17 because if this revenue account is excluded, the debit and credit balances in the remaining three accounts do not balance. At present, the debits and credits are equal to $12,000.

As previously stated, when a separate expense or revenue account is established, the bookkeeping equation, as shown in equation A or 5, does not balance. It is necessary to transfer the difference in the account balances between all expenses and revenues to the Fund Balance before the bookkeeping equation will balance. This transfer occurs only at the end of the financial year.

Exercise 2–4. Debiting and Crediting Revenues and Expenses

1. On the night on July 7, Twin Falls Art Center collects $975 on ticket sales to a production of *Ham & Letey* by Bill Shakepeers. Determine the account classification(s) to debit and credit. What are the names of these accounts?
2. Hanks Public Library received $3,000 in interest and dividends from its investments. Determine the account classification(s) to debit and credit. What are the names of these accounts?
3. Summitville Library recently leased a Xerox machine. The monthly rental of $300 is paid at the beginning of each month. Determine the account classification(s) to debit and credit for May 1. What are the names of these accounts?
4. Five hundred dollars worth of books were purchased *on account** by the Maysville–Wallis County Library for the Regional History Collection. Determine the account classification(s) to debit and credit. What are the names of these accounts?

*"On account" means no cash was paid.

Analyzing Transactions, Journalizing, and Posting

The bookkeeping equation and the T account analysis illustrate the effect of debits and credits on the various account classifications.

These methods are useful for illustrative purposes, but this is not the sequence of accounting procedures in a working accounting system. It is important to understand the proper sequence of accounting procedures used in an actual set of accounts. The fund accounting cycle (outlined earlier; see pp.9–10) lists the step-by-step procedures actually followed with a set of books. The first three steps in that cycle are of special concern at this point.

The first three steps in the fund accounting cycle are *analyzing* the transaction, *journalizing* it, and *posting* the journal entry to the ledger accounts. Although the bookkeeping equation is a concern when these transactions are recorded, it is not explicitly used in recording any transactions.

The first step in this series of procedures is to use transaction analysis to determine which accounts to debit and credit. (This technique is already familiar to the reader.) The second step is to record the transaction in a journal called the "general journal," where the initial entry is made for a transaction that enters the accounting system. All entries are recorded in the general journal in chronological order. The third step is to transfer the entry from the general journal to a ledger, called the "general ledger," which contains accounts that are very similar to the T accounts. The general ledger maintains all account balances for the organization in summarized form. One of its major purposes is to allow quick determination of the balance in every account in the accounting system.

In the journalizing process, specific accounts are selected to debit and credit. Examples of journal entries are illustrated in the general journal in figure 2–18, where each of the previous four transactions is journalized. They are recorded in the order they occurred in the chapter, with the date of the month corresponding with the transaction number. When an entry is made in the journal, the debit entry is always placed first; the credit entry, slightly indented, second. The entry is followed by an explanation to indicate the nature of the transaction for references at a later date, and the transaction date is recorded under the date column. The recorded date is the date of receipt of the document upon which the entry is based.[10]

Entries in the general journal are recorded in the time sequence in which they occur. This makes them very difficult to summarize according to account balances. For this summarization to occur efficiently, the journal entries are periodically transferred to the general

10. This assumes the use of an accrual accounting system and not a cash system. Under a cash system, the entries in the journal only occur when cash is paid out.

GENERAL JOURNAL

PAGE 1

Date	Items	Post. Ref.	Debit	Credit
MAY 1	CASH	10	50 —	
	DEPOSITS PAYABLE	21		50 —
	Recognition of obligation to repay patron's deposits			
MAY 2	DEPOSITS PAYABLE	21	50 —	
	CASH	10		50 —
	Repayment of deposit			
MAY 3	CASH	10	2000 —	
	USER'S FEE REVENUES	30		2000 —
	Receipt of cash for I.D. cards			
MAY 4	REPAIR EXPENSE	45	1500 —	
	CASH	10		1500 —
	Payment of roof repairs			

FIG. 2–18. Transactions 1–4 are journalized in General Journal

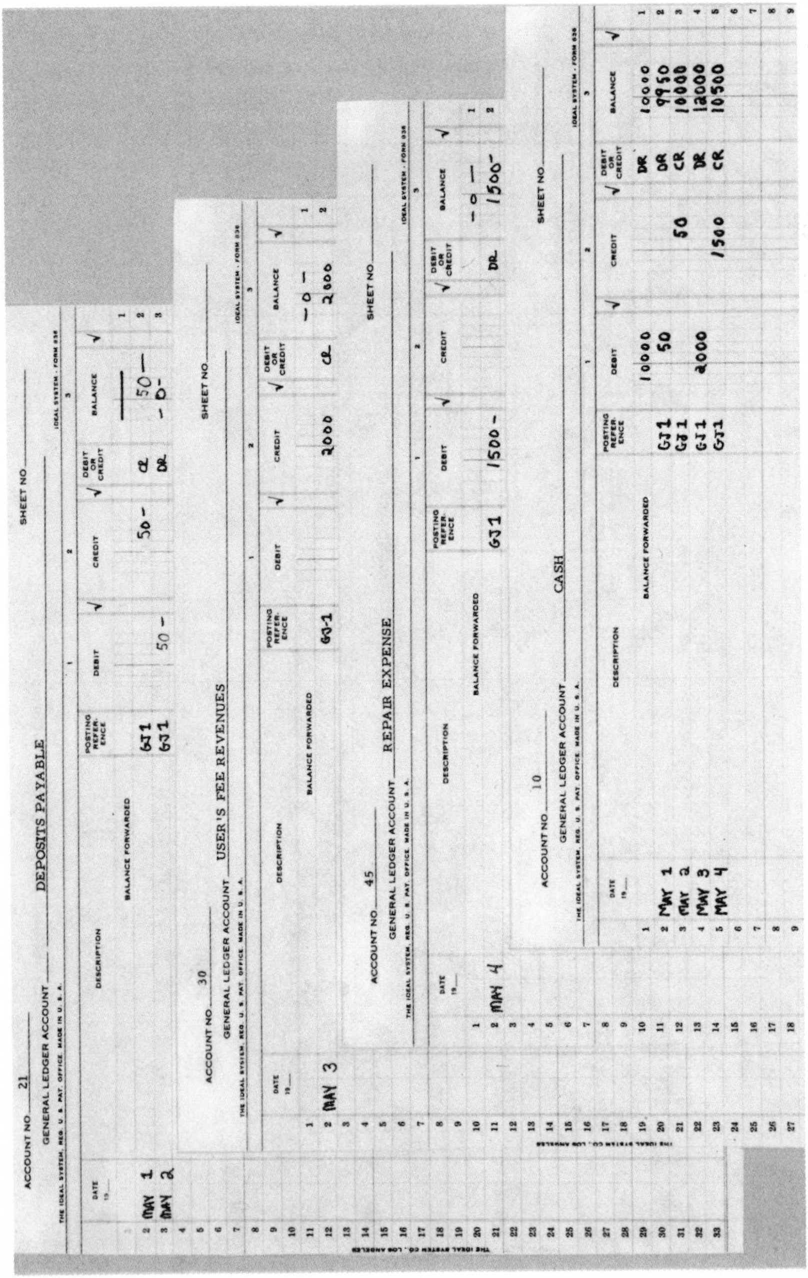

ACCOUNT NO. 21 — GENERAL LEDGER ACCOUNT: DEPOSITS PAYABLE

Date 19__	Description	Posting Reference	Debit	Credit	Debit or Credit	Balance
	Balance Forwarded					
May 1		GJ1		50-	CR	50—
May 2		GJ1	50-		DR	-0-

ACCOUNT NO. 30 — GENERAL LEDGER ACCOUNT: USER'S FEE REVENUES

Date 19__	Description	Posting Reference	Debit	Credit	Debit or Credit	Balance
	Balance Forwarded					-0-
May 3		GJ-1		2000	CR	2000

ACCOUNT NO. 45 — GENERAL LEDGER ACCOUNT: REPAIR EXPENSE

Date 19__	Description	Posting Reference	Debit	Credit	Debit or Credit	Balance
	Balance Forwarded					-0-
May 4		GJ1	1500-		DR	1500-

ACCOUNT NO. 10 — GENERAL LEDGER ACCOUNT: CASH

Date 19__	Description	Posting Reference	Debit	Credit	Debit or Credit	Balance
	Balance Forwarded				DR	10000
May 1		GJ1	10000		DR	9950
May 2		GJ1	50	50	CR	10000
May 3		GJ1	2000		DR	12000
May 4		GJ1		1500	CR	10500

FIG. 2–19. The General Ledger

ledger, which provides a summarization on an account-by-account basis so that the balances in all accounts are easy to determine. Figure 2–19 illustrates the four accounts as they appear in a general ledger. When the entries in the general journal are transferred to the general ledger, it is referred to as "posting to the general ledger." The frequency of posting depends on the number of transactions, but the longest interval between one posting and the next should be one month.

In order to use a set of books properly, cross-referencing is necessary between the general journal and the general ledger. The need for this arises any time it is necessary to trace a transaction through the books from the time it is journalized in the general journal to its entry in a specific account. (Of course, this tracing procedure is performed in the opposite direction also.) The cross-referencing procedures are presented in figures 2–18 and 2–19.

The posting-reference columns in the general ledger and the general journal (abbreviated *Post. Ref.* in the general journal) are used for cross-referencing. The posting reference from the journal to the ledger is the page number of the journal, which in this case is page 1. The cross-reference in the general ledger is shown as "G.J. 1." The ledger entry has a reference to the exact page number in the journal, as well as the date of entry in the journal. This provides a quick means of referring back to the journal from the ledger.

In the journal, the account number of the ledger account serves as the cross-referencing key. The account number is posted into the journal under the post-reference column. Here the account number for Cash is 10; for the liability, Deposits Payable, it is 21; for User's Fee Revenue it is 30; and for Repairs Expense it is 45. Before the posting process is complete, a final step ascertains that the date is recorded in the account in the ledger. Once this posting process is completed and the correct cross-references are in the journal and the ledger, it is possible to trace an entry from the time it enters the accounting system to its summarization in an account in the general ledger.

The other steps in the accounting cycle are not performed with the same frequency as the first three; so explanation of these latter procedures is saved for a later chapter.

Summary

This chapter is an introduction to the debiting and crediting of assets, liabilities, the Fund Balance, expenses, and revenues. Rather than maintain strict adherence to the accounting cycle to illustrate the debiting and crediting procedure, this process has been explained with the use of the bookkeeping equation and T accounts. Although the bookkeeping equation and T accounts are useful for illustrative purposes, the accounting cycle is actually used in a functioning accounting system.

Through reading the material in the chapter, familiarity with the various accounts should develop, but the reader cannot expect to understand all the mechanics of debiting and crediting accounts based on this chapter. The bibliography for this chapter includes several reference sources that are helpful for additional review. The basics with which the reader should be familiar before proceeding to the next chapters are in figure 2–20, where the effect of debits and credits is shown for the various account classifications, as well as the "normal" balances usually found in these accounts. It is necessary to be familiar with the debiting and crediting of accounts before full benefit, in terms of understanding, can be achieved in later chapters.

Account	Debit	Credit	Normal Balance
Asset	+	−	Debit
Liability	−	+	Credit
Fund Balance	−	+	Credit
Expenses	+	−	Debit
Revenues	−	+	Credit

FIG. 2–20. Debit and Credit Effects on Accounts

Exercise 2–5. Review Problems

1. Certain formal accounting documents correspond with specific steps in the fund accounting cycle. Name the internal accounting documents that are associated with (a) journalizing and (b) posting.

2. Sky Mountain Library has hired a new bookkeeper who recently completed Debit/Credit School at a local career college. The new bookkeeper is uncertain as to which accounts to debit and credit for the following transactions, which occurred during the month of June. Determine for the bookkeeper which accounts should be debited and credited

and write the entries in general journal form (see example). List the entries in chronological order.

Example: On June 1 the library paid $100 for roof repairs. The entry, recorded in "general journal" form:

June 1	Repairs Expense	$100	
	Cash		$100

June 5	Office Supplies for $725 received from previously placed order. (They will be paid for later in the month.)
June 7	Deposits of $85 received from patrons who checked out video tape equipment.
June 11	Paid $7 cash for delivery charges to UPS.
June 16	Check-out deposits of $50 returned to patrons when undamaged tape recording equipment was returned to Library.
June 27	Library collected $75 in fines during month of June.
June 27	Salaries of $7,500 paid by Library. (Ignore any taxes.)
June 27	Paid invoice on Office Supplies received June 5.

3. The new bookkeeper (question 2) is even more confused about the posting process. The journal entries on the following page have been taken from page 5 of the library's general journal. (a) Show the bookkeeper how to post these journal entries into T accounts. Include your posting reference in the T account. (b) Determine the "balance" in the Cash account after these entries are posted.

4. In question 3, the T accounts were used in place of what document in the formal accounting system?

5. The new bookkeeper assumed that the posting process had been completed in question 3, but when an attempt was made to trace an entry in the general journal to the general ledger, it could not be done. What part of the posting process remains to be completed?

6. Explain to the bookkeeper how it is possible to trace an entry from the general journal to the general ledger and from the general ledger to the general journal.

7. Without referring to figure 2–20, determine the effect of debits and credits on each of the following account classifications:

a) Assets   d) Expenses
b) Liabilities   e) Revenues
c) Fund Balance

GENERAL JOURNAL

PAGE 5

Date	Items	Post. Ref.	Debit	Credit
June 1	ACCOUNTS PAYABLE		250 —	
	CASH			250 —
4	SALARIES PAYABLE		750 —	
	CASH			750 —
5	CASH		1200 —	
	INTEREST REVENUE			1200 —
6	MISCELLANEOUS EXPENSES		50 —	
	CASH			50 —

Selected Bibliography

Matulich, Serge, and Heitger, Lester E. *Financial Accounting*. New York: McGraw-Hill, 1980.

Meigs, Walter B., and Meigs, Robert F. *Accounting: The Basis for Business Decisions*. 5th ed. New York: McGraw-Hill, 1981.

Walgenback, Paul H.; Dittrich, Norman E.; and Hanson, Ernest I. *Principles of Accounting*. 2nd ed. New York: Harcourt Brace Jovanovich, 1980.

Wilcox, Kirkland A., and San Miguel, Joseph G. *Introduction to Financial Accounting*. New York: Harper & Row, 1980.

3.

Which Accounting System Are We Using?

Chapter 2 provided a basic introduction to debits and credits that included an explanation of the various types of accounts in a typical NFP organization. Although the chapter provided an introduction to the basics of a fund accounting system, a major decision is necessary in regard to the foundation upon which that fund accounting system is based before those basics can be implemented. There are major choice differences as to the type of fund accounting system that can be established and the financial statements generated from these systems. In turn, these differences affect the type of decisions that are reached by those in charge of an NFP organization. Therefore, a consciously made decision about the type of fund accounting system is necessary.

This chapter compares and contrasts the three foundations upon which a fund accounting system can be based: the cash basis, the accrual basis, and the modified-accrual basis.[1] Each of these methods

---

1. Another possible method is the modified cash basis. This is a method where revenues are recognized on the cash basis and expenditures are recognized on the accrual basis, or it could also be that some revenues are recognized on an accrual basis and expenditures are recognized

is defined and explained in the chapter. The major difference between the three methods relates to the time at which a transaction is recorded in the journal.

Cash Basis versus Accrual Method

The cash basis of fund accounting requires the write up of a journal entry only when cash flows into or out of the organization. This method is very simple to use, compared with the accrual method, and is one we use in recording entries in our personal checkbooks. Although this method appears to be workable, especially in small organizations, there are serious difficulties in its use.

The accrual method of fund accounting records transactions as journal entries *when* they occur, rather than wait for the inflow or outflow of cash. This means that expenses and revenues are assigned to the time period in which they are incurred or earned, rather than the period in which they are paid or received.

To assist in distinguishing these accounting methods from one another, assume that the state government has provided Overdrew City Library with special restricted monies in the form of a grant. The $1,200 grant is for purchases of minority and ethnic books for the Genealogical Collection at the library. As a special, restricted grant, the monies can only be used for the purchase of minority and ethnic books. The grant has a one-year limitation: grant monies not used for the purchase of these books within the time period must be returned to the state. The period covered under the grant ends at the end of the current month, June. An invoice (billing statement) for $125 equal to the unexpended portion of the grant is received one day before the end of the month. The invoice does not require payment until a 30-day period has passed.

In a cash-basis system, no record of the purchase is made until the purchase is paid, and that may be up to 30 days after receipt of the invoice. If a purchase report is filed with the state before the $125 payment is made on the last purchase, it appears that not all the funds were used. In this case, the library has an obligation to repay $125 to the state because the accounting records do not indicate that all the monies have been used for the expressed purpose for which they had been granted.

---

on a cash basis. The basic idea is that there is a mixture of the accrual and cash basis under this system.

Under the accrual system, the $125 purchase under the grant is recorded as soon as the obligation for payment is incurred, that is, receipt of the invoice. An accrual system records the last of the grant monies as completely used on the date the invoice and materials are received.

Figure 3–1 shows the general journal entries under the cash basis and the accrual basis for the purchase of the books. In both cases, it is assumed that the library is not going to pay for the books prior to the time that payment is necessary—July 29.

On June 29, when the invoice is received, no entry is made under the cash system, as no cash has flowed out of the organization, but under the accrual system, an obligation for payment is recognized under the liability Accounts Payable. On July 29, both systems record the payment for the book purchase. The cash system records the expenditure, now that cash is flowing out of the library, and the accrual system shows the reduction in the obligation under Accounts Payable. Both systems show a reduction in the Cash account on this date. Note the use of the term "expenditures" under the cash system rather than "expenses." When a cash system (or a modified-accrual basis) is under consideration, *expenditures* are recognized rather than *expenses*. (See pp. 26–27 for a discussion of the differences between these terms.)

	Cash				Accrual		
June 29	No Entry			June 29	Book Expenses	125	
					Accounts Payable		125
July 29	Book Expenditures	125		July 29	Accounts Payable	125	
	Cash		125		Cash		125

FIG. 3–1. Cash Basis and Accrual Basis for Recording a Liability

In reviewing figure 3–1, it can be seen that under the cash system no liability is recognized on June 29. If the end of the financial year, also called the "fiscal year," is June 30, no liability for the purchase is recorded in the year-end financial statements. This results in liabilities and expenditures being understated, and the financial statements do not present an accurate picture of the organization. Expenditures are understated because no expenditure is recognized until July 29. If the end of the fiscal year is June 30, the expenditure will appear in a later year than it was incurred.

The net effect of using the cash basis to account for this particular transaction is to understate (1) liabilities and (2) expenditures, and in this case (3) to transfer expenditures to a fiscal year in which they were not incurred. None of these problems develops under the accrual system.

Accrual Basis versus Modified-Accrual Basis

The accrual system and the cash system are on opposite sides from one another on a continuum. The third method upon which a fund accounting system can be based is the modified-accrual method. On a continuum, this method is closer to the accrual basis than to the cash basis. It should be noted that, at the present time, the accrual method is the only recommended method to use with the NFP organizations discussed in this text.[2] Even though the accrual method is the recommended method of accounting, it is necessary to be familiar with these other methods of accounting, as they are widely used in NFP organizations.

The modified-accrual system is slightly different from the accrual basis. Under the modified-accrual system, revenues that have not been received in cash are not accrued, that is, journalized, unless they are either (1) material and there is a delay in their receipt[3] or (2) it is obvious they are "available." There are two terms in this explanation, "materiality" and "availability," which need to be fully described. The term "materiality" relates to the specific situation or financial data being considered; an item is determined to be material based on the judgment of the accountant. There are no specific percentage limits that will make an item material. An item is considered material if a financial or managerial decision would have been different if the information were known before the decision was made. Therefore, judgment must be used in determining whether an item is material or not.

2. American Institute of Certified Public Accountants, Statement of Position 78–10, *Accounting Principles and Reporting Practices for Certain Nonprofit Organizations* (New York: AICPA, 1979), p. 10.

3. Council of State Governments, *Preferred Accounting Principles for State Governments* (Lexington, Ky.: Council of State Governments, 1983), p. 64. The questions of materiality and delay of receipt are considered in this report.

"Availability" can be defined in several ways;[4] it can mean revenues will be considered available when the asset related to the revenue has been recognized in the books. For example, when the cash from a revenue item has been recorded, the revenue is also recognized. This method provides a cash orientation to the meaning of availability. At the end of a fiscal year, revenues are considered to be available when they are likely to be received in cash within 60 days. They are assumed to be available if they will be received in time to pay liabilities incurred in the fiscal year just ending.[5] Another, more obvious condition for revenues to be recognized is that they must be measurable. "Measurability" means that it must be possible to reasonably estimate the amount of revenues that will be received at a future date.

An example of such a revenue is a state library commission grant for $6,500 which is to be awarded July 15, 19x8, without restrictions, to Overdrew City Library. As of June 30, 19x8, the library's year-end, the grant has not been received, but it is receivable within two weeks. The criteria of materiality, normal receipt time, and availability are evaluated to determine whether grant revenue is recorded in the accounting records on June 30.

The question of measurability is not an issue because the amount of the grant is known. Determination of the materiality of the grant is a judgmental decision and is made by comparing the size of the grant with the total amount of revenues in the library. In this case, it is assumed not to be material. Determination of the normal receipt time of the grant revenues is obvious, as is stated in the award notification.

As it is unlikely that the award will be delayed, the first criteria of materiality and delay of receipt do not play a role in the decision to recognize revenues in the accounting records. The important criterion for deciding to record these revenues in the accounting records is availability. The cash from the grant has not been received, but it is anticipated in time to pay liabilities of the year just ending. Therefore, it will be recognized as a revenue in the accounts on June 30, 19x8. The criterion of availability, as defined here, has been met.

---

4. "In practice, some governments interpret 'available' to mean received in cash. Others interpret it to mean likely to be received in cash within 60 days. Still others assume that revenues are not 'available' until the period in which management *intends* to spend them." National Council on Governmental Accounting, *Governmental Accounting, Auditing, and Financial Reporting* (Chicago: Municipal Finance Officers Association, 1980), p. 14. The NCGA believes the best definition of availability recognizes revenues at the time the related current asset or the reduction in the related current liability is recognized.

5. This period should not extend beyond 60 days.

Another example of revenue recognition under modified accrual relates to book-fine revenues. The question of recognition relates to whether such revenues should be recorded before they are collected, and the decision revolves around the measurability of the fines before they are collected. Fine revenues have been defined as *not* measurable under the modified-accrual approach because they cannot be reasonably estimated before the fines are actually received.[6] Therefore, under the modified-accrual method, fine revenues are not journalized in the accounting records until they are received in cash, and the question of availability does not arise. In later chapters, the accrual method is used to illustrate journal entries for a library. Under this method, book fines are only recorded when they are received in cash for the same reason, that is, the question of measurability.

Figure 3–2 sets forth the decision criteria that are used under the three bases of accounting for determining when revenues are recognized in the accounting records. Notice that the major difference between the modified-accrual method and the accrual method is the question of availability of revenues and whether they are earned.

Availability of revenues under the modified-accrual basis has already been explained. This concept slightly contrasts with revenues that "are earned" as revenues may be available but "unearned." Revenues are earned at the point where the NFP organization has a right to expect to receive payment for "services" without the obligation of any further performance. The following are four examples of earned revenues: (1) contracted services have been provided; (2) the point at which a sale is made; (3) fines are received; and (4) interest revenues are receivable because of the passage of time. Although the two concepts overlap, availability of revenues concentrates on the period of collectibility, whereas the earnings of revenues focuses on the completion of performance.

In the modified-accrual basis, the method of recording expenditures is the same as recording expenses in chapter 2 on the accrual basis, except that interest on long-term debt is not recognized before the fiscal year in which it is actually paid and prepaid assets may not be recorded in the books other than as expenditures.[7] Supplies, a prepaid asset, may be considered an expenditure when they are purchased or when they are used. If they are considered expenditures when they are purchased, they are not recognized as prepaid assets.

Interest on long-term debt is not recorded until the fiscal year in

6. National Council on Governmental Accounting, *Governmental Accounting, Auditing, and Financial Reporting* (Chicago: Municipal Finance Officers Association, 1980), p. 14.
7. Ibid.

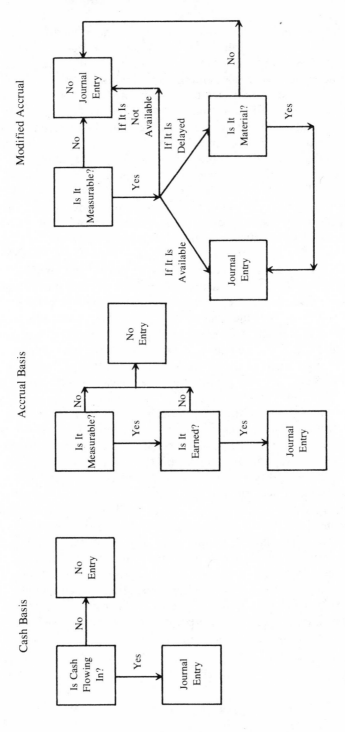

Fig. 3–2. Decision Criteria for Making Journal Entry for Revenues under the Three Methods of Accounting

which the interest is actually due because of the way monies are allocated by the governing board. For example, if the interest expenditures are journalized in the year ending December 31, 19x8, but they are not payable until January 15, 19x9, the following year, a deficit would be created, or at least contributed toward, in the Fund Balance. Recognizing the interest expenditures prior to the time they are due contributes toward a deficit because no monies are available through appropriations for the interest expenditures in 19x8. For the monies to be available, they need to be set aside by the governing board in a budget document, and this does not occur unless the interest expenditure is going to be paid in the current year. Creation of a deficit in the 19x8 Fund Balance serves no useful purpose because monies will be set aside through appropriations by the governing board in the following year, 19x9, for the interest expenditures. For this reason, the modified-accrual basis does not recognize a liability and expenditure for interest on long-term debt that is owed but not scheduled to be paid until the following year. The accounting for interest on long-term debt illustrates another difference between the accrual and modified-accrual systems of accounting.

Under the accrual method, an Interest Expense account and a liability account called Interest Payable would be increased for the amount of interest owed but not yet due on December 31, 19x8. As this interest is owed at the end of the year, it is recognized as both a liability and an expense in the fiscal period ending December 31, 19x8. This difference between the accrual and modified-accrual method is significant only for those NFP organizations with long-term debt outstanding. The third method of handling interest is the cash basis. Under this method, no journal entry is made until the interest expense is actually paid out. At that time, an expenditures account is increased and the cash in the Cash account is decreased for the amount of interest paid. This example for interest expense illustrates the differences that can arise in journalizing entries under the three methods of accounting. It should also indicate the differences that can develop in the financial statements prepared under the different accounting methods.

As indicated, another difference between the accrual and the modified-accrual bases of accounting occurs because the latter method does not have to recognize ''prepaid assets''—items that are paid for before they are used and that are recognized as assets with a short life under an accrual system. Under a modified-accrual system, they are recognized as expenditures of the current period. A common example of this type of item is insurance payments on a car or building. Payment of the insurance applies to a future period; it provides a benefit in the future, which is by definition an asset. Under the accrual system, it is recognized as an asset, Prepaid Insurance, but under the modified-accrual system it is recognized as an expenditure, Insurance Expenditures. When the asset account, Prepaid Insurance, is used, it is transferred to an expense classification bit by bit as the period covered by the insurance policy expires.

A commonly recognized prepaid asset under modified accrual is inventories. For control to exist over the use of inventories, they should be recognized as a prepaid asset and the actual physical counts of the inventory compared with the amounts shown in the accounts. Before the end of the year, the inventories may be considered expenditures when they are purchased or when they are consumed. At the end of the fiscal year the consumption method corresponds with the accrual method and an inventory is recognized in the books; whereas the purchase method is similar to the cash basis of accounting. The latter method expenses the inventories as they are purchased. All inventories are considered to be expenditures under this method, and no inventory account is recognized in the records. Obviously, if there are material amounts of inventory, footnotes to the financial statements should disclose their dollar value. Under the consumption method, any unused materials or supplies at the year end are disclosed as composing an asset called Material Inventory or Supplies Inventory. (Additional explanations about inventories are provided later in the chapter.)

Exercise 3–1. Cash, Accrual, and Modified-Accrual Systems (Assume fiscal year-end is June 30 in all cases)

1. The City of Tarrinton forwards monies for operational support to the city library each year. These monies are usually received in the first week of July. During the current year, budget revisions have delayed receipt of these monies, and as of the first week in July no monies have been received. Should a journal entry be made at the end of the first week in July for these monies under the following accounting methods?

    a) Cash
    b) Accrual
    c) Modified accrual

2. The Harry Carry Jr. Art Center has pledges receivable of $25,000 from a number of individuals who made pledges of support during a recent fund-raising drive. It is estimated that 10% of these pledges will never

be collected. After the pledges have been made, which of the following methods of accounting require a journal entry?

a)   Cash
b)   Accrual
c)   Modified accrual

3.   An NFP organization has a long-term debt of $100,000 and the interest rate on this debt is 14%. This debt requires a cash interest payment twice each year of $7,000, on July 1 and January 1 ($100,000 × .14 = $14,000/2 = $7,000). Under which method(s) of accounting should the organization recognize a $7,000 expense/expenditure on the June 30 financial statement for the interest payment on July 1?

a)   Cash
b)   Accrual
c)   Modified accrual

4.   The Stanley-Hanley County Library recently paid $250 for insurance on its bookmobile. How should this payment be recognized under the various methods of accounting?

a)   Cash
b)   Accrual
c)   Modified accrual

5.   What is the difference between the "purchases method" and "consumption method" of recording inventory expenditures?

Accounting under the Cash, Accrual, and Modified-Accrual Systems

The three foundations upon which a fund accounting system can be based have been briefly explained. This section goes into more detail by using the three methods to record a series of transactions and comparing the differences between them.

Whichever method is used in an NFP organization, it should be deliberately chosen and not used because "it's the one that was used before." Again, it should be noted that the only method that is recommended for NFP organizations is the accrual method. If the accrual method is *not* used to prepare financial statements and the limitations of the other methods are not understood, the financial statements can create misinterpretations. (The limitations of cash and modified-accrual financial statements are analyzed on pp. 68–77.)

Another reason for using the accrual method is related to the requirement that the books of an NFP organization be audited by an independent accountant. It is important to understand the effect on the audit of choosing a method other than accrual. The importance of a successful audit cannot be understated, and it is considered on page 78.

A series of transactions is used in this section to highlight the variations between cash, accrual, and modified-accrual accounting systems. Information about the transactions, in an entity called the Eclectic Organization, is contained in the following paragraphs (numbered 1 through 7). It is assumed that these transactions occurred during the year, and each is analyzed under the three different methods of accounting. It is further assumed that Eclectic's financial or fiscal year ends June 30.

> 1. On April 15, 19x8, an invoice was received from Acme Supply Company granting 30-day credit terms on a $10,000 purchase of supplies. The goods had been received by June 30. As of June 30, there was $2,000 of supplies inventory on hand, that is, unused. All these supplies had been purchased during the current year.

Figure 3–3 outlines the entries that are necessary on April 15 under the three methods of accounting. No entry is made under the cash basis for the purchase of supplies on April 15 because the supplies are purchased on credit. A cash-based system generates an entry only when cash flows into or out of the entity, and this does not occur when purchases are made on credit.

Cash
Apr. 15   No Entry

Accrual
Apr. 15   Supplies Expense   10,000
                    Accounts Payable   10,000

Modified Accrual
Apr. 15   Supplies Expenditures   10,000
                    Accounts Payable   10,000

Fig. 3–3.   Transaction 1

In the accrual and the modified-accrual bases, the entries are very similar. The accrual-based entry debits Supplies Expense[8] whereas

8. Under the accrual method, this debit entry could be made to Supplies Inventory, but for

the account debited under the modified-accrual method is Supplies Expenditures. (The differences between expenditures and expenses were explained on pp. 26–27.) In both cases the credit entry is to the liability account, Accounts Payable. It is assumed that the modified-accrual basis records inventories as an expenditure when they are purchased, and at the end of the year the amount of the unused inventory is recognized as a prepaid asset. At the same time, inventory expenditures are decreased. Whenever an inventory is recognized under the modified-accrual system, the consumption method is being used. Further explanation about the entries at the end of the year are provided on pages 63–64.

The major difference between the cash basis and accrual methods is that under accrual methods a liability is recognized for the amount owed to Acme Supply Company. It is obvious that use of the cash basis "hides" the liabilities of the organization.

> 2. The employees are paid every two weeks and the pay schedule is the first and third Friday of every month. The total to be paid for the next pay period is $24,000. (Any taxes, i.e., income taxes or social security taxes, are to be ignored at the present time.)

In a cash-basis system, no entry is made to record the organization's obligation to pay the employees. The employees' last payday was the third Friday in June, which means they have worked for a week without being paid. Salaries for that period are an expense of the current period and not the subsequent fiscal period. The cash-basis system records the expense when it is paid, not when it is actually owed or when the employees perform their tasks for the organization. The cash-basis system transfers the expense to the subsequent fiscal period. The salary expenditures for the year-end June 30, 19x8, are understated, and the salary expenditures for the fiscal year ending June 30, 19x9, will be overstated.

The accrual/modified-accrual systems record the amount owed and the expense on June 30, 19x8. Expenses/Expenditures for the first week of the two-week pay period are recorded in the fiscal year ending June 30, 19x8, and the second week's payroll is recorded as an expense of the following fiscal period. Figure 3–4 illustrates the debit and credit entries.[9] The accrual entry increases Personnel Expenses by $12,000, which is one-half of the two-week payroll, and

---

consistency in comparing the two methods, a debit is made to Supplies Expense. Either method is correct.

9. In effect, these are "adjusting" entries, explained on pages 61–67.

```
Cash
June 30      No Entry

Accrual
June 30      Personnel Expense              12,000
                Salaries Payable                        12,000

Modified Accrual
June 30      Personnel Expenditures         12,000
                Salaries Payable                        12,000
```

FIG. 3–4.   Transaction 2

Salaries Payable is increased by an equal amount. The only difference between the modified-accrual and the accrual methods is in the account names, Personnel Expenses and Personnel Expenditures, as shown in figure 3–4.

> 3. On July 2, Manual, Hang, Fanner & Jones, the investment banking firm that handles Eclectic Organization's bond and security investments, notified the organization that it earned $7,500 in interest income for the three-month period ending June 30, 19x8. The interest income will be forwarded to the organization on July 7, 19x8.

The journal entries to record this transaction under the accrual basis are a debit to Interest Income Receivable and a credit to Interest Revenue.[10] There is a credit to the Interest Revenue account, even though the revenues will not be received in cash until July. From an accrual viewpoint, this revenue is earned as of June 30, 19x8, and it needs accounting recognition in that period. The entry under the modified-accrual method is the same as the accrual entry. The revenue is recognized under modified accrual because it is considered to be available. These entries are shown in figure 3–5.

Under the cash system, the revenues are not recognized until the cash is received, which is scheduled for July 7, 19x8. The cash-basis

```
Cash
June 30      No Entry

Accrual
June 30      Interest Income Receivable      7,500
                Interest Revenue                        7,500

Modified Accrual
June 30      Interest Income Receivable      7,500
                Interest Revenue                        7,500
```

FIG. 3–5.   Transaction 3

10. This journal entry is also an adjusting entry.

procedures cause interest revenues of 19x7–19x8 to appear as revenues of 19x8–19x9, a later period. This is an incorrect classification, as the revenues are earned in the earlier period. This misclassification results in understating current-year revenues and overstating revenues in the subsequent year.

> 4. The Eclectic Organization has received confirmation that as of June 15, 19x8, it had been awarded a special grant from the federal government for a program for the handicapped. The grant is for $75,000, and is expected to be received shortly.

Under the accrual system, the grant needs to be recognized as a receivable in the current period. The grant has been awarded; so as soon as the Eclectic Organization is aware of the award, a receivable account, showing the amount owed to the organization by the federal government, is debited for $75,000. The amount owed to Eclectic Organization is its receivable until the monies are collected.

On the credit side of this journal entry, a liability, Deferred Restricted Contribution—Grants, is recognized. Remember, the monies receivable under this grant can only be used in a program to help the handicapped. If the organization does not use the monies for these purposes, the grant will have to be repaid. In this sense, the monies are unearned until they are expended. Grants accepted under such conditions create a contingent liability for the Eclectic Organization under which repayment may be necessary, and the contingency rests upon the proper spending of the monies. Due to the contingent nature of the grant, it is established as a liability until the monies are used for the designated purposes. As the monies are expended for helping the handicapped, the liability is reduced. The modified-accrual method adopts the same accounts as are used under the accrual method in this transaction. Figure 3–6 illustrates the entries for the two accounting methods.

```
Cash
June 15      No Entry

Accrual
June 15      Grant Receivable                          75,000
                 Deferred Restricted Contributions—
                     Grants                                     75,000

Modified Accrual                                      75,000
June 15      Grant Receivable
                 Deferred Restricted Contributions—     75,000
                     Grants
```

FIG. 3–6. Transaction 4

As illustrated in figure 3–6, there is no entry under the cash basis as no cash flows into or out of the organization. The cash method again understates the liabilities for the current year by not recognizing the liability under the grant. In addition, it understates assets by not recognizing the receivable from the federal government.

> 5. The Eclectic Organization has been required under a lease arrangement, signed on May 1, 19x8, to make a six-month prepayment of $12,000.

In this transaction, the same entries are used under the cash and the modified-accrual systems, and a different entry is used for the accrual method. The initial entry to record the payment of the rent under the cash and modified-accrual basis is shown in figure 3–7 as a debit to Lease Expenditures and a credit to Cash. Although the entry is the same under both methods, the reasons they are the same are slightly different. Under the cash basis, cash has flowed out of the organization, and this outflow triggers an entry in the accounting system. The prepayment of the lease is a prepaid asset, and in the modified-accrual method, prepaid assets are not recognized. Therefore, if an asset is not recognized in the debit portion of this entry, the expended cash for the lease is considered to be an expenditure.

Under the accrual method of accounting, the cash payment on the lease is recognized as a prepaid asset, Prepaid Rent. Prepaid assets have a short life and are soon consumed by the organization's operating activities. In this transaction, the cash and the modified-accrual methods record the same journal entry. This is an example of where journal entries for the modified-accrual method and the accrual method differ.

Cash			
May 1	Lease Expenditures	12,000	
	Cash		12,000
Accrual			
May 1	Prepaid Rent	12,000	
	Cash		12,000
Modified Accrual			
May 1	Lease Expenditures	12,000	
	Cash		12,000

Fig. 3–7. Transaction 5

6. On April 15, 19x8, season's ticket holders paid $50,000 for a ticket book, entitling them to attend six plays. Three of the plays had been produced as of June 30, 19x8.

Figure 3–8 illustrates the entries made on April 15. (The situation on June 30 will be considered later in the chapter.) The cash-basis system recognizes the inflow of $50,000 in cash on April 15 as a debit to Cash and a credit to Theatrical Revenues. The cash-based system recognizes the entire amount received for the tickets as revenues immediately. At this point the question should be asked, What happens if the plays are not produced? The most appropriate action is a refunding of the monies collected. This indicates that once cash is accepted for the tickets, the organization has an obligation either to produce the plays or, if they are cancelled, to repay the money. This type of obligation is a liability. These monies are collected in advance of the performance, and as of April 15 they are deferred. It would be possible to recognize revenues earned as each of the six plays is completed, but, in practice, revenues for the three completed plays are recorded only on June 30—at the end of the fiscal year. When the monies are collected, the liability account, Unearned Theatrical Revenue, is the account credited for $50,000 under both the accrual and modified-accrual systems.

Cash
Apr. 15   Cash   50,000
                  Theatrical Revenue   50,000

Accrual
Apr. 15   Cash   50,000
                  Unearned Theatrical Revenue   50,000

Modified Accrual
Apr. 15   Cash   50,000
                  Unearned Theatrical Revenue   50,000

FIG. 3–8. Transaction 6

In comparing the cash-based entries with the accrual entries, it is seen that the cash basis understates liabilities in the current period and overstates the revenues. Cash-based accounting systems will continually understate liabilities.

7. On June 28, 19x8, the Eclectic Organization made an award to a graduate student working on a master's in library science at a local university. The $1,000 award is for tuition support, and it is to be paid on September 2, 19x8, which is the beginning of the school year.

No entry is made for the award under the cash basis. The reason for not recording an entry is the same as before: no cash flowed into or out of the organization. Under the accrual basis, an expense, Award Expense, is recognized in the current period and a liability for the obligation to pay the award is also recognized in the account Award Payable. These entries appear in figure 3–9.[11]

Cash
June 28   No Entry

Accrual
June 28   Award Expense   1,000
                      Award Payable   1,000

Modified Accrual
June 28   Award Expenditure   1,000
                      Award Payable   1,000

FIG. 3–9. Transaction 7

The award is made in the period ending June 30, 19x8, but it will not be paid until the following period. This means that in June the Eclectic Organization has an obligation to make a payment to the student in September. This obligation is a liability. It is not known whether the monies for the award are to come from the current period or from monies available in the following period. It can be argued that if the monies come from those collected and received in the current fiscal year, the expenditures should be recognized in this earlier period. Let us assume that this is the situation. Then the entry in figure 3–9, under the modified-accrual method, follows the accrual entry; the only difference relates to use of the terms "expenses" and "expenditures," as is apparent in the name of the account debited.

11. It is assumed that the money for the award comes out of general operations, and it does not come out of a special award account.

**Exercise 3–2.   Journalizing Entries under Cash, Accrual, and Modi-
fied-Accrual Systems**

1.   Record in general journal form the proper entry for questions 2, 3, and
4 in exercise 3–1 under the cash, accrual, and modified-accrual bases.
2.   Assume Battell Library receives and pays for $750 worth of supplies on
May 1. The library uses the "purchases method" of recording supplies.
What is the correct journal entry on May 1 under the cash, accrual, and
modified-accrual methods?
3.   Assume the supplies described in question 2 are recorded under the
"consumption method." What is the correct journal entry under the
three different methods of accounting on May 1?

Adjusting Entries

The main objective of this chapter is to illustrate differences between
the three accounting methods that can be used for establishing a fund
accounting system. One important distinction that is necessary to
understand is the difference in the type of financial statements prepared under the cash, accrual, and modified-accrual systems. Before
preparation of any financial statements, it is necessary to make what
are called "adjusting entries," which are considered briefly in this
chapter and more fully when the preparation of financial statements is
explored. The major emphasis at this point is to highlight differences
between the three methods of accounting.

"Adjusting entries" are really "catch-up" journal entries, made
only at the end of the fiscal year, prior to preparing financial statements. In the case of Eclectic Organization, they are made on June
30, the year-end. The adjusting entries are year-end catch-up entries,
used to bring accounts up to date. As an example, consider the
Prepaid Rent which was recorded in figure 3–7 for the Eclectic
Organization. The entry for the rent was made May 1. From May 1
to the end of Eclectic's fiscal year, two months have passed, and an
adjustment to Prepaid Rent is necessary to bring the account up to
date. The adjustment is necessary because some of the prepaid rent
has been used up. It can no longer be said that the rent for Eclectic is
paid for the next six months, that is, the initial prepaid period. This
means that the asset Prepaid Rent needs to be reduced. In this case,
an adjusting entry can decrease the balance in an asset account, but

the adjusting entry can also reduce an expense, as will be shown shortly.

In explaining adjusting entries, each of the previous seven transactions is reviewed to determine which of the seven needs to be adjusted, which is not as difficult as it may appear. One reason is because none of the entries made under the cash basis needs any type of adjusting entry.[12] Only entries that used the accrual basis or the modified-accrual basis, when the latter follows accrual accounting, need to be considered for adjustment.

Each of the seven transactions is reviewed in figure 3–10 to determine which of them requires an adjusting entry. Figure 3–10 shows the transaction number of the item, the type of item, the date it was recorded in the journal, whether it needs an adjusting entry, and the reason it does or does not require an adjusting entry.

Transaction No.	Type of Item	Date Recorded in Journal	Does It Need Updating?	Reason for Update
1	Supplies	June 15	Yes	Passage of time
2	Salaries	June 30	No	Current as of June 30
3	Interest	June 30	No	Current as of June 30
4	Grant	June 15	No	Grant still not received
5	Rent	May 1	Yes	Passage of time
6	Revenues	Apr. 15	Yes	3 plays produced
7	Award	June 28	No	Award still not presented

FIG. 3–10. Considerations for Adjusting Entries in the Seven Transactions

The decision for making or not making an adjusting entry begins as a process of elimination. If a journal entry is dated as of June 30, it does not require an adjusting entry, because it is up to date as of the end of the fiscal year. On this basis, transactions 2 and 3 are eliminated. If the transactions involve a prepaid asset, and were recorded before June 30, an adjusting entry is required. On this basis, transactions 1 and 5, both dealing with prepaid assets, require adjusting entries.

12. It should be noted that adjusting entries may be made under the cash basis for corrections to the accounts.

The remaining transactions are analyzed individually to determine if they need to be updated since the time they were recorded in the journal. Transaction 4 records a grant that is to be received. If the monies from the grant have been received, an adjusting entry is necessary. In fact, the entry is made as soon as the monies are received—which is not necessarily as an adjusting entry at the end of the year. The point is academic as the grant monies have not been received as of June 30, and no entries are necessary.

In transaction 6, which deals with Theatrical Revenues, three plays out of six have been produced as of June 30. This means that some of the deferred revenues in the Unearned Theatrical Revenue accounts are now earned revenues; therefore, the liability needs to be reduced. The last transaction, 7, deals with the tuition award to the graduate student and it does not require an adjustment, because as of June 30 the award has not been transferred to the student. In other words, nothing has changed since the June 28 transaction.

The transactions that require accrual adjusting entries are 1, 5, and 6. Transactions 1 and 6 also require adjustments under the modified-accrual method. Each of these adjusting entries is analyzed in more detail in the remaining portions of this section.

As indicated in transaction 1, there are $2,000 worth of supplies in the inventory as of June 30. These supplies need to be reflected in the accounts as an asset. The adjusting entry necessary under both the accrual and the modified-accrual methods is reflected in figure 3–11. The only difference between the adjusting entries again relates to the differences in the account names, that is, "expenses" versus "expenditures." To minimize cross-referencing, the abbreviation *exp.* is used in the following paragraphs.

In the first entry in figure 3–11, the amount of supplies remaining at the end of the year is recorded as a debit to the Inventory of Supplies account. Without this entry, no record would be maintained as to the amount of the remaining supplies. This entry also reduces the Supplies Exp. by the amount of the ending inventory. This decrease in Supplies Exp. for the total of the unused inventory is necessary; otherwise the Supplies Exp. is overstated for the current fiscal year. The accounting for the inventory requires coordination with the employees who are responsible for keeping an inventory count of the supplies. The accounting supervisor must determine if there are discrepancies between the accounting records and the physical count made by the employees. Any significant differences require investigation. Without this type of coordination and recording procedures, there is little control over the supplies at the facility.

Cash
June 30   No adjusting entry*

Accrual
June 30   Inventory of Supplies   2,000
                    Supplies Expense   2,000

               Fund Balance   2,000
                    Reserve for Inventory
                    of Supplies   2,000

Modified Accrual
June 30   Inventory of Supplies   2,000
                    Supplies Expenditures   2,000

               Fund Balance   2,000
                    Reserve for Inventory
                    of Supplies   2,000

*It should be noted that when supplies are paid for, an entry is made under the cash system.

FIG. 3–11. Adjusting Entries for Transaction 1

The first adjusting entry reduces the Supplies Exp. by $2,000. This reduction in expenses causes the revenues to increase. In turn, when the $2,000 increase in revenues is transferred to the Fund Balance, it makes the Fund Balance higher. In the bookkeeping equation, it was shown (p. 17) that when an asset such as Inventory of Supplies increases, either a liability or the Fund Balance must increase for the equation to remain in balance. In this case, the Fund Balance increases. As a check on this unavailable increase, a reserve account is established in the Fund Balance. The reserve account restricts the Fund Balance so that the $2,000 increase is not available for use. Obviously, the only reason the Fund Balance increased was because an Inventory of Supplies account was established as an asset, but the inventory account does not provide more monies for potential spending in the Fund Balance, as it would appear to do without the reserve account. The reserve account shows that the $2,000 transfer to the Fund Balance is not available for use in supporting the operations of the Eclectic Organization.

The journal entry for establishing the reserve account is the second entry in figure 3–11, which reduces the Fund Balance by $2,000 and establishes a reserve account, Reserve for the Inventory of Supplies. The $2,000 in the reserve is still part of the Fund Balance, but it is not available for use in operating activities, as it has been restricted. The net effect of the two entries in figure 3–11 is to establish an Inventory of Supplies account for $2,000 and to set up a Reserve for Supplies Inventory in the Fund Balance for $2,000. As previously stated, the cash basis of accounting does not usually journalize any adjusting entries because no cash flows into or out of the NFP organization because of an adjusting entry. Therefore, an entry would be recorded for inventories under the cash basis only when the invoice is paid. At that time, an Expenditure account is debited and the Cash account is credited.

At this point, the Reserved accounts in the Fund Balance, which are restrictions of the Fund Balance, need to be further explained. In addition, a distinction between these restrictions of the Fund Balance and restrictions on accounts such as the Deferred Restricted Contributions for Grants and Unearned Theatrical Revenue should be made. The Fund Balance can consist of a number of reserved accounts. The purpose of these reserved accounts is to indicate to the reader of the Balance Sheet that these portions of the Fund Balance are not available for financing purposes. The reason they are not available for spending is that they are represented on the other side of the bookkeeping equation by noncash assets, such as supplies, or that they have been designated for a specific use by the board, such as the purchase of new equipment or some type of refund. In these cases, the amount available for spending purposes has been reduced. For example, spending needs to be done with cash and not supplies. Each time a reserve account is established within the Fund Balance, it reduces the portion of the Fund Balance that can be used for additional spending. The establishment of a reserve in the Fund Balance should be considered for representation of any noncash asset, and a reserve should be established for any board restrictions on the Fund Balance.

The major distinction between the Reserve account and restricted accounts such as the Deferred Restricted Contributions account is that the latter is a liability account. As such, the restrictions on a liability account are established by parties outside the NFP organization. In addition, if the obligation is not fulfilled, the monies which have been or will be received may have to be returned to the granting agency or the donor.

The next transaction requiring an adjusting entry is number 5, which deals with prepaid rent. The entries for this transaction are different under the accrual and modified-accrual methods.

In this transaction, the rent was initially paid for a six-month period, beginning May 1 and ending November 1, 19x8. As of June 30, two months of that rental period have passed. The passage of the two-month period provides a means for determining what portion of the rent has changed from a prepaid asset to an expense. Two months of the prepaid asset ($4,000) are considered an expense for the period ending June 30, 19x8, and the remaining four months' rent ($8,000) is still a prepaid asset. In figure 3–12, a debit is made to Rent Expense and a credit is made to the Prepaid Rent account. The debit and credit are both for $4,000, which is the prepaid rent which has become an expense over the two-month period ending June 30, 19x8. The effect of this entry is to reduce the Prepaid Rent account to an $8,000 balance, after the $4,000 credit is posted to the ledger, and to increase the Rent Expense account by $4,000.

Cash
June 30   No adjusting entry

Accrual
June 30   Rent Expense   4,000
                   Prepaid Rent   4,000

                   Fund Balance   8,000
                   Reserve for Lease
                   Prepayment   8,000

Modified Accrual
June 30   No adjusting entry

FIG. 3–12. Adjusting Entries for Transaction 5

In the second entry, a reserve account is established in the Fund Balance to indicate to anyone who reads the financial statements that there is a restriction on the Fund Balance for $8,000. Just as with the supplies inventory, a restriction is placed on the Fund Balance for the amount in the Prepaid Rent account to indicate that $8,000 of the Fund Balance is not available for future spending.

Under the modified-accrual method, no adjusting entry is made as the entire amount paid for the lease is recognized as an expenditure at the time of payment. This is the same procedure used in the cash basis. When prepaid assets are involved in a transaction, the modified-accrual method usually follows cash-basis accounting procedures.[13] Compared with the accrual method, the modified accrual and

13. Supplies and rent are both prepaid assets, but the procedures for handling them usually differ under the modified-accrual method.

the cash basis record higher amounts of lease expenditures in their financial statements for the fiscal year ending June 30, 19x8.

The final transaction requiring an adjusting entry is number 6, which deals with the collection of ticket revenues before production of the plays. As of June 30, three of the plays have been produced, and an adjusting entry is necessary to bring the amount of earned revenue up to date. Since half the plays have been produced, only half the cash received still needs to be considered a liability; the rest has been earned as a revenue item. The initial entries for the accrual and modified-accrual methods used the same accounts, and the adjusting entries apply to both of these methods. The adjusting entry, shown in figure 3–13, reduces the balance of the Unearned Theatrical Revenue account by $25,000 and transfers the $25,000 to the Theatrical Revenue account. This $25,000 now represents earned revenues rather than a potential liability. The $25,000 is equal to half of the total advance ticket sales, and it is removed from the liability account, Unearned Theatrical Revenues, because half of the plays have been produced.

Cash
June 30   No adjusting entry

Accrual
June 30   Unearned Theatrical Revenue   25,000
                   Theatrical Revenue   25,000

Modified Accrual
June 30   Unearned Theatrical Revenue   25,000
                   Theatrical Revenue   25,000

FIG. 3–13. Adjusting Entries for Transaction 6

This section demonstrates the use of adjusting entries under the three methods of accounting that can be used in a fund accounting system. Under the cash basis, no adjusting entries are necessary. This demonstrates that the cash system is easy to use, although it does not provide for correct reporting. The modified-accrual method requires adjusting entries when it records an entry in the same fashion as the accrual method, but when a transaction is recorded in the manner used under the cash basis, no adjusting entry is made. The accrual method more accurately assigns assets, liabilities, Fund Balance reserves, revenues, and expenses to the proper accounting period, and this method makes extensive use of adjusting entries.

Financial Statements

Financial statements are different when they are prepared under the three different methods of accounting. To illustrate the differences that arise in the financial statements, it is assumed that Eclectic Organization's financial statements for the year ending June 30, 19x7, appear in figure 3–14.

The differences in the types of financial statements prepared under the cash, modified-accrual, and accrual methods will be illustrated in the following sections. Major emphasis is not placed on how the differences arose but what they are, as well as their potential effects on decision making. Prior to considering the differences, attention needs to be focused on the two new financial statements in figure 3–14: the Balance Sheet and the Statement of Receipts and Expenditures.

The Balance Sheet for the Eclectic Organization (figure 3–14) is formulated on a cash basis. The balance sheet for an NFP organization represents a listing of all asset accounts, liability accounts, and the Fund Balance. It represents the balance in these accounts at one point in time, which is the date on which the statement is prepared. The complete Balance Sheet for an NFP organization is usually prepared only at the end of each fiscal year. It should be noted that the bookkeeping equation is represented in the Balance Sheet because the total of the asset balances is always equal to the total of the liabilities and the Fund Balance accounts. Under the cash system, no liabilities are recognized, but the total of the assets and the Fund Balance equals $109,000 in the cash-based Balance Sheet for the Eclectic Organization.[14]

Under the cash basis, the Statement of Receipts and Expenditures represents receipts as all the cash collected during the current year and expenditures as all the cash actually paid out during the year.[15] The Statement of Receipts and Expenditures for the Eclectic Organization for the year ending June 30, 19x7 (figure 3–14), is reflective of transactions over the entire year whereas the Balance Sheet is representative of only one point in time. The bottom line in the Statement of Receipts and Expenditures is referred to as Excess of Receipts over Expenditures, and it is transferred to the Balance Sheet at the end of each fiscal year. With the Eclectic Organization, the "Excess," in this case $56,000, is transferred to the Fund Balance

---

14. Some liabilities might be recognized in a cash system, although accounts and salaries payable are not recognized. An example of the type of liability that might be recognized is notes payable.

15. In a commercial enterprise, this statement is referred to as an "income" statement.

Eclectic Organization
Balance Sheet
June 30, 19x7

Assets		Liabilities & Fund Balance	
Cash	$109,000	Liabilities	$ —
		Fund Balance	109,000
		Total Liabilities &	
Total Assets	$109,000	Fund Balance	$109,000

Eclectic Organization
Statement of Receipts and Expenditures
for Year Ended June 30, 19x7

Receipts:			
	Support	$1,110,000	
	Revenues	35,000	
Total Receipts			$1,145,000
Expenditures:			
	Personnel	$1,068,000	
	Other Expenditures	21,000	
Total Expenditures			1,089,000
Excess of Receipts over Expenditures			$ 56,000

FIG. 3–14. Balance Sheet and Statement of Receipts and Expenditures for Eclectic Organization for Fiscal Year Ending June 30, 19x7 (Base Year)

and added to the existing balance (see figure 2–9).[16] For the Balance Sheet to balance (i.e., assets equal liabilities plus the Fund Balance), the transfer of the Excess must have been completed. This makes it important to prepare the Statement of Receipts and Expenditures prior to preparing the Balance Sheet. This transfer occurs only once a year, when the financial statements are prepared, and means that the Fund Balance is adjusted once every year.

16. The balance in the Fund Balance prior to the $56,000 transfer was equal to $53,000, determined as follows: Balance after Excess Transfer ($109,000) less Excess ($56,000) = Balance before Excess Transfer ($53,000).

Comparisons between Accrual- and Cash-based Financial Statements

In figures 3–15 and 3–16 the financial statements for the Eclectic Organization for June 30, 19x9 are presented on an accrual basis. The cash-based statements for the Eclectic Organization for the same period are presented in figure 3–17. All the statements update the financial statements in figure 3–14 by incorporating the seven transactions previously described. In addition, it is assumed that total personnel costs, paid out in cash during the year, amounted to $1,489,000, and the Eclectic Organization had received monies for support during the year equal to $1,400,000.

One immediate difference that is apparent in comparing the two systems is a change in one of the statement names under the accrual system. The Statement of Receipts and Expenditures, under the cash-basis system, is called the Statement of Support, Revenue, and Ex-

Eclectic Organization
Statement of Support, Revenue, and Expenses
for Year Ended June 30, 19x8

Support and Revenue:		
Support	$1,400,000	
Theatrical Revenue	25,000	
Interest Revenue	7,500	
Total Support and Revenue		$1,432,500
Expenses:		
Personnel	$1,501,000	
Supplies	8,000	
Award	1,000	
Rent Expense	4,000	
Total Expenses		1,514,000
Deficiency of Support and Revenue over Expenses		$ (81,500)

Fig. 3–15. Accrual-based Statement of Support, Revenue, and Expenses for Eclectic Organization for Fiscal Year Ending June 30, 19x8

Eclectic Organization
Balance Sheet
June 30, 19x8

Assets		Liabilities	
Cash	$ 58,000	Accounts Payable	$ 10,000
Grant Receivable	75,000	Salaries Payable	12,000
Interest Income Receivable	7,500	Deferred Restricted	
Prepaid Rent	8,000	Contributions—Grants	75,000
Inventory of Supplies	2,000	Unearned Theatrical	
		Revenue	25,000
		·Award Payable	1,000
		Total Liabilities	$123,000
		Fund Balance	
		Unrestricted	$ 17,500
		Restricted:	
		Reserve for Lease	
		Prepayment	8,000
		Reserve for Inventory	
		of Supplies	2,000
		Total Fund Balance	$ 27,500
		Total Liabilities &	
Total Assets	$150,500	Fund Balance	$150,500

FIG. 3–16. Accrual-based Balance Sheet for Eclectic Organization for Fiscal Year Ending June 30, 19x8

penses under the accrual system. This change is due to the way cash flows are recognized under the two systems.

A second difference relates to the manner in which the Cash balance is viewed under the two systems of accounting. Under the cash basis (figure 3–17), it appears that there are no claims on the cash of $58,000 as of June 30, 19x9, which means that the governing board is likely to want to use this cash for operating activities in the subsequent year.

It is apparent that there are claims against the cash under the accrual-based statement. After the balance in the Deferred Restricted Contributions—Grants account is matched against the balance in the Grants Receivable account, the remaining liabilities total to $48,000.

Eclectic Organization
Balance Sheet
June 30, 19x8

Assets		Liabilities & Fund Balance	
Cash	$58,000	Liabilities	$ —
		Fund Balance	58,000
		Total Liabilities &	
Total Assets	$58,000	Fund Balance	$58,000

Eclectic Organization
Statement of Receipts and Expenditures
for Year Ended June 30, 19x8

Receipts			
	Support	$1,400,000	
	Theatrical Revenue	50,000	
Total Receipts			$1,450,000
Expenditures:			
	Personnel Expenditures	$1,489,000	
	Lease Expenditures	12,000	
Total Expenditures			$1,501,000
Deficiency of Receipts over Expenditures			$ (51,000)

FIG. 3–17. Cash-based Balance Sheet and Statement of Receipts and Expenditures for Eclectic Organization for Fiscal Year Ending June 30, 19x8

These liabilities consist of $48,000 worth of claims against the cash, $58,000. When the Cash balance is considered together with the liabilities it will be used to pay, it changes any decision to spend a large portion of the $58,000. The liabilities that are listed will shortly have to be paid, and the balance in the Cash account will be applied against those liabilities.[17]

If a decision is made to spend the $58,000, it places the organization in a difficult position regarding the availability of monies to pay the outstanding liabilities when they come due. The amount of

17. This relationship is investigated in chapter 12 through financial ratio analysis.

"free" cash (i.e., with no liability claims against it) amounts to $10,000. In addition, there is a receivable for interest income of $7,500 that appears on the accrual-based Balance Sheet. The total amount available for reallocation by the governing board for the subsequent year is $17,500, which is equal to the free cash ($10,000) and the receivable interest income ($7,500). This amount is also equal to the unrestricted portion of the Fund Balance. In effect, the unrestricted or unreserved portion of the Fund Balance is the amount of monies that are available for use by the board ($17,500) in a subsequent year.

The accrual-based Balance Sheet records all the liabilities and assets of the organization, and it clearly shows the amount of monies available for use in a subsequent fiscal period. The amount shown in the Fund Balance as unrestricted accurately corresponds with the amount of monies available for the organization's use, whereas in the cash-based Balance Sheet this information is not easy to determine. It should be clear that the different bases for establishing a fund accounting system can affect decisions about the use of monies.

Several other differences are apparent when the two balance sheets are compared. The accrual-based Balance Sheet has a more complete listing of the organization's assets than the cash-based Balance Sheet. A listing of these assets allows for better control over them. For example, under the cash-based system there is no record of supplies. In other words, after the supplies are purchased, there is no accounting for them or control over them.

Both the Statement of Receipts and Expenditures and the Statement of Support, Revenue, and Expenses show expenditures/expenses as being higher than receipts/revenues and support. Note the change this causes in figure 3–17. The Excess is no longer called the Excess of Receipts over Expenditures, as it had been called in figure 3–14; because expenditures are higher now, it is called the Deficiency of Receipts over Expenditures. A similar change is apparent in figure 3–15 for the Statement of Support, Revenue, and Expenses. When this Deficiency is transferred to the Fund Balance, it decreases the credit balance in that account. In the cash-based statement, the decrease is $51,000, to a balance of $58,000, and under the accrual statement the decrease is $81,500, to a balance of $17,500.[18]

Another difference is apparent when the Statement of Receipts and Expenditures is compared with the Statement of Support, Revenue, and Expenses. There is a $30,500 difference in the Deficiency be-

18. This $17,500 is computed as follows: Beginning Fund Balance ($109,000) less Deficiency in figure 3–15 ($81,500) less Reserves in the Fund Balance ($10,000) = $17,500.

tween the two statements, increasing from $51,000 to $81,500 on the cash- and accrual-based statements, respectively. This is because of the increase in expenses that are recognized under the accrual method. The $30,500 difference between the statements is equivalent to about a 37 percent decrease, based on the Deficiency of Support and Revenue over Expenses in figure 3–17. This significant change from one method of accounting to the other illustrates the point that adoption of the accounting method for a fund accounting system requires a conscious choice by management. This decision should not be left only to the individual who is responsible for the accounting records.

The significant differences between the cash and accrual bases indicate that careful consideration needs to be given to the choice, but there is a third choice: the modified-accrual method.

Exercise 3–3. Financial Statements

1. Define the balance sheet.
2. Explain the major differences in balance sheets prepared under the cash method and the accrual method.
3. Explain the differences in the terms "Excess of Receipts over Expenditures" and "Excess of Support and Revenue over Expenses."
4. What is the major difference between the terms "Excess of Support and Revenue over Expenses" and "Excess of Expenses over Support and Revenue"?
5. What is a major problem in using cash-based financial statements in making decisions about the allocation of monies?

Modified-Accrual Statements Compared with Cash and Accrual Statements

The major difference between the accrual basis and the modified-accrual basis is that the latter method does not recognize a liability for certain items in the current period for which monies are going to be made available in the subsequent year.[19] For example, interest on long-term debt that is due at the end of the fiscal year is not recognized as being owed, because it is in the subsequent year that the

19. This is called an "appropriation" in later chapters.

board sets aside monies for the interest payment. Also, the modified-accrual method does not recognize revenues unless it is clear that they are "available" (or they are material and delays have arisen in collection). The most significant difference beween the modified-accrual and full-accrual bases of accounting, as they relate to the seven transactions in this chapter, is in the area of prepaid items. Under a modified-accrual basis, prepaid items other than (possibly) supplies are not recognized in the accounts. This practice is apparent when the Balance Sheet in figure 3–19 is compared with the accrual-based Balance Sheet in figure 3–15. The Prepaid Rent account for $8,000 is "missing" from the modified-accrual Balance Sheet.

Ramifications from the $8,000 difference also are apparent in the totals on the two balance sheets in figures 3–15 and 3–19. One difference occurs because the Prepaid Rent account is not recognized as an asset, and there is no Reserve for Lease Prepayments in the Fund Balance in figure 3–19. The $8,000 difference between the Deficiency on the Statement of Support, Revenue and Expenses and the Statement of Support, Revenue, and Expenditures (figure 3–18)

Eclectic Organization
Statement of Support, Revenue, and Expenditures
for Year Ended June 30, 19x8

Support and Revenue:		
Support	$1,400,000	
Theatrical Revenue	25,000	
Interest Revenue	7,500	
Total Support and Revenue		$1,432,500
Expenditures:		
Personnel	$1,501,000	
Supplies	8,000	
Award	1,000	
Lease	12,000	
Total Expenditures		1,522,000
Deficiency of Support and Revenues over Expenditures		$ (89,500)

Fig. 3–18. Modified-Accrual based Statement of Support, Revenue, and Expenditures for Eclectic Organization for Fiscal Year Ending June 30, 19x8

Eclectic Organization
Balance Sheet
June 30, 19x8

Assets		Liabilities	
Cash	$ 58,000	Accounts Payable	$ 10,000
Grant Receivable	75,000	Salaries Payable	12,000
Interest Income Receivable	7,500	Deferred Restricted	
Inventory of Supplies	2,000	Contributions— Grants	75,000
		Unearned Theatrical	
		Revenue	25,000
		Award Payable	1,000
		Total Liabilities	$123,000
		Fund Balance	
		Unrestricted	$ 17,500
		Restricted:	
		Reserve for Inventory	
		of Supplies	2,000
		Total Fund Balance	$ 19,500
		Total Liabilities &	
Total Assets	$142,500	Fund Balance	$142,500

FIG. 3– 19. Modified-Accrual based Balance Sheet for Eclectic Organization for Fiscal Year Ending June 30, 19x8

occurs because Rent Expenditures are higher under the modified-accrual basis.

The $8,000 greater Deficiency in the modified-accrual over the accrual basis Statement of Support, Revenue, and Expenses in figure 3– 17 is about a 10 percent change. Although this is an important change, it is not as significant as the $30,500 difference between the cash and accrual methods. This is especially true since the cash basis creates a more favorable financial picture by reducing the expenditures.

Under the modified-accrual basis, the amount of the unrestricted Fund Balance is still $17,500, which is the same as under the accrual method. An overallocation of cash by the board is not likely to be made under the modified-accrual basis because the limitations on cash are apparent in the Fund Balance. The modified-accrual basis uses slightly different accounting procedures than the accrual basis, but it has the advantages similar to those of the accrual basis in this example.

When the modified-accrual basis is compared with the cash-based statements, all points that were made between the cash and accrual statements still hold true. The modified-accrual statements provide management with a better instrument than cash-based statements for making financial decisions.

Exercise 3–4. Account Classification

Place checkmarks in reference to the accounts listed below to indicate what type of balance sheet they would likely be found on.

Balance Sheet Prepared under:

	Cash Basis	Accrual Basis	Modified-Accrual Basis
Cash			
Interest Income Receivable			
Prepaid Insurance			
Reserve in Fund Balance			
Accounts Payable			

Audits of NFP Organizations

This chapter highlights some questions which need to be asked regarding the type of accounting system adopted in a particular NFP entity. If the organization is small enough, it may be possible to maintain the accounting records on a cash basis.[20] Of course, if it is decided to maintain the records on a cash basis, another problem may develop, because the results of any type of independent audit of the records of an NFP organization that uses a cash-based accounting

---

20. "For numerous nonprofit organizations, complex accounting procedures may be neither practical nor economical, and reporting based essentially on cash receipts and disbursements may be adequately informative. If financial statements prepared on the cash basis are not materially different from those prepared on the accrual basis, the independent auditor may still be able to conclude that the statements are presented in conformity with generally accepted accounting principles." American Institute of Certified Public Accountants, Statement of Position 78–10, p. 10.

system are not likely to be satisfactory. The major purpose of this section is not to describe the procedures in an audit but to indicate the effect of an audit of use of a cash-based accounting system.[21]

Before we proceed to the audit opinion, an explanation is needed of the function of an audit and the importance of the opinion rendered by the independent public accountant who performs the audit. An audit is an examination of the books and records of say, an NFP organization to determine whether generally accepted accounting principles (GAAP) were followed in preparing the financial statements. GAAP, the established body of rules and guidelines that should be followed in the preparation of financial statements, is formed around the pronouncements of such organizations as were described on pages 6–7. If the accounting firm that performs the audit discovers, through its investigation of the records, that the organization is not following GAAP, a satisfactory opinion is not provided.[22] This type of opinion is called a "qualified opinion" whereas an opinion that is considered satisfactory is called an "unqualified opinion." The unqualified opinion certifies that the accounting system has been adequately examined and GAAP is being followed. One GAAP recommendation for NFP organizations is that the financial statements be prepared on an accrual basis rather than a cash or modified-accrual basis.[23]

The requirement for an accrual system relates to the financial statements, but the accounting records themselves can be maintained on a cash basis, with conversion to an accrual basis at the end of the fiscal year. If this conversion is properly handled, the statements should receive an unqualified opinion. Of course, this conversion is time consuming and expensive.

There may be some question as to the reason an audit is required. In many cases it is required by a regulatory agency which provided a grant to the organization that is audited. Some other granting agency could also require this kind of audit. In addition, the NFP organization may want an audit performed as a further assurance of proper use of the monies for which it has responsibility.

AICPA has issued an audit guide, *Audits of Certain Nonprofit Organizations,*[24] for accountants who perform audits on nonprofit

21. Although this section compares the audit effects of using cash or accrual methods, the modified-accrual method can also result in less than a satisfactory audit opinion.

22. There can be other reasons for an opinion that is not satisfactory besides not following generally accepted accounting principles.

23. Again, note that there may be an exception for "small" organizations.

24. American Institute of Certified Public Accountants, *Audits of Certain Nonprofit Organizations* (New York: AICPA, 1981).

organizations such as libraries, museums, civic art organizations, botanical societies, and fourteen other nonprofit organizations.[25] An audit guide provides recommendations to be followed in auditing an organization in a specialized type of industry, such as NFP organizations. Recommendations in the audit guide relate to the specific type of opinion required for an NFP organization that follows GAAP and those that do not follow it.

Following is the type of opinion recommended for issuance by independent accountants who examine financial statements that are based on GAAP:

[Scope Paragraph]

We have examined the balance sheet of XYZ Nonprofit Organization as of December 31, 19x2, and the related statement[s] of activity [and of changes in financial position] for the year then ended. Our examination was made in accordance with generally accepted auditing standards and, accordingly, included such tests of the accounting records and such other auditing procedures as we considered necessary in the circumstances.

[Opinion Paragraph]

In our opinion, the financial statements referred to above present fairly the financial position of XYZ Nonprofit Organization at December 31, 19x2, and the results of its operations [and the changes in its financial position] for the year then ended, in conformity with generally accepted accounting principles applied on a basis consistent with that of the preceding year.[26]

Below is the type of opinion issued by independent auditors after examining a set of books prepared under the cash basis, that is, a qualified opinion:

[Scope Paragraph]

We have examined the statement of cash receipts and disbursements of ABC Association for the years ended December 31, 19x2 and 19x1. Our examinations were made in accordance with generally accepted auditing standards and, accordingly, included such tests of the accounting records and such other auditing procedures as we considered necessary in the circumstances.

[Explanatory Paragraph]

As described in Note X, the statement of cash receipts and disbursements is a summary of the cash activity of the association and does not present certain transactions that would be included in financial state-

25. Refer to pages 6–7 for a complete list of these organizations.

26. American Institute of Certified Public Accountants, *Audits of Certain Nonprofit Organizations* (New York: AICPA, 1981), pp. 43–44.

ments of the association presented on the accrual basis of accounting, as contemplated by generally accepted accounting principles. Accordingly, the accompanying statement is not intended to present financial position or results of operations in conformity with generally accepted accounting principles.

[Opinion Paragraph]

In our opinion, the accompanying statement presents fairly the cash receipts and disbursements of ABC Association for the years ended December 31, 19x2 and 19x1.[27]

The qualification, in the middle paragraph of the opinion, is related to the cash basis of accounting, which is not considered acceptable under GAAP.

In many cases, a small public library's accounting system is audited as part of a city's or county's accounting system, not as a separate entity from the city or county. If the library's accounting system is judged part of the larger system, the library may not have a significant impact on the entire organization's audit report. Therefore, it is possible that cash-basis accounting in a public library that is a small part of a larger accounting system could occur without serious audit problems.

Although it may be possible to use a cash basis of accounting without problems, instances may arise where separately audited statements are required. If a separate audit is required, it may still be possible to use the cash basis. As previously stated, if a cash-based system is converted to an accrual system at the end of the year, the criteria for an unqualified opinion can be met.

The possible consequences of using a cash-based system should be clear to the administrators of a public library or other NFP organization that is audited as a separate entity. Otherwise, if a public library is audited as part of a larger organization's accounting system, the use of a cash-based system may not seriously affect the type of opinion that is rendered. Therefore, from an audit standpoint, a cash-based system may be utilized within an NFP organization where the unit is an insignificant part of a larger governmental unit or where conversion to an acceptable accounting method is done at the end of the fiscal year. But the recommended method is accrual.

There is one final factor which should be considered before a library unit or other NFP organization decides to adopt a cash-basis

27. American Institute of Certified Public Accountants, *Audits of Certain Nonprofit Organizations* (New York: AICPA, 1981), pp. 50–51. "Note X" refers to a footnote in the notes, which typically follow the financial statements.

system. Although this factor does not affect the audit opinion, it is important from a public relations viewpoint. If the prepared financial statements are used beyond the immediate organization's boundaries, consideration should be given to adoption of GAAP because of the confusion that cash-based statements are likely to create.

Summary

This chapter has presented the basic differences between cash-basis accounting, accrual-based systems, and systems based on modified accrual. The differences between these methods can affect managerial decisions. In addition, use of the cash basis can affect the type of audit opinion that is rendered by the independent accountant. Therefore, establishing an accounting system should be a well-considered decision. The decision should not be left to the accounting personnel alone. If improper funding decisions are made because of the decision to use a cash-based accounting system, the responsibility for these inadequacies rests with the director of the organization and possibly with the board. This does not mean that the cash basis should be ruled out entirely. It *does* mean that the limitations of the cash basis should be understood and corrected by the director and the board prior to making funding decisions. Figure 3–20 provides a summary of the differences between the three accounting methods.

Exercise 3–5. Converting a Balance Sheet

The balance shown below is for Outer Banks Pirate Museum. It is a cash-based balance sheet.

Outer Banks Pirate Museum
Balance Sheet
June 30, 19x5

Assets		Liabilities & Fund Balance	
Cash	$75,000	Liabilities	$ —
		Fund Balance	75,000
	———	Total Liabilities	———
Total Assets	$75,000	& Fund Balance	$75,000

Item	Cash	Accrual	Modified Accrual
Assets	Recognized if cash paid	Assets recognized as received & title passes	Usually no recognition of prepaid assets; capital additions recognized as expenditures
Liabilities	Not recognized	All liabilities recognized as incurred	Most liabilities recognized as incurred, but not on long-term debt
Revenues & Expenses/Expenditures	Not assigned to correct fiscal period where earned or incurred	Correctly assigned to fiscal period where earned or incurred	Not always assigned to correct fiscal period where earned or incurred
Inventory Costs	Recognized when cash paid	Recognized when used	Recognized when purchased or when used
Fund Balance Reserve	Not used	All prepaid assets require a reserve	Only used for supplies inventory
Auditing Effect	Qualified opinion likely	Unqualified opinion	Qualified opinion likely
Adjusting Entries	Not "normal" procedure	Required	Required
Bookkeeping Equation	Assets = Fund Balance	Assets = Liabilities + Fund Balance	Assets = Liabilities + Fund Balance

FIG. 3–20. Summary of Major Differences between the Three Foundations for an Accounting System

The museum is on an island that can only be reached by boat; so it was not an active year for the museum. Assume that the following transactions are the only ones that occurred during the year:

February 15—Purchased $825 worth of supplies. On June 30, 19x5, there are $500 worth of supplies remaining. (Assume no beginning inventory was in existence.)

June 15—The Museum has received notification of the award of a $12,500 grant from the Smithzonen National Museum to be used for the preservation of ship relics. (The grant has not been received as of June 30.)

June 30—As of June 30, 19x5, salaries owed to employees are equal to $3,700.

Required: Convert the cash-based balance sheet to accrual-based balance sheet by incorporating the additional three transactions as necessary.

Selected Bibliography

American Institute of Certified Public Accountants. *Audits of Certain Nonprofit Organizations*. New York: AICPA, 1981.

American Institute of Certified Public Accountants, Statement of Position 78–10. *Accounting Principles and Reporting Practices for Certain Nonprofit Organizations*. New York: AICPA, 1979.

Financial Accounting Standards Board, Statement of Financial Accounting Concepts No. 4. *Objectives of Financial Reporting by Nonbusiness Organizations*. Stamford, Conn.: FASB, 1980.

National Council on Governmental Accounting. *Governmental Accounting, Auditing, and Financial Reporting*. Chicago: Municipal Finance Officers Association, 1980.

4.

Making Budget Dollars Make Sense

The budgetary accounts assist the managers of an NFP organization keep track of the monies that have been provided for the use of the NFP organization by the governing board. This can be very important as in some NFP organizations it may be a violation of law if more monies are spent than are provided at the beginning of the period. Therefore, use of budgetary accounts provide a vital service.

Budgetary accounts (listed in figure 4–1) can be used under most types of accounting systems. The effects of debits and credits on these accounts are also shown in figure 4–1. These accounts relate specifi-

Budgetary Accounts	Debit	Credit
Estimated Revenues	+*	–
Appropriations	–	+*
Encumbrances	+*	–
Reserve for Encumbrances	–	+*

* "Normal" balance of account classification

FIG. 4–1. Budgetary Accounts

cally to the budget handed down by the board of the NFP organization. Those accounts which have been discussed in previous chapters relate specifically to the financial operations, rather than the budgetary operations, of the organization. Accounts concerned with financial operations are called "proprietary accounts." Both budgetary accounts and proprietary accounts appear on the financial statements.

Use of a budgetary accounting system in conjunction with the Expense account provides answers to the following questions:

> How much money do I have left for my department?
>
> Can monies be transferred from supplies to book purchases?
>
> Do we need additional funds to complete our operating year?
>
> Will we have to curtail our program for disadvantaged readers at the end of the month?

All these questions relate to the availability of monies, and the budgetary system will provide the answers.

Estimated Revenues and Appropriations

The budget action of the governing board in approving monies for spending in an NFP organization is incorporated into the accounting system with a journal entry. This entry actually incorporates the approved budget into the formal accounting system. An entry of this type is shown in figure 4–2, as a debit to the Estimated Revenues account and a credit to the Appropriations account for $425,000. The Appropriations account simply shows the amounts that have been approved by the board for spending. In this example, the estimated revenues to be collected, in the Estimated Revenues account, are equal to the amount approved for spending, that is, $425,000 in the Appropriations account. This equality does not occur in all cases, as will be explained shortly.

When the budget is approved or passed by the governing board, it means that the organization has been provided with spending authority for the year. This authority can be allocated to the organization as a whole, as shown in the entry in figure 4–2, or the spending authority can be allocated on a departmental level, as is usually the case. In both cases, the spending authority or the budget must be approved by the board. The illustration in figure 4–2 is a simplified example and, as such, does not divide the appropriation of $425,000 among other

July 1   ESTIMATED REVENUES   425,000
                       APPROPRIATIONS   425,000
              Initial entry to record budget

General Ledger

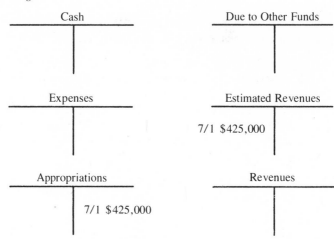

FIG. 4–2. Initial Journal Entry to Record Budget, and Posting to General Ledger

categories, such as supplies, departments, or programs. Further division of the budget is necessary for adequate financial planning.

In the entry in figure 4–2, the Estimated Revenue account is used as a debit. (This account is different from the Revenue account, as was explained on pp. 29–33.) Estimated revenues are projected amounts that are expected to be received from various funding sources throughout the year, whereas revenues are recognized when the estimated revenues actually become available to the organization. Although some projections of estimated revenues are very accurate, such as amounts expected to be received from funding agencies, other projected amounts, such as investment income, are not likely to be as accurate. Regardless of accuracy, the total amount of predicted revenue is used as a base to make appropriations among the various activities of the organization for the budget year. Once the budget appropriations are approved, each program's spending level in the current year is set. Any difference between the amounts recorded as Estimated Revenue and the actual Revenue collected is recorded in the Fund Balance at the end of the fiscal year. In figure 4–2, for example, if the estimated revenues of $425,000 do not materialize, the difference between $425,000 and the amount collected decreases the balance in the Fund Balance. In such a situation, it would be possible for a debit balance to develop in the Fund Balance.

It may appear that providing a reserve in the Fund Balance account for any possible decrease is good financial practice. By not appropriating all the estimated revenues projected, it is possible to provide for a reserve. Such a policy assures that some of the estimated revenues are "set aside" for emergencies. But the main objective of an NFP organization is to provide a service to the public, and if the organization withholds services only to ensure that it maintains a credit balance in its Fund Balance, it is probably not meeting its service objective. It is not considered acceptable practice to retain resources only for the purpose of maintaining or increasing the Fund Balance account. Increases in the Fund Balance are justifiable only when the NFP organization has attempted to provide a full level of services to the public. Therefore, the recommended procedure is to attempt to predict estimated revenues accurately and to base appropriations for programs on a full-service concept.

After the journal entries to record the budget have been made, it is necessary to post them to the ledger accounts. The general ledger and the posting process were explained on pages 36–39, but, as a reminder, the posting process transfers the amounts debited and credited in the journal to accounts in a ledger. The ledger summarizes all journal entries with the current balance of that account. The account contains summarizations of all debits and credits recorded in the journal relative to that account, and this difference is called the balance. Figure 4–2 contains ledger accounts for Cash, Due to Other Funds, Appropriations, Revenues, Expenses, and Estimated Revenues, as well as the initial journal entry. (This ledger is another example of a general ledger.) The journal entry in figure 4–2 has been posted to the proper accounts in the general ledger, and these are the only two accounts with balances in them.

The transaction in figure 4–2 introduces the concept of appropriations and estimated revenues on a simple basis, because there are no additional divisions of appropriations and only one funding source is assumed. Normally, there is more than one funding source, and the appropriations are subdivided among many categories, such as supplies, maintenance, salaries, and employee benefits. When a budget appropriation is separated into detailed appropriation divisions, the accounting system is expanded to incorporate subsidiary ledgers, which are subdivisions of a specific general-ledger account. Subsidiary ledgers provide detailed information about general-ledger accounts that are more easily maintained outside the general ledger. By using subsidiary ledgers, detailed information related to general-ledger accounts does not have to be kept in the general ledger. The total of a specific account balance is maintained in the general ledger, but detailed information about the account is kept in the subsidiary ledger. When each subsidiary account is totaled, it should equal the debit or credit balance in the general-ledger account to which it is related.

Assume that the authorized budget is journalized to specific appropriation accounts. Under this assumption, specific appropriations for items such as salaries and supplies are posted to the subsidiary-ledger accounts. At the same time, the total of the appropriations is posted to the Appropriations account in the general ledger. Due to this dual posting to accounts in both ledgers, the total of the detailed appropriation accounts in the subsidiary ledger should equal the balance of the Appropriations account in the general ledger. The general-ledger accounts serve as a check on the subsidiary accounts. For this reason, they are known as "control accounts."

Without a control account and a subsidiary ledger, detailed information about appropriations would have to be recorded in the general ledger, which would be tedious. Therefore, a subsidiary ledger is a consideration for any general-ledger account where extensive detailed account information can be eliminated from the general ledger.

Figures 4–3 and 4–4 expand the initial recording of the budget entry to include the use of subsidiary accounts. The journal entry in

July 1	ESTIMATED REVENUES	425,000		
	City of X		200,000	
	County Commission		125,000	
	State Grant		100,000	
	APPROPRIATIONS			425,000
	Personnel Salaries			250,000
	Employee Benefits			39,000
	Book Purchases			48,000
	Standing Orders			7,950
	Supplies			9,350
	Maintenance			48,000
	Publicity			6,000
	Miscellaneous Utilities			10,000
	Staff Development			6,700

Fig. 4–3. Initial Entry to Record Budget at Beginning of Fiscal Year

General Ledger

Estimated Revenues	Appropriations
$425,000	$425,000

Revenue Ledger*   *Appropriation-Expense Ledger***

City of X	Personnel Salaries	Maintenance
$200,000	$250,000	$48,000

County Commission	Employee Benefits	Publicity
$125,000	$39,000	$6,000

State Grant	Book Purchases	Misc. Utilities
$100,000	$48,000	$10,000

Standing Order	Staff Development
$7,950	$6,700

Supplies
$9,350

*Total debit balance in Revenue Ledger is equal to $425,000.
**Total credit balance in Appropriation-Expense Ledger is equal to $425,000.

FIG. 4–4. Relationship between General Ledger and Subsidiary Ledgers after Postings from Journal

figure 4–3 is the same as the one in figure 4–2 except for the listing of three debit subsidiary accounts under Estimated Revenues and nine credit subsidiary accounts under Appropriations. The procedure for entering these accounts in the journal entry is to place them, slightly indented, under the proper control account. The indentation indicates that they are subsidiary accounts. In figure 4–3, the $200,000 of estimated revenues projected to be received from the City of X is recorded as a debit, slightly indented under the control account Estimated Revenues. In a similar fashion, subsidiary accounts are recorded under the Appropriations control account. All the dollar amounts in these journal entries require posting to the general ledger or the subsidiary ledgers.

The three debits to the subsidiary accounts under Estimated Revenues add up to the amount debited to the Estimated Revenues account, and the credits to the nine subsidiary accounts are equal to the total credited to the Appropriations account. The subsidiary account's balances will always add up to the balance in a control account in the General Ledger.

There can be several layers of subsidiary accounts below a designated control account. Subsidiary financial information can be maintained on a departmental level and further subdivided to specific expenses within a department. As a new subsidiary level is added below the control account, an additional indentation serves to distinguish that subsidiary level in the journal entry. The indentation system in the subsidiary accounts works much like the indentation system in a formal outline. An outline starts with roman numerals representing the major headings or the control accounts in the General Ledger. Lesser topics or departmental financial information are *indented* below the roman numerals and represented by arabic numbers. Still lesser topics or specific expenses in a department are *indented* and represented by letters in the outline. The decision of how many layers of subsidiary accounts to use is a decision that should be related to the information needs of management. As more levels are added more detailed information is available, but in a manual accounting system the addition of more than two levels below the General Ledger control accounts makes the system tedious to maintain. At any rate, each subsequent division of subsidiary accounts should total to the control account in the level above it. This upward balancing is apparent in all journal entries in this chapter. The upward control becomes more apparent in figure 4–5 when department levels are used as a subsidiary level between the General Ledger control accounts and lower subsidiary accounts.

Finally, the credit entry to the Appropriations account is posted to the general ledger. (See figure 4–4.) The subsidiary accounts—Personnel Salaries, Employee Benefits, Book Purchases, Standing Orders, Supplies, Maintenance, Publicity, Miscellaneous Utilities, and Staff Development—are posted to the subsidiary ledger. The amounts allocated to each of these subsidiary accounts indicate the manner in which total estimated revenues have been budgeted. It is important to record the approved budget in the books as a means to ensure that spending is limited by the amount of the appropriations that have been approved by the governing board. This initial recording of the budget provides control points for limitations on future spending. More information is provided later about these control features, but as an example, consider the $6,700 that has been authorized for the Staff Development account. This account provides monies for attending seminars and professional meetings. Recording this budget appropriation in the subsidiary accounts provides a spending limit for staff development.

One of the subsidiary ledgers that is used with an NFP's general ledger is known as the Appropriation–Expense ledger, and it is illustrated in figure 4–4. One of its purposes is to record detailed information about the allocation of the $425,000 appropriation. The posting procedure to this ledger is also illustrated in figure 4–4. The Appropriations account in the general ledger is a control account for the Appropriation–Expense ledger. Once the postings have been made to the general ledger and the subsidiary, the balance in the Appropriations account and the total of all the subsidiary accounts are equal to $425,000. If postings to both ledgers are up to date, the balance in the control account should always equal the total of the balances in the subsidiary ledger. This relationship between a control account and its related subsidiary ledger allows for easier detection and isolation of errors in the account balances.

In addition to the introduction of subsidiary accounts under the Appropriations credit entry, the journal entry in figure 4–3 introduces subsidiary accounts for estimated revenues. The three subsidiary accounts are the City of X, the County Commission, and the State—the sources of funding for the NFP organization. All three funding sources are posted to a subsidiary ledger called the "revenue ledger," which is illustrated in figure 4–4. The $425,000 debit entry in the journal for estimated revenues is posted to the Estimated Revenues account in the general ledger, and this account acts as the control account over the revenue ledger. The balances in the three subsidiary accounts in the revenue ledger are equal to the Estimated

Revenue account in the general ledger. Again, this illustrates the relationship between a control account and its subsidiary ledger.

The journal entry illustrated is adequate for an NFP organization that does not require any departmental or program budget information or control. If an organization requires more detailed information about departments and programs, the entries require the introduction of another subsidiary account, based on a departmental or program classification. For example, an account such as Circulating Library is a program classification.

Before we proceed to the next entry, which incorporates additional accounting information about programs and departments, an assumption must be made about the relationship between a program and a department. When a program, such as an audio-visual program, is established, it is assigned, as nearly as possible, to one department. The reason for this one-on-one relationship is to ensure that control and responsibilities are clearly established for the program. When program activities are spread over a number of departments, the primary responsibility for the program becomes less clear. In addition, any allocation of central administration's salary costs to programs that are partially run by two or more departments can lead to difficulties.[1] Finally, assignment of a program to a single department should result in less duplication of effort. (Numerous examples exist in the federal government, where a program is assigned to several agencies and there is much duplication of efforts.) Although this problem would not be expected in a small NFP organization, assignment of a program to several departments tends to contribute to its development. Therefore, for our purposes, the assumption is made that programs are assigned *within* departments. For example, the program that relates to children is considered to be part of the Children's Library, a separate department in the main library.

In the next series of journal entries, illustrated in figure 4–5, departmental divisions have been introduced as new accounts in the subsidiary ledgers. The departments are listed as Audio-Visual, Regional History, and Children's Library. The specific appropriations are separately entered in the journal under each departmental account. The detailed appropriation accounts under each departmental account are equal to the total departmental appropriation. For example, in the Audio-Visual Department the total appropriation is $25,000, and this amount is equal to the total appropriations for personnel, books, and

---

1. The cost allocation method is explained in chapter 13.

	Debits		Credits

		Debits	Credits
July 1	ESTIMATED REVENUES 55,500		
	City of X	28,500	
	County Commission	15,000	
	State Grant	12,000	
	APPROPRIATIONS		55,500
	Audio-Visual		25,000
	Personnel		12,000
	Books		10,500
	Supplies		2,500
	Regional History		12,500
	Personnel		6,700
	Books		4,800
	Supplies		1,000
	Children's Library		18,000
	Personnel		12,500
	Books		3,700
	Supplies		1,800

FIG. 4–5. Initial Entry to Record Budget Includes Departmental Accounts

supplies. All these amounts are posted to the proper accounts in figure 4–6. The number of specific appropriations under each department has been limited for illustrative purposes.

The entries to the Estimated Revenue control account and its subsidiary accounts in figure 4–5 are the same as in figure 4–3, except the dollar amount has changed. As there is no major difference (except the change in dollar amounts), the posting process for the Estimated Revenue account and its subsidiary accounts is not illustrated in figure 4–6, where the general ledger and the Appropriation–Expense ledger are presented.

The manner in which the accounts are in the Appropriations–Expense subsidiary ledger should be noted. Each account is classified to a department by the first two digits in the account code, and the decimal digits indicate whether the credit is for supplies, books, or a personnel item. For example, account number 14.02 indicates the account is part of the Regional History Department (14), and the specific item is a book purchase (.02).

Figures 4–5 and 4–6 disclose budget information according to departments. As is apparent in the journal entry in figure 4–5, the departmental budget information is subcategorized between the Appropriations credit entry and specific appropriation accounts, such as

General Ledger

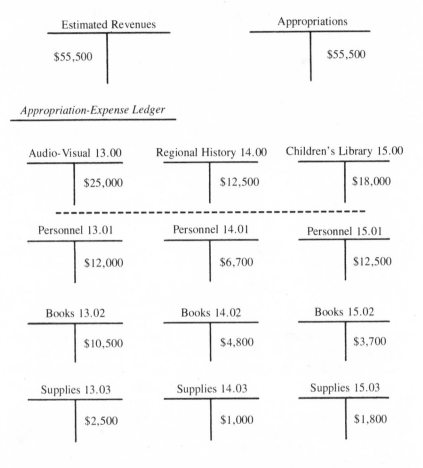

FIG. 4–6. Postings to Appropriation-Expense Ledger and General Ledger, with Departmental Accounts

Supplies and Books. Supplies and books are called "object" classifications of appropriation or expenses. The departmental account is maintained in the subsidiary ledger, along with the specific appropriation accounts for supplies, etc. The department accounts act as a control account over the expenses of each department, and the total of all departments equals the total in the Appropriations account in the general ledger.

This method of categorizing departmental budget information utilizes another layer of accounts in the subsidiary ledger. These additional accounts are useful if this information is needed or frequently requested (on a total departmental basis) by the director or the board. If the information is needed only by the separate appropriations in each department, such as Supplies and Books, it is possible to eliminate the departmental accounts.

It is always possible to separate the specific appropriation accounts with the use of account numbers. For example, the Supplies account for Administration could be classified as account number 16.03, whereas the Supplies account for the Regional History Collection could use account number 14.03. It would be obvious to which department the supplies appropriation belongs without having a separate departmental control account. The major difference in an accounting system without departmental control accounts is that departmental information, in total, could be generated only by adding all the department's specific object appropriations. This information is already available in a system that uses departmental accounts. If accounting is requested on a total department basis, without classifications as to appropriations, a departmental control account should be utilized, as it will save tedious work; otherwise, it should be eliminated.

Exercise 4–1. Journalizing Initial Budget Entry

In the current budget year the Montclair Heritage Art Center has received or will be receiving monies from the following sources: (1) investment income, $75,000, (2) federal awards for general operations, $25,000, and (3) anticipated collections in a fund-raising campaign, $10,000. In its June meeting, these monies received final approval for spending as follows:

Personnel	$75,000
Administrative Supplies	4,500
Craft Supplies	5,200
Utilities	10,100
Staff Development	1,100
Publicity	1,200
Repairs and Maintenance	4,000

a)   Journalize in general-journal form the entry necessary to record the budget, assuming departmental account classifications and subsidiary expenditure ledgers are not used.

b)   Journalize in general-journal form the entry necessary to record the budget, assuming departmental account classifications are not used but subsidiary expenditure ledgers *are* used.

c)   If the accounts are maintained without some sort of departmental information on expenses, what type of problems can arise?

d)   Assume that a Craft Education and Exhibit Department are added to the organization structure of the Art Center. Furthermore, assume that the expenses are divided equally between them. How would this change the journal entry necessary to record the budget?

Estimated Revenues, Revenues, and the Revenue Ledger

Previously, it was stated that estimated revenues are projections of funding that will become available to the organization. When these funds actually become available, they are recognized as revenues. The journal entry for recording estimated revenues has been illustrated, and after the estimated revenues are recorded in the accounts, the monies are received from various funding sources. Prior to the time they are received, a receivable is recognized in the accounts. When the funds are actually received, Cash is debited in the journal and the receivable is canceled.

In figure 4–7, a debit and credit entry is made to the account Due from the City of X and Revenues, respectively, to recognize an increase in revenues. This type of entry can be made for any of the funding sources. The journal entry for the City of X should be made shortly after the estimated revenues from the city have been recognized, on July 1, in figure 4–5. The receivable Due from the City of X will appear in an account in the general ledger. The credit entry will be posted to the Revenue account in the general ledger. Also, recorded in the journal entry is a credit to the subsidiary account City of X. The amount credited to this account will be posted to the revenue ledger.

July 2	DUE FROM CITY OF X	28,500		
	REVENUES		28,500	
	City of X			28,500
July 5	CASH	7,125		
	DUE FROM CITY OF X		7,125	

FIG. 4–7. Recognition of Revenues for Subsidiary Account, City of X

Although this journal entry used the receivable account Due from City of X, a receivable is not always used in recording revenues. In many cases the funds are received in cash. If no previous receivable had been recognized in the accounts, a receipt of cash is recognized as a debit to Cash and a credit to Revenues and the City of X account.

In the second journal entry in figure 4–7, the cash from the City of X is received in the form of a quarterly payment. The cash receipt increases the cash available and decreases the amount receivable from the City of X. Both of these accounts are posted to the general ledger, and no subsidiary ledger accounts are affected by this transaction.

In using a revenue ledger it is necessary to consider the format of the accounts incorporated in the ledger. Figure 4–8 illustrates one type of format for the account, City of X, that can be used in the revenue ledger (which records the estimated revenues and revenues in the same account). The initial entry in this account is the estimated revenues projected for this funding source at the beginning of the fiscal year. For the City of X, this amount is $28,500. As the actual revenues are received in cash, or recognized as a receivable, they are recorded in the account and the balance in the account is reduced. This is seen when the July 2 entry for $28,500 is posted into the revenue ledger, causing the balance in the Balance of Estimated Revenues column to decrease to zero.[2]

At the end of each fiscal year, a schedule should be prepared to show the differences between estimated revenues projected at the beginning of the year and the actual revenues received. The purpose of this comparison is to show the accuracy of the revenue projections and to indicate where adjustments may be necessary in subsequent-year projections.

As the Revenue account and the Estimated Revenues account in the general ledger are temporary accounts, they must be "closed" at the end of the year. (The process used to close temporary accounts is illustrated in chapter 5.) Basically, the process results in any temporary accounts with a debit or credit balance being reduced to a zero balance by transferring the current balance to the Fund Balance account. This procedure is said to "zero balance" an account.

Two closing procedures can be followed with the revenue ledger. It, too, can be zero balanced at the end of the fiscal year, or it can

---

2. Although this balance is reduced to zero, this reduction does not always immediately occur. In the case of some revenues (such as fines), it takes longer to collect the estimated revenues for the year as they are recognized only when the cash is received; that is, they are not recognized as a receivable.

REVENUE LEDGER:
Account No: **27** City of X

Year: 1987 – 1988

Date	Description	Post. Ref.	Estimated Revenues	Actual Revenues	Balance of Estimated Revenues
7/1	Initial budget entry	GJ 1	28,500		28,500
7/2	Recognition of receivable	GJ 1		28,500	- 0 -

Fig. 4–8. Format and Entries in Revenue Ledger Account

simply be filed away and a new ledger opened for the current year. The method selected is a matter of choice. In either case, the revenue ledger is relatively easy to maintain.

Encumbrances, Reserve for Encumbrances, and Expenses

The interrelationship of the three accounts, Encumbrances, Reserve for Encumbrances, and Expenses, is introduced at this point. Only Encumbrances and Reserve for Encumbrances accounts are part of the budgetary system, but an Expense account is also a necessary part of the accounting procedure to determine the amount of uncommitted monies. Therefore, it is included with the explanation of the two budgetary accounts.

In an NFP organization, the question continually arises as to the amount of monies still available for spending by the organization. Introduction of an encumbrance system into a fund accounting system allows this question to be answered without difficulty. For some NFP organizations, the answer to this question can extend beyond management needs to legal implications. In some cases, expending more funds than have been appropriated can raise the question of legal action against the official responsible. Fortunately, overexpending is not likely to result with use of an encumbrance system.

An "encumbrance" discloses a commitment of monies for an anticipated purchase at the time the purchase order is *issued*. If purchase orders are not used, any commitment of monies creates an encumbrance. A journal entry for an encumbrance is made prior to the time the ordered items have become a liability or have been paid. The ordered items create a liability only when the billing statement is received and accepted. At the time a purchase order is issued, an entry is made in the journal, debiting the Encumbrances account and crediting a Reserve for Encumbrances account. At this time, the funds have been "encumbered" by the debit to the Encumbrances account. The Encumbrances account in the general ledger acts as another control account over the accounts in the appropriation-expense ledger. It should be noted that in addition to the Encumbrances account's acting as a control account over the appropriation-expense ledger, the Appropriations and Expense accounts in the general ledger are also control accounts over this subsidiary ledger.

At the time the Encumbrances account is debited, the effect is to reduce the amount that has been appropriated for a specific account. As an illustration, assume a purchase order is issued for supplies in the amount of $300 and recorded in the journal as a debit to Encumbrances and a credit to Reserve for Encumbrances. As soon as these journal entries are posted to the ledgers, they reduce the appropriation for supplies. This procedure provides accurate information to the department head as to the amount of monies available for future spending in this supplies account.

The Reserve for Encumbrances account acts as a restriction on the Fund Balance, indicating that not all funds are available for use by the entity. The role of the Reserve for Encumbrances in the Fund Balance is the same as the other reserve accounts, such as the Reserve for Inventory of Supplies (explained on pp. 64–65).

The typical entries that are used in an encumbrance system are illustrated in figure 4–9, where issuance of a purchase order on July 15 results in a journal entry debiting the Encumbrance account and the Audio-Visual account (the latter being slightly indented to indicate it will be posted to a subsidiary ledger), as well as crediting the Reserve for Encumbrance account. The debit to Encumbrances and the credit to Reserve for Encumbrances will be posted to the general ledger.

After the vendor receives the purchase order and accepts the order, the goods are shipped and a sales invoice (or billing statement) is sent to the purchasing organization. When the purchasing organization receives the sales invoice and the goods, it is necessary to approve the invoice and make payment on it. At the time of payment, two situations can develop. The amount of the invoice is assumed to be equal to the amount of monies which had previously been encumbered, in which case the original encumbrance entry is simply re-

July 15	ENCUMBRANCES	37	
	Audio-Visual Supplies	37	
	RESERVE FOR ENCUMBRANCES		37
	Recording initial obligation on appropriation for Purchasing Order #11		
Aug. 10	RESERVE FOR ENCUMBRANCES	37	
	ENCUMBRANCES		37
	Audio-Visual Supplies		37
	Recording reversal of encumbrances		
Aug. 10	EXPENSES	40	
	Audio-Visual Supplies	40	
	CASH		40
	Recording payment of cash for supplies received		

FIG. 4–9. Typical Sequence of Entries for Encumbrance System

versed and the invoice is paid. The journal entry to record the payment of the invoice is a debit to the Expense account and a credit to the Cash account. The second type of situation occurs when the invoice is *not* equal to the amount that had previously been encumbered. Under these conditions, the same accounts are debited and credited, but although the dollar amount for the reversal of the encumbrance is the same as the amount originally encumbered, the amount on the invoice is different. This difference is reflected in figure 4–9 for the entry on August 10, where it can be seen how the $3 difference between the amount originally encumbered and the actual amount paid is handled in the journal entries. This difference will also be reflected in the postings to the subsidiary ledger. There must be an adjustment for the difference to the subsidiary account balance in the appropriation-expense ledger so that it will properly reflect the amount available for future spending.

Before these transactions are posted to the ledgers, a new format for the subsidiary accounts needs to be illustrated. The new format is used to save recording time and effort. Encumbrances, expenses, and appropriations are all recorded in the appropriation-expense ledger. If the standard form of account is used in the ledger, as represented by the T accounts in figures 4–4 and 4–6, it makes the recording process difficult because an account has to be established for the appropriations in supplies (for example), another account for the expenses in supplies, and a third account for the encumbrances in supplies. To determine the amount of funds available, all three accounts have to be consolidated and compared. To avoid this cumbersome process, encumbrances, appropriations, and expenses are *not* separated into three different accounts; instead, they are combined into one account. The balance in that account is the amount of appropriated monies still available. In other words, the account balance provides the answer to the question, How much money do we have available to spend?

The type of format for this account is illustrated in figure 4–10— one of several formats that can be used to combine appropriations, expenses, and encumbrances into one account. The first columns of the account contain information about the date, type of transaction, post reference, and purchase-order number. The first column, under "Encumbrances–Issued," records the journal entry debiting the encumbrance, and the second column, "Liquidated," records the credit entry which reverses the initial encumbrance entry. The third column, "Outstanding Balance," maintains the total amount of the appropriation that is encumbered or committed. (These headings can be retitled to use names other than the ones chosen here.)

APPROPRIATION-EXPENDITURE LEDGER

Year: *198A - 1988*
Fund: *Gen. Fund*

Account No.: *13.03*
Account Title: *Audio-visual supplies*
Appropriation: *$2,500*

Date	Description	P. Ref.	Purchase Order Number	ENCUMBRANCES			Expense	Unencumbered Balance
				Issued	Liquidated	Outstanding Balance		
7/1	Appropriation							2500
7/5	Cleaning Supplies		7	225		225		2275
7/15	Cataleg Cards		11	37		262		2238
7/25	Cleaning Supplies		7		225	37	220	2243
8/10	Cataleg Cards		11		37	0	40	2240

Fig. 4—10. Account Form in Appropriation-Expense Ledger Contains Information about Appropriations, Encumbrances, Expenses

Following the three encumbrance columns is another column which records the amount of the actual expenses. This amount is recorded at the same time the encumbrance is reversed, which usually occurs when the invoice has been approved for payment. The last column in the account contains the information which answers the question of the department head or director: How much of the appropriation remains for future spending? The portion of the appropriation that has not been spent or obligated is called the "unencumbered balance."

The first entry on July 1 in the account in figure 4–10 relates to the initial appropriation which was allocated for supplies in the Audio-Visual Department by the governing board. The appropriated amount is equal to $2,500, and it is the same amount that was shown in the T account for Audio-Visual Supplies in figure 4–6. The T accounts in figure 4–6 were used to provide an introduction to the material, but the account in figure 4–10 is an example of the actual type of account that could be used in the appropriation-expense ledger. In the initial entry, the appropriation is equal to the unencumbered balance, but as encumbrances and expenses are made, the appropriation is reduced.

The July 5 entry in the account has been posted from a journal entry that is not shown, but the entry records Purchase Order 7, for cleaning supplies. It is recorded under the "Encumbrances–Issued" column, and it reduces the amount of unencumbered funds to $2,275. This indicates to anyone who uses the account that the appropriation has been reduced by the amount of the purchase order, and that the purchase order is considered a commitment of these funds. (It is not a liability.)

The July 15 entry in the account corresponds with the journal entry on July 15 in figure 4–9, in response to issuance of another purchase order, and it is recorded in the same manner as the previous entry. It, too, reduces the unencumbered balance, indicating a further commitment of funds.

On July 25, the invoice for the July 7 purchase of cleaning supplies is approved for payment and paid. This transaction (which has not been illustrated as a journal entry) liquidates the $225 outstanding encumbrance, and it is entered under the "Encumbrances–Liquidated" column. After this liquidation, a balance of $37 remains encumbered. At the same time that the $225 encumbrance is liquidated, the expense is recorded for the actual amount of the invoice. The *actual* amount that was paid for the purchase was $220, rather than the $225 that was encumbered.

It is not uncommon to find that the amount of the original encumbrance is different from the invoice that is forwarded by the vendor. These differences can arise from price changes. To ascertain that any differences between encumbered amounts and invoices are recognized, a comparison should always be made between the two dollar amounts. Any difference can be easily accounted for by subtracting or adding it to the unencumbered balance. In this case, the encumbrance was for more than the invoiced amount; therefore, $5 is added to the unencumbered balance. At this point, the amount of funds available for additional purchases of supplies is equal to $2,243.

On August 10 the invoice for the catalog cards ordered under Purchase Order 11 is approved for payment and paid. The journal entries for this transaction are recorded in figure 4–9, where it can be seen that the first entry on August 10 is a reversal of the entry on July 15. The reversal occurs because the invoice is being paid and the unencumbered funds are no longer obligated under an encumbrance; instead, these funds are affected by the actual expense. In figure 4–9, under the control account, Encumbrances, the entry to the Audio-Visual Supplies account is recorded. The $37 encumbrance reversal is entered in the subsidiary ledger account in figure 4–10 under the "Encumbrances–Liquidated" columns. The date, description, and purchase-order number are also entered under the proper columns. This entry in the "Liquidated" column of the Audio-Visual Supplies account removes the remaining $37 encumbrance and results in a zero balance in the "Encumbrances-Outstanding Balance" column.

The journal entry to record the payment of the invoice is shown in figure 4–9. In that final journal entry, a debit is made to the control account, Expenses, and a credit to Cash in the general ledger. Beneath the debit to the Expenses account, another debit is made to the Audio-Visual Supplies account in the appropriation-expense ledger. This entry is recorded in the account in figure 4–10, under the "Expense" column, as the $40 entry. It should be noted that the $3 difference between the amount that was encumbered and the amount of the actual expenses is deducted from the unencumbered balance. When the expended amount is *more* than the encumbered amount, the difference must be *deducted* from the unencumbered balance; when the encumbrance is *higher,* the difference is *added* to the unencumbered balance.

The introduction of the subsidiary ledger in this chapter changes the relationship between the accounts as was illustrated in chapter 2, where no subsidiary accounts were used and all expenses were maintained in the general ledger. With introduction of the subsidiary ledger, specific expense account classifications are transferred to the subsidiary ledger accounts and a control summarization account for each subsidiary ledger is maintained in the general ledger. A budgetary system and subsidiary accounts are required parts of a fund accounting system if control is to be maintained over the spending of appropriations, to ensure that appropriations are not overexpended.

Summary

This chapter has explained the function of budgetary accounting in a fund accounting system. A fund accounting system can be established without budgetary accounts, but budgetary accounts, used in conjunction with expenses, allow for quick determination of the amount of monies left in each appropriation classification. It allows the director and the head of a department to easily determine how much money is available for spending. This is particularly important at the end of the fiscal year, when overspending of the year's appropriation can have serious consequences.

As part of the budgetary accounts, the use of two subsidiary ledgers—the revenue ledger and the appropriation-expense ledger—was explained. In addition, the presentations in this chapter introduced a more extended type of account format to use in these subsidiary ledgers. Through these techniques, determination of the amount of monies still available need not involve an extensive search through the records. With budgetary accounting, the amount of remaining monies can be quickly found.

Exercise 4–2. Using the Appropriation-Expense Account

1. The Hennin County Library has recently introduced a budgetary system in its fund accounting system. The bookkeeper was not happy about the change and has resigned. However, the bookkeeper used the new account format for a while, and the director is afraid mistakes were made in the accounts.

    You have been asked to review a typical account—Craft Supplies—to determine if the accounts were properly handled. Craft Supplies records expenditures for supplies that are used to decorate the library. The transactions in this account for the last several months are described below; the Craft Supplies account is also shown. As you review the transactions and the account, correct the bookkeeper's mistakes. Also, make a recommendation to the director as to whether you think there are other mistakes in the budgetary accounting system.

Year: 19×8 – 19×9
Fund: General

APPROPRIATION-EXPENDITURE LEDGER
Account No.: 72-734
Account Title: Craft Supplies
Appropriation: $975

Date	Description	P.R.e.f.	Purchase Order Number	ENCUMBRANCES			Expense	Unencumbered Balance
				Issued	Liquidated	Outstanding Balance		
July 1	Budget Approp.							975
July 15	Craft Supplies		15	185		185		790
July 25	Invoice Rec.		15		185	—		790
Aug. 1	Returned Damaged Goods/ Reduced Approp.		15					765 –25
Aug. 15	Supplies		18	240		240		525
Sept. 5	$300 transferred to Regional History						(300)	825
Sept. 9	Supplies		25	225		225		600
Oct. 3	Invoice Rec.		25		225	—		600

July 1   Budget approved at $975 for Craft Supplies.

July 15   Issued Purchase Order #15 for Craft Supplies for $185.

July 25   Received and approved payment invoice on Purchase Order #15. Invoice was for $200.

Aug. 1   It was discovered that some of the craft supplies received under Purchase Order #15 were damaged, and adjustment was requested (and granted) from vendor for $25.

Aug. 15   Issued Purchase Order #18 for $240 for Office Supplies.

Sept. 5   Money was transferred from Craft Supplies account to Regional History account. Amount was $300.

Sept. 9   Issued Purchase Order #25 for $225 for purchase of craft supplies.

Oct. 3   Received and approved for payment invoice on Purchase Order #25. Invoice was for $250.

2. The Muskegon Art Center is represented by the following organization chart and the dollar amounts appropriated by the board are shown under each organizational unit. The monies to operate the Art Center are received from one major source, investment income. In addition, earned monies are received from play ticket sales, craft education tuition, and receipts from trip ticket sales. These revenues amount to $25,000, $57,000, and $12,200, respectively.

Journalize the initial budget entry, which should be divided down to a divisional level on the Art Center; that is, departmental accounts should be used in the entry. The following description of each organization unit provides an indication of the type of activities taking place in each department. Assume the initial budget entry contains a credit entry to the Fund Balance for $6,600. You will have to estimate the amount of other appropriations in each department (besides those for personnel salaries).

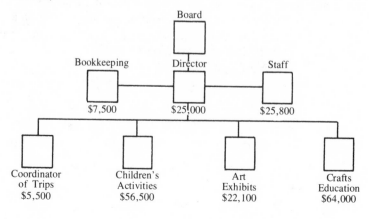

Bookkeeping. This function is staffed by a part-time bookkeeper who maintains the ledgers and handles mailing of purchase orders, as well as receipt of invoices. He works with the auditor, who comes in once a year to audit the records. The bookkeeper's salary is $6,700, and the remainder of the budget is used for supplies.

Director and Staff. This position is held by an individual with an art-center management background who makes $25,000 a year. She has a staff of two secretaries; one is full time and the other is part time. Together, they earn a total of $16,000. The director and staff are responsible for publicity, telephone charges, the entire organization's training program, and the payment of professional fees to the auditor.

Coordinator of Trips. The Art Center sponsors bus trips to see major theatrical productions in New York City. This position is staffed by one part-time person who earns $4,000. This person also has responsibilities under the Crafts Education Department. The trip scheduling requires reservation deposits for bus transportation.

Children's Activities. This department is staffed by a full-time production director and an assistant. Their salaries are $17,800 and $14,700, respectively. Their activities involve the production of plays, including the construction of sets for plays.

Art Exhibits. This department opens selected art works to the public for viewing. It includes paintings and crafts of local artists as well as occasional traveling art exhibits. It is staffed by one full-time employee who earns $15,100 per year.

Crafts Education. A series of classes and workshops is continually conducted in the Art Center. These classes range from stained-glass making to calligraphy. The faculty for the classes is hired from local artists and some supplies are provided by the Art Center. Eventually, each of these classes must be self-supporting through the tuition that is collected. The part-time coordinator of trips works half-time in scheduling classes for Crafts Education and earns $6,500.

5.

End of a Year: Closing Entries

One consideration of any type of accounting system is division of the financial history of an organization into equal time periods. It is necessary to subdivide the life of an organization into equal periods to measure its progress from one period to the other or to evaluate its expenditure pattern between periods.

These periods are either *calendar* years or *fiscal* years. The calendar period follows the January–December calendar year whereas the fiscal year is a twelve-month period that more closely corresponds with the activities of the organization. For example, in an agriculture-related business the most active period is the summer months and the least active is the winter. A fiscal year for this type of business might be the twelve months from the beginning of March to the end of the following February. This period is considered a *fiscal* year rather than a *calendar* year. A common business practice is to schedule the end of the financial year with the end of a business cycle, so that inventories are low and it will be easier to count the ''ending'' inventories.

In an NFP organization, the fiscal year usually begins July 1 and ends on the following June 30, because this period is likely to correspond with sessions of state legislatures and approval of the budget.

Although a July–June fiscal year is common in NFP organizations, the example in the chapter adopts a January–December calendar year.

At the end of a fiscal or calendar year, certain accounting procedures occur. Usually this is the time when financial statements, as described in chapter 3, are prepared. The end of the year is also the time when "closing entries" are prepared, and this chapter explains the process of making those entries.

Previously, it had been mentioned that a number of accounts are considered temporary accounts; that is, they are closed at the end of the fiscal year. Temporary accounts are established only to reflect financial events during the current fiscal year; therefore, their balances should not be carried into the next year. For example, if a governing board approves the budget appropriations for the current fiscal year and they are recorded in the ledgers for the current year, there is no reason to continue to carry these balances or add to them in subsequent years. The objective of temporary accounts is concentrated on the current year, and there is no useful purpose in carrying forward current-year balances in temporary accounts. To eliminate these balances from the accounts, they are closed or "zero balanced" at the end of the year.

Budgetary accounts, as well as accounts for expenditures and revenues, are considered temporary accounts, and all are closed at the end of the fiscal year. This closing process results in transfers to the Fund Balance. Any unexpended appropriations are added to the Fund Balance, and any excess expenses over appropriations contribute to a deficit in the Fund Balance. A difference between estimated revenues and actual revenues also affects the Fund Balance account. The remaining portions of this chapter deal with the entries that must be made to close the temporary accounts.

Closing Temporary Accounts

In a commercial enterprise, the closing process results in credits to all expense accounts and debits to the revenue accounts. Any difference between the debits and credits is transferred to the retained earnings section of the balance sheet. In an NFP organization, the difference is also transferred to the balance sheet, but in this case to the Fund Balance account. The determination and final handling of the difference is more complicated in an NFP organization than in a commercial enterprise because of the conditions upon which the *initial appropriation* is issued.

An appropriation is considered to be either a lapsing or nonlapsing appropriation. A lapsing appropriation can be considered to be an appropriation that is not encumbered by the NFP organization during the fiscal year and therefore is returned to the granting agency. In a completely nonlapsing appropriation, the NFP organization is allowed to keep whatever monies remain from unexpended appropriations during the fiscal year. Many motivational implications are associated with lapsing and nonlapsing appropriations, but only the difference in accounting for these appropriations is presented here.

In this chapter the assumption with a lapsing appropriation is that any *unexpended* appropriations are returned. Although this is generally the case, there may be variations from this assumption in some NFP organizations. Under nonlapsing appropriation authority, it is assumed that any *unencumbered* monies are returned, but monies encumbered at the end of the fiscal year are not returned to the agency that granted the NFP organization its spending authority. The assumption could be changed so that no monies are returned to the agency that granted the spending authority. If the monies do not have to be returned, they automatically create an increase in the Fund Balance in the year-end closing entries. Thus nonreturnable appropriations are the easiest to handle.

The closing entries for the two types of appropriations are illustrated in figures 5–1 and 5–3. In those examples, the entries are presented for the entire fiscal year in a consolidated form. The initial entry is recorded on January 1, 19x8, to record the budget. On November 30 the encumbrances are recorded for the entire year, and on December 15 all expenses are paid. The entire year's transactions are consolidated into these few entries to illustrate the closing process. The closing process is illustrated by the December 31 entries.

When an account is described as "closed," it refers to the process of putting a zero balance in the account and carrying the balance that was in the account to the Fund Balance. For example, the entry on January 1 put a $320,000 credit balance in the Appropriations account in the general ledger. At year-end, the Appropriations account is debited for $320,000, which eliminates any balance in this account. In figures 5–2 and 5–4, the entries shown in figures 5–1 and 5–3 are posted to T accounts to illustrate more fully the closing process. Review of these accounts quickly reveals accounts that have zero balances—that is, those accounts that have been closed.

The closing entries, shown in figure 5–1, are for lapsing appropriations. Under the assumptions of the lapsing appropriation, all funds that are not expended must be returned to the agency that granted the spending authority. The granting agency can use the

19x8

Jan. 1	ESTIMATED REVENUES	325,000	
	APPROPRIATIONS		320,000
	FUND BALANCE		5,000
	Recording the budget		

Nov. 30	ENCUMBRANCES	320,000	
	RESERVE FOR ENCUMBRANCES		320,000
	Recording total encumbrances during the year in one entry		

Dec. 15	RESERVE FOR ENCUMBRANCES	305,000	
	ENCUMBRANCES		305,000
	Reversal of encumbrances at time invoice is paid		

Dec. 15	EXPENSES	305,000	
	CASH		305,000
	Recording payment of invoice		

Dec. 20	CASH	331,000	
	REVENUES		331,000
	Recognition of receipt of estimated revenues previously projected		

Dec. 31	APPROPRIATIONS	320,000	
	RESERVE FOR ENCUMBRANCES	15,000	
	EXPENSES		305,000
	ENCUMBRANCES		15,000
	FUND BALANCE		15,000
	Closing entries		

Dec. 31	REVENUES	331,000	
	ESTIMATED REVENUES		325,000
	FUND BALANCE		6,000
	Closing entries		

Dec. 31	FUND BALANCE	15,000	
	CASH		15,000
	Return of the cash to granting agency		

FIG. 5–1. Sequence of Accounting Entries for Lapsing Appropriations

(General Ledger)

Estimated Revenues	
1/1 $325,000	12/31 $325,000
Bal. $0	

Encumbrances	
11/30 $320,000	12/15 $305,000
	12/31 15,000
	Bal. $0

Appropriations	
12/31 $320,000	1/1 $320,000
	Bal. $0

Reserve for Encumbrances	
12/15 $305,000	11/30 $320,000
12/31 15,000	
	Bal. $0

Expenses	
12/15 $305,000	12/31 $305,000
Bal. $0	

Revenues	
12/31 $331,00	12/20 $331,000
	Bal. $0

Cash	
12/20 $331,000	12/15 $305,000
	12/31 15,000
Bal. $ 11,000	

Fund Balance	
12/31 $15,000	1/1 $ 5,000
	12/31 15,000
	12/31 6,000
	Bal. $11,000

FIG. 5–2. Posting Closing Entries to General Ledger Accounts

previous year's unexpended funds by reallocating them in the subsequent year in any manner.

Reviewing the entries in figure 5–1, we see that $320,000 was appropriated under the current year's budget and the remaining estimated revenues of $5,000, anticipated to be collected during the year, were credited to the Fund Balance. On November 30, $320,000 was encumbered, but only $305,000 was paid on the invoices by December 15, as is apparent by the debit to the Expense account. On the same date, a reversal of the encumbrance occurs.

If we assume that no additional payments were made from December 15 to December 31, this leaves encumbered, but unexpended, funds equal to $15,000. The closing entries on December 31 indicate how this $15,000 is handled with a lapsing appropriation. It can be seen in the December 31 entry that the $15,000 is transferred into the Fund Balance, and the Encumbrances and Reserve for Encumbrances accounts, which had balances of $15,000, are closed. This is also apparent in the T accounts in figure 5–2. At this point, the $15,000 can be returned to the granting agency. Return of the cash to the granting agency is shown as a journal entry by debiting the Fund Balance and crediting Cash for $15,000 on December 31. The granting agency would then determine where these monies are to be used in the subsequent year. If this last entry were not made, the balance in the Fund Balance would be $15,000 too high.[1]

The December 31 entries contain the closing entries for a lapsing appropriation. The first entry, on December 31, closes the Appropriations, Reserve for Encumbrances, Expenses, and Encumbrances accounts. The effect of all these closings is apparent in figure 5–2. It should be noted, as was illustrated by the fund accounting cycle (pp. 9–10), that closing entries are journalized after the financial statements are prepared. This is the necessary sequence of accounting events because it would be impossible to prepare a Statement of Support, Revenue, and Expenses after the closing entries had been journalized and posted to the ledger, as all the temporary accounts would have zero balances. Remember, revenues, support and expenses are temporary accounts.

The second entry on December 31 relates to closing the Revenues and Estimated Revenue accounts, which are also temporary accounts. The Estimated Revenue account was debited on January 1 for the amount of revenues projected to be collected during the year, $325,000. During the year, $331,000 was collected in actual revenue. The entry recorded on December 20 is a cumulative entry of the entire year's revenue collections. As of December 31, these accounts need to be closed. The accounts are closed by "reversing out" the amounts previously placed in them. This is done on December 31 by debiting Revenues for $331,000 and crediting Estimated Revenues for $325,000. The difference, $6,000, which is the increase in actual revenues collected over those estimated, is entered as a credit to the Fund Balance account.

Up to now, these entries have illustrated the lapsing appropriation; the next illustrations are concerned with nonlapsing appropriations.

---

1. It is assumed that the $11,000 remaining in the general ledger accounts is not part of the appropriation from the granting agency.

19x8

Jan. 1	ESTIMATED REVENUES		325,000	
		APPROPRIATIONS		320,000
		FUND BALANCE		5,000
Nov. 30	ENCUMBRANCES		320,000	
		RESERVE FOR ENCUMBRANCES		320,000
Dec. 15	RESERVE FOR ENCUMBRANCES		305,000	
		ENCUMBRANCES		305,000
Dec. 15	EXPENSES		305,000	
		CASH		305,000
Dec. 20	CASH		331,000	
		REVENUES		331,000
Dec. 31	APPROPRIATIONS		305,000	
		EXPENSES		305,000

Closing those amounts that are unencumbered
or expended

Dec. 31	REVENUES		331,000	
		ESTIMATED REVENUES		325,000
		FUND BALANCE		6,000

Closing entries

FIG. 5–3. Sequence of Accounting Entries for Nonlapsing Appropriations

Figure 5–3 illustrates a situation slightly different from figure 5–1 because the assumption is made that if the funds are encumbered, they do not have to be returned to the agency which granted the spending authority. The entries and dollar amounts are the same in figures 5–3 and 5–1 until the first closing entry is made on December 31. In figure 5–3, the debit and credit entries in that closing entry are equal to the appropriations which have been *expended*. The amount of the expended appropriations is equal to the expenses, which total $305,000 for 19x8. The remainder of the appropriations are kept open in the appropriations-expense ledger's subsidiary accounts and the Appropriations control account in the general ledger until the encumbered amounts are either paid or canceled.

General Ledger

Estimated Revenues			Encumbrances	
1/1 $325,000	12/31 $325,000		11/30 $320,000	12/15 $305,000
Bal. $0			Bal. $ 15,000	

Appropriations			Reserve for Encumbrances	
12/31 $305,000	1/1 $320,000		12/15 $305,000	11/30 $320,000
	Bal. $ 15,000			Bal. $ 15,000

Expenses			Revenues	
12/15 $305,000	12/31 $305,000		12/31 $331,000	12/20 $331,000
Bal. $0				Bal. $0

Cash			Fund Balance	
12/20 $331,000	12/15 $305,000			1/1 $ 5,000
				12/31 6,000
Bal. $ 26,000				Bal. $11,000

FIG. 5–4. Posting Closing Entries to General Ledger Accounts

These open accounts are apparent when the T accounts in figure 5–4, which represent the postings from the journal entries in figure 5–3, are reviewed. It can be seen that the Encumbrances, Reserve for Encumbrances, and Appropriations accounts all have $15,000 balances. These balances represent the amount of outstanding encumbrances at the end of the year. If the appropriation were a lapsing appropriation, all these accounts would have zero balances. This difference is clear when these accounts are compared with one another in figures 5–2 and 5–4.

The three temporary accounts with balances can be labeled with the year in which the encumbrance originated, or as "Prior Year" accounts. If this alternative is not satisfactory, the account can be closed—and reopened as a new account with a new name. There is room for choice in this matter; see the appendix to this chapter.

Depending on the size of the accounting system, the procedures may transfer the outstanding balances into new accounts specifically established for these prior-year amounts. This change is made at the beginning of the new year. It is an easy process that involves closing out the balances in the accounts from the previous year and recording these same balances in new accounts, with such names as Appropriations—Prior Years, Encumbrances—Prior Year, and Reserve for Encumbrances—Prior Year. If this process seems unnecessary, it may be possible to keep the old accounts open and relabel them. If the accounting system is a large one, new accounts should be established, but in a small accounting system it can be a matter of choice.

Exercise 5–1. Lapsing and Nonlapsing Appropriations

The Herchal Public Library completed its fiscal year as of June 30, 19x8. Its accounts and the balances in those accounts as of June 30, 19x8, are listed below.

Debits		Credits	
Cash	$ 15,000	Accounts Payable	$ 25,700
Grants Receivable	18,000	Revenues	118,000
Inventory	2,200	Appropriations	120,000
Investments	125,000	Reserve for:	
Estimated Revenues	120,000	Encumbrances	5,000
Encumbrances	5,000	Inventory	2,200
Expenses	122,500	Fund Balance	136,800
	$407,700		$407,700

a) Journalize in general-journal form the closing entries, assuming a lapsing appropriation.

b) Journalize in general-journal form the closing entries, assuming a nonlapsing appropriation.

c) In the case of a nonlapsing appropriation, should accounts payable be equal to encumbrances?

d) Prepare a balance sheet for Herchal Public Library after the closing entries have been made under both a lapsing and nonlapsing appropriation assumption.

e) What are the differences and similarities between these two balance sheets?
f) How much is the difference between projected revenues at the beginning of the year and the actual revenues collected? If there is a difference, is it a serious difference?

Outstanding Encumbrances in Subsequent Year

With a nonlapsing appropriation, the 19x8 encumbered monies will be used to pay invoices received on outstanding encumbrances in the subsequent year, 19x9. This is not a concern with lapsing appropriations as all unexpended monies are returned. Figure 5–5 contains the 19x9 entries for the payment of invoices with the 19x8 encumbered funds from figure 5–3. When the payment is made from the previous year's encumbered amounts, three types of situations could develop between expenses and encumbrances. Although expenses could be exactly equal to encumbered monies, the journal entries illustrate those other two cases where the expenses are not equal to the amount encumbered.

In figure 5–5, case 1 represents expenses that are less than the amount encumbered, and case 2 represents expenses for more than the encumbered amounts. It is apparent that they are journalized in the year following the one in which they were encumbered. In 19x8, the Encumbrances and Reserve for Encumbrances accounts had been left open at the end of the year for the $15,000 that was encumbered. When these amounts are paid, in the early part of 19x9, the encumbrance entries are reversed (as always) and the expense is recorded. If the actual amount of the expense is not equal to the amount of the funds that were encumbered, the difference affects the Fund Balance. In case 1, the February 1 entry reverses the encumbrances and recognizes the expense. These expenses should be clearly separated from the 19x9 expenses by having the date, "19x8," appended to the account's name.

The posting process from the February 1 journal entry for Encumbrances and Reserve for Encumbrances is made in the previous year's general-ledger control accounts as the balances in these accounts are assumed to have remained open. The new account, Expense, 19x8, is maintained in the current year's general ledger, as the Expense ac-

Case I

(If expenses are less than encumbered amounts, the Fund Balance will increase.)

19x9

Feb. 1	RESERVE FOR ENCUMBRANCES, 19x8	15,000	
	ENCUMBRANCES, 19x8		15,000
	Reversal of encumbrances from previous year occurs when invoice is paid in 19x8		

Feb. 1	EXPENSES, 19x8	12,000	
	CASH		12,000
	Recording payment of invoice		

Dec. 31	APPROPRIATIONS, 19x8	15,000	
	EXPENSES, 19x8		12,000
	FUND BALANCE		3,000
	Closing entry for appropriations left open from previous year		

Case II

(If expenses are more than encumbered amounts, the difference will contribute toward a deficit in Fund Balance.)

19x9

| Feb. 1 | RESERVE FOR ENCUMBRANCES, 19x8 | 15,000 | |
| | ENCUMBRANCES, 19x8 | | 15,000 |

| Feb. 1 | EXPENSES, 19x8 | 17,000 | |
| | CASH | | 17,000 |

Dec. 31	FUND BALANCE	2,000	
	APPROPRIATIONS, 19x8	15,000	
	EXPENSES, 19x8		17,000

FIG. 5–5. Closing Entries for Nonlapsing Appropriations in Subsequent Year

count from the previous year was closed. In all cases, where journal entries are made that relate to these previous-year transactions, the year should be appended to the account name so that these expenses are not confused with current-year expenses and make it appear that appropriations for the current year are being overexpended. Any 19x8 expenses should clearly be shown as expending the portion of that year's appropriations which remained open on the books at the end of the previous year. This separation should be reflected in the preparation of financial statements.

On December 31, 19x9, the closing entry is made. This entry closes the account Appropriations, 19x8, which was left open from the previous year; it also closes out the account Expenses, 19x8, which contains the expenses paid in 19x9 for 19x8 encumbrances. Any differences between the two accounts are transferred to the Fund Balance account.

In case 2, journal entries for the accounts are the same as case 1, except that the expense is for more than the amount encumbered in the previous year. The $2,000 increase is apparent in the entries for the February 1 journal entry. When the expense for the purchase is more than the encumbrance, payment of this additional amount may require approval from the governing board because there are insufficient prior-year appropriations available to pay for the more costly purchase.

In case 2, the remaining 19x8 appropriations were $15,000, but the invoice was for $17,000. The $2,000 increase in purchase cost has an effect on the Fund Balance, as can be observed in the December 31 entry. In this entry, the Fund Balance is decreased with a $2,000 debit entry when the Expenses, 19x8, and Appropriations, 19x8, accounts are closed. To make the payment on the more costly purchase, approval may be necessary from the governing board which grants the governmental unit its spending authority. (This requirement for board action varies with organizations.)

When outstanding encumbrances from the previous year are considered, the interests of the organization are best served if a policy (with guidelines) is instituted as to when all prior-year purchase orders are to be canceled if the orders have not been received. Without such a policy, monies are committed to encumbrances and appropriations that can be used elsewhere. A policy might require that all purchase orders from the previous year be canceled after a two-month period if the materials have not been received. When a purchase order is canceled, the encumbrance is reversed and the remaining appropriations that applied to the canceled orders are closed with a debit entry to Appropriations. The corresponding credit entry is made to the Fund Balance.

The closing entries for an NFP organization have been illustrated in this chapter and these entries will be used again in chapters 6

through 11. Before we begin chapter 6, a brief review of the procedures introduced in the first five chapters is in order.

Review

The fund accounting cycle (pp. 9–10) outlines the steps that are
followed and the order in which they are followed in a typical accounting system. Step 1, analysis of transactions, was explained in chapter
2. Step 2, the journalizing of transactions, was covered in chapters 2
through 5. The posting process, step 3, was explained in chapter 2.
The adjusting entries, described in step 4, were covered in chapter 3.
Two financial statements were described in chapter 3, and chapter 5
illustrated the closing entries for an NFP organization.

The only part of the fund accounting cycle which has not been
illustrated is preparation of a *trial balance,* which is simply a totaling
of the debit and credit balances in the accounts in the general ledger
to ensure that they are equal. As shown in the fund accounting cycle,
trial balances are prepared after the adjusting entries have been posted
to the accounts and, later, after the closing entries have been posted.
Preparing a trial balance after the adjusting entries are posted ensures
that the accounts are in balance prior to preparing the financial statements. If all the debits and credits in the general ledger are not equal,
there is probably an error in the accounts, and if it is not corrected, it
will be carried into the financial statements.

A trial balance is also prepared after the closing entries have been
posted. This ensures that all the debits and credits are equal prior to
beginning the journalizing process in the new fiscal year. If an error
is carried forward into the new year, it is very difficult to find it
without reopening the prior year's records.

Besides preparing trial balances after the posting of adjusting and
closing entries, a trial balance should be prepared at the end of each
month during the fiscal year to ensure that debit and credit errors are
caught at the end of each month, rather than later. Preparing a trial
balance at the end of each month is a good procedure to follow to
detect debit and credit errors at reasonable intervals during the fiscal
year.

The trial balance can be a formal statement, with all accounts and
their balances listed and totaled (as in figure 5–6), or it can be an
informal document. If a formal document is not considered necessary, it is possible to use an adding-machine tape, which provides a
simple, running total of debit and credit balances in the general-
ledger accounts. The tape should be dated, initialed by the preparer,
and kept in the records for future reference. In any case, it is not

always necessary to prepare a formal statement. Use of the trial balance will be discussed again in chapter 11 and additional illustrations will be provided.

Figure 5–6 represents the trial balance for Ronald Library on June 30, 19x7, after the closing entries have been posted. The library receives a nonlapsing appropriation each year, and the trial balance shows the balances in the budgetary accounts which have not been closed at the end of the fiscal year because of outstanding encumbrances. The debit and credit balances in the accounts are equal to a total of $127,000, and this equality indicates that the journalizing process can begin in the new year with the accounts in balance.

Ronald Library
Trial Balance
June 30, 19x7

Cash	$ 25,000	
Marketable Securities	20,000	
Due from Other Governments	35,000	
Inventory	12,000	
Prepaid Items	18,000	
Encumbrances, 19x7	17,000	
Appropriations, 19x7		$ 17,000
Reserve for Encumbrances, 19x7		17,000
Reserve for Inventory		12,000
Fund Balance		81,000
	$127,000	$127,000

FIG. 5–6. Trial Balance for Ronald Library on June 30, 19x7

Summary

This chapter explains the concept of closing temporary accounts. It is necessary to close accounts that are used only to reflect the current year's financial activities. The budgetary accounts are related to the current year's budget; therefore, these accounts are considered temporary. The revenue and expense accounts are related to the current year's financial activities only in the sense that the balances in these accounts do not accumulate from year to year. Therefore, they are temporary accounts also. The accounting procedure for closing these accounts was presented and adapted to situations where the appropriations are either lapsing or nonlapsing. The procedures outlined in this chapter assist in allocating funding sources to the correct fiscal year. The closing entries are not really the end of anything, as the accounting cycle immediately begins again, once the closing entries have been posted and a trial balance has been prepared.

Exercise 5–2. Nonlapsing Appropriations in a Subsequent Year

1. The Andes Public Library has a nonlapsing appropriation. Its balance sheet for the fiscal year ending June 30, 19x1, is reproduced below.

Andes Public Library
Balance Sheet
June 30, 19x1

Assets

Cash	$ 7,500
Prepaid Assets	8,000
Inventory	6,700
Investments	69,700
Total Assets	$91,900

Liabilities, Appropriations, & Fund Balance

Liabilities		
Accounts Payable		$15,000
Appropriations	$12,700	
Less: Encumbrances	12,700	—
Fund Balance		
Unreserved		49,500
Reserved for:		
Encumbrances		12,700
Inventory of Supplies		6,700
Prepaid Assets		8,000
Total Liabilities, Appropriations,		
& Fund Balance		$91,900

a) On July 1, 19x1, open new accounts for outstanding encumbrances as of June 30, 19x1.

  b) An invoice for $13,200 is received and paid on July 15 for out-
      standing encumbrances on June 30, 19x1. Journalize the proper
      general journal entry on July 15.
  c) Journalize the closing entries on June 30, 19x2.

2. The John Able Free Library has a nonlapsing appropriation. The bal-
    ance sheet for the June 30, 19x1, fiscal year is reproduced below. The
    library has a policy of canceling all outstanding encumbrances from the
    previous year on August 31 of the current year.

John Able Free Library
Balance Sheet
June 30, 19x1

Assets

Cash	$ 9,300
Prepaid Assets	4,100
Inventory	5,500
Investments	23,100
Total Assets	$42,000

Liabilities, Appropriations & Fund Balance

Liabilities		
Accounts Payable		$ 4,000
Appropriations	$7,500	
Less: Encumbrances	7,500	
Fund Balance		
Unreserved		20,900
Reserved for:		
Encumbrances		7,500
Inventory of Supplies		5,500
Prepaid Assets		4,100
Total Liabilities, Appropriations,		
& Fund Balance		$42,000

  a) On July 21, 19x1, an invoice for $7,100 is received and paid for
      $7,100 of encumbrances outstanding as of June 30, 19x1. This is
      for the actual amount that was encumbered under the purchase
      order. Journalize the proper general-journal entry for July 21.

b)   Journalize the proper general-journal entry on August 31, the cut-off date (assuming no additional invoices were received since July 21).

c)   Journalize any necessary closing entries on June 30, 19x2.

3.   The Burgburg City Library has outstanding encumbrances at the end of the June 30, 19x2, fiscal year as follows:

Encumbrances	$7,300
Reserve for Encumbrances	7,300

An amount equal to $7,300 has been left in the Appropriations account. The library has a policy of canceling all outstanding encumbrances from the previous year on August 31 of the current year. During the first two months of the new year, the following transactions affecting encumbrances occurred:

July 16   A $1,200 invoice is received and paid on a purchase order encumbered for $1,250.

July 31   A purchase order for $525 is canceled.

Aug. 10   A $5,500 invoice is received and paid on a purchase order encumbered for $5,175.

Aug. 31   The remainder of purchase orders encumbered and unfilled from the June 30, 19x2, fiscal year are canceled.

a)   Open new accounts for the old encumbrances and appropriations on July 1, 19x2.

b)   Journalize the transactions for July and August in general journal form.

c)   Make any necessary closing entries on June 30, 19x3.

Appendix

If the Appropriations and Encumbrances accounts in the current year are to be closed when there are outstanding encumbrances, the following entries are made on December 31, 19x8. These entries are for a nonlapsing appropriation.

APPROPRIATIONS	320,000	
EXPENSES		305,000
FUND BALANCE		15,000

Closing the Appropriations account to zero balance

FUND BALANCE	15,000	
ENCUMBRANCES		15,000

Closing Encumbrance out to Fund Balance

The only account which contains the outstanding encumbrances at the end of 19x8 is the Reserve for Encumbrances account. This account is closed to a new account, which indicates that these encumbrances are from the previous year. This entry is also made on December 31, 19x8.

RESERVE FOR ENCUMBRANCES	15,000	
RESERVE FOR ENCUMBRANCES, 19x8		15,000

Opening new, dated Reserve for Encumbrances account

When the invoice is received in the following year, assume it is for $15,000, and the expense is recognized as a 19x8 expense. At the end of the fiscal year the Expense, 19x8 account is closed to the Reserve account.

EXPENSE, 19x8	15,000	
CASH		15,000

Recognizing Expense for prior-year encumbrances

RESERVE FOR ENCUMBRANCES, 19x8	15,000	
EXPENSE, 19x8		15,000

The closing entry

Part 2.

Accounting for the Three Major Funds

The chapters in part 2 introduce the types of funds found in an NFP organization and provide examples of financial statements for each of these funds, as well as combined financial statements for the entire organization. Each dated transaction in the next six chapters will be used in the formulation of financial statements for the H. K. Fines Library, a case study of a public library.

6.

The Operating Fund:
Introduction

The definition of a fund accounting system (p. 4) describes it as a set of self-balancing account groups, called "funds," organized within one NFP organization. The self-balancing set of accounts is composed of assets, liabilities, the Fund Balance, expenses, and revenues. Each of these accounts is "assigned," so that each fund in a fund accounting system has its own set of financial statements (such as those described in chapter 3 under an accrual system).

The previous five chapters, concerned with the basics of fund accounting, explained the account types: assets, liabilities, etc., as well as debits and credits, the different foundations upon which an accounting system can be established, budgetary accounts, and how to make closing entries. These topics are preliminary to introduction of the typical funds actually used in a NFP fund accounting system. This chapter begins the introduction of those funds with the Operating Fund.

The Operating Fund accounts for the daily, routine activities of an NFP organization and, therefore, it is the most widely used type of fund. The financial statements in the Operating Fund are the Balance Sheet; the Statement of Support, Revenue, and Expenses and

Changes in the Fund Balance (SREF); and the Statement of Changes in Financial Position. The first two financial statements were introduced in earlier chapters, and the Statement of Changes in Financial Position is explained in this chapter.

Many typical transactions in the Operating Fund, as well as periodical accounting procedures, were introduced in part 1. Even so, there are unique aspects of accounting for the Operating Fund. Therefore, chapters 6 and 7 explain the specific functioning of the Operating Fund. Chapter 6 explains the financial statements used by the Operating Fund and chapter 7 uses a series of transactions to illustrate the workings of the fund.

Before we begin the explanation of the financial statements, one unique aspect of the Operating Fund needs to be considered. The fund is composed of two subclassifications of accounts, known as "unrestricted" accounts and "restricted" accounts. Unrestricted accounts are expended upon *any* daily operations of the organization whereas restricted accounts are used only for designated purchases. Although these purchases are specifically designated, they are also part of the daily operations of the organization. Due to this distinction between these account groups, unrestricted accounts must be maintained separately from restricted accounts. This generates two distinct account classifications within the Operating Fund. For example, there is a Cash account for both Unrestricted Cash and Restricted Cash. All three financial statements illustrated in this chapter divide the Operating Fund into these two distinct account groups.

Restricted accounts have been designated for specific purposes in the daily operations of the organization because the monies in these accounts have been contributed by donors who have restricted their use. These donors allow the NFP organization to make only certain types of purchases with the monies they have contributed. In order for the NFP organization to provide documentation that these monies have been properly used, separate accounts must be maintained. For example, a monetary gift (under a restricted account classification) would be given to a library for the purchase of certain types of books. These monies cannot be used to purchase *any* book, but the type specifically designated by the donor. These restricted contributions, a unique aspect of NFP fund accounting, must be taken into consideration in preparing financial statements for the Operating Fund.

Operating Fund Financial Statements

Three basic statements compose the financial statements of the Operating Fund. Two of these statements, the Balance Sheet and the

SREF, were introduced in "preliminary" form in chapter 3. The third statement, the Statement of Changes in Financial Position, which has not yet been introduced, provides information about the sources and uses of the organization's resources during the fiscal year. The statements in figures 6–1, 6–2, and 6–3 have been prepared for a hypothetical library, the "Harold Know Fines Library." The Statement of Changes in Financial Position is illustrated in figure 6–3; the SREF and the Balance Sheet appear in figures 6–1 and 6–2, respectively; and all three statements are typical of the financial statements prepared under an actual accounting system.

The SREF and the Balance Sheet are prepared as comparative financial statements that allow the reader to make comparisons between the current year and the previous year. For example, on the SREF in figure 6–1 it can be seen, by comparing the amount of Government Grants received in the year ending June 30, 19x1, with the total received in the year ending June 30, 19x2, that there was an increase in governmental grants of $5,000. In addition, it can easily be seen that total support increased by $18,500. This type of financial statement allows for easy comparison between two years so that trends can be highlighted.

The financial statements for the H. K. Fines Library are arranged to separate the unrestricted accounts from the restricted accounts. Although both of these account groups are within the Operating Fund, they are separated from one another in the financial statements. As previously stated, this separation is important as the restricted accounts can only be used for specific purchases within the Operating Fund. To provide documentation that restricted funds are not used for *all* types of purchases in the Operating Fund, they must be maintained separately from the unrestricted accounts.

STATEMENT OF SUPPORT, REVENUE, AND EXPENSES AND CHANGES IN FUND BALANCES

In this statement, Support and Revenue are separated from each other. "Support" is considered to be contributions received by the library through grants and gifts, such as pledges or bequests, under the settlement of an estate. "Revenues" come from items upon which the library has earned an income, rather than received monies as part of a grant or contribution. Typical of these items are sales revenues that the library might earn as a result of book sales and charging for photocopying or other services, as well as the amounts received from book fines, sales of gift items, a charge for a user's card, or interest and dividends from investments.

H. K. FINES LIBRARY
Operating Fund
Statement of Support, Revenue, and Expenses and Changes in Fund Balance
Year Ended June 30, 19x2
(with Comparative Totals for 19x1)

	Unrestricted	Restricted	Total	June 30 19x1 Totals
Support and Revenue				
Support				
Grants (Note 1)*				
Governments	$ 90,000	—	$ 90,000	$ 85,000
Other	3,500	—	3,500	11,000
Contributions and Bequests	9,000	$15,000	24,000	3,000
Total Support	$102,500	$15,000	$117,500	$ 99,000
Revenue				
Book Fines and Sales	$ 2,100	—	$ 2,100	$ 3,000
Photocopying	3,785	—	3,785	4,000
Investment Income, incl. net gains	3,000	—	3,000	2,700
Total Revenue	8,885	—	8,885	9,700
Total Support and Revenue	$111,385	$15,000	$126,385	$108,700
Expenses (Note 4)*				
Program Services:				
Reference	$ 25,000	$ 8,000	$ 33,000	$ 34,000
Children's Library	13,000	4,300	17,300	15,000
Circulation	32,000	—	32,000	28,000
Regional History	11,000	2,700	13,700	12,000
Total Program Services	$ 81,000	$15,000	$ 96,000	$ 89,000

Supporting Services				
Administration	$ 24,000	—	$ 24,000	$ 40,000
Total Expenses	$105,000	$15,000	$120,000	$129,000
Excess (Deficiency) of Support and Revenue over Expenses	$ 6,385	—	$ 6,385	$ (20,300)
Prior-Year Expenses on Prior-Year Encumbrances (Note 6)*	$ 5,700	—	$ 5,700	$ 100
Excess (Deficiency) of Support and Revenue over Expenses in Current Year	$ 12,085	—	$ 12,085	$ (20,200)
Fund Balance at Beginning of Year	235,190	—	$235,190	$270,490
Transfers	(190,000)	—	(190,000)	(15,000)
Less: Prior-Year Expenses (Note 6)*	(5,700)	—	(5,700)	(100)
Fund Balance at End of Year	$ 51,575	—	$ 51,575	$235,190

* Notes are included in figure 6—4.

Fig. 6—1. Statement of Support, Revenue, and Expenses and Changes in Fund Balances for H. K. Fines Library

The expenses on the SREF are maintained on a program basis—and programs in the H. K. Fines Library are defined on a departmental basis. It is possible to have program definitions overlap departments, as long as expense responsibility can be clearly assigned. The division of expense between two departments is sometimes more difficult than making program definitions along departmental lines. Also, it is advantageous to provide expense information on an "object" basis. (Object expenses are classified according to such uses as maintenance, supplies, or personnel services.) For internal reporting, the accounting system should provide expense information on both a program basis and an object basis. Both forms of reporting are necessary to maintain control over the costs of a library and to detect any trends in expenses. Departmental or program division of expenses is called a "functional" classification.

Reviewing the expenses of the library from 19x1 to 19x2, it can be seen that a cutback in *total* expenses of $9,000 occurred and that Administration had a reduction of $16,000. An object classification of Administration's expenses would provide additional information on the extact reasons for this decrease. Was the cutback due to a reduction in personnel services, due to elimination of a position, or was the reduction due to other reasons? An object classification of expenses would provide the answer to this question. In 19x1 there was a deficiency of Support and Revenue over Expenses by $20,300, but in 19x2 this deficiency was reduced and an excess of $6,385 was achieved, largely through the reduction in expenses.

Another reason why it is important to keep track of expenses is to determine if expenses are maintained within budget guidelines established at the beginning of the year. The board had established expenditure guidelines through its approval of the budget, and if the board established guidelines on a program basis, the individual department heads need to stay within those guidelines. Although it may be possible to transfer monies from one department to another, unapproved expenditures beyond those established by the board, in any area, constitute a serious problem. Even if guidelines are maintained, it is important to review costs on an object basis to determine if certain costs, such as supplies or personnel services, require monitoring—if, say, spending for them is increasing at a rapid rate. This type of analysis should be performed *before* the fact, rather than trying to determine the reason for cost coverages after a program has gone beyond budgeted amounts.

In the SREF, $5,700 is described as "Prior Year Expenses on Prior Year Encumbrances" for 19x2. This amount shows the exact amount used to pay off the preceding year's outstanding encumbrances. The $5,700 is shown as an addition and later as a deduction without any lasting impact on the statement. It can be seen that the $5,700 is added to the Excess, then deducted prior to computing the balance in the year-end Fund Balance. The major purpose for including this figure in the SREF is to show the reader the amount of prior-year encumbrances that are paid in the current year. The purpose of providing this information on the SREF is to disclose the cost of accepting outstanding orders under prior year encumbrances. As previously indicated, prior year encumbrances may be more or less than the actual expense incurred for the purchase. In the H. K. Fines Library, the amount expended is more than the encumbrance, as disclosed in footnote 6.

The $51,575 in the Fund Balance on the SREF at the end of the 19x2 fiscal year should be equal to the amount of the year-end Fund Balance on the Balance Sheet in figure 6–2. Note that the Fund Balance on the Balance Sheet is divided into a restricted and unrestricted portion. (This division should not be confused with the division of the Operating Fund as a whole into a restricted and unrestricted portion, as is shown at the column headings atop the financial statements. The two divisions are unrelated.)

The division on the Fund Balance section of the Balance Sheet provides the board with information as to the exact amount of money that is available for use (i.e., the amount that can be appropriated) in the subsequent fiscal year. For example, in reviewing the Balance Sheet for the Fines Library in 19x2, it can be seen that only $11,180 of the Fund Balance is available for appropriation. This is the amount of the Fund Balance that is undesignated. Although the unrestricted portion of the Fund Balance is equal to $33,125 ($4,945 + $17,000 + $11,180), $4,945 of this unrestricted portion has been designated by the board for the purchase of office equipment and $17,000 is designated for investments. Although the board designated a portion of the Fund Balance for the purchase of office equipment and investment purposes, this is a discretionary assignment, and it can be reversed by board action.

For Fund Balance amounts to be completely unavailable to the board, they must be part of the *restricted* Fund Balance. The restrictions under this section of the Fund Balance for the library are typical of the restricted Fund Balance section of any NFP organization. The restrictions are for outstanding encumbrances, which are a potential commitment of monies, and for the amount reserved for inventories that are already committed and cannot be otherwise expended by the board. Unlike the designated Fund Balance, these amounts are truly restricted and cannot be expended by the board. Therefore, it is important to review the Unrestricted Fund Balance to determine the amount available for appropriation in a subsequent year.

It is also useful to study the changes that occur in the Fund Balance components from year to year. The largest change in the library's Fund Balance occurred in the unrestricted section; the total in this section decreased by $200,165 from June 30, 19x1 to June 30, 19x2. This is a large decrease, compared to the other changes in the components of the Fund Balance, and additional investigation into its causes would be justified.

When the total of the Fund Balance account is reviewed, the reasons for the $200,165 change can be isolated. In 19x2 a significant decrease occurred in the Fund Balance because of the transfer of $190,000 in that year to the Plant Fund, which is another fund in the Library. The transfer was made because the Plant Fund is part of a program to which the Operating Fund provides monies for the purchase of long-lived assets, such as buildings and equipment. At periodic intervals, these transfers are made to the Plant Fund. (More detailed information will be provided about the transfer in chapter 10, which deals with the Plant Fund.) Various types of transfers can occur between the funds in an NFP organization, and this is only one example.

As previously stated, the SREF also separates unrestricted and restricted accounts from one another. Restricted accounts are composed of support and expenses; support is received from contributions and bequests and expenses are made to meet the stipulations under which the contribution or bequest was received. Each year, the amounts of recognized support and restricted expenses are equal, because it is necessary for an expense to be made before the monies that have been contributed for a designated purpose can be recognized as a contribution or bequest. Therefore, expenses should be exactly equal to the amount of support, and a zero balance will always exist in the Restricted Fund Balance. Expenses in the restricted portion of the SREF indicate where expenditures were made for program support. In most cases, these expenditures are for the purchase of books for a specific portion of the collection.

BALANCE SHEET

The Balance Sheet represents the assets, liabilities, and the Fund Balance of an organization. The Balance Sheet in figure 6−2 for the H. K. Fines Library is similar to the balance sheets prepared in the earlier chapters except for two major differences: (1) there is an

H. K. FINES LIBRARY
Operating Fund
Balance Sheet
June 30, 19x2
(with Comparative Totals for 19x1)

	Unrestricted	Restricted	Total	June 30 19x1 Totals
Current Assets				
Cash, including interest-bearing savings accounts	$17,000	$14,700	$31,700	$212,190
State Grant Receivable	16,000	—	16,000	7,100
Pledges Receivable, at estimated net realizable value (Note 1)*	7,200	—	7,200	—
Prepaid Assets and Other Current Assets	6,750	—	6,750	900
Total Current Assets	$46,950	$14,700	$61,650	$220,190
Investments (Note 2)*	$17,000	—	$17,000	$ 40,000
Total Assets	$63,950	$14,700	$78,650	$260,190
Liabilities and Fund Balance				
Current Liabilities				
Accounts Payable	$12,375	—	$12,375	$ 15,000
Deferred Restricted Contributions (Note 3)*	—	$14,700	$14,700	$ 10,000
Total Current Liabilities	$12,375	$14,700	$27,075	$ 25,000
Fund Balances				
Unrestricted				
Designated by Board for:				
Office Equipment	$ 4,945	—	$ 4,945	—
Investments	17,000	—	17,000	$ 40,000
Undesignated	11,180	—	11,180	193,290
Restricted				
Encumbrances (Note 1)*	11,700	—	11,700	1,000
Inventory	6,750	—	6,750	900
Total Fund Balance	$51,575	—	$51,575	$235,190
Total Liabilities and Fund Balance	$63,950	$14,700	$78,650	$260,190

* Notes are included in figure 6–4.

FIG. 6–2. Balance Sheet for H. K. Fines Library

unrestricted and a restricted division of the accounts, and (2) the Balance Sheet is a comparative statement. Despite these differences, the Balance Sheet is the same basic statement as those prepared in chapter 3 under the accrual basis.

As previously stated, it is necessary to divide accounts into an unrestricted and a restricted portion so that it can be clearly shown that restricted monies are being used only for the purposes designated by the donors. A comparative Balance Sheet is a convenience that tells the reader of changes that have occurred from the previous year. For example, there is a change in Prepaid Assets and Other Current Assets of $5,850 between the two years. In this case, this account is composed of the library's inventories, and the reason for such a large change in the inventory should be investigated. At present, it is impossible to tell if the 19x1 inventory was significantly *under* the normal balance or if the 19x2 inventory is *higher* than the normal balance.

Another change that should always be reviewed is the change in the cash balance. If there had been a significant decrease in the Cash account balance, this would be easily detected through comparison of the Cash account in the comparative Balance Sheet. When the change in the Cash account is computed, it is equal to $180,490, which is a significant change from one year to the next for the library. The reason for this large change can be attributed to the cash transfer to the Plant Fund.

As stated, the Fund Balance total on the Balance Sheet should always be equal to the Fund Balance total on the SREF. For the period ending June 30, 19x2, these two totals are equal to $51,575. In addition, the total of the restricted portion of the Fund Balance, other than the portion restricted for Encumbrances, is equal to the amount in the Prepaid Asset account. This is apparent in the H. K. Fines Balance Sheet where the Prepaid Asset and Other Current Assets balance of $6,750 (which represents the amount of supplies unused at the end of the 19x2 year) is equal to the portion of the Fund Balance restricted for the Inventory.[1] This same equality exists between the amount recorded as an asset under Investments and the Unrestricted Fund Balance designated by the board for investments.[2]

1. This account could contain other prepaid items besides inventories. Additional types of prepaid assets would require additional restrictions in the Fund Balance.

2. The Investments account relates to long-term commitments of monies, but if monies are invested into securities for only a short period, the Marketable Securities account should be used to record the investments. When using the Marketable Securities account, it is not necessary to establish a reserve in the Fund Balance, as these securities can be sold and used for spending purposes.

There is a differentiation between unrestricted and restricted accounts on the Balance Sheet. As those account classifications are reviewed, it should be noted that the unrestricted group uses more accounts than the restricted group, because the restricted portion of the Balance Sheet records only cash (and possibly investments) as an asset that is equal to the amount of liabilities. This equality is a characteristic of the way liabilities are recorded here. In the H. K. Fines Library, the Cash account of $14,700 is equal to Deferred Restricted Contributions, a liability. This latter account records the obligation incurred by the library in accepting monies which can only be expended as specified by a donor. These two amounts should be equal, as the liability account, Deferred Restricted Contributions, is reduced only when cash is expended on a qualified purpose which has been specified by the donor who contributed monies to the library. Therefore, restricted accounts are usually composed of only one asset, Cash, and one liability, Deferred Restricted Contributions.

STATEMENT OF CHANGES IN FINANCIAL POSITION

The third financial statement that is prepared for the Operating Fund is the Statement of Changes in Financial Position, an important financial statement which discloses information that is unavailable through reviewing the Balance Sheet or the SREF. The basic purpose of the Statement of Changes in Financial Position is to provide a summary of sources and uses of resources during the year. This statement provides information as to where resources were used during the year and from what sources they were generated. Resources are generated for an NFP organization from contributions, borrowed money, investment income, bequests, and earnings, and are used to make purchases of various types or transfers to other funds. Using the Statement of Changes in Financial Position, the reader can quickly determine how the resources received during the year were used or whether they were not used. This information cannot be easily obtained from any other financial report, and therefore any set of financial statements prepared without the Statement of Changes in Financial Position is incomplete.

The general term "resources" has been purposely used in the preceding paragraph because the resources concept in the Statement of Changes in Financial Position can be defined in different ways. In this chapter, "resources" will be synonymous with "working capital," which refers to the difference between current assets and

H. K. FINES LIBRARY
Operating Fund
Statement of Changes in Financial Position
Year Ended June 30, 19x2

	Unrestricted	Restricted	June 30, 19x1 Totals
Sources of Working Capital:			
Excess of support and revenues over expenses	$ 6,385	—	$ 6,385
Less: Net Gain on Sale of Investments	2,690	—	2,690
Working Capital provided by operations	$ 3,695	—	$ 3,695
Sale of Investments (including gain on sale of $2,690)	25,690	—	25,690
Deferred Restricted Contributions Received	—	$ 15,000	15,000
Total Sources of Working Capital	$ 29,385	$ 15,000	$ 44,385
Uses of Working Capital:			
Transfer to Plant Fund	$ (190,000)	—	(190,000)
Deferred Restricted Contributions recognized as support	—	$ (15,000)	(15,000)
Total Uses of Working Capital	$ (190,000)	$ (15,000)	$ (160,615)
Increases (Decrease) in Working Capital	$ (160,615)	—	$ (160,615)
Changes in Working Capital Components:			
Increase (Decrease) in current assets:			
Cash	$ (185,190)	$ 4,700	$ (180,490)
State Grant Receivable	8,900	—	8,900
Pledges Receivable	7,200	—	7,200
Prepaid Expenses	5,850	—	5,850
	$ (163,240)	$ 4,700	$ (158,540)
(Increase) Decrease in current liabilities:			
Accounts Payable	$ 2,625	—	$ 2,625
Deferred Restricted Contributions	—	$ (4,700)	(4,700)
	$ 2,625	$ (4,700)	$ 2,075
Decrease in Working Capital	$ (160,615)	—	$ (160,615)

FIG. 6–3. Statement of Changes in Financial Position for H. K. Fines Library

current liabilities and is a common method for measuring changes in resources.

It should be remembered that "current assets" are cash or other assets that are expected to be converted to cash within one year or that result in cash from operations within that year. "Current liabilities" are obligations that are expected to be liquidated with current assets or by incurring additional current liabilities. When current assets are more than current liabilities, a "positive" working capital balance exists. This balance can be used in the operations of the NFP organzation before long-term financing is needed or before the organization must sell assets (such as investments or equipment) to finance its operations.

When working capital is evaluated, increases and decreases from one year to the next are used to measure its changes. For example, assume that the balance in the Cash account, a current asset, decreases $6,000 during the year. During the same period, Accounts Payable, a current liability, decreases by $7,000. The overall effect of these changes is a decrease in the working capital of $1,000, which shows that the NFP organization used more resources than it received. The important question is where did the additional resources come from to pay the Accounts Payable. Was an asset given up in exchange for a reduction of the amount owed to a creditor? Was money borrowed? The answer is very important for it has implications for the future functioning of the organization.

If an organization obtains the additional resources through the generation of support and revenues, it is in better financial shape than a similiar organization which has to sell its furniture and other assets to generate the additional inflow of resources to pay its accounts payable. Although this is an extreme example, it illustrates the importance of knowing where the NFP organization receives its inflows of resources to finance its operations. The Statement of Changes in Financial Position makes these sources and uses apparent.

The Statement of Changes in Financial Position for the H. K. Fines Library (figure 6–3) is composed of two basic sections. The top part lists the sources and uses of working capital and cumulates the increase or decrease in working capital during the year. The bottom section is a schedule of changes in current assets and current liabilities during the year. This schedule cumulates in the same increase or decrease in working capital as determined in the upper portion.

In the top part of the statement a distinction is made between working capital generated from operations, in this case $3,695, and working capital generated from "other sources." In the case of the

Fines Library, the "other sources" is sale of investments, for $25,690, and a distinction must be made between these two sources. They are separated from one another to show the amount of resources generated from the normal operations of the organization which arise largely from support and revenue. These sources are distinguished from other, nonrecurring sources, such as the sale of investments. This distinction allows the reader of the statement to recognize resources that are likely to be continual sources.

The H. K. Fines Library has had a decrease in working capital of $160,615 in the year ending June 30, 19x2. This decrease, which arose from the $190,000 transfer to the Plant Fund, was reduced by working capital from operations ($3,695) and the sale of investments ($25,690). In the lower portion of the statement, the effect of this transfer on the Cash account is shown. A decrease occurred in the Cash account balance from the previous year that is almost equal to the entire amount of the transfer.

Through a review of the statement it can be determined whether an NFP organization is using working capital to finance long-term operations, but it is also important to know what sources of working capital are used to finance long-term operations. In the case of the library, the transfer was the largest use of working capital, and it was financed through the Cash account. This analysis could have shown that it was financed through borrowing, which might have left the library with a significant debt to carry into future years. At the present time, the library does not have any difficulty financing its operations, but it is unlikely that in the current year it would be able to make a transfer of the size it made in the year just ended.

In reviewing the Statement of Changes in Financial Position, it should be noticed that the net gain of $2,690 on the sale of the temporary investment is deducted from the working capital generated from operations. At first this may appear confusing, but it must be deducted; otherwise the gain will be double-counted in the statement. The easiest way to explain the reason for this deduction is to review the entry when the stock was initially sold. The stock was sold for $25,690 in cash, and this sale resulted in a net gain of $2,690. The entry to record the sale follows:

CASH	$25,690	
INVESTMENTS		$23,000
GAIN ON SALE OF INVESTMENTS		2,690

Recording the sale of investments with an original cost of $23,000

The gain is recorded under revenues on the SREF and becomes

part of the Excess of Support and Revenue over Expenses. Therefore, the net gain of $2,690 is part of the Excess of $6,385.

In presenting the sources of working capital, it is necessary to show the complete resource inflow generated from each source. The sale of the investment generated an increase in working capital of $25,690, which is shown separately from the sources generated from operations. The problem arises because the gain of $2,690 is now contained in both the Excess, $6,385, and the sale of the investment for $25,690. To correct this situation, the gain is deducted from the Excess and included only as a source of working capital received from the sale of the investment. Without this adjustment, the gain would be double-counted. Losses are handled in opposite fashion, that is, as an addition to the Excess.

The schedule at the bottom of figure 6–3 shows the changes that occurred in the components of working capital, that is, current assets and current liabilities. The increase/decrease in working capital that is computed in this schedule should be equal to the change in the top portion of the statement. It can be seen that there were increases in all current assets during the year, except for the $185,190 decrease in Cash. These changes resulted in a decrease in current assets of $163,240. The change in current liabilities was equal to a decrease of $2,625. All of this change was accounted for by the decrease in Accounts Payable, indicating that the balance in this account had been reduced by cash payments. The decrease in current liabilities is deducted from the decrease in current assets to arrive at a decrease in working capital of $160,615, which is equal to the change in sources and use of working capital previously computed. The decrease in Accounts Payable is a use and the decrease in assets is a source. For that reason, they are deducted from one another.

Just as changes in working capital are computed for the unrestricted accounts, changes in working capital must be determined for the restricted accounts. In reviewing figure 6–3, it can be seen that the changes in the restricted accounts eliminate each other, so that the net effect of the changes is zero. In the Statement of Changes in Financial Position, the restricted accounts recognize $15,000 as support from Deferred Restricted Contributions and as a use of working capital. In the lower portion of the statement the Cash account increased $4,700 from the donors' contributions and the liability account, Deferred Restricted Contributions, also increased by $4,700 because of the obligations generated by acceptance of the donors' contributions, to be used only for a specific purpose. The net result of all these changes in restricted accounts is always zero, and this pattern is typical for these accounts.

NOTES TO FINANCIAL STATEMENTS

An integral part of the previously described financial statements is the notes to these statements. (The notes for the H. K. Fines Library are presented in figure 6–4). These footnotes provide additional disclosures about the financial activities of the organization that cannot be conveniently placed in the financial statements themselves.

Note 1 relates to the significant accounting policies followed by the library, because the basis upon which financial statements are prepared needs to be described. In this case, the accrual basis is used. If a library does not use the accrual basis of accounting, it should be disclosed in two places. First, if the financial statements are audited, the use of an accounting method other than the accrual method is likely to be disclosed as a qualification in the audit opinion rendered by the independent public accountant.[3] Second, it should be disclosed in the first note to the financial statements. The first footnote describes the significant accounting policies used by the organization, and part of that disclosure relates to the method of accounting.

In addition to the accounting method, the first footnote should disclose the following:

1. Is fund accounting followed?
2. Explanation of restricted resources
3. How grant income is recorded
4. How income from gains and losses on investments is handled
5. How amounts received under pledges are recorded
6. If contributed facilities are used, their fair rental value
7. Contributions that are recognized as contributed services of lay personnel, with expense charge for their services
8. Descriptions of encumbrances.

Note 2 for the H. K. Fines Library is concerned with its investments, and this information needs to be expanded upon in the footnotes to the financial statements. The disclosures in note 2 in figure 6–4 are required for either long-term or temporary investments in marketable equity securities. The distinction between long-term and temporary investments is that the latter are held for less than one year. Marketable equity securities are defined as any instrument representing ownership shares (e.g., common, preferred, and other capi-

3. See page 78.

NOTE 1, *Summary of Significant Accounting Policies*

The financial statements of H. K. Fines Library have been prepared on the accrual basis. The significant accounting policies followed are described below to enhance the usefulness of the financial statements to the reader.

Fund Accounting

To ensure observance of limitations and restrictions placed on the use of resources available to the library, the accounts of the library are maintained in accordance with the principles of fund accounting. This is the procedure by which resources for various purposes are classified for accounting and reporting purposes into funds established according to their nature and purposes. Separate accounts are maintained for each fund.

The operating funds, which include unrestricted and restricted resources, represent the portion of expendable funds that is available for support of library operations.

Expendable Restricted Resources

Operating funds restricted by the donor, grantor, or other outside party for particular operating purposes are deemed to be earned, and reported as revenues of operating funds when the library has incurred expenditures in compliance with the specific restrictions. Such amounts received but not yet earned are reported as restricted deferred amounts.

Grants

The library records income from unrestricted grants in the period designated by the donor.

Other Matters

All gains and losses arising from the sale, collection, or other disposition of investments and other noncash assets are accounted for in the fund that owned the assets. Ordinary income from investments, receivables, and the like is accounted for in the fund owning the assets.

Legally enforceable pledges less an allowance for uncollectible amounts are recorded as receivables in the year made. Pledges for support of current operations are recorded as operating fund support. Pledges for support of future operations and plant acquisitions are recorded as deferred amounts in the respective funds to which they apply. Encumbrances represent obligations in the form of purchase orders, contracts, or other commitments which have been appropriated, but for which no liability has yet been incurred.

NOTE 2, *Investments*

Investments are presented in the financial statements in the aggregate at the lower of cost (amortized cost, in the case of bonds) or fair market value.

Continued

FIG. 6–4. Footnotes to 19x2 Financial Statements of H. K. Fines Library

	Cost	Market
Operating Fund	$17,000	$21,000

Investments are composed of the following:

	Cost	Market
Corporate Stocks	$ 7,000	$11,000
U.S. Government Obligations	10,000	10,000
	$17,000	$21,000

Fair market value is determined by aggregating all current marketable securities. At June 30, 19x2, there was unrealized gain of $4,000 pertaining to the current portfolio. This portfolio had a cost on June 30, 19x1, of $30,000, and a market value of $32,300.

A net realized gain of $2,690 on the sale of marketable equity securities was included in the determination of Excess (Deficiency) of Support and Revenue over Expenses for 19x3. The cost of the securities sold was based on a first-in, first-out method in both years.

NOTE 3, *Changes in Deferred Restricted Amounts*

Balances at beginning of year	$10,000
Additions:	
Contributions and Bequests	8,000
Investment Income	1,700
	$19,700
Deductions—Funds expended during year	5,000
Balance at end of year	$14,700

NOTE 4, *Functional Allocation of Expenses*

The costs of providing the various programs and other activities have been summarized on a functional basis in the statement of support, revenue, and expenses and changes in fund balances. Accordingly, certain costs have been allocated among the programs and supporting services benefited.

NOTE 5, *Commitments and Contingencies*

The library receives a substantial amount of its support from federal, state, and local governments. A significant reduction in the level of this support, if this were to occur, may have an effect on the library's programs and activities.

NOTE 6, *Current Year Expenditures on Prior-Year Encumbrances*

The amount encumbered at the end of the 19x1 year was $5,000. During the 19x2 fiscal year, $5,700 was expended on these encumbrances.

FIG. 6–4. (Continued)

tal stock).[4] If the investments represent something other than owner-ship interests, these securities are not considered marketable equity securities.

In effect, this division allows four types of investments: (1) marketable equity (ownership) securities—short term; (2) marketable equity (ownership) securities—long term; (3) marketable debt securities—short term; and (4) marketable debt securities—long term. Generally, the investments of the Operating Fund are for temporary investments of idle cash, and they represent marketable equity securities—short term. In the case of the Fines Library, the investment is not classified under current assets and, therefore, it is a long-term marketable equity security. This classification provides more illustrative information about handling gains and losses on securities in the Statement of Changes in Financial Position. In most cases, however, investments of the Operating Fund are classified as current assets and called marketable securities rather than investments. As each of the four types of investment requires somewhat different accounting treatment, each will be considered separately in the following descriptions.

Prior to consideration of the difference in these types of securities, a feature they have in common needs to be considered: the means that can be used to evaluate them. There are two basic ways all marketable equity securities and short-term marketable debt securities can be valued.[5] Either the market value or the lower of cost or market can be used. With marketable debt securities—long term, three methods can be used to determine value: amortized cost, market value, or lower of amortized cost or market.[6]

Securities that are purchased on a national stock exchange are bought for the market price when they are initially acquired, but changes occur in that market price on a daily basis, so that a difference occurs between the price paid for the securities (cost) and the current market price on those same securities. The market value of a security is its current market price, and when the market-value method is used for evaluating securities, the market price is recorded in the accounting records. This is an acceptable procedure for NFP organizations.

4. "Accounting for Certain Marketable Securities," *Statement of Financial Accounting Standards No. 12* (Stamford, Conn.: FASB, 1975), par. 7.

5. American Institute of Certified Public Accountants, Statement of Position 78–10, *Accounting Principles and Reporting Practices for Certain Nonprofit Organizations* (New York: AICPA, 1979), par. 79.

6. Ibid.

A second way in which securities can be valued is by using the lower of cost or market. Under this method, if the cost paid for the security is lower than the year-end market price, the purchase cost is the value at which the investments are listed on the Balance Sheet. If the market price is lower, the securities should be carried at the lower market price on the Balance Sheet.

Another way of valuing securities is based on amortized cost.[7] In this case, cost valuation does not make changes in the carrying value of securities due to market-price changes (unless those market-price changes are assumed to be permanent). These price changes are not considered permanent, unless the organization in which these investments have been made has suffered a financial upheaval, such as bankruptcy, causing the investments' value to fall.

It is required that a decision be made as to the method to use with each of the four classes of securities,[8] and the method has to be used consistently throughout the organization's investments, regardless of whether they appear as part of the Operating Fund or another fund.

The decision to choose a method to value an investment also affects the way in which gains and losses on that security are recognized. A security can have "realized" or "unrealized" gains and losses. A realized gain or loss occurs when the security is either sold for more than was paid for it—a realized gain—or for less than was paid for it—a realized loss. This type of gain or loss occurs in a security exchange external to the NFP organization. An unrealized gain or loss, on the other hand, does not involve a party outside the NFP organization. Unrealized gains or losses occur when, at year-end, there is a difference between the market value of the security and the cost or price paid for that security. If the cost is lower than the market value, an unrealized gain has occurred, and if the market price is lower than the cost paid, an unrealized loss has occurred.

If the market-value method of evaluation is used, the difference between the market value and the cost price of the security at the end of the fiscal year is recognized on the SREF as an unrealized gain or loss in the same manner as if it were a realized loss. If a security is sold during the year, the gain or loss that is recognized is the difference between the last evaluation date, at the previous year-end, and the price at which the security was sold. For example, if a security is

---

7. The term "amortized cost" will be explained in more detail shortly.

8. The four groups of securities are: (1) Marketable Equity Securities—short term; (2) Marketable Equity Securities—long term; (3) Marketable Debt Securities—short term; and (4) Marketable Debt Securities—long term.

purchased for $75 and at year-end it has a market value equal to $100, a $25 gain is recorded on the SREF. If, after the year-end, the security is sold for its market value, which has declined to $85, this results in a loss of $15 being recognized on the sale. Therefore, this method of evaluation recognizes unrealized gains and losses on the SREF as well as realized gains and losses when the security is sold.

If the lower of cost or market method is used to value the securities or, in the case of long-term debt, the lower of amortized cost or market, a different situation arises. A distinction is made between unrealized and realized gains and losses. In the example of a security purchased at $75, with a year-end market value equal to $100, the unrealized gain is not recognized and the security is valued at the lower of cost or market, which in this case is the cost value of $75. If the security is sold for $85, a realized gain of $10 is recognized in the accounts. This method works differently if the market value of the security had declined below the cost price. For example, if a security is purchased for $75 and has a market value at the end of the year equal to $60, this results in an unrealized loss of $15 being recognized under the lower of cost or market method. Under this method, the security is listed on the Balance Sheet at $60.

The important point to remember is that the lower of cost or market method recognizes unrealized losses but not gains, whereas the market value method recognizes both. Both of these methods are handled in more detail in the following illustrations.

MARKETABLE EQUITY SECURITIES—SHORT TERM

Before we consider the valuation of short-term marketable equity securities, the term "valuation allowance" needs to be explained.[9] In dealing with short-term marketable equity securities, it may be necessary to establish a "valuation account." The need for this account arises when the market value of the marketable equity securities in the aggregate has declined below the total cost of those securities. This type of accounting can be considered "as if" accounting, and is used to record transactions *as if* they occurred, when actually they have not occurred. Accounting of this nature is used in certain cir-

---

9. Although FASB Statement No. 12 does not apply to NFP organizations, many of the disclosures required by Statement No. 12 are similar to those required for NFP organizations that value their investments at the lower of cost (amortized cost) or market. The financial statements prepared in chapter 6 meet the requirements for NFP organizations, and in addition provide disclosures about gains and losses on each balance sheet date, as well as information about changes in valuation allowances.

cumstances, as when the market price of marketable equity securities drops below the cost paid for those securities.

To illustrate how a valuation account can be established, assume that Frisk Library has purchased, as a temporary investment in the Operating Fund, shares of stock in T & M Corporation for $4,500 and in ABC Corporation for $5,700. This investment is made on the advice of an investment advisor as a temporary, short-term investment. It is accounted as using the lower of cost or market method. At the Balance Sheet date of June 30, 19x5, the investment in T & M is worth $4,700, but the investment in ABC is worth only $5,000. These changes require disclosure in the footnotes and establishment of a valuation account.

Footnote disclosures require that the amount of unrealized gains and losses be shown. There is an unrealized gain on T & M stock of $200, but an unrealized loss on ABC stock of $700. These unrealized gains and losses should be disclosed in the notes to the financial statements. If there were more than two securities, the gross unrealized gain can be determined and the unrealized loss can also be totaled. These two totals, for unrealized losses and gains, would be shown as separate figures in the notes, and the totals should not be combined except to establish a valuation account.

For this investment, a valuation account needs to be established, recognizing the decrease in the value of stocks as the difference between their market value and the purchased cost of the investment at the year-end Balance Sheet date. Determination of the amount to write off is made as follows:

June 30, 19x5	Cost	Market	Unrealized Gain (Loss)
ABC Corporation	$5,700	$5,000	($700)
T & M Corporation	4,500	4,700	200
	Unrealized Loss		($500)

With these two stocks there is an aggregate unrealized loss of $500. In an actual situation, where the loss was only $500, there would be some question as to the materiality of this amount and whether it is necessary to record the $500 in the accounting records; it is expected that recording an unrealized loss would involve amounts more significant than $500. Assuming that the $500 is recorded in the books, it would be recorded with the following entry:

UNREALIZED LOSS ON SECURITIES	$500	
ALLOWANCE FOR UNREALIZED LOSS ON SECURITIES		$500

Recording the valuation account on the books

Unrealized Loss on Securities is shown on the SREF as a deduction from the revenues, but it should not be deducted directly from the Fund Balance. The Allowance for Unrealized Loss on Securities account appears on the Balance Sheet as a deduction from the Marketable Securities account,[10] and brings the balance in that account down to the aggregate market value of the securities, $9,700. These procedures incorporate "as if" accounting in the sense that there has not been a *realized* loss, that is, an actual sale has not occurred, but the unrealized loss is still deducted on the SREF. The unrealized loss is treated *as if* it were an actual loss on the SREF.

Although recognition of an unrealized loss on the SREF seems to be a rather severe approach, one aspect of this type of "as if" accounting makes the recognition easier to accept, because the loss of one year can be recovered in the following year. As an example, assume that in the second year the Frisk Library still owns ABC Corporation stock, but it sold the T & M Corporation stock for $4,800 and purchased XYZ Company stock. The entry to record the sale of the T & M Corporation stock follows:

CASH	$4,800		
MARKETABLE SECURITIES		$4,500	
T & M Stock			$4,500
GAIN ON SALE OF STOCK		300	

Recording the sale of stock and recognizing a realized gain

This entry recognizes the sale of T & M stock and a realized gain on the sale equal to $300. The unrealized gains and losses recorded at the end of the year are not affected by the sale of stock during the year as the unrealized gains and losses are based on the total portfolio results and not on the performance of one stock in that portfolio.

The cost and market information for the year ending June 30, 19x6, on the stocks in the current portfolio follows:

June 30, 19x6	Cost	Market	Unrealized Gain (Loss)
ABC Corp.	$5,700	$5,000	($ 700)
XYZ Co.	3,000	5,100	2,100
Unrealized Gain			$1,400

The ABC stock has retained the same market value from the previous year, but the XYZ stock, which was purchased during the current

---

10. The account Marketable Securities is used with short-term investments.

year, increased substantially in price. This increase resulted in an aggregate unrealized gain of $1,400. Due to the unrealized gain in 19x6, the unrealized loss of the previous year can be recovered. It is important to note that an unrealized gain cannot be recognized on the books;[11] it is useful only to the extent it can be used to recover an unrealized loss from the previous year, but is limited to countering the effect of that loss. This means that recovery of a loss can only be up to, and not beyond, the amount of the loss recognized in a previous year, even if the gain is more than the loss. The loss from the previous year, 19x5, is completely recovered in the current year. This $500 recovery is equal to the balance in the valuation account, Allowance for Unrealized Losses on Securities, on the Balance Sheet. The entry to record the recovery and cancel the valuation account follows:

ALLOWANCE FOR UNREALIZED LOSS ON SECURITIES $500
    RECOVERY OF UNREALIZED LOSS ON SECURITIES $500

Recording the recovery of the loss on securities

After the posting of this entry to the general ledger, the Allowance account on the Balance Sheet is closed and the Marketable Securities account will contain a balance equal to the cost of the securities, $8,700. The account Recovery on Unrealized Loss on Securities will appear on the SREF before the Excess of Support and Revenue over Expenses in the Current Year, and along with (but not consolidated with) any other realized gains and losses. The $500 in the Recovery of Unrealized Loss on Securities becomes part of the Excess. This has the effect of increasing the dollar amount transferred from the SREF to the beginning Fund Balance.

Several points need to be emphasized about this procedure. First, the investment in the example is a temporary investment and not a long-term investment. Second, none of the unrealized gain for the year ending June 30, 19x6, has been recognized, and the gain has only been used to recover the previous year's loss. Third, if the unrealized gain in 19x6 had been only $400, a recovery of only $400 would have been recognized in a journal entry, like the last one. Fourth, this is an investment change, evaluated by fund groups and not the organization as a whole. Fifth, this investment was carried on the books at the lower of cost or market rather than at market value.

11. The only time an unrealized gain would be recognized is when the market value method of investment valuation is used.

MARKETABLE EQUITY SECURITIES — LONG TERM

These securities are purchased for long-term appreciation in the securities themselves, and not for temporarily investing idle cash. The disclosures that are necessary for these securities are the same as those for temporary marketable equity securities:

1. Total cost and total market value for securities for each Balance Sheet date presented need to be disclosed.
2. Amount of gross unrealized losses and gross unrealized gains needs to be disclosed as of latest Balance Sheet date.
3. (a) For each period in which an income statement is presented, net realized gain or loss in Excess of Support and Revenue over Expenses is to be disclosed; (b) method used to determine cost of the securities needs to be disclosed; and (c) any change in "valuation allowance" is to be disclosed.

In fact, both types of securities are treated in the same fashion, except for one aspect of their accounting procedure. When the valuation account is established as a loss for long-term investments, it is recorded as a deduction from the Fund Balance rather than a deduction in arriving at the Excess on the SREF. Also, when a recovery of the previous unrealized loss is recognized, it is recorded as an addition to the Fund Balance. Therefore, the major change in accounting for long-term investments is that any unrealized loss or recovery of that loss is recorded directly in the Fund Balance. It should be noted that it is also possible to value these securities at market value.

MARKETABLE DEBT SECURITIES — SHORT TERM

If temporary investments of cash are made in government securities, such as U.S. Treasury Bills, or if the investment is made in bank financial investments that do not represent equity ownership, such as Certificates of Deposit, they are considered to be marketable debt securities. These securities are valued at either market value or the lower of cost or market. Use of the latter method has already been explained for both long- and short-term marketable equity securities, and since its use would be the same with marketable debt securities, its explanation will not be repeated here.

Short-term marketable debt securities can be valued by the market value method. Assume that a debt security has been purchased for $12,000 during the year as a short-term investment, and it is valued by using the market-value method. At the end of the year, but before its maturity, the debt security has a market value equal to $11,500.

The $500 difference between the purchase price and the market value is handled like a realized loss that is recognized on the SREF. The following entry records that loss:

LOSS ON SECURITIES $500
    MARKETABLE SECURITIES $500
Recording a loss on marketable debt securities

This entry would be made only as a year-end adjusting entry. Once the entry is made, the securities have a value on the books equal to $11,500. The reason the Marketable Securities account was used instead of Investments is because this sale deals with a short-term investment. If a gain had occurred, instead of a loss, the Marketable Securities account would have been increased by the amount of the gain and a Gain account would have been credited.

Whenever the market value method is used, any changes from market at the end of each period are recorded on the SREF as part of revenues or reductions in revenues. The notes to the financial statements should disclose the amount of realized gains and losses associated with the securities. For complete disclosure, this information should be shown for each date a Balance Sheet is presented.

MARKETABLE DEBT SECURITIES—LONG TERM

The major difference between the evaluation of long-term and short-term marketable debt securities is that, besides using market value as a valuation method, the amortized cost and the lower of amortized cost or market value are also acceptable valuation methods. The lower of amortized cost or market value is handled in the same manner as the lower of cost or market value method once the amortized cost is determined.

A marketable debt security can be valued at *amortized* cost, but this term has no meaning for marketable equity securities. It should be noted that a debt security is issued for a specific period, and when the end of that period arrives, the holder of the bond is paid back the face value of the bond. This amount is also called the "maturity" value of the bond. The purchaser of the debt has received interest payments for holding the debt, and at the bond's maturity date, the face value is repaid to the purchaser. Amortized cost arises when a debt security is purchased at more or less than its face value.

For example, a $10,000 bond (the "face" value) may be purchased for $9,700, which results in its being purchased at a "discount." If the same bond were purchased for $10,300, it would have been purchased at a "premium." At the maturity of the bond, the purchaser receives its face value, $10,000. The purchaser who paid $10,300 loses $300 over the period the bond was held whereas the purchaser who paid $9,700 gains $300. There are various reasons for premiums or discounts on bonds, and one common reason is differences in the current rate of interest for this type of bond and the rate that bond is paying. For example, if the bond is paying a rate of 4 percent and the current rate of interest for this type of bond is 12 percent, no one would be willing to buy the bond at its face value of $10,000, and the only way the bond could be sold is for less than $10,000.

The amortized cost of a bond can be computed whether the bond is sold for a premium or a discount. If a $10,000 bond is sold for a $300 discount (or $9,700), the holder of the bond, when it matures, will receive the entire $10,000 maturity value of the bond, which results in a $300 "gain." The gain should not be recognized at the maturity date. Accounting procedures require that the $300 gain be spread over the life of the bond from the time it was purchased. If the bond was purchased June 30, 19x1, and will mature in five years, or on June 30, 19x6, the discount of $300 is written off to revenues over each of the five years on an equal basis of $60 per year. The amortized cost of this bond is 19x2, $9,760; 19x3, $9,820; 19x4, $9,880; 19x5, $9,940; and in the last year, 19x6, it will reach its maturity value, $10,000. Therefore, the amortized cost of a bond is determined by writing off any discount or premium associated with the bond. At the end of each of the five years, the following entry is made to recognize this change:

INVESTMENT	$60	
Marketable Debt Security		$60
INTEREST REVENUE		$60

Recording the yearly write off of the discount on debt securities

If a $300 premium had been involved, the debit to the Investment account and the credit to Interest Revenue would have been reversed. Therefore, when a long-term marketable debt security is valued by amortized cost, the premium or discount must be used to compute the amortized cost.

It is expected that a long-term investment would be held to maturity, but if it is not, the realized gain or loss is the difference between the selling price of the security and its amortized cost. For example, if the previous debt security had been sold in 19x3 for $9,900, an $80 gain would have been recognized. This is the difference between the amortized cost of $9,820 and its selling price.

The amortized cost method recognizes a "write-down" on an investment only when a permanent reduction in the investment's value has occurred. Under such conditions, the Investment account is written off by an amount equal to the reduction in value, and a realized loss is debited. Therefore, when a cost method of valuation is used, such as the amortized cost method, the losses that are recognized are realized losses. It should be noted that long-term marketable debt securities can be valued by using the amortized cost or market method.

In preparing notes to the financial statements, it is important to understand the meaning of unrealized and realized gains and losses as they relate to the method used to value the investments. In the case of the H. K. Fines Library, the marketable equity securities are valued at the lower of cost or market and the long-term marketable debt securities are valued at the lower of amortized cost or market.

In reviewing the financial statements for the H. K. Fines Library, it can be seen that no valuation account was recognized because the library's investments had a market value that was higher or equal (as in the case of marketable debt securities) than the cost paid for these investments. No unrealized gain is recognized as a recovery as there are no unrealized losses from the previous year to recover. The library made the necessary disclosures (p. 153), as is required for both short- and long-term investments.

In comparing the required disclosures about marketable securities and the disclosures made by the library, it can be seen how the required disclosures are made in the footnotes. The library's disclosures are listed in the same order as listed on page 153, and they are all contained in note 2 in figure 6–4.

1. The total cost and total market value for the securities for each Balance Sheet date are shown in the schedule for June 30, 19x2, at a cost of $7,000 and a market value of $11,000. The respective information for the previous year, 19x1, is also given, as $30,000 and $32,300, respectively.

2. The amount of unrealized losses and unrealized gains as of June 30, 19x2, is only relevant in regard to unrealized gains, as there is no unrealized loss. The unrealized gain is equal to $4,000, which is the difference between the market value and the purchase price of the stock.

3. (a) For each period an income statement is presented, the net realized gain or loss is disclosed. For the H. K. Fines Library, there was only a gain in the year ending June 30, 19x2. In that year, the library had a gain on the sale of a portion of its investment of

$2,690. If a realized gain or loss had occurred in the period ending June 30, 19x1, it needs to be disclosed.

(b) The method used to determine the cost of the securities is disclosed as the first-in, first-out method. Under this method of costing an investment, the stocks of a corporation that were purchased first are recorded as being sold first. This information would be important if one company's stock were purchased at different times and at different costs.

(c) No valuation account was used by the library and no information about a valuation is recorded.

The necessary disclosures for marketable securities is one of the most extensive areas of disclosure for an NFP organization. The highlights of the accounting procedures to follow with marketable securities, both equity and nonequity, are outlined in figure 6–5.

Another area of disclosure in the notes relates to changes that have occurred in the Deferred Restricted Amounts of the restricted accounts over the year. The type of disclosure that should be shown here relates to the changes that have occurred since the previous year. Note 3 in the H. K. Fines Library's footnotes provides adequate disclosures for the changes in this account. The beginning balance, $10,000, is shown as increasing through the addition of contributions, bequests, and investment income. The funds expended during the year reduce the balance in the account to the balance shown on the Balance Sheet, $14,700. This information provides the reader of the notes with adequate information as to what caused the changes in this account from the previous year.

Note 4 to the financial statements discloses how the expenses are allocated. For the H. K. Fines Library, it is along functional lines, that is, programs. The last sentence in this note indicates that because of this functional division, some costs have been allocated among programs and supporting services. This statement means that certain costs which are not clearly related to a program or service as a functional expense have been assigned as a cost of that program or service on some logical allocation basis. (The use of this method of cost allocation is explained on pp. 397–410.) As an example of this method of cost allocation, travel costs could be allocated to the programs and services based on the employees involved in the travel, and general telephone charges could be allocated on the basis of extension telephones.

Note 5 relates to commitments and contingencies, and should disclose any contingencies about the operation of the library. A "contingency" can be considered as a set of circumstances, involv-

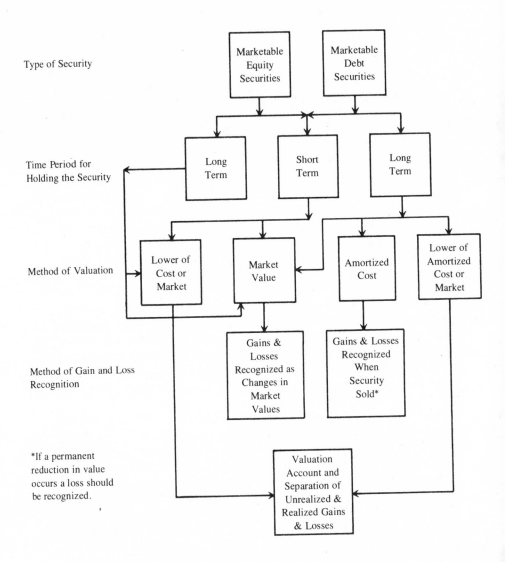

Type of Security

Time Period for
Holding the Security

Method of Valuation

Method of Gain and Loss
Recognition

*If a permanent
reduction in value
occurs a loss should
be recognized.

FIG. 6–5. Highlights of Accounting for Marketable Securities. The two securities groups and
their selection methods are: (1) long-term marketable debt which uses market value, amortized
cost, or lower of amortized cost or market; and (2) short-term or long-term marketable equity
and short-term debt securities which select from lower of cost or market or market value. A
selection must be independently made within each of the two groups and that decision applies to
all investments in that group throughout the organization's funds. This decision should be
applied consistently from one year to the next.

ing uncertainty to an organization, that will be decided upon through the occurrence of various future events. Note 5 should also disclose important commitments that the library has made and that are not disclosed in the accounting records. A "commitment" can be considered as a future obligation that the library has committed itself to fulfilling. This obligation has a potential claim on the resources of the organization. An example is a preliminary agreement to purchase an expensive piece of equipment, such as a bookmobile. Once the purchase contract is signed, it becomes a commitment (or encumbrance), but prior to the signing of that purchase contract, any preliminary agreement should be disclosed in the notes to the financial statements.

Note 5 discloses the fact that a large portion of the library's support is received from federal, state, and local governments. Therefore, the library's future operations are dependent upon this support. Without this support, the library would have to curtail its operations severely. (This type of information is considered a contingency.) The effect of a cutback in this support of the library's operations could be a serious problem, and a contingency disclosure is necessary in the notes.

The final note to the financial statements, note 6, discloses the amount encumbered at the end of the previous year and the amount expended on those encumbrances in the current year. If this information is not significant, it does not have to be footnoted in the financial statements.

Exercise 6–1. The Operating Fund

1. Define the function of the Operating Fund for an NFP organization.
2. Explain the differences in the terms "restricted" and "unrestricted" as they are used in account groups and in the Fund Balance.
3. Name the three financial statements that are needed to describe the financial activities of the Operating Fund.
4. Distinguish between revenue and support items as shown on the Statement of Support, Revenue, and Expenses and Changes in fund balances.
5. What are discretionary board restrictions in the Fund Balance?
6. Explain the purpose of the restricted account group in the Operating Fund.
7. What additional information is available to a reader of the financial reports of an NFP organization if a Statement of Changes in Financial Position is included in the reports?
8. What is working capital?
9. If an organization's temporary, nonequity investments have a market

value of $12,000 and an initial purchase price of $15,000, at what value should they be recorded on the Balance Sheet? Assume the decline is permanent, and the market value method of valuation is used.

10. Define unrealized gains and losses. Where are these gains and losses recorded?

11. The Oxford County Public Library has periodically had idle cash. When this cash was available, a portion of it was invested in marketable equity securities. The market values on June 30, 19x4 and 19x5, as well as the initial purchase price of the securities, follow.

19x4	Market	Cost
Texas Oil Co.	$1,600	$1,500
Mushroom Cloud Energy, Inc.	400	900

19x5	Market	Cost
Texas Oil Co.	$1,750	$1,500
Air & Space Technology, Inc.	750	1,050

On September 15, 19x4, the investment in Mushroom Cloud Energy was sold for $450. Assume the lower of cost or market method of security valuation is used to value the investments, and prepare the year-end journal entries required as of June 30, 19x4, and June 30, 19x5. Also, prepare the journal entry to record the sale of the securities on September 15, 19x4.

12. Prepare the footnote that should appear in the Oxford County Public Library's financial statements for the securities in question 11 for the year ending June 30, 19x5. (Assume that comparative financial statements are prepared.)

13. Prepare the proper footnote disclosures and any necessary journal entries for the following two events:

a) During the 19x5 fiscal year, the Pole Town Library transferred $75,000 of monies restricted for remodeling the library to the Pole Town City Commission, which used the money to buy snow removal equipment. At the present time, the library is being sued by the donor's estate for return of the monies. The library's attorney has indicated that the library has a high probability of losing its case.

b) During the 19x5 fiscal year, the Mason-Dixon Library has been party to a lawsuit brought against the library by a patron who fell and broke his arm in the library. The suit is for damages of $125,000. The library's attorney has indicated that the library is not likely to have to pay these damages, and when the case is settled the amounts likely to be paid are in the range of $1,000 to $3,000.

Preparing the Statement of Changes in Financial Position

The Statement of Changes in Financial Position (introduced in this chapter) is an important statement that rounds out the financial activities of an NFP organization. In order to better understand the importance of this statement, its formulation as related to the Operating Fund is explained in this section.

As previously stated, the Statement of Changes in Financial Position is concerned with the changes that occur in working capital (which is defined as the difference between current assets and current liabilities). This difference is computed over two fiscal years. For example, assume that ABC Library's current assets and current liabilities for the fiscal years ending June 30, 19x1, and June 30, 19x2, are recorded in the books as follows:

	June 30, 19x1	June 30, 19x2
Current Assets	$17,900	$23,000
Current Liabilities	8,100	9,000
Working Capital	$ 9,800	$14,000

The difference in the working capital between the two years is $4,200, and this means that during the year the working capital increased by $4,200. Although this information by itself is important, it is equally important to determine what caused this change in working capital. Did the increase arise from the Excess on the SREF, or was part of it from the Excess and the remainder from the sale of some asset? This determination can only be made through development of a formal Statement of Changes in Financial Position which isolates the sources and uses of working capital.

The easiest method in developing this type of statement is the worksheet method. To continue with the above example, assume that ABC Library's Excess of Support and Revenue over Expenses is $4,200 and that there are no long-term assets and liabilities. This means that the effect of all changes in assets and liabilities is contained in the changes in the current assets and current liabilities, that is, working capital changes.

Figure 6–6 is a simple illustration of the use of a worksheet in developing the Statement of Changes in Financial Position. The basic purpose of the worksheet is to determine the changes that occur in the accounts listed in the upper portion of the worksheet and classify them as sources or uses in the lower portion of the worksheet.

ABC Library
Worksheet for
Statement of Changes in Financial Position

	19x1	Dr.	Cr.	19x2
Working Capital	$9,800	@ $4,200		$14,000
Fund Balance	9,800		1) $4,200	14,000

	Working Capital	
	Source	Use
Increase in Working Capital		@ $4,200
Excess	1) $4,200	
Total	$4,200	$4,200

FIG. 6–6. Worksheet for Statement of Changes in Financial Position for ABC Library

Changes in the upper portion are listed as debit or credit changes, and as these changes are determined, they are assigned as sources or uses of working capital in the lower portion of the worksheet. The basic rule to follow with this worksheet is: If a debit is made to an account, it is a use of working capital and it belongs under the Use column in the lower portion of the worksheet; if a credit is made to an account, it is a source of working capital, and it belongs under the Source column. Any type of transaction that affects a current asset and current liability has already been accounted for in the net change in the working capital balance. Therefore, if a transaction incorporates a debit and credit to the Accounts Payable account and Cash account, respectively, that transaction should not be entered into the worksheet as it has already been incorporated through the change caused in the working capital balance.

In the first step of the procedure to develop the worksheet, working capital, long-term assets and liabilities, and the Fund Balance are listed, along with their ending balances for the two fiscal years, 19x1 and 19x2, in the upper section. In figure 6–6, ABC Library only has a Fund Balance account. The increase in the Fund Balance over the period is $4,200, which is equal to the Excess on the SREF that was transferred to the Fund Balance at the end of the 19x2 fiscal year. All changes in current assets and current liabilities are accumulated in the net change in the working capital. In figure 6–6, this net change was determined by listing the working capital balance for 19x1 and 19x2, then finding the difference between these two amounts. For the ABC Library, this difference is equal to $4,200.

The working capital increase of $4,200 from 19x1 to 19x2 is recorded as a debit in the top portion of the worksheet. In the bottom part, it is therefore listed in the opposite column in the line "Increase in Working Capital." Similarly, in a year in which current liabilities decreased without changes in other accounts, such as assets or the Fund Balance, Increase in Working Capital might appear as a use of working capital at the bottom of the worksheet, if it represented the entire change in working capital for the year. In either case, the remainder of the worksheet is used to examine the sources of the accumulated change in working capital. In the case of ABC Library, the source is the 19x2 Excess of $4,200, recorded as a debit in the bottom part of the worksheet. The purpose of using an increase or decrease in working capital in the lower portion of the worksheet is as a balancing figure to ensure that the amounts under the Source and Use columns are equal. Once the two columns are "in balance," the worksheet has been correctly prepared.

On the other hand, an overall decrease in working capital would appear at the bottom of the worksheet under the Source column because this amount of working capital has been "eaten away" during the year. The rest of the worksheet would summarize the transactions of the year which caused the institution to use its own working capital as a source this year.

In effect, the change in the working capital is the "answer" to the Statement of Changes in Financial Position because the changes that occur over the year must balance to this total. In this simple worksheet, the increase in working capital is completely accounted for by the Excess of Support and Revenue over Expenses of $4,200. This amount is shown as increasing the Fund Balance, and it is recorded in the lower portion of the worksheet as a source obtained from the Excess. The "sources" and "uses" on the bottom portion of the worksheet must always be equal. Although the bottom totals should be equal, it is only coincidental if the debits and credits in the top portion of the worksheet are equal.

If the totals at the bottom are not equal, an error was made. To help avoid these errors, cross-referencing letters should be made between debits and credits in the top portion of the worksheet and the corresponding sources and uses in the lower portion. The reason for this cross-reference procedure becomes more important as the number of entries between the two sections of the worksheet increases. The change in working capital is cross-referenced as an @, largely because this is the "answer" to the Statement of Changes in Financial Position.

In preparing the worksheet, a rule which can be used to determine if a transaction should be recorded on the worksheet is applicable to most (but not all) transactions. *If a transaction crosses debits and credits in a journal entry from a current account classification to a long-term or Fund Balance account classification, it needs to be recorded on the worksheet. If a transaction crosses debits and credits in a journal entry between two current account classifications, it does not have to be recorded on the worksheet.* This rule does *not* cover situations where the two account classifications are long-term items.[12] The best policy to follow in these latter situations is to record the transaction on the worksheet. (In these cases, the entries will only appear in the top portion of the worksheet.)

The worksheet approach is relatively easy to use to calculate the sources and uses of working capital for an organization. One purpose of finding the change in working capital is to determine how the financing of operations is occurring. Does it arise from internal sources (i.e., the Excess or selling investments and assets) or from amounts obtained from external sources, such as the issuance of debt, as could occur in some NFP organizations? In addition, the Statement of Changes in Financial Position should show where all the changes in working capital were used. In many cases, the uses are for purchasing assets.

In the H. K. Fines Library, the worksheet for establishing the Statement of Changes in Financial Position for the unrestricted portion of the library is illustrated in figure 6–7. The SREF and the Balance Sheet are used to arrive at the amounts shown in the upper portion of the worksheet. The decrease in working capital is a credit in the upper portion and is shown as a source of working capital in the lower portion. When a decrease in working capital occurs, it is always a source. The $6,385 Excess of Support and Revenue over

---

12. These types of transactions have to be analyzed to determine whether they should be included in the Statement of Changes in Financial Position as both sources and uses of working capital. For example, if debt is incurred and used to purchase equipment, the source is the debt and the use is the purchase of equipment in the statement. Both these accounts involve long-term items, i.e., long-term debt and a long-lived asset.

H. K. FINES LIBRARY
Worksheet for
Statement of Changes in Financial Position

	19x1	Dr.	Cr.	19x2
Working Capital	$195,190*		@ $160,615	$34,575**
Fund Balance	235,190†	3) $190,000	1) 6,385‡	51,575†
Investments	40,000†		2) 23,000	17,000†

	Working Capital	
	Source	Use
Decrease in Working Capital	@ $160,615	
Excess	1) 6,385	
Gain on Sale§ — Deduction	2) (2,690)	
Sale of Investment	2) 25,690	
Transfers Out		3) $190,000
Total	$190,000	$190,000

* The difference between current assets and current liabilities on the Balance Sheet in figure 6–2 for 19x1 is $195,190 ($220,190 − $25,000).

**The difference between current assets and current liabilities on the Balance Sheet in figure 6–2 for 19x2 is $34,575 ($46,950 − $12,375).

† These amounts are taken off the Balance Sheet for their respective years.

‡ This amount is taken off the SREF for June 30, 19x2, in figure 6–3.

§ The entry to record the sale of the investment is:

Cash		25,690	
	Investments		23,000
	Gain on Sale of Investments		2,690

FIG. 6–7. Worksheet for Statement of Changes in Financial Position for H. K. Fines Library

Expenses is shown as a credit to the Fund Balance and a source of working capital in the lower portion of the worksheet.

The difference between this worksheet and the previous one (for the ABC Library) arises from the sale of investments (journalized in the last footnote to figure 6–7). It can be seen (from the footnote) that the increase in working capital from sale of the investment is $25,690, which was received in the form of cash. The gain on the sale of the investment is recorded on the SREF and becomes incorporated as part of the Excess. Therefore, the Excess of $6,385 contains $2,690 which is part of the working capital received from the sale of the investment.

The purpose of the Statement of Changes in Financial Position is to show all the sources and uses of working capital. The sale of the investment generated a source of working capital in the form of cash to the organization of $25,690, and it should be shown at this amount. If the sale of the investment is shown as generating re-sources of $25,690, the gain that is included as part of the Excess will be double-counted—as part of the Excess and as part of the working capital generated from the sale of the investment. To prevent double-counting, the gain on the sale is subtracted from the Excess (on the lower portion of the worksheet under the column headed "Sources" in figure 6–7), and it is part of transaction 2.

The entry for transaction 2 records the effect of the sale of the investment in three accounts: (1) the Investment account, a long-term asset, is reduced by $23,000, which is the original cost of the invest-ment; (2) Sale of Investment, a source of working capital, is recog-nized under the Sources column at $25,690; and (3) the $2,690 Gain on the Sale of the Investment is deducted from the Excess in the Sources column.

If the investments are composed of short-term securities, the Gain on the Sale would not be recognized in the worksheet as the net effect of the gain would be recognized in the net change in working capital between the two years. This situation occurs because the change in the Cash account, as well as the short-term investments, are current assets, and changes in current assets are summarized in working capital changes.

The Excess is always carried to the Fund Balance as a debit or a credit. Transaction 1 shows that the Excess for the year ending June 30, 19x2, increases the balance in the Fund Balance. If the Excess had been a Deficiency, it would have decreased the balance in the Fund Balance. In the worksheet, the only decrease in the Fund Bal-ance account occurs as a result of the transfer. The $190,000 transfer shown on the worksheet is determined by finding the difference in the Fund Balance account between the two years after taking into account the increase caused by the Excess. In other words, there had to be a $190,000 debit to the Fund Balance account to arrive at the ending balance for the current year. It is also shown as a use of working capital in the lower portion of the worksheet.

The worksheet in figure 6–7 shows the reasons for the $160,615 decrease in working capital. This decrease is the same as that in figure 6–3. The net difference between current assets and current liabilities between the two years is attributed to several changes, the first of which is the net increase in working capital from the operations of the organization (equal to $3,695 after the $2,690 gain is deducted). The second item is the working capital received from the sale of the investment, $25,385. These two sources of working capital total $29,385. Countering this increase is the $190,000 transfer to the Plant Fund, which is a use of working capital. In this worksheet, it can be seen that the decrease in working capital was caused by the transfer to the Plant Fund. In addition to the decrease in working capital, the transfer was provided for by the Excess, the gain and the sale of the investments.

The H. K. Fines Library had a gain on the sale of its investment, but it would also be possible for a loss to occur on the sale of an investment. In that case, the dollar amount of the loss is added to the Excess from the SREF. As an example, assume that the investment was sold for $21,000, rather than $25,690, which would result in a $2,000 loss on the sale. The entry to record this loss follows:

LOSS ON SALE OF INVESTMENT	2,000	
CASH	21,000	
INVESTMENTS		23,000
Sale of the investment for $21,000		

In this transaction, the total amount generated from the sale of the investment is $21,000; this amount should be shown on the worksheet as the working capital generated by the sale. Therefore, on the worksheet $25,690 would be replaced by $21,000. The reduction in the Investment account would be shown at the same amount, $23,000.

Before proceeding further, a question should be asked about how much of an outflow of resources occurred because of the loss? In other words, did the loss result in an outflow of cash to anyone? The answer is no. There is no outflow of resources or use of working capital because of a loss on the sale. It simply means that the investment was sold for less than its original cost.

If there was no outflow of resources, should the Excess be reduced by the amount of the loss? Again, the answer is no. But the Excess has already been reduced by the loss because the loss appears on the SREF as one of the deductions from Support and Revenue. Therefore, to correct for this deduction on the Statement of Changes in Financial Position, the loss would be added to the Excess of $6,385 on the worksheet in figure 6–7. Of course, the worksheet will not balance if these changes are made, because a loss will create other changes in the accounts. (As this is only an illustration of how a loss is handled on the worksheet, this discussion of changes is not to be extended into the worksheet in figure 6–7.)

Once the worksheet is complete, it is used to prepare the formal Statement of Changes in Financial Position, which is shown in figure 6–3 for the H. K. Fines Library. In reviewing that statement, it can be seen that it is basically a recasting of the worksheet in figure 6–7. In addition, at the bottom of the Statement of Changes in Financial Position in figure 6–3, the components of working capital are shown with the changes that occurred in those accounts during the one-year period.

Summary

This chapter is an overview of the financial statements that are prepared for the Operating Fund, which is one of the most important fund groups in an NFP organization because so many transactions are recorded in it.

Although the Balance Sheet and the Statement of Support, Revenue, and Expenses and Changes in Fund Balances were discussed in an earlier chapter, the Statement of Changes in Financial Position is a new statement, introduced in this chapter. The preparation of a Statement of Changes in Financial Position was explained through a worksheet procedure. In addition, this chapter introduces the type of footnotes that should accompany the financial statements of an NFP organization. As part of that introduction, the recording of unrealized and realized gains and losses on marketable securities was explained. This explanation is important because these methods will be used with all NFP investments, whether they appear in the Operating Fund or the Endowment Fund. The latter fund will be explained in chapter 8—and again, it will be important to remember how to account for unrealized gains and losses.

Exercise 6-2. Statement of Changes in Financial Position

The Kellogg Library's comparative balance sheets reveal the following changes from June 30, 19x7, to June 30, 19x8:

	Unrestricted	Restricted
Cash	$ 7,000 increase	$5,000 increase
State Grants Receivable	30,500 increase	—
Inventories	400 increase	—
Investments	20,000 decrease	—
Accounts Payable	5,000 decrease	—
Deferred Restricted Contributions	—	5,000 increase

The following additional information is available for the period ending June 30, 19x8.

1. Excess of Support and Revenue over Expenses was $17,200 for the period ending June 30, 19x8.
2. There was a realized gain on the sale of investments of $2,100. The investment originally cost $20,000.
3. An unrealized loss was recorded on June 30, 19x8, of $5,700.
4. Deferred Restricted Contributions, recognized as support, was $11,000.

Prepare the Statement of Changes in Financial Position and changes in the components of working capital for the Operating Fund of the Kellogg Library.

7.

The Operating Fund with Journal Entries

Although a number of accounting transactions in the Operating Fund are typical of those discussed before, there are enough unique aspects to these transactions that they deserve separate consideration. These transactions are considered in this chapter, in the context of the Operating Fund, to provide a number of illustrative journal entries for the H. K. Fines Library that are typical of those in the Operating Fund of an NFP organization. Special attention should be paid to these transactions, as they will be used to revise the financial statements in chapter 6 into a set of new financial statements for the H. K. Fines Library for the period ending January 30, 19x3 (in the appendix to chapter 7).

Allotments

In the previous chapter, restricted and unrestricted assets were distinguished from each other; and there is another type of restriction that can occur in an NFP organization's Operating Fund: "allotments."

The allotment is a self-imposed restriction on appropriations by higher management or the board. If an allotment system is used, the appropriation dollars are designated for use in specific periods. For example, the appropriation for the Reference Department may be divided into four quarterly allotment periods. If the total appropriation is for $70,000, each quarter's allotment is $17,500. The spending plans developed by the head of the Reference Department are required to stay within the quarterly allotment of $17,500.

Thus the allotment is a restriction on spending. This type of system is used where additional controls are desired over the spending patterns of departments. When this system is in use, adherence to the allotment schedule should be enforced.

Use of an allotment procedure introduces another account into the general ledger—the Allotment account, which acts as a temporary holding account from which the appropriation is allocated to each period. If we assume that a $125,000 budget appropriation is made to Flavor Library and is divided into four equal quarterly allotments, the following entries record the accounting for allotments.

ESTIMATED REVENUES 125,000			
ALLOTMENTS	125,000		
Reference		48,000	
Children's Library		35,000	
Circulation		27,000	
Regional History		15,000	

Recording initial budget entry as allotment

ALLOTMENTS	31,250		
Reference	12,000		
APPROPRIATIONS		31,250	
Reference		12,000	
Personnel			8,000
Travel			250
Supplies			1,700
Maintenance			800
Book Purchase			1,250

Recording first-quarter allotment to Reference Department. This is a partial entry.

These entries are based on the journalizing format used in chapter 4, with subsidiary accounts slightly indented under the general-ledger Control accounts. The subsidiary accounts provide detailed information about the allotments to each department, as well as the specifics of the quarterly appropriations.

The first entry journalizes the initial budget. The debit to the Estimated Revenues account and the credit to the Allotments account is recorded in the general ledger. The various department accounts act as subsidiary accounts under the general-ledger control account, Allotments. In the second entry, the first quarterly allotment is credited to the departments and to the object expenses of that department (in the illustration, only the Reference Department's appropriations are shown). The amount credited to subsidiary departmental accounts are recorded in the Appropriation-Expense ledger, as explained on pages 89–94 and 101–5. The illustration shows the yearly allotment evenly divided into quarterly amounts.

The equality of these allotments should depend on the cycle of activity in the organization. If there are peaks of activity, it is not a good idea to divide the appropriation into equal allotments, as more monies are expended during peak activity periods during the year. For example, the summer session is a slower period for a private elementary school, and the appropriations should be divided so that the largest allotments occur during the school year.

The second entry also contains a debit to the Allotment account and a reduction in the Reference Department's allotment in the subsidiary account. This debit entry records the amount by which the allotments have been reduced in the first quarter.

The entries for the library's Operating Fund, shown in the remaining portions of the chapter, will not use an allotment system. The major reason for using this type of system is more control over the organization's use of appropriations.

Unrestricted Account Group

As indicated, unrestricted assets in the Operating Fund are available for use in the daily, routine activities of an NFP organization. They have not been restricted for specific uses. The unrestricted account group of the Operating Fund is the first consideration in the chapter, followed by an explanation of transactions in the restricted account group. Journal entries for the unrestricted account group of the Operating Fund are used to illustrate unique aspects of this account group.

RECORDING THE BUDGET

The H. K. Fines Library has had its 19x3 budget approved by the governing board of the library, and on July 1 the budget is recorded in the general journal with the following entry. (For additional explanation of this entry, see pp. 88–91 and 96–99.)

July 1	ESTIMATED REVENUES		183,500	
	City of Fines	78,000		
	Backlog County	66,000		
	State Grant	26,000		
	Book Fines	2,500		
	Book Sales	3,000		
	Photocopying	8,000		
	APPROPRIATIONS		171,000	
	Administration			45,000
	Reference Department			35,000
	Children's Library			37,000
	Circulation			40,000
	Regional History			14,000
	FUND BALANCE		12,500	

Recording the 19x3 budget

In this entry, the appropriations are made to the departments in the library and are not further subdivided into object expense accounts, such as supplies or maintenance. (This simplification makes the example a workable illustration.) The departmental accounts in the July 1 entry are maintained in the Appropriation-Expense ledger, a subsidiary ledger.

REVISING THE BUDGET

Shortly after the budget was recorded in the accounts, it was learned that the City of Fines would be able to contribute only $68,000 to the library. In response to this $10,000 appropriation reduction, the library revised its budget. The revised budget reduces the amount that had been appropriated to the Reference and Circulation departments by $1,500 each, the Fund Balance is reduced by $7,000, and Estimated Revenues is reduced, along with the estimated revenues to be available from the City of Fines. Although there was a $10,000 reduction in estimated revenues from the city, the appropriations were reduced by only $3,000 because amounts in the Fund Balance were used to make up the difference of $7,000.

July 7	FUND BALANCE	7,000		
	APPROPRIATIONS	3,000		
	Reference		1,500	
	Circulation		1,500	
	ESTIMATED REVENUES			10,000
	City of Fines			10,000

Recording revision of original budget

Budget revisions, because of reductions in anticipated support from various governments or from changes in the way the budget was originally appropriated among departments and programs, are not unusual.

RECEIPT OF CASH FROM GOVERNMENTS

On July 14, 19x3, the monies from all three governments are received in cash and recorded in the general journal.

July 14	CASH	160,000	
	REVENUES		160,000
	City of Fines		68,000
	Backlog County		66,000
	State Grant		26,000

Recording receipt of revenues from governments that support the library

As indicated in chapter 4, portions of the estimated revenues available from a government may not be immediately receivable in the form of Cash. The amounts that are not quickly available should be recognized as a receivable by debiting a "Due from" account. As the estimated revenues are received in the form of cash, the receivable is reduced. In the case of the H. K. Fines Library, the monies are received quickly enough so that a "due from" receivable is not established.

ISSUANCE OF PURCHASE ORDERS

The recording of purchase orders is assumed to occur with one entry—for illustrative convenience. The library issued $33,450 worth of purchase orders during the fiscal year for books, periodicals, supplies, and repairs. Each encumbrance is assigned to a departmental account, based on the department responsible for originating the purchase order. The encumbrances are posted to the departmental accounts in the Appropriation-Expense subsidiary ledger. (For additional information about recording this entry, see pp. 99–101.)

August 15	ENCUMBRANCES	33,450	
	Administration	6,950	
	Reference Dept.	8,000	
	Children's Library	5,500	
	Circulation	9,000	
	Regional History	4,000	
	RESERVE FOR ENCUMBRANCES		33,450

Recording purchase orders issued during entire year

PRIOR-YEAR ENCUMBRANCES

There are $11,700 of outstanding encumbrances at the end of June 30, 19x2, and invoices for them are received, approved for payment, and paid during the year ending June 30, 19x3. The invoices are for a total of $11,900, or $200 more than the amount that was encumbered at the end of the previous year. The library has a policy of canceling unfilled encumbrances two months after the beginning of a new year, but all the encumbrances were filled by that time.

The invoices approved for payment are $200 more than the outstanding encumbrances from the prior year. This means that $200 of current-year appropriations, or a portion of the Fund Balance, has to be used to pay for last year's encumbrances. The following entries records the reversal of the encumbrances and the payment of the prior-year expenses. The entry to close the expenses is not made until the end of the fiscal year, and that closing entry is shown in the appendix to chapter 7.

```
August 1  RESERVE FOR ENCUMBRANCES—Prior Year    11,700
              ENCUMBRANCES—Prior Year                        11,700
                  Reference                                                6,700
                  Circulation                                             5,000

          Reversal of prior year's encumbrances

August 1
          EXPENSES—Prior Year                      11,900
              Reference                                   6,700
              Circulation                                 5,200
              CASH                                                         11,900

          Payment of invoices on prior-year encumbrances
```

RECORDING THE PAYROLL

Unlike payments on purchase orders, the payroll is not encumbered, because the amount of the payroll is known at the beginning of the year and significant changes in this amount are not likely. Unlike a payroll expense, the amount encumbered under a purchase order can increase, or decrease, from the time the purchase order is issued to the time the invoice is paid.

When the Fines Library pays its payroll, certain deductions must be made from employees' pay for social security, state and federal income taxes, insurance, and possibly a retirement plan. Such deductions are owed to the various agencies from the time the payroll entry is recorded. These amounts are considered liabilities from that date, and they need to be recorded as liabilities until they are paid. The payroll for the H. K. Fines Library is $88,000 for the year, and it is assumed that deductions are made only for federal and state government liabilities.

```
June 20  PAYROLL EXPENSES                          88,000
             Administration                              20,000
             Reference Dept.                             12,000
             Children's Library                          28,000
             Circulation Dept.                           20,000
             Regional History                             8,000
                 DUE TO FEDERAL GOVT.—FICA                               14,000
                 DUE TO FEDERAL GOVT.—Income Tax                         14,000
                 DUE TO STATE GOVT.—Income Tax                           10,000
                 WAGES PAYABLE                                           50,000

         Recording the payroll
```

In some library accounting systems, the payroll is handled by a local governmental agency, such as the city. This may occur even if the monies for the library payroll are provided by the resources of the library. If this is the case, the library's accounting records would show the transfer of monies to the agency responsible for making the actual payment of the payroll as well as a credit to cash.

The June entry is posted to the departmental accounts in the Appropriation-Expense subsidiary ledger. Just as the issuance of a purchase order is a reduction of the appropriation, the payment of a departmental payroll is also a reduction of this appropriation. The liabilities owed to the federal government are composed of Federal Insurance Contribution Act (FICA) contributions (or social security taxes, as it is more commonly called) and federal income taxes; the amount owed to the state is for state income taxes. Wages Payable records the employee's net pay.

The June 20 entry is recorded on the employee's payday. As employees cash their checks and the library starts to receive the canceled checks, the Wages Payable account is reduced and the Cash account is credited. Assuming all payroll checks had been cashed by June 25, the following entry would be made:[1]

June 25	WAGES PAYABLE	50,000	
	CASH		50,000

Recording the cashing of payroll checks by employees

A common occurrence at the end of the fiscal year is for the organization to owe employees for a partial payroll, because the employees have worked a portion of a pay period in one year but payment for that pay period will not be received until the following year. These wages are a real liability of the NFP organization, and are required to be recorded in the same fashion as any other liability. If this entry is not recorded, liabilities and expenses will be understated on the financial statements. This entry is usually made as an adjusting entry at the end of the fiscal year (see pp. 61–67 for a discussion of adjusting entries). If we assume that the H. K. Fines Library owes $1,500 in payroll expenses at the end of the 19x3 fiscal year, the following entry would be made. (The June 30 entry has not recognized liabilities for the state and federal governments as they are not due until the wages are paid.)

---

1. With the payroll procedure, a separate Cash account is usually established for the payroll checks. All payroll checks are then cleared through this one account. After all the payroll checks have been cashed by the employees, the balance in this account should be equal to zero.

```
June 30  PAYROLL EXPENSE                        1,500
              Administration                300
              Reference Dept.               400
              Children's Library            400
              Circulation                  300
              Regional History             100
                   WAGES PAYABLE                        1,500
```

Recording year-end liability for payroll expenses

EMPLOYER'S PAYROLL EXPENSES

In addition to tax deductions from an employee's gross pay, certain payroll taxes are charged directly against the library that must be paid to federal and state governments. One such tax is FICA for social security; the library must match the employee's FICA deduction. The library must also pay an unemployment compensation charge to the state to support payments to qualified out-of-work wage earners. The rate charged the organization usually varies with the number of former employees of the organization who have made successful claims for unemployment compensation. In addition, the library has to make payments to an employee retirement and insurance plan. All these payments are the *employer's* payroll expenses.

The FICA deduction from the employees' pay was $14,000; therefore, the library's FICA expense is also $14,000. The library makes a contribution to the employee's retirement and insurance plan of $6,700, and a payment to the state's unemployment compensation plan of $6,000. These amounts are recorded when the payroll entry for the employees is recorded on June 20.

```
June 20  PAYROLL EXPENSE                          26,700
              Administration                8,000
              Reference Dept.               9,700
              Children's Library            2,200
              Circulation Dept.             5,100
              Regional History              1,700
                   DUE TO FEDERAL GOVT.—FICA                14,000
                   DUE TO RETIREMENT & INSURANCE             6,700
                   DUE TO STATE UNEMPLOYMENT
                        COMPENSATION PLAN                    6,000
```

Recording employer's payroll expense

These employer expenses are recorded in each of the subsidiary departmental ledger accounts. They are the additional cost of hiring an employee, above the costs of his salary or wage earnings.

CURRENT-YEAR ENCUMBRANCES

Invoices for $32,000 were received on $30,000 of the current year's encumbrances of $33,450. They were approved for payment but not immediately paid. For additional discussion about this entry see pages 100–1.

June 20	RESERVE FOR ENCUMBRANCES	30,000		
	ENCUMBRANCES		30,000	
	Administration			3,500
	Reference Dept.			8,000
	Children's Library			5,500
	Circulation Dept.			9,000
	Regional History			4,000
	Reversing encumbrances			
June 20	EXPENSES	32,000		
	Administration		3,500	
	Reference Dept.		9,000	
	Children's Library		5,500	
	Circulation Dept.		10,000	
	Regional History		4,000	
	ACCOUNTS PAYABLE			32,000
	Recording current-year expenses and recognizing them as liability			

In both the above entries for June 20, postings are made to the Appropriation-Expense ledger. The first posting to the departmental account reduces the encumbrance, and the second posting records the actual expense. Notice that the expenses approved for payment in the Reference and the Circulation departments are both $1,000 more than was encumbered. Before the expense was approved, the Appropriation-Expense ledger would have to be checked to ensure that there is sufficient departmental appropriation remaining to cover this additional expense. The Accounts Payable account records the amount owed under the approved expenses.

COLLECTION OF CASH FROM BOOK FINES AND BOOK SALES

During the 19x3 fiscal year, the library collected $2,700 in book fines and $2,800 in book sales revenues. The book sales revenues were collected by Friends of the Library. The entry to record these revenues is:

June 25	CASH	5,500		
	REVENUES		5,500	
	Book Fines			2,700
	Book Sales			2,800

Recording collection of book fines and book sales

PAID LIABILITIES

The library paid $32,000 of its Accounts Payable:

June 25	ACCOUNTS PAYABLE	32,000	
	CASH		32,000

Recording the payment of liabilities

Usually the Accounts Payable account acts as a control account over the individual vendors to whom the $32,000 is owed. This additional subsidiary ledger is not used in the illustration.

REIMBURSING PETTY CASH ACCOUNT

Many NFP organizations establish a Petty Cash account for small, miscellaneous expenses. An example of this type of expense is delivery charges. When a payment is made from the Petty Cash account, a receipt and any supporting documents are placed in the fund's file, showing the reason for the expenditure and making it easy to assign the expenses to object and program classifications. One person is usually made responsible for the Petty Cash account; if more than one person is involved in control of the account, it is difficult to assign responsibility for shortages.

The Petty Cash account should be thought of as a subdivision of the Cash account. This relationship is clearly shown in the entry by the library in initially establishing the Petty Cash account for $500:

July 4	PETTY CASH	500	
	CASH		500

Establishing the Petty Cash account.

This entry should only be made when the account is established, and "reversed" only when the account is no longer needed. If it is decided to increase the amount in the Petty Cash account, Petty Cash is again debited and Cash is credited for the amount of the increase. Replenishment of the account does not affect the amount in the Petty Cash account.

On December 17, the Petty Cash account was low and it was decided that the account should be replenished. Payments out of the fund were equal to $475 and the money in the Petty Cash drawer was equal to $25; so all the cash was accounted for, with no shortages in the account. If shortages had occurred, they would have to be recorded as expenses of the period. The expenses that were incurred, with payments from Petty Cash, should be assigned to the various departments in the subsidiary ledger in the same manner as other expenses are handled. The entry to reimburse the Petty Cash account is a debit to Expenses control account and a debit to the departmental accounts in the Appropriation-Expense subsidiary ledger. A credit is made to the Cash account. This entry indicates that monies from the Cash account are being transferred into Petty Cash.

December 17	EXPENSES	475	
	Administration	350	
	Reference	15	
	Circulation	60	
	Regional History	50	
	CASH		475

Reimbursing petty cash account

INVENTORY OF SUPPLIES

The inventory at the end of the year is determined through a physical count of the items in the inventory. Through this count, it is determined that there is $250 more inventory on June 30, 19x3, than there was on June 30, 19x2, the last time the inventory was counted. (The entry for the inventories was explained on p. 54 with transaction 1.)

If the ending inventory is more than the beginning inventory (the June 30, 19x2, ending inventory is the July 1, 19x2, beginning inventory), adjustment is required. In this case, the inventory needs to be increased by $250, and the Reserve for Inventory of Supplies in the Fund Balance also needs to be increased.

June 29	INVENTORY OF SUPPLIES		250	
	EXPENSES			250
	Administration			250
June 29	FUND BALANCE—Undesignated		250	
	RESERVE FOR INVENTORY OF SUPPLIES			250

Recording increase in inventories and restricted reserve of fund balance

The items in the inventory can be maintained on a departmental basis or by one person in Administration. If supplies are maintained in Administration, they are issued to the other departments on properly signed requisitions for supplies. In either case, control should be maintained over the supplies to prevent their unauthorized use. The best control is achieved when there is one central source for supplies, and they are not distributed to departmental inventories.

BUYING REPURCHASE AGREEMENTS

Repurchase agreements are purchased from a bank for short-term investments of cash that otherwise would be idle. After a period of up to three months, the bank returns the cash, with a premium. This is one method that can be used to invest the idle cash of the library and earn a return on it. The following entry illustrates the buying of the repurchase agreement:

May 1	REPURCHASE AGREEMENTS	25,000	
	CASH		25,000

Recording the investment in repurchase agreements

If it is known at the beginning of the year that idle cash is going to be invested in repurchase agreements, the amount of revenues expected to be received should be estimated and incorporated into the Estimated Revenues entry at the beginning of the year.

In the May 1 transaction, the premium received on the three-month maturity date (August 1) needs to be divided between the year ending June 30, 19x3, and the following year. This division is necessary under the accrual system of accounting because the revenues are required to be assigned to the period in which they are actually earned, rather than the period in which the cash is received.

Two months of the period for which the repurchase agreements are held fall in the year ending June 30, 19x3, and one month falls in the fiscal year ending June 30, 19x4. If we assume a premium of $3,750 is paid by the bank at the maturity date of the repurchase agreement (August 1), two-thirds of it is recognized as revenue in the year ending June 30, 19x3. This amount is equivalent to a percentage equal to two months of the three-month maturity period. The remainder of the premium will be recognized as revenue in the following year. The adjusting entry to recognize the two months of earned revenues is as follows:

June 30 REPURCHASE PREMIUM RECEIVABLE	2,500	
REPURCHASE REVENUES		2,500

Recording the accrual of revenues receivable on the repurchase agreement

For additional discussion of adjusting entries, such as the one for repurchase agreements, see page 56.

In the June 30 entry, a receivable is recognized for the premium, and this receivable will remain on the books until the premium is received on August 1, 19x3. In addition, revenues are recognized for the earned portion of the premium. Under the accrual system, it is necessary to recognize the accounting event during the fiscal period it actually affects, rather than wait for the collection or disbursement of cash. Two months of the premium have actually been earned in the period ending June 30, 19x3; therefore, revenues need to be recognized on the books.

PAYING "DUE TO" ACCOUNTS

At periodic intervals during the year, the amounts owed to the federal government, the state government, and the retirement plan are paid. The H. K. Fines Library paid $18,000 owed on social security, $14,000 on federal income taxes, $10,000 on state income taxes, $3,000 on employment insurance, and the entire amount owed on the retirement and insurance plan, $6,700. The journal entry follows.

March 31	DUE FEDERAL GOVT. — Income Taxes	14,000	
	DUE FEDERAL GOVT. — FICA	18,000	
	DUE STATE GOVT. — Income Taxes	10,000	
	DUE RETIREMENT & INSURANCE	6,700	
	DUE STATE UNEMPLOYMENT		
	COMPENSATION PLAN	3,000	
	CASH		51,700

Recording payment of liabilities on payroll

RECEIPT OF UNRESTRICTED BEQUEST

The estate of Estes Parson was recently settled. In her will, Ms. Parson left $2,300 to the library to be used for the general operations of the library, without restrictions on its use. The library has been notified of the bequest, and it is awaiting the payment from the trustee bank. The entry to record the bequest in the general journal is as follows:

| June 1 | DUE FROM ESTATE FOR E. PARSON | 2,300 | |
| | SUPPORT — Bequests | | 2,300 |

Recording the receipt of a bequest

The "Due from" account is a receivable, recognized on the books until the cash is actually collected from the trustee bank. The "support" is an item that will be recognized on the SREF as of June 30, 19x3.

The journal entry for this type of bequest is a relatively straightforward entry, but it is not always this simple. If the library is aware of the possible receipt of a bequest, but the actual amount is unknown (because the estate has not been settled), the situation is a little more complex. In such a case, an entry cannot be made until the amount receivable from the estate is determined. Therefore, a description of the events should be made as a footnote to the Balance Sheet. A footnote of this nature would resemble the following:

> The estate of the late Sybil Lawrence, currently being settled, has bequeathed an 11% interest in such estate to the H. K. Fines Library. The exact amount of this interest is not known at the present time. Trustees for the estate have indicated that they estimate it to be between $275,000 and $550,000.

This footnote to the Balance Sheet provides an indication that an amount is collectible from an estate. If a range of the amount collectible can be estimated with reasonable probability, it should be stated in the footnote; otherwise, the amounts should be omitted.

RENTALS ON EQUIPMENT

A duplicating machine has recently been rented from ABC Business Machines Company by the library. The machine is located in the administrative offices of the library, but it is available for each department to use. A system has been established so that a department's use of the machine can be charged against that department's appropriation. This departmental charge is used to pay the rental contract. The rental charge is part of the Administration's budget appropriation, and it was allocated at the beginning of the year. Rental on the machine is $700 a year, and the charges to the various departments are as follows: Reference Department, $202; Children's Library, $178; Circulation, $189; and Regional History, $89. The journal entries to record the signing of the contract, and the transfer of monies within the departments follows.

May 1	ENCUMBRANCE	700		
	Administration		700	
	RESERVE FOR ENCUMBRANCES			700

Recording the signing of the machine rental contract

May 10	RESERVE FOR ENCUMBRANCES	700		
	ENCUMBRANCES		700	
	Administration			700

Reversing encumbrances

May 10	EXPENSES	700		
	Administration		700	
	CASH			700

Recording the receipt of the invoice

June 30	EXPENSES	658		
	Reference		202	
	Children's Library		178	
	Circulation		189	
	Regional History		89	
	EXPENSES			658
	Administration			658

Recording transfer of expenses from Administration to other departments, based on usage

The effect of signing the rental contract is the same as the issuance of a purchase order. Even though this rental contract is not a purchase of supplies or books, it is recorded as an encumbrance at the time of the signing. This entry is shown on May 1. The May 10 entry records the reversal of the encumbrance and the recording of the expense; this entry occurs when the ABC Business Machines Company bills the library.[2] Notice that the entire contract price is charged to Administration's subsidiary account because the expense had originally been part of Administration's appropriations.

The June 30 entry charges the various departments that have been using the duplicating machine for the copies they have run on the machine. At the same time, it reduces the charge of $700 to Administration by $658. This system has been established to control the use of the duplicating machine. Each department knows that it will be charged for its usage of the machine, and this knowledge (it is hoped) will help to control costs. This is especially true if the machine has been used for a number of years and comparisons of usage costs can be presented to each department, illustrating the trend of costs over several periods.

This type of reporting system requires that supplemental records be maintained in Administration regarding each department's use of the machine. These records can become part of the regular accounts, but they are easier to maintain outside the ledger accounts by one person who is responsible for the machine.

LEASE PAYMENTS

Leases can be of two basic types: an "operating lease" or a "capital lease." Only the operating lease is considered here. The main difference between the operating lease and the capital lease is that the latter type is a purchase arrangement whereby the lessee assumes the risks of ownership. Unlike the capital lease, the operating lease is simply a means of allowing the lessee the right to use the property over a period of time without transferring the rights of ownership.

The H. K. Fines Library has entered into a lease for a small building as a branch library. As demand for a library in this community is uncertain, it was decided to rent building facilities rather than purchase them. The lease has been signed for a three-year period, with no rights to purchase the building at the end of that time (this is

2. If it is very clear that the amount on the contract is certain and that the contract will be completed within one year, an encumbrance entry could be omitted.

a characteristic of an operating lease). The lease payments are $6,000 for each of the first two years, and $6,700 in the third year. The first payment was made on July 31, 19x2, for a twelve-month period. When the payment was made, the following was entered.

```
19x2
July 31   RENT EXPENSE                    6,000
              Administration                        6,000
                  CASH                                         6,000

          Recording one-year payment on lease
```

As the period covered by the payment is for twelve months and the remaining months in the year (from July 31) are only eleven, the rent is pro-rated between the 19x3 and 19x4 fiscal years. The monthly rental is $500, and for the 19x3 period of eleven months, this is equal to a rental expense of $5,500. The remaining $500 of the rental fee that was paid is a prepaid asset. (For additional discussion on this type of transaction, see p. 58, transaction 5.) The entry to record the prepaid asset reduces the amount of expense in the year ending June 30, 19x3, by $500 and recognizes a prepaid asset for that amount.

```
19x3
June 30   PREPAID LEASE                    500
              RENT EXPENSE                          500
                  Administration                             500

          Recording prepaid portion of lease as an adjusting entry
```

In addition to this entry, there must be another entry to restrict a portion of the Fund Balance for the amount of the Prepaid Lease account. This restriction indicates to a reader of the Balance Sheet, reviewing the Fund Balance, that the amount restricted for leases is not available for appropriations. The journal entry that places this restriction in the Fund Balance is recorded as an adjusting entry on June 30:

```
June 30   FUND BALANCE—Undesignated          500
              RESERVE FOR LEASES                         500

          Recording a restriction of the Undesignated Fund Balance
```

COLLECTION OF RECEIVABLES

The H. K. Fines Library collected several receivables during the 19x3 fiscal year for $23,200: a state grant for $16,000 and pledges for $7,200. The entry to record these collections is as follows:

Aug. 10 CASH	23,200	
STATE GRANT RECEIVABLE		16,000
PLEDGES RECEIVABLE		7,200

Recording the collection of receivables

As shown on the library's Balance Sheet in figure 6–2, the pledges receivable are recorded at their net amount. This means that the pledges are recorded at the amount that is actually expected to be collected, even if that amount is different from the amount initially pledged. The initial entry to record the pledges, along with the uncollectible amount, was recorded in the entry:

PLEDGES RECEIVABLE	8,000	
PLEDGE REVENUE		7,200
ESTIMATED UNCOLLECTIBLE PLEDGES		800

Recording the receivable on pledges

The amount on the 19x2 Balance Sheet in figure 6–2, $7,200, is shown net of the $800, which is expected to be uncollectible. From past experience, it is anticipated that 10 percent or $800 of the pledges will not be collected. The uncollectible portion should not be allowed to increase revenues or estimated revenues; and without the credit to the Estimated Uncollectible Pledges account, an increase in revenues and estimated revenues would occur. As a specific pledge becomes uncollectible, it is written off as a receivable and the Estimated Uncollectible Pledges account is debited in the following manner.

ESTIMATED UNCOLLECTIBLE PLEDGES	xxx	
PLEDGES RECEIVABLE		xxx

Writing off an uncollectible pledge

In a subsidiary ledger, or as information supplemental to the accounting records, the actual names of the individual uncollectible pledges also are written off. If, at the end of the year, there is a balance in the Estimated Uncollectible Pledges account, it means that the amount estimated to be uncollectible is different from the actual amount written off. Furthermore, it means that the rate used to estimate uncollectibles, 10 percent, may have to be changed. There are two ways that this difference can be adjusted, depending on whether the pledge process in the NFP organization is a yearly event or a less-than-yearly program. If the pledge process occurs less frequently than one year, the Estimated Uncollectible Pledges credit balance should be closed to the Pledge Revenue account. The credit balance means that the uncollectible pledges (written off) were less than the amount estimated. If the pledge process occurs with less frequency than every year and a debit balance exists in the Estimated Uncollectible Pledges account, the balance should be closed to an expense account, like Uncollectible Pledges Expense, or to Pledge Revenue. A debit balance in the Estimated Uncollectible Pledges account means that there were more uncollectible pledges during the year than had been estimated. These situations are illustrated in the two following journal entries.

ESTIMATED UNCOLLECTIBLE PLEDGES	xxxx	
PLEDGE REVENUE		xxxx

Closing credit balance in Estimated Uncollectible Pledge account to revenue account

UNCOLLECTIBLE PLEDGE EXPENSE	xxxx	
ESTIMATED UNCOLLECTIBLE PLEDGES		xxxx

Closing debit balance in Estimated Uncollectible Pledge account to an expense account

If the seeking of pledges by an NFP organization is a yearly event, the debit or credit balance in Estimated Uncollectible Pledges is handled in a different manner. Regardless of a debit or credit balance in the account, the account is brought up to the 10 percent uncollectible balance that should exist in the Estimated Uncollectible Pledge account after the pledge period is over. For example, if the pledges receivable after the pledge period are equal to $1,000 and the uncollectible rate is still 10 percent, there should be a $100 balance in the Estimated Uncollectible Pledges account. If there is a $100 balance in the account, no entry needs to be made. If there is a $300 credit balance in the account, an entry is required to change the $300 credit balance to a $100 credit balance. The entry to record the proper amount in the uncollectible account when there is already a $300 credit balance in the account is as follows:

| ESTIMATED UNCOLLECTIBLE PLEDGES | 300 | |
| PLEDGE REVENUE | | 300 |

Closing uncollectible pledges to revenue account

PLEDGES RECEIVABLE	1,000	
ESTIMATED UNCOLLECTIBLE PLEDGES		100
PLEDGE REVENUE		900

Recording current year's pledges

The effect of these journal entries is a kind of "catch-up" adjustment because in the prior year the pledges that were written off were not equal to the estimated amount; that is, actually written-off pledges were less than the amount estimated to be uncollectible. Therefore, the Estimated Uncollectible Pledges account had a credit balance. This credit balance is reduced, and the net effect is that a total of $1,200 in pledge revenues is recognized.[3]

If the Estimated Uncollectible Pledge account had a debit balance of $200, the adjustment would be just the opposite than when a $300 credit balance exists in the account. The reason for a $200 debit balance is that more pledges were written off as uncollectible than had been estimated to be uncollectible in the prior year. Again, if $1,000 in pledges is receivable in the current year and uncollectibility is 10 percent, there should be a $100 credit balance in the Estimated Uncollectible Pledges account. The following entries are necessary journal adjustments for a $100 credit balance to exist in the account:

| PLEDGE REVENUE | 200 | |
| ESTIMATED UNCOLLECTIBLE PLEDGES | | 200 |

Closing uncollectible account to revenue account

PLEDGES RECEIVABLE	1,000	
ESTIMATED UNCOLLECTIBLE PLEDGES		100
PLEDGE REVENUE		900

Recording current year's pledges

3. This entry could also be recorded as follows, just as long as $1,200 in pledge revenue is recognized at the time the transaction is recorded.

| PLEDGES RECEIVABLE | 1,000 | |
| PLEDGE REVENUE | | 1,000 |

Recording current year's pledges

| ESTIMATED UNCOLLECTIBLE PLEDGES | 200 | |
| PLEDGE REVENUE | | 200 |

Adjusting Estimated Uncollectible Pledge account to proper balance of $100

The net effect of these entries is that revenues that are earned in one period are recognized in another period. Under the accrual basis of accounting, revenues should be recognized in the books during the accounting period in which they are earned. Although these adjustments create a situation where this does not occur, the effect is so small as to be insignificant. In every case, it is important to make the best possible estimate of uncollectible pledges because a difference between the amount that is estimated and the amount that actually becomes uncollectible may mean that the revenues estimated for the period are either under- or overstated. The consequences could result in changes in the way appropriations are made.

A final point about pledges is related to the period in which the pledge revenue should be recognized. If a donor had designated a portion of his or her pledge for the NFP organization's use in the subsequent year, the portion of the pledge designated for the subsequent year should not be recognized as revenue *until* that year. Until it is recognized as revenue, it is recognized in the accounts as a deferred revenue, which is a liability.

MISCELLANEOUS ENTRIES

The outstanding balance in the Accounts Payable account in the Fines Library's Balance Sheet (figure 6–2) is reduced with a cash payment of $10,375. In addition to this transaction, cash of $8,000 was received from photocopying revenues during the year. Both of these transactions are recorded in the accounts as follows:

July 21	ACCOUNTS PAYABLE		10,375	
	CASH			10,375

Recording cash payment on Accounts Payable

June 29	CASH		8,000	
	REVENUE			8,000
	Photocopying Revenue			8,000

Recording photocopying revenue for year

In addition to these two entries, a final entry in the unrestricted account group relates to action the board took during the year. The board removed the $4,945 portion of the Fund Balance that was designated for the purchase of office equipment. Originally, this portion of the Fund Balance had been designated for the purchase of certain office equipment, including a new copy machine, but this equipment was donated to the library by a local office equipment manufacturer. Recording such a donation does not affect the Operating Fund, and this type of transaction is discussed in chapter 9.

The board of directors has a right to designate a portion of the Fund Balance for specified purposes. This is a discretionary type of restriction and not a legal one; therefore, the monies can be transferred back to the unrestricted portion of the Fund Balance by board action. The entry to record this transfer back to the unrestricted portion of the Fund Balance is as follows:

June 30   DESIGNATED FUND BALANCE   4,945
                    UNDESIGNATED FUND BALANCE   4,945

> Transferring the designated portion of the Fund Balance back into the undesignated portion

This entry closes the Designated Fund Balance for the purchase of office equipment and transfers $4,945 back into the undesignated portion of the Fund Balance account. This transfer makes an additional $4,945 available for use in the general operations of the library through additional appropriations.

Exercise 7–1. Unrestricted Account Group of the Operating Fund

The Sexton Library has just ended its 19x7 fiscal year, on June 30. The bookkeeper is uncertain how to handle several transactions and has come to you, as director of the library, to ask your advice on handling these transactions. Tell the bookkeeper how the following transactions should be recorded in the books.

a)   There were prior-year encumbrances from the previous year for $15,200 that had not been reversed. Invoices had been received for $14,700. These invoices had been approved and paid. They represented $14,000 of issued purchase orders from the previous year. The remainder of the previous year's outstanding purchase orders had not been filled or canceled as of the end of the 19x7 fiscal year. Assuming that the entries at the end of the previous fiscal year had been properly made, but no entries had been made relating to these transactions during the 19x7 fiscal year, journalize the proper journal entries.

b)   The employees are paid $34,000 on the 15th of each month. Presently, two weeks' gross pay is owed to the employees. Included as part of this gross payroll are $7,250 of federal income taxes and a FICA tax equal to 7% of the employees' gross pay. There is also a deduction for medical insurance of $473.20. Also, the library's payroll expenses, as an employer, need to be recorded for this period. The library must match the employees' medical deduction. Record the correct adjusting entry.

c)   The Petty Cash Fund, which was established with a $400 balance, needs to be replenished. The receipts and supporting documents showed $315 had been used for expenditures from the monies in the fund. At the present time, there is $75 in cash in the fund.

d)   The lease that the library entered into on a yearly basis, beginning December 1, 19x6, is renewable for each of the next three years at $3,600. Record the correct entry for June 30, 19x7.

e)   During March, April, and May, a pledge campaign had been conducted. This is a yearly campaign for funds. Pledges had been received for $7,500 at the end of the pledge period, and a 5% uncollectibility rate exists for pledges. Record the proper entry as of June 30, 19x7. As of that date, it is known that $120 of these pledges is uncollectible.

f)   The board has decided to designate $9,000 of the Fund Balance for the purchase of a van. The board's action has not been recorded in the books. If an entry is necessary, record it.

Restricted Group

The restricted assets of an organization are those assets that are not available for the organization to use in its daily operations without meeting certain stipulations. The donors of these assets have restricted their use to a specific aspect of the general operations of the organization. If any assets are contributed to the organization with restrictions upon their use, these assets must be accounted for separately from the unrestricted assets in the Operating Fund.

In addition to the separation of the restricted assets from the unrestricted assets, another concern is at which point the contributed restricted assets should be recognized as support on the SREF. If a gift, bequest, or grant is given to an organization with restrictions on it, it is not recognized as support for the organization until those restrictions have been fulfilled. Before that time, the organization has a commitment to fulfill the restriction, and the commitment is recognized in the accounts as a liability. For additional discussion on this type of asset see page 57, transaction 4.

Two final points need to be emphasized: (1) restrictions on gifts, bequests, or grants have to be established by the donor, not by the NFP organization, and (2) gifts, bequests, or grants are usually designated for some activity that is part of the routine operations of the organization.

Accounting in the restricted asset group of the Operating Fund does not involve establishment of a budget with appropriations to specific accounts because all the monies in this account group have been designated for specific purposes. The H. K. Fines Library has restricted assets which have been established as an account group in the name of the donor. The monies in these restricted account groups are to be used for the purchase of specific types of books for the library. Although these monies are not, technically, funds, because they are part of the Operating Fund, they will be referred to as "funds" in the remainder of the chapter. In addition to these donor fund groups, a federal grant was received this year to develop a program for the handicapped.

TIM RIM FUND

Several years ago, the library received $5,000 to be used to purchase books on home construction, repair, and maintenance. The monies were designated for this single purpose and, as such, are part of the restricted account group of the Operating Fund. The monies have been placed in a savings account in the local bank to earn interest. As no specific use was designated for any interest earned on the contributed monies, the interest is used for the general operations of the library. As of June 30, 19x3, $200 of interest earnings are transferred to the unrestricted Cash account. In addition, $2,100 worth of books on home construction and maintenance were purchased during the year by the library. Before these two transactions are journalized, the original entry for receipt of the donation is recorded on July 3 as shown:

July 3	CASH		5,000	
	DEFERRED RESTRICTED CONTRIBUTIONS			5,000
	Tim Rim Fund			5,000

Recording the receipt of the contribution

The Deferred Restricted Contribution account is a liability account that indicates the library has an obligation either to spend the monies for the purpose for which it was donated or return the monies. During the current year, $2,100 of these monies were used to purchase books on home construction and maintenance. They are considered part of the reference collection. Once the expenditure has been made, the liability can be reduced. All entries, from issuance of the purchase order to payment of the order, are illustrated in the following entries.

Sept. 1 ENCUMBRANCES   2,100
      Tim Rim Fund   2,100
        RESERVE FOR ENCUMBRANCES   2,100
    Recording issuance of purchase order

Sept. 10 RESERVE FOR ENCUMBRANCES   2,100
      ENCUMBRANCES   2,100
      Tim Rim Fund   2,100
    Recording reversal of encumbrances upon receipt of invoice

Sept. 11 EXPENSES—Restricted   2,100
      Tim Rim Fund   2,100
      ACCOUNTS PAYABLE   2,100
    Recording approval of invoice for payment

Sept. 11 DEFERRED RESTRICTED CONTRIBUTIONS 2,100
      Tim Rim Fund   2,100
      CONTRIBUTION—Support   2,100
    Recording reduction of liability and recognition of support

Sept. 17 ACCOUNTS PAYABLE   2,100
      CASH   2,100
    Recording payment of invoice

The liability, Deferred Restricted Contributions, is reduced when the expense for the book purchase is incurred. Only at that time can the contribution be recognized as support, because at that time the library has fulfilled its obligation to purchase the books specified by the donor. The Tim Rim Fund is maintained in a subsidiary ledger that is like the Appropriations-Expense ledger, with multiple columns to keep track of Deferred Restricted Contributions as well as encumbrances and expenses of the Tim Rim Fund.

During the year, interest was earned on the balance maintained in the Tim Rim Fund. The initial entry to record the receipt of the interest in the savings account would be recorded in the Cash account of the restricted account group with the following entry:

Restricted Account Group

Mar. 31 CASH—Restricted   200
      INTEREST REVENUES—Restricted   200
    Recording interest earned on the savings account

The $200 earned as interest on the balance of the Tim Rim Fund during the year needs to be transferred from the restricted Cash account to the unrestricted Cash account in the Operating Fund. If the transfer is not made immediately, there is a receivable and a liability between the restricted and unrestricted account groups in the Operating Fund. This receivable and liability would be recognized as:

Unrestricted Account Group

Apr. 1   DUE FROM RESTRICTED GROUP   200
                  TRANSFER FROM RESTRICTED GROUP   200

Recording receivable in unrestricted section of Operating Fund

Restricted Account Group

Apr. 1   TRANSFER TO UNRESTRICTED GROUP   200
                  DUE TO UNRESTRICTED GROUP   200

Recording liability in restricted section of Operating Fund

The accounts "Transfer from" and "Transfer to" are used in place of Revenues and Expenses, respectively. This type of transfer from one section of the Operating Fund to another section should not be considered a revenue or expense item. If these transfers are considered revenues, it would be possible to generate revenues within the NFP organization just by transferring cash between account groups. It does not make sense for an NFP organization to have more revenues or expenses because of internal cash transfers; therefore, the Transfer account is used in the journal entry. Transfer accounts are considered temporary accounts, and are closed in the same manner as other temporary accounts.

Once the cash is transferred from the restricted to the unrestricted portions of the Operating Fund, the following entries are made:

Unrestricted Account Group

Apr. 4   CASH—Unrestricted   200
                  DUE FROM RESTRICTED GROUP   200

Recording receipt of cash from restricted account group

Restricted Account Group

Apr. 4   DUE TO UNRESTRICTED GROUP   200
                  CASH—Restricted   200

Recording payment of cash to unrestricted account group

The April 4 entry in the unrestricted section of the Operating Fund records the receipt of cash and the closing of the balance in the receivable, Due from the Restricted Group. The entry in the restricted section of the Operating Fund records the transfer of cash to the unrestricted account group and the elimination of a liability, Due to the Unrestricted Group. Once this entry is journalized, the unrestricted account group of the Operating Fund has an additional $200 in cash that it can use on any of the general operations of the library.

It may appear that unnecessary work is involved in the use of these accounts, but the outlined procedure sets up a trail of accounting entries that show exactly which monies were transferred out of the restricted account group. [4] This journalized record shows that monies given to the library to purchase books are not being used for the daily operations of the library.

CHARLES ROAST MEMORIAL FUND

The late Charles Roast, a meat cleaver magnate, left the library $12,000. The money and any interest earned on these monies are to be used to purchase books on butchering meat. During the current year, $1,200 was earned in interest on the monies and only $750 was spent on books about butchering meat. They are considered part of the reference collection. The entries to record the transactions for the Charles Roast Memorial Fund are the following:

June 29   EXPENSE—Restricted   750
               C. Roast Memorial Fund   750
                    ACCOUNTS PAYABLE   750
        The invoice on the purchase is approved for payment

June 29   DEFERRED RESTRICTED CONTRIBUTIONS   750
               C. Roast Memorial Fund   750
                    CONTRIBUTIONS—Support   750
        Reducing liability by cost of books

June 30   ACCOUNTS PAYABLE   750
               CASH   750
        Paying the invoice

4. Arguments can be made that there should not be transfers between unrestricted and restricted funds, that the interest income should be recognized only in the unrestricted portion of the Operating Fund. See M. J. Gross and S. F. Jablonsky, *Principles of Accounting and Financial Reporting for Nonprofit Organizations* (New York: Ronald Press, 1979), p. 145. This

The entry on June 29 records the reduction of the Deferred Restricted Contributions account, a liability, by the same amount for which an expense is recognized. At the same time, support from contributions is recognized as being earned. This entry is the same as the entry that was made on September 11 in the Tim Rim Fund.

The recognition of interest earned on the savings account is journalized as follows:

```
June 30   CASH—Restricted                          1,200
               DEFERRED RESTRICTED CONTRIBUTIONS  1,200
                         C. Roast Memorial Fund                1,200
```

Recording the increase in the liability from the interest earnings

The receipt of the cash in interest earnings increases the fund's liabilities because the monies can only be used for the purchase of books on butchering meat. Until those books are purchased, the library has an obligation to fulfill.

FEDERAL GRANT PROGRAM

Under this federal grant program, $15,000 is to be received to provide operating expense support for a program to bring reading materials to handicapped individuals who are unable to use the library's facilities. The grant was awarded on June 18, but the monies receivable under the grant have not yet been received. Before receipt of the monies, the library expended $7,500 of cash from the unrestricted account group for handicapped purposes which would qualify under the grant. These expenditures had been made in anticipation of receiving the grant. The entries to record these payments are the following:

Unrestricted Account Group

```
June 10   EXPENSES                              7,500
               Administration                        7,500
                         ACCOUNTS PAYABLE                   7,500
```

Invoice is approved for payment

---

argument is generally made for endowment funds. As the current entry occurs in the Operating Fund, a transfer will be shown. On pages 218–25, which deals with the Endowment Fund, transfers for unrestricted investment income will not be made; instead, the investment income will be immediately recognized as part of the unrestricted Operating Fund revenues. This assumes that this investment income is not to remain part of the endowment principal.

| June 13 | ACCOUNTS PAYABLE | 7,500 | |
| | CASH | | 7,500 |

Recording payment of invoice

The June 10 and 13 entries record the expenses incurred before receipt of the grant. The monies expended were taken from the unrestricted Cash account, and are reimbursable to the unrestricted account group from the restricted account group after the grant is received. It may appear that the reimbursement entry is the same as for the transfers in the Tim Rim Fund, but the unrestricted account group is reimbursed for an expenditure it made for the restricted account group. On June 18, when it is learned that the grant has been awarded, the entry in the unrestricted account group should recognize a receivable from the restricted account group and a reduction in expenses. The entry is:

Unrestricted Account Group

June 18	DUE FROM RESTRICTED GROUP	7,500	
	EXPENSES		7,500
	Administration		7,500

Recording a receivable from the restricted account group

Usually monetary transfers between account groups or funds are recorded in "Transfer to" or "Transfer from" accounts, but in the case of reimbursable expenses, the expense must be recorded in the accounts. Also, this expense must be a charge against the proper account group or fund. When cash is transferred from the reimbursing account group to the reimbursable account group, or a receivable is recognized in the account group to be reimbursed, the expenses in the reimbursable account group should be reduced. The entry on June 18 is such an entry, and it records a receivable and a reduction of expenses in a reimbursable account group. In this case, the reimbursable account group is the account group that incurred the initial expense—the unrestricted account group.

Shortly after the June 18 notice of the award is received, the restricted account group recognizes an expense and a liability to the unrestricted account group with the following entry:

Restricted Account Group

June 20	EXPENSES	7,500	
	Federal Grant		7,500
	DUE TO UNRESTRICTED GROUP		7,500

Recording the increase of expenses previously incurred

This June 20 entry records $7,500 of previously incurred expenses in the restricted account group where the federal grant will be recorded. The liability and receivable between the two account groups will be canceled when cash is transferred from the restricted account group Cash account to the unrestricted account group Cash account.

As previously stated, on June 18 the library received notice that it had been awarded the grant from the federal government, and the following entry is made in the restricted account group on June 20:

Restricted Account Group

| June 20 | FEDERAL GRANT RECEIVABLE | 15,000 | |
| | DEFERRED RESTRICTED CONTRIBUTION—Grant | | 15,000 |

Recording liability under grant

| June 20 | DEFERRED RESTRICTED CONTRIBUTIONS—Grant | 7,500 | |
| | SUPPORT—Grant | | 7,500 |

Recognizing support equal to amount previously expended

The first entry on June 20 records the receivable from the federal government. The second entry recognizes as earned support the amount that had already been expended on the handicapped program out of the unrestricted monies on June 15 and recorded as an expense in the restricted account group on June 20. It is proper to record the reduction of a liability such as Deferred Restricted Contributions when money has been expended for the specific purposes of the grant before receipt of the grant. This is especially true when the expenditures are made in anticipation of receipt of the grant. (For additional discussion about the recognition of liability on receipt of a federal grant, see p. 57, transaction 4.)

Receipt of the grant monies on June 28 requires the write-off of the receivable from the federal government and recognition of an increase in cash:

Restricted Group

| June 28 | CASH—Restricted | 15,000 | |
| | FEDERAL GRANT RECEIVABLE | | 15,000 |

Recording the receipt of Federal Grant monies

Summary

This chapter has presented an overview of typical entries in the Operating Fund. Some of these entries had been highlighted in earlier chapters, but additional explanation of these entries, as well as the ones that were introduced for the first time, are helpful to the reader in understanding the Operating Fund. The importance of the Operating Fund cannot be overemphasized as the majority of journal entries in a NFP organization occur in this fund. It is hoped that the last two chapters have clarified the use of this fund. Additional illustrations are provided in the appendix to chapter 7, where the 19x2 financial statements for the H. K. Fines Library are brought up to date by incorporating the dated entries on pages 170–200.

Exercise 7–2. Restricted Account Group of Operating Fund

1. On May 1, 19x9, the Harold Miner Fund at the Atwood Library was established, with $6,000. The $6,000, and any interest earned on it, are to be used for the purchase of books on ecclesiasticism. By June 15, 19x9, $1,700 had been used for the purchase of these books. Journalize the necessary entries in general-journal form.
2. On June 19, 19x9, notice was received that a $2,000 federal grant had been awarded to the Morganville Library, but as of June 30, 19x8, the year-end, it had not been received. The grant was awarded for the purchase of ethnic materials for the Regional History Collection. In anticipation of receiving the grant, a $500 purchase had been authorized and paid for out of Regional History monies on June 10, 19x9. Record in general-journal form the correct entries between the unrestricted and restricted account group.

Appendix

The financial statements for the H. K. Fines Library have been prepared for the fiscal year ending June 30, 19x3, using all the *dated* transactions in pages 170–200 of the chapter, and the financial statements prepared in figures 6–1 through 6–3, as well as the Notes to the Financial Statements in figure 6–4. It is recommended that T accounts be opened for the accounts in the financial statements for the period ending June 30, 19x2, and the dated entries from chapter 7 be posted to these T accounts. A trial balance of the balances in these T accounts should be taken before the financial statements are prepared.

H. K. FINES LIBRARY
Operating Fund
Statement of Support, Revenue, and Expenses and Changes in Fund Balance
Year Ended June 30, 19x3
(with Comparative Totals for 19x2)

	Unrestricted	Restricted	Total	June 30, 19x2 Totals
Support and Revenue				
Support				
Grants (Note 1)				
Governments	$160,000	$ 7,500	$167,500	$ 90,000
Other	—	—	—	3,500
Contributions and Bequests	2,300	2,850	5,150	24,000
Total Support	$162,300	$10,350	$172,650	$117,500
Revenue				
Book Fines and Sales	$ 5,500	—	$ 5,500	$ 2,100
Photocopying	8,000	—	8,000	3,785
Investment Income	2,500	$ 200	2,700	3,000
Total Revenue	$ 16,000	$ 200	$ 16,200	$ 8,885
Total Support and Revenue	$178,300	$ 10,550	$188,850	$126,385
Expenses (Note 4)				
Program Services				
Reference	$ 38,017	$ 2,850	$ 40,867	$ 33,000
Children's Library	36,278	—	36,278	17,300
Circulation	40,849	—	40,849	32,000
Regional History	13,939	—	13,939	13,700
Handicapped Services	—	7,500	7,500	—

Total Program Services	$129,083	$10,350	$139,433	$ 96,000
Supporting Services Administration	$ 37,442	—	$ 37,442	$ 24,000
Total Expenses	$166,525	$10,350	$176,875	$120,000
Excess (Deficiency) of Support and Revenues over Expenses	$ 11,775	$ 200	$ 11,975	$ 6,385
Prior Year Expenses on Prior Year Encumbrances (Note 6)	$ 11,900	—	$ 11,900	$ 5,700
Excess (Deficiency) of Support and Revenues over Expenses in Current Year	$ 23,675	$ 200	$ 23,875	$ 12,085
Fund Balance at Beginning of Year	51,575	—	51,575	235,190
Transfers	200	(200)	—	(190,000)
Less: Prior Year Expenses on Prior Year Encumbrances	(11,900)	—	(11,900)	(5,700)
Fund Balance at End of Year	$ 63,550	—	$ 63,550	$ 51,575

(Notes are included in figures 6–4 and 7A–4.)

Copyright © 1979 by the American Institute of Certified Public Accountants, Inc.

FIG. 7A–1. Statement of Support, Revenue, and Expenses and Changes in Fund Balances for Operating Fund

H. K. FINES LIBRARY
Operating Fund
Balance Sheet
June 30, 19x3
(with Comparative Totals for 19x2)

	Unrestricted	Restricted	Total	June 30 19x2 Totals
Assets				
Current Assets				
Cash, including interest bearing savings account	$17,750	$33,050	$ 50,800	$31,700
Petty Cash	500	—	500	—
Marketable Securities (Note 2)	25,000	—	25,000	—
Repurchase Premium Receivable	2,500	—	2,500	—
State Grant Receivable	—	—	—	16,000
Pledges Receivable, at estimated net realizable value	—	—	—	7,200
Due from Restricted Fund	7,500	—	7,500	—
Due from Estate of E. Parsons	2,300	—	2,300	—
Prepaid Expenses and Other	7,500	—	7,500	6,750
Total Current Assets	$63,050	$33,050	$ 96,100	$61,650
Investments (Note 2)	17,000	—	17,000	17,000
Total Assets	$80,050	$33,050	$113,100	$78,650

Liabilities and Fund Balance				
Accounts Payable	$ 2,000	—	$ 2,000	$12,375
Due to State Unemployment	3,000	—	3,000	—
Due to Federal Government—FICA	10,000	—	10,000	—
Due to Unrestricted Fund	—	$ 7,500	7,500	—
Deferred Restricted Contributions (Note 3)	—	25,550	25,550	14,700
Wages Payable	1,500	—	1,500	—
Total Current Liabilities	$16,500	$33,050	$ 49,550	$27,075
Fund Balance				
Unrestricted				
Designated by Board for				
Office Equipment	—	—	—	$ 4,945
Investments	$17,000	—	$ 17,000	17,000
Undesignated	35,600	—	35,600	11,180
Restricted				
Encumbrances	3,450	—	3,450	11,700
Inventory	7,000	—	7,000	6,750
Rent	500	—	500	—
Total Fund Balance	$63,550	—	$ 63,550	$51,575
Total Liabilities and Fund Balance	$80,050	$33,050	$113,100	$78,650

(Notes are included in figures 6–4 and 7A–4)

FIG. 7A–2. Balance Sheet for Operating Fund

H. K. FINES LIBRARY
Operating Fund
Statement of Changes in Financial Position
Year Ended June 30, 19x3
(with Comparative Totals for 19x2)

	Unrestricted	Restricted	Totals	June 30 19x2 Totals
Sources of Working Capital:				
Excess (Deficiency) of Support and Revenues over Expenses	$11,775	$ 200	$ 11,975	$ 6,385
Less: Net Gain on Sale of Investments	—	—	—	2,690
Working Capital Provided by Operations	$11,775	$ 200	$ 11,975	$ 3,695
Sale of Investments	—	—	—	25,690
Deferred Restricted Contributions Received	—	$ 10,350	$ 10,350	15,000
Total Sources of Working Capital	$11,775	$ 10,550	$ 22,325	$44,385
Uses of Working Capital:				
Deferred Restricted Contributions Recognized as Support	—	$ (10,350)	$ (10,350)	$15,000
Transfers between Funds	$ 200	(200)	—	—
Total Uses of Working Capital	$ 200	$ (10,550)	$ (10,350)	$15,000
Increase (Decrease) in Working Capital	$11,975	—	$ (11,975)	$29,385

Changes in Working Capital Components				
Increase (Decrease) in Current Assets				
Cash	$ 750	$ 18,350	$ 19,100	$21,210
Petty Cash	500	—	500	—
Marketable Securities	25,000	—	25,000	—
Repurchase Premium Receivable	2,500	—	2,500	—
State Grant Receivable	(16,000)	—	(16,000)	8,900
Pledges Receivable	(7,200)	—	(7,200)	7,200
Due from Restricted Fund	7,500	—	7,500	—
Due from Estate of E. Parsons	2,300	—	2,300	—
Prepaid Expenses	750	—	750	(5,850)
	$16,100	$ 18,350	$ 34,450	$31,460
(Increase) Decrease in Current Liabilities				
Accounts Payable	$10,375	$ —	$ 10,375	$ 2,625
Due to State Unemployment Fund	(3,000)	—	(3,000)	—
Due to Federal Government	(10,000)	—	(10,000)	—
Due to Unrestricted Fund	—	(7,500)	(7,500)	—
Deferred Restricted Contributions	—	(10,850)	(10,850)	(4,700)
Wages Payable	(1,500)	—	(1,500)	—
	$ (4,125)	$(18,350)	$(22,475)	$(2,075)
Increase (Decrease) in Working Capital	$11,975	$ —	$ 11,975	$29,385

(Notes are included in figures 6–4 and 7A–4.)

FIG. 7A–3.   Statement of Changes in Financial Position for Operating Fund

These notes incorporate the necessary changes that have occurred during the fiscal year only.

Note 2, Investments

Investments are presented in the financial statements in the aggregate at the lower of cost (amortized, in the case of bonds) or fair market value.

	Cost	Market
Operating Fund	$42,000	$46,500

Investments are composed of:

	Cost	Market
Corporate Stocks	$ 7,000	$11,500
U.S. Government Obligations	10,000	10,000
Repurchase Agreements	25,000	25,000
	$42,000	$46,500

The determination of fair market value is calculated by aggregating all current marketable securities. At June 30, 19x2, there was an unrealized gain of $4,500 pertaining to the current portfolio. The portfolio had a cost on June 30, 19x2, of $17,000 and a market value of $21,000. The cost of the securities sold was based on a first-in, first-out method in both years.

Note 3, Changes in Deferred Restricted Contributions

Balances at beginning of year	$14,700
Additions:	
Contributions, Bequests, and Grants	20,000
Investment Income	1,200
	$35,900
Deductions:	
Funds expended during year	(10,350)
Balance at end of year	$25,550

Note 6, Current-Year Expenditures on Prior-Year Encumbrances

The amount encumbered at the end of the 19x2 year was $11,700. During the fiscal year ending June 30, 19x3, expenditures on these encumbrances totaled $11,900.

FIG. 7A–4. Notes to the Financial Statements. (These notes update the notes in chapter 6; therefore, they are not the complete notes to the financial statements. The complete notes incorporate the material shown here with the information in chapter 6.)

Unrestricted Accounts

19x3				
June 30	REVENUES		173,500	
		ESTIMATED REVENUES		173,500
	Closing Revenue and Estimated Revenue accounts			
	REPURCHASE REVENUES		2,500	
		FUND BALANCE		2,500
	Closing revenues to Fund Balance			
	TRANSFER FROM RESTRICTED GROUP		200	
		FUND BALANCE		200
	Closing transfer account to Fund Balance			
	SUPPORT—Bequests		2,300	
		FUND BALANCE		2,300
	Closing bequest to Fund Balance			
	APPROPRIATIONS		164,550	
		EXPENSES		154,625
		FUND BALANCE		9,925
	Closing Appropriation and Expenses account to Fund Balance			
	FUND BALANCE		200	
	APPROPRIATIONS		11,700	
		EXPENSES—Prior Years		11,900
	Closing prior-year expenses to Fund Balance			

Restricted Accounts

	INTEREST REVENUE—Restricted		200	
	SUPPORT—Grant		7,500	
	CONTRIBUTORS—Support		2,850	
		EXPENSES—Restricted		10,350
		TRANSFER TO UNRESTRICTED GROUP		200
	Closing all the temporary accounts in the unrestricted account group with one entry.			

FIG. 7A–5. H. K. Fines Library Closing Entries (These entries are made after the financial statements have been prepared, but they are needed to determine the proper balance in the Fund Balance at the end of the year.)

8.

The Endowment Fund

This chapter deals with another fund common to the NFP organization, the Endowment Fund, which is responsible for the maintenance of assets such as cash, debt, or equity securities. These assets have either been contributed to the organization by a donor or designated by the board as an endowment. They are called the "principal" of an Endowment Fund, and a common characteristic of the "principal" is that its value must be maintained.

The principal of an endowment fund is largely composed of securities that earn some type of income in the form of interest or dividends. The interest and dividends are usually made available to the Operating Fund for spending purposes, but this income can also be reinvested as part of the principal of the fund.

Another characteristic of an endowment's investments is that there may be restrictions on the type of investments that can be made. These legal restrictions may or may not exist, but any restrictions on the type of investments allowed under the endowment should be investigated.

Another name for this type of fund is Trust Fund, which is more descriptive of the functions of this fund: to maintain a trust into perpetuity. When donors contribute assets to an endowment, their intention is that the assets will be maintained intact by the organization.

210

In the previous chapter, the restricted portion of the Operating Fund was explained. The main distinction between the restricted portion of the Operating Fund and the Endowment Fund is that the principal in the endowment must be maintained intact whereas the monies contributed to the restricted portion of the Operating Fund can be used (in their entirety) for the purposes specified by the donor.

The Operating Fund is the most active fund in an NFP organization, in terms of the number of accounting transactions, but an NFP organization's financial picture is not complete without the Endowment Fund. Therefore, this chapter should be considered as important as those that dealt with the Operating Fund.

Endowment Fund Assets

The assets of an endowment fund have been contributed to the NFP organization for maintenance and not for spending purposes. At least this is the general case with endowments. Two exceptions to this type of endowment are the "term endowment" and the "quasi endowment." The major distinction between the different types of endowments relates to the access the organization has to the endowment's principal.

As stated, the principal of the typical endowment cannot be used by the NFP organization, and must be maintained intact; that is, it cannot be spent. With a term endowment, at the occurrence of a future event or future date the principal becomes available to the NFP organization for its use. This event may be based upon the death of the donor or that of an heir to the donor. When a quasi endowment is established, it permits the board of the NFP organization to use the assets of the organization to establish an endowment. These assets form the principal of the endowment, but this principal does not have to be maintained intact. These board-contributed assets have not been restricted by an outside donor; for that reason, it is a simple matter for the board to change its policy and remove the assets from the endowment for use in normal activities of the organization. This endowment is based on discretionary decisions of the board, which can be reversed without great difficulty.

The principal in any endowment may be handled by the NFP organization or by a trustee, such as a bank, which does the actual investing. In such cases, only the investment income would be transferred to the NFP organization. The donor may have stipulated, as a condition of the contribution, that the principal is not to be transferred to the organization, but is to be maintained by a specific trustee with only its income forwarded to the organization.

Regardless of the handling of the principal of an endowment, the result is the generation of income, as well as gains and losses, and these are the next considerations. The income of an endowment is usually considered to be the dividends and interest earned on the principal; and this amount is usually made available for either the general operations of the organization or for some specified use. Under the latter situation, income from the endowment is recorded in the restricted portion of the Operating Fund as a deferred revenue item. If the income is used for the general, daily operations of the organization, it is recognized as revenue in the unrestricted portion of the Operating Fund. This is true for either a "regular" endowment or a quasi endowment.

Although income from an endowment is considered to be the dividends and interest earned on its principal, the concept of income can be broadened to include realized gains and losses, and even *un*realized gains and losses. "Total return" is another way in which endowment income can be defined. Under this concept of income, appreciation on the securities in the endowment's principal is considered to be part of the income on the endowment. This makes the appreciation available for spending, just as the dividends and interest are available for spending. As part of this approach, a "spending rate"—the portion of the total return that can be used for spending purposes—has to be set by the board. In other words, it is the total of dividends, interest, and appreciation that can be spent. Before this method can be adopted by an endowment, an NFP organization would have to obtain the advice of legal counsel to determine whether this method is available for use by a particular endowment.

Another common characteristic of endowment funds is that the assets of the various endowments can be combined into one investment pool, which allows for more efficient decision making in the investment process. Also, if the amounts that are invested are large enough, it can result in lower commission charges in making investments. Another effect of the pooling process is that it reduces the risk of a bad investment to an individual endowment by spreading the risk among all the endowments in the pool. When investments are pooled in this fashion, it is still necessary periodically to distribute the income and realized gains to the various endowments in the pool. This is a simple record-keeping task when the endowments are maintained separately from each other, but when they are combined into a pool, it becomes more complex.

A method that can be used to distribute the income and realized gains and losses of the pooled investments is called the "market unit method," which uses the market value of the investments as the basis for establishing a per share allocation procedure. This method is used to determine each endowment's balance in the pool and the number of shares received upon the contribution of new securities or cash to the pool. (This allocation procedure is explained in detail on pp. 226–30.) It can be thought of as similar to a percentage distribution of gains and losses to endowments in an investment pool.

A final characteristic of endowments that should be noted is that they do not recognize appropriations, estimated revenues, or budget entries in their accounts. The reason is that the endowment is not involved in spending the income earned on its principal, and therefore no need exists for these accounts.

Therefore, the major accounting questions surrounding endowments relate to the handling of income, as well as realized gains and losses on the endowment's principal. In addition, there is a question of the division of these amounts when an investment pool is formed.

Endowment Fund's Financial Statements

Financial statements for the Endowment Fund are relatively simple, compared with the Operating Fund's financial statements. The financial statements for the Endowment Fund consist of a Statement of Support, Revenue, and Expenses and Changes in Fund Balances (SREF) and a Balance Sheet. These financial statements for the year ending June 30, 19x2, are illustrated in figures 8–1 and 8–2, respectively, for the H. K. Fines Library. The Statement of Changes in Financial Position has not been prepared for the Endowment Fund, as the sources and uses of working capital are readily apparent.[1]

The SREF in figure 8–1, prepared for the H. K. Fines Library's three endowment funds, is a financial statement much like those prepared for the Operating Fund of the library, except for Capital Additions at the bottom of the statement and the fact that no support, revenue, or expenses are recognized in any of the three endowments.

---

1. Actually a statement of changes in financial position prepared for the endowment fund would be prepared on a "cash" basis rather than a "working capital" basis as there are no current liabilities and the only current asset is cash.

H. K. FINES LIBRARY
Statement of Support, Revenue, and Expenses
and Changes in Fund Balances for Endowment Fund
Year Ended June 30, 19x2
(with Comparative Totals for 19x1)

	Endowments A	Endowments B	Endowments C	Totals	June 30 19x1 Totals
Support and Revenue	—	—	—	—	—
Expenses	—	—	—	—	—
Excess (Deficiency) of support and revenue over expenses before capital additions	—	—	—	—	—
Capital Additions:					
Gifts and Grants	—	—	—	—	$ 23,000
Net Investment Income	—	$ 25,000	—	$ 25,000	—
Net Realized Gains (Losses)	$ (2,000)	10,000	—	8,000	12,000
Total	$ (2,000)	$ 35,000	$ —	$ 33,000	$ 35,000
Excess (Deficiency) of support and revenue over expenses after capital additions	$ (2,000)	$ 35,000	$ —	$ 33,000	$ 35,000
Fund Balances at Beginning of Year	100,000	725,000	150,000	975,000	940,000
Fund Balances at End of Year	$ 98,000	$760,000	$150,000	$1,008,000	$975,000

FIG. 8–1. Statement of Support, Revenue, and Expenses and Changes in Fund Balances for Endowment Fund

Even though there is no support, revenue, or expense, the statement is presented in a form that can be easily integrated with the Operating Fund's SREF when a combined SREF is prepared for the total organization in chapter 11.

The use of capital additions on the statement needs to be explained. Capital additions are the income, or the gains and losses, on the endowment's investment that become part of the principal of the endowment. This means that it is not expended; rather, it becomes part of the "capital" of the endowment fund.[2] It is added to the Fund Balance of the endowment, as can be seen in figure 8−1, and it remains as part of the endowment's principal. Capital additions can also include gifts, grants, or bequests that become part of the principal of an existing endowment.

There are three endowments in the H. K. Fines Library's Endowment Fund. Endowment A allows the *income* generated from the endowment to be used for scholarship grants for students in library science at the local university. The *realized gains and losses* from the investments are part of the capital additions of this endowment. Endowment B requires that all the *income,* as well as the *realized gains and losses* on the investments, be returned to the endowment as capital additions. Endowment B is a term endowment, and it was contributed to the library with the condition that no expenditures would be made from it until the donor's death. Endowment C is a quasi endowment, established by the board, and, as such, all its investment income and its net gains are available to be used by the unrestricted portion of the Operating Fund for the daily, routine operations of the library. The library has not pooled its investments, and each endowment is accounted for separately.

The Balance Sheet for the Endowment Fund (figure 8−2) is a relatively simple statement, compared with the Balance Sheet prepared for the Operating Fund. The Endowment Fund's Balance Sheet consists of a listing of the assets of the fund. These assets are usually composed of equity and debt securities, as well as some cash. The accounts listed on the Balance Sheet are control accounts that are supported by detailed information on the investments in a subsidiary ledger. The subsidiary ledger should have specific information on the types of securities that are held by the endowment. The method of

2. These changes in the principal can be net gains or capital additions, and the examples in the chapter are largely oriented toward net gains on the endowment. However, it should be noted that it is possible for the principal to incur a capital deduction due to incurring net losses. When this occurs, the principal of the endowment is reduced.

H. K. FINES LIBRARY
Endowment Fund
Balance Sheet
June 30, 19x2
(with Comparative Totals for 19x1)

	Endowment A	Endowment B	Endowment C	Totals	June 30 19x1 Totals
Assets:					
Cash	—	$ 40,000	—	$ 40,000	—
Investments (Note 2)	$98,000	720,000	$150,000	968,000	$975,000
Total Assets	$98,000	$760,000	$150,000	$1,008,000	$975,000
Liabilities and Fund Balance:					
Liabilities	—	—	—	—	—
Fund Balances:					
Restricted— Nonexpendable	$98,000	$760,000	$150,000	$1,008,000	$975,000
Total Fund Balance	$98,000	$760,000	$150,000	$1,008,000	$975,000

FIG. 8—2. Balance Sheet for Endowment Fund

valuing these investments should be disclosed in the notes to the financial statements. As was explained in chapter 6, there are several ways that these types of securities can be valued.

The Balance Sheet for the H. K. Fines Library presents the amount of cash and investments in each of the three endowments. The Fund Balance should be equal to the total amount of cash and investments. The information in the Balance Sheet in figure 8—2 should not be considered alone, but in conjunction with the information in the Notes to the Financial Statements in figure 8—3.

The Notes to the Financial Statements in figure 8—3 consist of only supplemental notes. They are specifically related to the Balance Sheet in figure 8—2, but they are not the complete notes for the organiza-

Note 1, Summary of Significant Accounting Policies

Endowment Funds represent the type of funds that are subject to restrictions requiring in perpetuity that the principal be invested and the income only can be used.

Note 2, Investments

Investments are presented in the financial statements in the aggregate at the lower of cost (amortized, in the case of bonds) or fair market value.

	Cost	Market
Endowment A	$ 98,000	$ 99,000
B	720,000	735,000
C	150,000	163,000
	$968,000	$997,000

Investments composed of the following:

	Cost	Market
Corporate Stocks and Bonds	$790,000	$800,000
U.S. Government Securities	168,000	187,000
Municipal	10,000	10,000
	$968,000	$997,000

The determination of fair market value is made by aggregating all current marketable securities. At June 30, 19x2, there was unrealized gain of $29,000 pertaining to the current portfolio. The portfolio had a cost on June 30, 19x1, of $975,000 and a market value of $995,000.

A net realized gain of $8,000 on the sale of marketable equity securities was included in the determination of the Excess (deficiency) of Support and Revenue over Expenses after Capital Additions for 19x2. The cost of the securities sold was based on a first-in, first-out method in both years.

FIG. 8–3. Notes to Financial Statements Relative to the Endowment Fund

tion. The Notes to the Financial Statements of the H. K. Fines Library, included in figure 6–4, should be considered along with the additional notes in figure 8–3. The information which needs to be disclosed in the notes about investments is listed on page 153, and the disclosures in figure 8–3 are very similar to those in figure 6–4.

As these investments are still part of the library's investments, even though they are part of the Endowment Fund rather than the Operating Fund, they all should be valued in the same manner. In other words, the method of security valuation that is chosen should apply consistently to all the organization's investments, regardless of their fund classification. In the case of the H. K. Fines Library, the marketable equity securities are valued by using the lower of cost or market, and the debt securities are valued by using the lower of amortized cost or market value. It needs to be emphasized that when one fund's marketable equity securities are valued by the lower of cost or market value, a second fund with marketable equity securities should not value these securities based on market value alone.

Exercise 8–1. The Endowment Fund

Explain the following terms:

a) Capital additions
b) Total-return concept
c) Quasi endowment
d) Spending rate
e) Investment pool

Typical Entries for Endowment Fund

Typical entries for an Endowment Fund depend on the type of endowment. As previously stated, if a quasi-endowment fund is involved, the income and the net gains that are used by the unrestricted portion of the Operating Fund are recognized as revenue on the SREF for the Operating Fund. There is no recognition of these amounts on the SREF of a quasi-endowment fund. This relationship is illustrated in figure 8–4.

In figure 8–4, the path for net income and net gains, to be recognized on the unrestricted portion of the Operating Fund's SREF, is illustrated.[3] When these amounts appear as revenues on the Operating Fund's SREF, they follow path 1–2, or 4–6, and become part of the

---

3. The term "net gains" refers to the difference between losses and gains incurred during the fiscal year. When the difference between gains and losses is a positive amount, it is called a "net gain." If the difference is negative, it is called a "net loss."

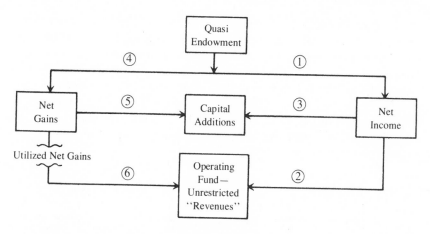

FIG. 8–4. Quasi-Endowment Fund and Its Net Gains and Income

unrestricted revenues of the Operating Fund. If these amounts are to be returned to the endowment (which is not usually the case with a quasi endowment), they follow paths 1–3, or 4–5, and become capital additions on the Endowment Fund's SREF.

In the quasi endowment for H. K. Fines Library, Endowment C, all the net gains and net income are used by the unrestricted portion of the Operating Fund. During the year ending June 30, 19x3, net gains and net income for this endowment amounted to $11,250 and $8,750, respectively. The following entries record these amounts in Endowment C:

Endowment C

June 1 19x3	CASH	8,750	
	DUE TO OPERATING FUND—Unrestricted		8,750
	Recording net income received by endowment		

June 1 19x3	CASH	61,250	
	GAIN ON SALE OF INVESTMENTS		11,250
	INVESTMENTS		50,000
	Recording realized gains on sale of investments		

These aggregated entries for all the income and gains are recorded on June 1 in Endowment C. The first entry records the net income during the 19x3 period. The second entry records the realized net gains that have been received in the buying and selling of investments during the year. This is a net amount, which means that losses and any commission charges for buying and selling of stock have been deducted. Realized gains and income are not supposed to appear in the SREF of the Endowment Fund. As the entries now appear, a gain would be recognized on the Endowment's SREF, along with a liability to the Operating Fund. These accounts should be eliminated from the SREF. The following entry accomplishes that result when cash is forwarded to the Operating Fund:

Endowment C

June 30	GAIN ON SALE OF INVESTMENTS	11,250	
19x3	DUE TO OPERATING FUND—Unrestricted	8,750	
	CASH		20,000

Forwarding cash to the Operating Fund and writing off the liability and the gain

The entry on June 30 eliminates the gain and the liability from Endowment C. At the same time that these entries are recorded in the Endowment Fund, the Operating Fund records corresponding entries. The following entry is recorded in the Operating Fund on June 1:

Operating Fund—Unrestricted

June 1	DUE FROM ENDOWMENT C	20,000	
19x3	REVENUE ON INVESTMENTS—Endowments		20,000

Recognizing as revenues the amounts received on Endowment C investments

This entry records the amounts due from Endowment C as of June 1. These amounts are recorded as revenues from the Endowment. It should be noted that this is one type of entry that occurs simultaneously in the two funds. Another simultaneous entry occurs on June 30 in both funds when the monies are forwarded to the Operating Fund:

Operating Fund—Unrestricted

June 30	CASH	20,000	
19x3	DUE FROM ENDOWMENT C		20,000

Recording the receipt of cash from Endowment C

The results of these two journal entries in Endowment C are that the income earned on the investments and the net gains on the sale of investments are transferred to the Operating Fund as revenue of that fund. Although the income and gains are first received by the endowment, they are never recognized as revenue in Endowment C.

As the board has complete discretion in the operation of a quasi endowment, its gains and income are usually recognized as revenues in the unrestricted portion of the Operating Fund. The board could have set a policy that allowed only investment income to be available to the Operating Fund. This change means that net gains would become part of Endowment C's principal, rather than being transferred to the Operating Fund. In this situation, net gains would follow path 4–5 in figure 8–4. In such a case, the Gain on the Sale of Investments account is still eliminated, except this time it is recognized as a capital addition to the principal of the Endowment Fund. The entry to record this change is as follows:

Endowment C

GAIN ON SALE OF INVESTMENTS	11,250	
CAPITAL ADDITIONS—Net Realized Gains		11,250

Recognizing a capital addition equal to the net gains on investments

The $11,250 in Capital Additions is shown on the SREF below the Excess before Capital Additions. Any amounts that contribute to increases in the endowment's principal should be recognized as capital additions and not as gains or revenue to the Operating Fund.

As stated, the board's policy toward the quasi endowment is completely discretionary, and it may set a policy that all *un*realized net gains can be used by the unrestricted portion of the Operating Fund. This amount is determined by netting the unrealized gains and losses against each other and making the result (which is assumed to be a net gain) available for use by the unrestricted portion of the Operating Fund. This procedure may raise the question as to how unrealized gains can be used when they have not been realized. The answer is that unrealized gains become usable once the endowment sells the marketable securities with an unrealized gain for cash. The endowment's investments are readily marketable and they can be quickly sold. This type of policy requires the conversion of marketable securities to cash in order to transfer an unrealized gain to the Operating Fund. In effect, this is a policy which forces the realization of an unrealized gain through a sale if the cash balance is insufficient to cover the transfer.

If the cash in the endowment's Cash account is equal to the amount of the unrealized gain, it can be tranferred to the Operating Fund. The net effect of this cash withdrawal is a reduction in the endowment's principal, and this transaction is recorded as a debit to a Transfer account and a credit to a Cash account. Later, when the unrealized gain is realized, it will increase the balance of the principal. Of course, withdrawal of cash without the sale of the securities equal to the unrealized gain is a risky policy, as an unrealized gain can quickly disappear with changes in market conditions. Once this occurs, the principal will be permanently reduced, as the unrealized gain will never be recognized.

The H. K. Fines Library's Endowment Fund also contains Endowment A and Endowment B, which are not quasi endowments. The rules under which they operate have been established by an outside donor. Endowment A's net realized gains and losses are part of the endowment's principal, but the net investment income is available to the restricted portion of the Operating Fund. This arrangement requires that the net realized gains or losses be recognized as capital additions or deductions in the endowment's SREF, and that the investment income be recognized as deferred revenue in the restricted portion of the Operating Fund's SREF. Figure 8–5 outlines the path that net income and net gains follow. In Endowment A, the investment income follows the path marked 1–3–4 whereas the net gains follow the path 6–7.

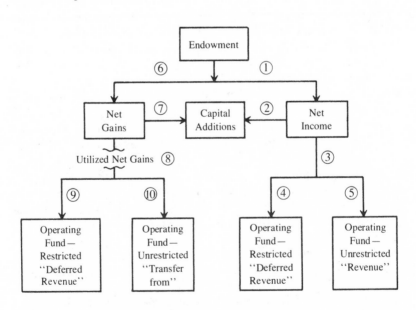

Fig. 8–5. The Endowment and Its Net Gains and Income

Assume that during the fiscal year ending June 30, 19x3, net realized gain was equal to $5,500 and net income was equal to $8,900. Further assume that a previous entry credited the Gain account for $5,500 when a security with a value, at cost, of $10,000 was sold.[4] The following entry would be recorded in the journal to eliminate the Gain account from the endowment's records:

Endowment A

June 30   GAIN ON SALE OF INVESTMENTS   5,500
            CAPITAL ADDITIONS—Net Realized Gains   5,500

    Recognizing a capital addition equal to the net gains on the investment

The investment income of $8,900 from the endowment is recognized in the restricted portion of the Operating Fund with the following entry:

Operating Fund—Restricted

June 30   CASH   8,900
            DEFERRED RESTRICTED REVENUE   8,900

    Recognizing a liability on the cash received from Endowment A

The account Deferred Restricted Revenue is a liability, and it will remain a liability until the money received from the endowment is spent for the scholarship grants for which it was intended. Note that the investment income will not be recognized in the accounts of Endowment A. Even if it had been recognized as a "Due to" account in the endowment, this liability would have been canceled once the cash was forwarded to the Operating Fund. The net effect on the cash received as revenue on Endowment A's account balances is zero.

The last endowment, Endowment B, requires a slightly different accounting treatment than the previous two endowments. In this endowment, both the net income and net gains are to be recognized as increases in the principal of the endowment. If figure 8–5 is re-

---

4. The sale of the security was recorded with the following entry.

Endowment A

June 30   CASH   15,500
            GAIN ON SALE OF INVESTMENTS   5,500
            INVESTMENTS   10,000

    Recording sale of investments for a gain

viewed, it can be seen that investment income and net gains from this endowment follow paths 1–2 and 6–7, respectively. The accounting for this endowment is simpler than for the other two endowments because all the entries can be handled within the Endowment Fund, and they do not affect the Operating Fund.

For example, assume that during the fiscal year ending June 30, 19x3, there is net investment income of $27,750 and net realized gains of $13,000. Both of these amounts are used to increase the endowment's principal as a capital addition. This increase is journalized with the following entry:

Endowment B

June 30	CASH	27,750	
	CAPITAL ADDITIONS—Investment Income		27,750

Recording increase in capital additions from investment income

June 30	GAIN ON SALE OF INVESTMENTS	13,000	
	CAPITAL ADDITIONS—Net Realized Gains		13,000

Recording increase in capital additions from net realized gains

The first entry recognizes the cash received as investment income in the capital additions section of the endowment's SREF. This addition is added to Endowment's A principal. The second entry cancels a previously recognized gain from the sale of investments with a value, at cost, of $50,000[5] and transfers the gain to the realized gain section of the capital additions. None of the net income or gains is recognized in the Operating Fund.

These three endowments in the H. K. Fines Library illustrate three combinations that can occur with net gains and income in an endowment fund. It should be pointed out that net gains usually become a capital addition to the principal, and investment income is used either by the unrestricted or restricted portion of the Operating Fund.

As previously indicated, when the total-return concept is followed, net gains and (in some cases) unrealized gains are utilized by the

---

5. The sale of the security was recorded with the following entry.

Endowment B

June 30	CASH	63,000	
	GAIN ON SALE OF INVESTMENTS		13,000
	INVESTMENTS		50,000

Recording sale of investments for a gain

Operating Fund to achieve the spending rate which has been set by the board. An endowment that operates under the total-return concept is illustrated in figure 8–5. For the net gains to be utilized by the restricted portion of the Operating Fund, they would follow path 6–8–9. This results in the net gains being recognized as deferred revenue in the restricted portion of the Operating Fund. In the Endowment Fund, these amounts are recognized in a transfer account, such as Transfers to the Operating Fund. Therefore, when the net gains are made available to the Operating Fund, recognition as a transfer is recommended in the Endowment Fund.

In figure 8–5, net gains utilized by the unrestricted portion of the Operating Fund follow the path 6–8–10 to be recognized in a transfer account such as Transfer from the Endowment Fund. This transfer is recorded in the Endowment Fund at the same time as a Transfer to the Operating Fund. Unlike the restricted portion of the Operating Fund, which recognizes these net gain transfers as deferred revenue, the unrestricted portion of the Operating Fund recognizes these same amounts in a transfer account. Therefore, when net gains are made available to another fund from an endowment that is not a quasi endowment, consideration needs to be given to transfer accounts. These transfer accounts appear below the Excess on all SREFs.

Exercise 8–2. Endowment's Journal Entries

1. The Cross Endowment consists of a $500,000 quasi endowment which is not part of an investment pool. During the current fiscal year, the endowment earned $30,000 in investment income and recognized a net gain of $27,000. The income is made available to the restricted portion of the Operating Fund, and the net gain increases the principal of the endowment. A Due to Operating Fund account had been established in the endowment. Record the correct journal entries for both funds, as completely as possible, with the available information. Assume the entries are recorded at the end of the fiscal year, on June 30, 19x9.

2. The Lord Harold Library has a quasi endowment which has been established by the board with a $150,000 investment. All the gains and income from the endowment are available to the unrestricted portion of the Operating Fund. During the current year, $5,000 in net gains were received on the sale of $30,000 of securities, and $6,000 in income earned on the endowment as of the third quarter. Record all entries for the endowment and the Operating Fund as of the end of the third quarter, on October 1, 19x7.

3. The Morelane Library Board has adopted the total-return concept with its Ross Endowment, which consists of $250,000 in investments, at cost. The board adopted a spending rate of 10% of cost. The return from the endowment was composed of net gains of $2,000, net income of $18,000, and unrealized gains of $8,000. Ten percent of the endowment was made available to the unrestricted portion of the Operating Fund. Record the correct journal entries in the Ross Endowment and the Operating Fund for the transfer *of cash* on July 1, 19x5, only.

Investment Pools

It may be to the advantage of the NFP organization to form an investment pool with its endowment assets. An investment pool is formed when the assets of all the endowments are merged into one large fund, rather than account for each endowment separately (as was done with the H. K. Fines Library's endowment). This investment pool's financial statements are prepared like any other endowment fund, but the assets are not assigned to a specific endowment. The assets are assigned to the investment pool as a whole.

The investment pool is either invested into securities by the organization itself, or it is handled by a trustee outside the organization. In either case, at periodic intervals (perhaps quarterly) the amounts of realized gains and losses, as well as the income from the investments, are allocated to all the endowments in the pool through their fund balances. Each endowment in the pool has a Fund Balance account on the investment pool's Balance Sheet. In a separate calculation, the market value of each endowment's assets is determined. Unrealized gains and losses are included in this calculation because whenever the market value of an asset is determined, it will always incorporate all unrealized gains and losses in that group of assets.[6]

This results in two sets of records being maintained on the endowment's investments. Unless the books are based on market value, different dollar values will be attributed to the endowment's investment on the pool's Fund Balance at cost from the market value of those same securities. From the material in chapter 6, it was apparent

---

6. It needs to be emphasized that the cost basis does not recognize unrealized gains and losses, and for this reason a difference exists between cost and market valuation methods, as the latter method *does* recognize unrealized gains and losses.

that an NFP organization can use any of the following methods to value its investments: (1) cost, (2) market, (3) lower of cost or market, and (4) lower of amortized cost or market. If the pooled investments are valued by the cost method, it means that the actual accounting records are kept on a cost basis. At the same time, when a determination of the amount of each endowment's market value is made, a different dollar value is obtained. If the market value is higher than the cost value and the endowment withdraws its securities from the investment pool, it means that the dollar amount withdrawn from the fund is more than the amount at which the investment is carried on the books, that is, its cost. The difference between these amounts—cost basis versus market basis—is divided among the endowments remaining in the pool in the same manner as realized gains and losses and investment income are divided among them.

As an example of how an investment pool functions, assume that the investments and cash in the H. K. Fines Library's three endowments are placed into an investment pool. The amounts contributed by each of the endowments appeared on the Balance Sheet in figure 8–2 and consist of the following assets:

Endowment A: $98,000 in investments; market value $99,000

Endowment B: $40,000 in cash and $720,000 in investments; market value $735,000

Endowment C: $150,000 in investments; market value $163,000

Furthermore, assume that a share in the investment pool is arbitrarily set at $100. This amount is set arbitrarily when the pool is initially established. Once this share value is set, the number of shares held by each endowment in the investment pool can be determined as follows:

	No. of Shares
Endowment A	999
Endowment B	7,750*
Endowment C	1,630
Total	10,370

* Cash plus market value of securities

If a new endowment were added to the investment pool at this point, the market value of its investments and cash would be divided by the market unit value of $100 to determine the number of shares it would have in the pool. For example, if a new endowment were added to the investment pool and it had securities with a market value of $100,000, it would have a total of 1,000 shares in the investment pool. It is important that all allocations from the investment pool be based on market values.

As a further example, assume that the same endowment, with $100,000 in market value securities, enters the investment pool after the investments held by the three endowments already in the pool have doubled in value. This doubling of investment values would increase the market value of each share to $200. The result is that a new endowment that enters the investment pool with $100,000 in market value securities would only receive 500 shares in the investment pool. Correspondingly, it receives a smaller proportion of any gains, losses, and investment income.

As purchases and sales of securities occur in the investment pool, realized gains and losses also occur. These realized gains and losses should be netted against one another, and the result is distributed to the shares in the investment pool at periodic intervals. The most frequent distribution of these amounts is quarterly, but it could occur on a yearly basis.

As an example of how the distribution process is handled, assume that during the first quarter of a fiscal year, securities with a value on the books of $3,000 are sold for $3,500, which results in a realized gain of $500. To record this sale, the following entry should be made:

CASH	3,500	
RESERVE ON REALIZED GAINS AND LOSSES		500
INVESTMENTS		3,000

Recording the sale of investment pool securities

The credit to the control account, Investments, is tied in with a subsidiary-ledger entry. (The subsidiary ledger contains all the detailed information on the securities.) The $3,000 credit in the entry should also cause a decrease in the securities in the subsidiary ledger by an equal amount. The account Reserve on Realized Gains and Losses acts as a holding account. The amount of gains is credited to this account, and the amount of losses is debited to it. After a certain time has passed, the amount accumulated in the account is allocated to the various endowments on a per share basis. When a gain or loss occurs on the sale of a security, it is recorded in the Reserve account, but this amount does not immediately have to be allocated to the various endowments in the pool.

As an example of how the amount in the Reserve on Realized Gains and Losses is distributed to the endowments in the investment pool, assume that the balance in this account has accumulated to a $5,185 credit balance. (This balance includes the previous gain of $500.) This amount is to be distributed to Endowments A, B, and C on the basis of the per share figures previously shown. By dividing the total number of shares (10,370) into the amount in the Reserve account ($5,185), the amount of gain attributed to each share is determined ($.50). When the $.50 per share amount is multiplied by the number of shares held by each endowment, the total amount of gain allocated to each endowment is determined. The following table shows these results.

Endowment	Allocated Gain	Computation
Endowment A	$ 495	990 × .50
Endowment B	3,875	7,750 × .50
Endowment C	815	1,630 × .50

The increase in each of the endowments is recorded as an increase in the Fund Balance of each endowment in the investment pool. This allocation procedure does not affect the percentage of shares allotted to each of the endowments, but it does increase the dollar value attributed to each of the shares in the pool. The results of this distribution are recorded as follows in the Fund Balance accounts of the investment pool:

RESERVE ON REALIZED GAINS AND LOSSES	5,185	
FUND BALANCE—Endowment A		495
FUND BALANCE—Endowment B		3,875
FUND BALANCE—Endowment C		815

Recording the net gains and losses allocated to each endowment

This entry divides the net realized gains among the endowments. When the investment pool receives investment income, it is periodically divided among the endowments by the same procedure.

The total amount in the Fund Balance of the endowments is the amount that can be withdrawn by the endowment from the investment pool. If the investments are valued on the books at market value, any endowment's withdrawal from the pool will withdraw an amount equal to the balance in the Fund Balance account. If the investments are valued at cost, which is less than market value, then an endowment's withdrawing its investments from the pool would withdraw more than the amount in the Fund Balance. This situation occurs because the endowment is allowed to withdraw an amount equal to the market value of its securities, not their cost value. The market value information about the investments is maintained as supplemental information when the accounts on the books are kept on the cost basis.

As an example of these procedures, assume that the Kirwin Library has an investment pool and the May Endowment is going to withdraw from that pool. The investments are accounted for at cost on the books of the pool, and market information on each endowment's investments is maintained separately from the books. The endowment's Fund Balance on the books is equal to $120,000 and the market value of the endowment's investments is equal to $150,000. Obviously, the endowment should be able to withdraw the market value of its investments from the investment pool. It is recommended that the difference between these two amounts be distributed among the endowments remaining in the investment pool in the same manner as net gains and income are distributed. The entry to record the withdrawal follows:

RESERVE FOR REALIZED GAINS AND LOSSES	30,000	
FUND BALANCE—May Endowment	120,000	
CASH		150,000

Recording the May Endowment's withdrawal from the investment pool

The balance in the account Reserve for Realized Gains and Losses will be distributed to the fund balances of the endowments remaining in the investment pool. If the difference between market value and cost is large enough, the difference should be reported in an account separate from the Reserve account.

If the May Endowment were not going to completely withdraw from the investment pool, the amount it could withdraw is established in terms of the shares it holds. The dollar amount withdrawn might represent 10 percent of its shares. At this time, the reduction in the Fund Balance is set at 10 percent. Again, these 10 percent portions are equal to different monetary amounts. This difference in monetary amounts is debited to the Reserve account, and that balance is allocated to the fund balance of the endowments remaining in the pool.

Summary

The Endowment Fund is required to maintain a patron's donation intact. The donation is termed the "principal" of the Endowment Fund, and this amount must not be spent. This is the major characteristic of an Endowment Fund. The principal of the endowment is invested to earn a return, and its securities are purchased and sold to achieve a gain. The accounting for receipt of income, realized gains and losses, and the formation of investment pools have been explained in the chapter.

The H. K. Fines Library's financial statements, as presented in figures 8–1 and 8–2, as well as the Notes to the Financial Statements in figure 8–3, are updated in the appendix to chapter 8. This updating procedure incorporates all the dated entries in the chapter as they relate to the Endowment Fund, the entries in the footnotes to the chapter, and the two journal entries noted in the appendix. These financial statements have been updated to the period ending June 30, 19x3. Dated entries in this chapter that involve the Operating Fund are taken into account in preparing the H. K. Fines Library's comprehensive financial statements in chapter 11, but not in preparation of the financial statements in the appendix.

Exercise 8–3. The Investment Pool

1. An investment pool has been formed by two endowments. Endowment X has securities listed at a cost value of $89,000 (market value of $110,000). Endowment Y has cash of $15,000 and securities with a cost value of $37,000 (market value of $57,000).

   a) The market unit value is set at $75. Determine how many shares each endowment receives.

   b) Assume that at the end of the first quarter, investment income is equal to $17,000 and net gains have been $20,000. Allocate these amounts to the two endowments.

2. An investment pool is composed of four endowments. The investments are valued at cost on the books. The Fund Balance section on the investment pool's Balance Sheet appears as follows:

	Cost Value	Shares
Fund Balance—Endowment A	$125,000	500
Fund Balance—Endowment B	78,000	400
Fund Balance—Endowment C	48,000	600
Fund Balance—Endowment D	67,000	500

It has been decided that Endowment A will withdraw $59,000 (market value) from the investment pool. This withdrawal will reduce the endowment's shares by 200 shares. In terms of its cost value, this withdrawal is equal to $50,000.

a)   Journalize the withdrawal by Endowment A.

b)   Distribute the difference between the cost and market valuations to the endowments remaining in the investment pool with journal entries.

c)   What are the balances in the fund balances after the distribution?

3. Why are unrealized gains and losses automatically part of any market valuation of investment securities?

Appendix

The financial statements for the H. K. Fines Library have been prepared for the fiscal year ending June 30, 19x3, using all the *dated* entries occurring in pages 219–30, the following two entries, and the financial statements in figures 8–1 and 8–2, as well as the Notes to the Financial Statements in figure 8–3. It is recommended that T accounts be opened for the accounts in the financial statements for the period ending June 30, 19x2, and the dated entries be posted to these T accounts. A trial balance of the balances in these T accounts should be taken before the financial statements are prepared.

ADDITIONAL INVESTMENTS

One objective of the endowment is to keep its assets earning a return. Assets such as cash do not earn a return; therefore, Endowments B ($120,000) and C ($45,000) have reduced their cash balances by making the following investments during the fiscal year ending June 30, 19x3. The entries to record the purchase of these investments follow:

Endowment B

May 15	INVESTMENTS	120,000	
	CASH		120,000

Endowment C

May 15	INVESTMENTS	45,000	
	CASH		45,000

H. K. FINES LIBRARY
Endowment Fund
Statement of Support, Revenue, and Expenses and Changes in Fund Balances
Year Ended June 30, 19x3
(with Comparative Totals for 19x2)

	Endowment A	Endowment B	Endowment C	Total	June 30 19x2 Totals
Support and Revenue	—	—	—	—	—
Expenses	—	—	—	—	—
Excess (Deficiency) of support and revenue over expenses before capital addition	—	—	—	—	—
Capital Additions:					
Gifts and Grants	—	—	—	—	—
Net Investment Income	—	$ 27,750	—	$ 27,750	$ 25,000
Net Realized Gains (Losses)	$ 5,500	13,000	—	18,500	8,000
Total	$ 5,500	$ 40,750	$ —	$ 46,250	$ 33,000
Excess (Deficiency) of support and revenue over expenses after capital additions	$ 5,500	$ 40,750	—	$ 46,250	$ 33,000
Fund Balances at Beginning of Year	98,000	760,000	150,000	1,008,000	975,000
Fund Balance at end of Year	$103,500	$800,750	$150,000	$1,054,250	$1,008,000

FIG. 8A–1. Statement of Support, Revenue, and Expenses and Changes in Fund Balances for Endowment Fund

H. K. FINES LIBRARY
Endowment Fund
Balance Sheet
June 30, 19x3
(with Comparative Totals for 19x2)

	Endowment A	Endowment B	Endowment C	Total	June 30, 19x2 Totals
Assets:					
Cash	$ 15,500	$ 10,750	$ 5,000	$ 31,250	$ 40,000
Investments (Note 2)	88,000	790,000	145,000	1,023,000	968,000
Total Assets	$103,500	$800,750	$150,000	$1,054,250	$1,008,000
Liabilities and Fund Balance:					
Liabilities	$ —	$ —	$ —	$ —	$ —
Fund Balances:					
Restricted—Nonrefundable	103,500	800,750	150,000	1,054,250	1,008,000
Total Fund Balance	$103,500	$800,750	$150,000	$1,054,250	$1,008,000

FIG. 8A–2. Balance Sheet for Endowment Fund—

Note 1, Summary of Significant Accounting Policies

Endowment funds represent the type of funds that are subject to restrictions requiring in perpetuity that the principal be invested and the income only can be used.

Note 2, Investments

Investments are presented in the financial statements in the aggregate at the lower of cost (amortized, in the case of bonds) or fair market value.

	Cost	Market
Endowment A	$ 88,000	$ 99,000
B	790,000	820,000
C	145,000	160,000
	$1,023,000	$1,079,000

Investments composed of the following:

	Cost	Market
Corporate Stocks and Bonds	$ 849,000	$ 884,000
U.S. Government Securities	164,000	185,000
Municipal Bonds	10,000	10,000
	$1,023,000	$1,079,000

The determination of fair market value is made by aggregating all current marketable equity securities. At June 30, 19x3, there were unrealized gains of $56,000 pertaining to the current portfolio. The portfolio had a cost on June 30, 19x2, of $968,000 and a market value of $997,000.

A net realized gain of $29,750 on the sale of marketable equity securities was included in the determination of the Excess (deficiency) of Support and Revenue over Expenses after Capital Additions for 19x3. The cost of the securities sold was based on a first-in, first-out method in both years.

FIG. 8A–3. Notes for Endowment Fund

19x3
June 30

CAPITAL ADDITIONS — Net Realized Gains		5,500	
FUND BALANCE — Endowment A			5,500

Closing capital additions to Fund Balance

CAPITAL ADDITIONS — Investment Income		27,750	
FUND BALANCE — Endowment B			27,750

Closing capital additions to Fund Balance

CAPITAL ADDITIONS — Net Realized Gains		13,000	
FUND BALANCE — Endowment B			13,000

Closing capital additions to Fund Balance

FIG. 8A–4. H. K. Fines Library Closing Entries (These entries, made after the financial statements have been prepared, are used to determine the proper balance in the Fund Balance at the end of the year.)

9.

The Plant Fund: An Introduction

This chapter discusses the last type of fund that is commonly found in an NFP organization, the Plant Fund. Besides being used in NFP accounting, the Plant Fund is also part of the fund system for hospitals and universities, but it is not used in state and local governmental accounting.[1] The Plant Fund maintains a record of the values assigned to the long-lived assets of the NFP organization. These types of assets have a life longer than one year, and they include land, buildings, and equipment. They are also referred to as "fixed assets." Although many NFP organizations do not record these assets in their accounting records, they must be recorded if there is to be responsible control over them.

The Plant Fund is also responsible for the indebtedness incurred to purchase these fixed assets. In addition, the periodic payments that must be made on this indebtedness are accounted for in the Plant Fund. If the organization follows a systemic policy of setting aside monies for the construction and renewal of assets, these amounts are

1. National Council on Governmental Accounting, *Governmental Accounting, Auditing, and Financial Reporting* (Chicago: Municipal Finance Officers Association, 1980).

recorded in the Plant Fund. Finally, it is possible to incorporate into the Plant Fund the necessary accounting entries to record the building or renewal of fixed assets for the NFP organization.

As previously stated, the fund accounting system for hospitals and universities contains a Plant Fund. Unlike these NFP organizations, state and local government accounting uses four separate funds to account for the activities that appear in the Plant Fund. The assets of a state and local government are recorded in the Fixed Asset account group. The indebtedness of the organization is accounted for in the Long-Term Debt account group, and the payment of interest and principal on that debt is recorded in the Debt Service fund.[2] The construction of fixed assets is handled in the Capital Projects fund. Therefore, a state and local government uses at least four separate funds and account groups for the accounting transactions that are recorded in the Plant Fund of an NFP organization. The recommended accounting for an NFP organization requires the use of a Plant Fund, and that fund will be explained in this chapter.

Recording Depreciation

Before we consider the financial statements and typical entries in the Plant Fund, several new concepts that are used in this fund need to be considered. First, the characteristics of the assets recorded in this fund need to be emphasized. Fixed assets are not like the assets recorded in previous funds. For example, a major difference between inventories of supplies and a fixed asset like buildings is that supplies are used up quickly. In other words, benefits received from the inventory of supplies cannot last very long without being replenished. Therefore, the distinction between these two types of assets relates to length of life. An inventory of supplies has a relatively short life, compared to a building, which means that the reduction of a supplies inventory can easily be related to its use. With a building or equipment, it is more difficult to see this relationship; yet it exists. The value of a building or equipment is reduced over time through wear and tear on the asset, as well as through obsolescence. When the processes that cause reduction in the value of an asset are recognized in the accounts, it is called "depreciation."

2. For an explanation of the Long-Term Debt account group and the Debt Service Fund, see Leon E. Hay, *Accounting for Governmental and Nonprofit Entities* (Homewood, Ill.: Richard D. Irwin, 1980), chapters 7 and 12; Edward S. Lynn and Robert J. Freeman, *Fund Accounting: Theory and Practice* (Englewood Cliffs, N.J.: Prentice-Hall, 1983), chapters 8 and 10.

Depreciation is a means of assigning the value of a long-lived asset to the periods over which that asset provides a service to the organization. This assignment of values should be determined on a rational and consistent basis. Usually the cost of an asset (i.e., its value) is assigned to yearly time periods in the asset's estimated life. For example, if an asset with an original cost of $1,000 has an estimated life of five years, $200 of its cost is recognized as depreciation in each of the next five years. This is determined by dividing the cost, $1,000, by the estimated life of five years. This is not a cash allocation method for the replacement or renewal of assets, but simply a method to allocate the benefits received from the use of the asset over the asset's life. No cash is involved in this transaction. The $200 depreciation is recognized as an expense of the current fiscal period, and it reduces the recorded value of the asset. (This is explained in more detail in the pages that follow.)

At the end of their useful life, many assets still have a value, which is called the asset's "salvage" or "residual" value. If an asset has salvage value, the amount of that salvage must not become part of the asset's depreciation. To prevent the salvage value of an asset from being depreciated, it is deducted from the original cost of the asset before determining the yearly depreciation. For example, if an asset with a $1,000 cost has a salvage value of $200, the amount of this asset which can be depreciated is equal to $800. This amount is divided by the estimated life of the asset, which is assumed to be five years, and the yearly depreciation is computed to be $160. This method of depreciation is called the "straight-line" method, and it can be used in all NFP organizations.

In all types of organizations, there is one long-lived asset that cannot be depreciated. Land that is not used as a natural resource, such as a mine, is not depreciated. The characteristic of land which makes it different from other long-lived assets is that it is inexhaustible. In general, land will not lose its value through wear and tear or obsolescence. In NFP organizations, certain other long-lived assets do not have to be depreciated because they share this characteristic of inexhaustibility. These assets are landmarks, monuments, cathedrals, historical treasures, and houses of worship. In addition, some collections of museums, art centers, art galleries, and libraries also share the characteristic of inexhaustibility.

The term "collection" refers to books, works of art, and other similar items. It is understandable that placing a value on these collections is difficult—if it is possible at all to do so. Therefore, asset values for collections do not have to be recorded at a specific dollar value in the accounting records; in fact, no value has to be shown for these types of collections. If no value is recorded for a collection, it is recommended that the collection be listed on the Balance Sheet under an asset classification "Collections," without any dollar value recorded for it. In addition, a reference note should be made as to the policy that is being followed to recognize the value of the collection. The note should disclose that the NFP organization has not recorded a dollar value on the collection.[3] Furthermore, the note should disclose the dollar value of any accessions and decessions related to the collection during the current period if these amounts are significant.

Summarizing this procedure: an NFP does not have to record a value for inexhaustible collections and, consequently, no depreciation is recorded. Of course, in considering the need for depreciation and the recording of asset values, similar policies can be followed for certain exhaustible assets. For example, if part of a library's collection is considered to be exhaustible within one year, such as the circulating library, no depreciation would be recorded for it either, as it would be completely written off within the one-year period (without the need for a depreciation calculation).

The entry to record depreciation is usually made as an adjusting entry, which means that it is recorded on the last day of the fiscal year. The entry for depreciation requires a debit to the account Depreciation Expense and a credit to an account called Accumulated Depreciation in the following manner:

DEPRECIATION EXPENSE   XXXX
        ACCUMULATED DEPRECIATION—Buildings   XXXX
        ACCUMULATED DEPRECIATION—Equipment   XXXX

Recording depreciation as an adjusting entry on June 30, 19xx

The depreciation expense appears on the SREF as a reduction of revenue and support. The Accumulated Depreciation accounts appear on the Balance Sheet. This account increases in value each year, and it maintains a running total of the amount of depreciation that has accumulated on each asset separately, such as buildings and equipment. These amounts are further subdivided in a subsidiary ledger as to each specific asset. The amounts in the Accumulated Depreciation accounts are subtracted from each asset such as buildings or equipment to show the net or book value of that asset. For example, if an

3. Although a collection may be insured for a specific dollar value, the collection may not be recorded at a specific value on the financial statements because of the collection's inexhaustibility.

asset was purchased at a cost of $2,000 and its Accumulated Depreciation account has a balance of $500, its net or book value would be $1,500.

Exercise 9–1. Straight-Line Depreciation

1. Compute the amount of straight-line depreciation on each of the following assets for one year.

Asset	Cost	Life	Salvage Value
a) Truck	$12,500	5 years	$2,500
b) Office equipment	3,000	10 years	250
c) Exhaustible collection	90,000	4 years	None

2. Record the journal entry for the depreciation expense for the above assets. Your journal entry should reflect the use of subsidiary accounts.

Reasons for Recording Asset Values

When it comes to recording values for the fixed assets of an NFP organization, many organizations face difficulties because no value has ever been recorded for their assets and there are no records of the original cost of these assets. It may appear that recording asset values and the subsequent depreciation is not worth the difficulty it presents in determining these values; but before this decision is reached, several factors should be considered. First, it is difficult to be sure that easily removed assets will not be stolen. If no asset record is kept, it is easy for departing employees to depart with less conspicuous assets. Second, without some type of control over assets, it is difficult to establish a maintenance program for them. Some assets may be purchased with a maintenance contract, but those that are not should also be maintained on a regular basis. At the minimum, recording asset values increases awareness of the need for an asset-maintenance policy.

Third, the financial statements are misleading if they do not show the dollar value of the assets held by the organization. Fourth, without a record of the assets owned by an NFP organization, it is difficult to plan for the replacement of assets as they wear out. For employees to request new equipment when old equipment wears out is *not* a satisfactory policy of asset replacement. Such a "system" does not allow for replacement of assets in a consistent and systematic manner. Finally, without an accounting record of assets owned by an NFP organization, the organization cannot receive an unqualified audit opinion.[4] Therefore, the recording of asset values is considered an important function of any accounting system which presents the organization's financial situation without misleading results.

Establishing a Fixed-Assets Policy in the NFP Organization

The first consideration of an NFP organization that has not reported the amount of its long-lived assets in previous years is, How do we determine the values to place on these assets? The best answer is to use historical cost of the original asset, but, unfortunately, the original cost of the asset may not be known. If this information is not available, alternatives need to be substituted for historical cost, such as appraisals which have been developed for insurance purposes or an independent appraisal for specifically determining a value for the assets. In some cases, it may not be possible to value each asset separately, and it may be necessary to place a value on a group of assets.

If the historical cost is thought to be determinable, it is necessary to know what costs are included in the original historical cost of an asset. The original cost of an asset is considered to be more than its list price. In addition to the list price, the total or depreciable cost of an asset is equal to the total of such other items as sales tax, freight cost, and installation costs. (Cash discounts for early payment of the purchase price should be *deducted* from the cost of a fixed asset.) Once these additions and deductions are made to and from the list price, the result is the depreciable cost of the asset.

When valuation has been determined for the asset, still other decisions must be made about the assets. The "life" of the various assets must be established. Published guidelines for the estimated life of assets, or appraisal firms, should be able to provide guidance in this area. With any method of depreciation that is established (i.e., straight-line or other), the life of the asset will determine how much

---

4. This assumes the fixed assets are a significant dollar value of the total assets of the NFP organization, which is usually the case.

depreciation is charged to the financial statements in any single year. Without any attempt to manipulate this charge, the life of the asset should be estimated so that the benefits received from the asset are spread over the useful life of the asset.

After the lives of assets are established, other policy decisions must be made. For example, a standard accounting convention is to take a whole year's worth of depreciation in the first year of the asset's life and none in the last year, or to take half a year's depreciation in the first year and the same amount in the last year of an asset's life. This convention allows the recording of depreciation in a more consistent manner. For example, if four depreciable assets with the same estimated life are purchased at the same price at the beginning of each week during July, the *exact* amount of depreciation accumulated at the end of the year on each of these assets would be different, due to the weekly differences in their expired lives. Furthermore, in order to calculate the exact amount of depreciation on each asset purchased at these different times, a separate calculation is necessary for each asset. When this situation is compounded by all the depreciable assets within an organization, the potential for an enormous workload develops. To avoid an unnecessary and tedious situation, the depreciation convention of "full year—half-year" is adopted. As depreciation is always an estimate, the sacrifice of exactness is not considered a serious deviation. At any rate, a policy decision needs to be made as to which convention is to be followed.

Another decision which needs to be made is whether small, low-cost asset purchases will be recorded as assets or expenses. For example, if a pencil sharpener is purchased for less than $10, should this asset be depreciated over its 15-year life or should it be immediately written off as an expense in the current period? It seems that a small item such as a pencil sharpener should be written off as an expense of the period. A policy decision will have to be made about the dollar level to determine the difference between recording an asset or an expense. For example, a policy could be established to "expense" all asset purchases under a cost of $75.

Another side of this question requires an accounting distinction to be made between repairs (or maintenance) and betterments. Repairs or maintenance are the costs incurred to keep an asset in working order—the charges for painting a building, inspection charges for elevators, the cost of repairing a broken window or fixing a leaking roof. These types of charges are recorded as expenses of the current period. For example, repair of a broken window is recorded as a debit to Miscellaneous Expenses and a credit to Cash. On the other hand, if a cost is considered to be a betterment of an asset, it extends the life of that asset. Examples of these types of costs are replacement of a roof, rather than repairs, or replacement of a motor in a vehicle, rather than repairs to the engine. These types of betterments extend the life of the asset, and are not accounted as expenses.

The easiest way to handle betterments is to debit the Accumulated Depreciation account related to the asset and to credit the Cash account. It must be remembered that a betterment extends the life of the asset; therefore, the remaining asset value is to be written off over the new, longer life of the asset. Additionally, it should be remembered that the effect of the Accumulated Depreciation account's being debited for the cost of the betterment increases the asset's book value. In effect, this results in an increased asset value being written off over a longer period.

For example, assume that a bookmobile with an original life of 8 years and an original cost of $18,000 is written off at $2,250 a year ($18,000/8). In the beginning of the sixth year, the engine is replaced on the vehicle, and the life of the bookmobile is extended by 4 years. The cost of the engine replacement is $1,275. The amount in the Accumulated Depreciation account prior to replacing the engine is equal to five years of depreciation, or $11,250. This total is the amount of the accumulated depreciation prior to recording the depreciation for the sixth year. The cost of the engine relacement ($1,275) is debited to the Accumulated Depreciation account, leaving a balance of $9,975 in that account. The amount of the bookmobile that remains to be depreciated after this entry increased by $1,275 to $8,025, from the $6,750 balance before the engine replacement. In addition to this change, the life of the bookmobile has been extended by 4 years over the original estimate of 8 years. Therefore, counting the sixth year, the bookmobile has a 7-year life remaining. When the remaining life (7 years) is divided into the book value of $8,025, the yearly depreciation is computed to be $1,146.86 or $1,147. The entries to record these changes in the depreciation accounts follow.

ACCUMULATED DEPRECIATION—Bookmobile	1,275	
CASH		1,275

Recording payment for engine replacement as a debit to Accumulated Depreciation account

DEPRECIATION EXPENSE	1,147	
ACCUMULATED DEPRECIATION—Bookmobile		1,147

Recording depreciation expense on bookmobile at end of sixth year

There is a need to separate charges for repairs and maintenance from betterments. For the former, these amounts are recorded as expenses, and for the latter, the amounts are used to increase the book value and the life of the asset affected by the change.

An NFP organization may not have recorded any value for its assets in prior years, nor any depreciation. As previously indicated, values to place on these assets, if unavailable through records, can be determined through appraisals. Once a value is recorded for an NFP organization's assets, the organization is faced with determining the accumulated depreciation on these assets from the time they were acquired. This type of calculation is called a "retroactive adjustment," and it has two accounting effects. First, it reduces the carrying value of any assets recorded in the accounts. Second, it reduces the balance in the Fund Balance of the Plant Fund. As an example of this effect, assume that a building, acquired 15 years ago, has a life of 10 more years after the end of the current fiscal year. The original cost of the building was $100,000. If the building had not been recognized on the books previously, it would be recorded in the books with the following entry:

| BUILDING | 100,000 | |
| FUND BALANCE | | 100,000 |

Recording the original cost of the building in the accounts

Journalizing this transaction results in the building's being carried on the books at a value of $100,000. At the same time, a retroactive adjustment must be made to account for the depreciation which has not been recorded for the past 15 years. Initially, the building had a life of 25 years; therefore, its yearly depreciation is equal to $4,000. Fifteen years' worth of depreciation is recorded in the books as a retroactive adjustment with the following entry:

| FUND BALANCE | 60,000 | |
| ACCUMULATED DEPRECIATION—Building | | 60,000 |

Recording depreciation on the building for the last 15 years as a retroactive adjustment

This entry recognizes that $60,000 of usage benefits have been received from the building. Without this entry, the assets and the Fund Balance in the Plant Fund are overstated. After the retroactive entry is made, yearly depreciation entries are recorded on the building.

The inclusion of depreciation in an accounting system is not restricted to finding a value for these assets, recording it, and writing it off over an estimated life. Other decisions must be made if these assets are to be properly maintained. Another interrelated consideration is the funding policy that is to be followed by the board of the NFP organization. Recording depreciation is not an asset-funding policy. A funding policy is established when it is determined how the assets which are being used are going to be replaced. This policy may mean that a certain amount of monies is transferred to the Plant Fund from the Operating Fund each year. The amount of this transfer is determined by the board. This transfer could be established at a fixed amount or it could be established as a certain percentage of the depreciation that is recorded in the fiscal year. Once the Plant Fund receives these monies, they are set aside and invested until they are used for the purchase of new assets to replace the assets which can no longer function. This is an example of a funding policy.

A funding policy is instituted to prevent a budget situation where it is necessary to reduce departmental appropriations in order to replace assets which have "suddenly" become unusable.

To establish a fixed-asset policy in an NFP organization, a number of decisions need to be made, in addition to the amount of depreciation that is to be recorded. The following eight steps should be incorporated into the decision to include fixed-asset accounts in an accounting system.

1. Determine the values to assign to the assets.
2. Estimate the usable life of the assets.
3. Calculate any salvage value on the assets.
4. Determine whether a full-year or half-year depreciation policy will be followed.
5. Make all necessary retroactive adjustments.
6. Establish a minimum dollar level of asset purchases to record as assets.
7. Establish a policy on the distinction between repairs or maintenance and the betterment of assets.
8. Establish a funding policy to provide for the replacement of assets.

These are the major steps to follow when asset values and depreciation are recorded in the accounting system. Of course, it would be possible to establish a value for the assets of an NFP organization in the Plant Fund without recording depreciation. In fact, many NFP organizations do not record depreciation on their assets, even though they record values for their assets. However, recording asset values and depreciation is the recommended procedure by the AICPA[5]—and recording a value for assets without recording depreciation on them is *not* a recommended procedure. It is also possible to have an accounting system that does not record the value of assets, but such a system is faulty because little control is maintained over the assets of the organization if they are not recorded in the accounts. The organization has a stewardship responsibility to the public which supplied the monies to purchase the organization's assets, and any organization which does not maintain accounting control over those assets is in violation of that stewardship trust.

Finally, it should be emphasized that proper accounting procedures require that asset values be recorded, as well as depreciation on those asset values.

Exercise 9–2. Asset Policy Decisions

1. In the year ending June 30, 1985, the Clear Springs Library decided to record depreciation on its assets. Although the library has recorded asset values in the books in prior years, this is the first time depreciation has been recorded. The library follows a policy of recording one-half of a year's depreciation in the first year that an asset is placed in service. The library also follows a policy of expensing all fixed-asset purchases of $400 or less. The following information has been collected about some of the library's assets.

	Asset	Cost	Life	Salvage Value	Year Acquired
a)	Automobile	$ 6,000	5 years	$1,500	1985
b)	Building*	60,000	60 years	None	1950
c)	Shelving	175	25 years	None	1985
d)	Plastic library cards	1,200	2 years	None	1985

*This building is valued at $1,000,000 at current prices.

Required: Determine the book value of the assets after the depreciation for 1985 is recorded. Record the proper journal entries for the depreciation on each of these assets for the period ending June 30, 1985. Do not use subsidiary accounts.

5. American Institute of Certified Public Accountants, Statement of Position 78–10, *Accounting Principles and Reporting Practices for Certain Nonprofit Organizations* (New York: AICPA, 1979), par. 107.

2. On July 1, 1987, the Shakey Wells Library had the roof on the building housing the main library replaced. The cost of the roof replacement was $75,000. The building was originally purchased on July 1, 1962, for $121,000, and its estimated life at the time was 55 years, with no salvage value. Replacement of the roof was a major construction project, and it is estimated that the new roof will extend the life of the building by 10 years. Record the entries for replacement of the roof and the depreciation expense entries on June 30, 1987, and June 30, 1988. Assume that a full year of depreciation is taken in the first year.

3. The director of the Stile Public Library has been discussing the possibility of establishing an asset replacement policy. The library's bookkeeper has stated that a replacement policy is already in place, as the accounting system records depreciation on the assets, and to establish an asset replacement policy would result in double-counting depreciation. The bookkeeper's statements have made the director uncertain of the desirability of such a policy. Comment on the bookkeeper's statements.

4. The Cowan Library made several fixed-asset purchases during the current year. The following information was collected about these purchases. Determine the value at which each of these assets should be recorded in the accounts.

   a) A building was purchased for $52,000. The closing costs of the sale were $1,200. Cost of renovating the building before it was placed into service was $17,000.

   b) Land was purchased for $19,500. The closing costs of the sale were $600. The cost of the title search was $120. An old building on the land had to be demolished before the land was ready for the library's use. The cost of demolishing the building was $2,500.

   c) A microcomputer and the software for maintaining an inventory of the collection was purchased for $5,700. There was a 5% sales tax on the purchases, and freight charges of $125 were paid on the microcomputer. It is estimated that the software package has a separate purchase price of $1,100. The software program was difficult to implement and costs of $525 were involved in testing and putting the software program into working order.

5. The Hansell-Comings County Library has used its library building for 25 years. Originally, the building had an estimated life of 50 years. During the current year, a new loading dock was added to the back of the building. The loading dock cost $4,500, and it has an estimated life of 30 years, with no salvage value. Record the depreciation expense entry for the loading dock, assuming an entire year's depreciation is recognized.

Plant Fund Financial Statements

The financial statements prepared for the Plant Fund are the same basic three statements that have been prepared for the Operating Fund. The Statement of Support, Revenue, and Expenses and Changes in Fund Balances (SREF), presented in figure 9–1 for the H. K. Fines Library, is similar to the previous ones in terms of the program and supporting-services expenses. These amounts are shown for the current period, with comparative amounts for the previous period, 19x1. This SREF also contains a section with Capital Additions, as did the SREF for the Endowment Fund. Capital Additions for the Plant Fund consist of various types of contributions and the investment income, with any net gains that were realized on the investments. During the current year, there were no gains realized on investments.

The changes in the Fund Balance at the bottom of the SREF include the addition of mandatory transfers of $190,000. These transfers are from the Operating Fund, and are used to pay the interest and principal on long-term debt of the Plant Fund. Any transfers need to be disclosed separately from the support and revenues provided to the fund. Transfers also can be made to the Plant Fund from the Operating Fund so that the former can make purchases of long-lived assets. The amounts in the unrestricted portion of the Plant Fund have not been restricted for the purchase of any specific assets, nor have they been restricted by a third-party donor outside the library.

A restricted portion of the SREF is shown in figure 9–1 for illustrative purposes, but no dollar amounts are shown in that part of the SREF. Although the H. K. Fines Library has donated monies which have been restricted for purchase of a specific type of asset, these amounts do not affect the SREF because none of the amounts have been spent. Until these amounts are used, they remain liabilities on the Balance Sheet. The restricted monies have been donated to the library for the specific purpose of constructing an annex. The original donation of $700,000, and any interest and net gains earned on the donation, are to be used for construction of this annex.

Finally, it should be noted that the format of the Plant Fund's SREF follows the same account classification pattern as illustrated in figure 6–1 for the Operating Fund's SREF. The same pattern is followed because it will make it easier to integrate the financial statements for all three funds in chapter 11, when the overall financial statements are prepared for the library. At that time, the departmental expenses of the Operating Fund are combined with the depreciation and interest expense that compose the departmental expenses in the Plant Fund.

H. K. FINES LIBRARY
Plant Fund
Statement of Support, Revenue, Expenses and Changes in Fund Balance
Year Ended June 30, 19x2
(with Comparative Totals for 19x1)

	Unrestricted	Restricted	Year Ended June 30, 19x1 Totals
Support and Revenue	—	—	—
Expenses (Note 4)			
Program Services:			
Reference	$ 2,500.00	—	$ 1,780.00
Children's Library	1,200.00	—	1,800.00
Circulation	750.00	—	1,370.00
Regional History	500.00	—	2,100.00
Total Program Services	$ 4,950.00	—	$ 7,050.00
Supporting Services:			
Administration	$ 39,012.50	—	$ 46,650.00
Total Expenses	$ 43,962.50	—	$ 53,700.00
Excess (Deficiency) of Support and Revenue over Expenses	$ (43,962.50)	—	$ (53,700.00)
Prior-Year Expenses on Prior-year Encumbrances	—	—	—

Excess (Deficiency) of Support and Revenue over Expenses before Capital Additions	$ (43,962.50)	$ (53,700.00)
Capital Additions:		
Contributions	37,000.00	—
Investment Income, including Net Gains (Note 2)	40,000.00	27,300.00
Contributed Materials, Equipment, etc.	—	5,700.00
	$ 77,000.00	$ 33,000.00
Excess (Deficiency) of Support and Revenue over Expenses after Capital Additions	33,037.50	(20,700.00)
Fund Balance at Beginning of Year	$1,198,750.00	$1,204,450.00
Mandatory Transfers— Principal of Indebtedness and Acquisitions	190,000.00	15,000.00
Fund Balances at End of Year	$1,421,787.50	$1,198,750.00

FIG. 9–1. Plant Fund's Statement of Support, Revenue, and Expenses and Changes in Fund Balances

In the Balance Sheet for the H. K. Fines Library (figure 9–2) are a number of new accounts that have not been used in previously illustrated balance sheets. The first of these new accounts appears in the assets section of the Balance Sheet, in the Land, Buildings, and Equipment account. If the original cost of these assets is available, it is recorded in this account.[6] If the original cost is not known, appraisal values will be used to record a value for these assets. The amounts of yearly depreciation or retroactive depreciation are accumulated in the Accumulated Depreciation account, and the balance in this account is deducted from the Land, Buildings, and Equipment account. The remainder is the net asset value of the buildings, land, and equipment of the organization. In the case of the H. K. Fines Library, this balance is equal to $1,550,000.

Remember that although land is listed with the buildings and equipment, land is an inexhaustible asset and it is not depreciated. The amount of the accumulated depreciation is only for the buildings and equipment, and it is shown at $44,000 and $35,000, respectively. Also listed in this asset section is another new account, Inexhaustible Collections and Books. This account is listed on the Balance Sheet, although no dollar balance is recorded for it. It may be impractical to determine a value for the library's collection. Listing a dollar value for the collection is encouraged, but if it is undeterminable, the recommended procedure is to list this account on the Balance Sheet, followed by a reference which explains the accounting policy for the collection in Notes to the Financial Statements. Note that this is the procedure to follow with *in*exhaustible collections.

The liabilities section of the Balance Sheet also has several new accounts. The library has incurred long-term debt to purchase assets such as equipment and a temporary building for use as a branch library. Long-term debt is defined as that indebtedness which has a maturity date of over one year. The amount of long-term debt is disclosed in the Long-Term Debt Payable account. The debt is actually divided between two accounts. The current portion of this debt, the amount to be paid within the current year, is recorded under the current liabilities section in the account Current Portion of Long-Term Debt Payable. The debt which is payable in maturities longer than a year remains in the Long-Term Debt Payable account. It should be disclosed in Notes to the Financial Statements if any of the organization's assets have been used for collateral for this debt.

6. This account is usually separated into its various components (i.e., land, buildings, and equipment) in the ledger accounts. This separate listing is followed in the ledger accounts, even if the three assets are listed together on the Balance Sheet.

When the notes are reviewed, it can be seen that the H. K. Fines Library has used some of its assets for collateral.

Another new liability account in the Balance Sheet is the Interest Payable account. This account recognizes the amounts which are owed on the debt as of the end of the fiscal year, on June 30, 19x2, but which will not be paid until the following year. When a payable is recognized in the accounts prior to its payment, it is said to be "accrued." The interest is recognized as a liability on the Balance Sheet and an expense within the program classifications of the SREF. The entry for this adjusting entry is explained on page 281.

Several asset accounts in the Balance Sheet have been previously introduced. The Investment account and the Marketable Securities account are two of these, and both record investments in securities such as bonds or stocks. The major difference between the two accounts is that the Investment account is used for long-term investments and the Marketable Securities account is for short-term investments. The distinction between "short term" and "long term" is related to the objectives of the organization in making these investments.

Within the H. K. Fines Library, the Marketable Securities account is used when the Operating Fund makes transfers to the Plant Fund for the yearly interest which is to be paid on the debt, as well as the yearly principal payments. It is anticipated that these amounts are to be temporarily invested until they are used, and for that reason they are recorded in the Marketable Securities account. Until the interest and principal are paid, these investments earn a return for the library. In addition to these types of transfers, the Operating Fund may make transfers to the Plant Fund for the purchase of new assets and the payment of maturing debt, or if amounts have been accumulated to retire maturing debt, and they are insufficient, the transfer may be for the additional amount needed to retire the matured debt.

The debt agreement may require that the Operating Fund make fixed, periodic transfers to the Plant Fund. Furthermore, it may require that these amounts be accumulated to retire the maturing debt. The H. K. Fines Library makes yearly transfers from the Operating Fund to the Plant Fund for the yearly retirement of the principal on its debt and for the payment of interest on its debt.

The Investment account in the Balance Sheet in figure 9–2 records the amount which has been donated to the library for the construction of an annex. This amount is restricted, and it appears in the restricted portion of the Plant Fund. Until it is used for construction of the annex, it will be invested in securities. The management of the library anticipates that this donation will not be used for a period of at

H. K. FINES LIBRARY
Plant Fund
Balance Sheet
June 30, 19x2
(with Comparative Totals for 19x1)

	Unrestricted	Restricted	Total	Year Ended June 30, 19x1 Totals
Assets				
Current Assets				
Cash	$ 31,800.00	—	$ 31,800.00	$ 6,550.00
Marketable Securities (Note 2)	$ 171,000.00	—	$ 171,000.00	$ 170,500.00
Total Current Assets	$ 202,800.00	—	$ 202,800.00	$ 177,050.00
Investments (Note 2)	—	$712,000.00	$ 712,000.00	$ 700,000.00
Land, Buildings, and Equipment, at cost Less: Accumulated Depreciation of $44,000 and $35,000 respectively (Note 3)	$1,550,000.00	—	$1,550,000.00	$1,366,700.00
Inexhaustible Collections and Books (Note 7)	—	—	—	—
Total Assets	$1,752,800.00	$712,000.00	$2,464,800.00	$2,243,750.00
Liabilities and Fund Balances				
Current Liabilities				
Current Portion of Long-Term Debt Payable	$ 15,000.00	$ —	$ 15,000.00	$ 15,000.00
Interest Payable	1,012.50	—	1,012.50	—
Deferred Restricted Contributions (Note 5)	—	$712,000.00	$ 712,000.00	$ 700,000.00
Total Current Liabilities	$ 16,012.50	$712,000.00	$ 728,012.50	$ 715,000.00
Long-Term Debt Payable (Note 4)	$ 315,000.00	—	$ 315,000.00	$ 330,000.00
Total Liabilities	$ 331,012.50	$712,000.00	$1,043,012.50	$1,045,000.00
Fund Balance: Undesignated	$1,421,787.50	—	$1,421,787.50	$1,198,750.00
Total Fund Balances	$1,421,787.50	—	$1,421,787.50	$1,198,750.00
Total Liabilities and Fund Balances	$1,752,800.00	$712,000.00	$2,464,800.00	$2,243,750.00

Fig. 9–2. Plant Fund's Balance Sheet

least a year, and therefore the $700,000 donation, as well as the earnings on it, are recorded in the Investment account rather than the Marketable Securities account. It should be noted that the balance in the Investment account corresponds with the liability in the Deferred Restricted Contributions account. This equality, at $712,000, in the balances in these two accounts will exist until the monies are used for construction of the annex. It should also be noted that amounts transferred to the Plant Fund from the Operating Fund for the purchase of specific assets are not recorded in the restricted portion of the Plant Fund because the restriction on the use of monies must be made by a donor outside the NFP organization. (The recording of restricted contributions was explained when the restricted portion of the Operating Fund was explained on pp. 193–200.)

In the Statement of Changes in Financial Position for the H. K. Fines Library in figure 9–3, the amounts of the transfers from the Operating Fund are shown at $190,000 and $15,000 for the periods ending on June 30, 19x2 and 19x1, respectively. The Statement of Changes in Financial Position is used to show the sources and uses of working capital during the fiscal year. (For a complete discussion of the Statement of Changes in Financial Position, see pp. 139–43.)

The aspects of the Statement of Changes in Financial Position for the Plant Fund which are different from those for the Operating Fund or the Endowment Fund need to be considered. The first of these differences relates to the recording of depreciation on the statement in figure 9–3. Depreciation of $13,700 is shown as an addition to the Excess after Capital Additions of $33,037.50 for the 19x2 period. This $13,700 addition to the Excess is the amount of depreciation that is recorded as an expense in the current year. The amount recorded as an expense in the current year is a special type of expense because no cash is paid out of the organization and no cash is placed into any type of holding account. Depreciation expense is a consistent allocation of the original cost of the asset into the time periods over which it is estimated that the asset will be used. As no monies are actually paid out, the recording of yearly depreciation in essence allows this expense to remain in the organization. Therefore, they are added to the Excess on the Statement of Changes in Financial Position. Another way of relating this idea to the Statement of Changes in Financial Position is to realize that if depreciation expense were not recorded, the Excess would be $13,700 higher. For this reason, when depreciation is recorded, it must be added to the Excess to determine the correct amount of working capital generated from operations.

H. K. FINES LIBRARY
Plant Fund
Statement of Changes in Financial Position
Year Ended June 30, 19x2
(with Comparative Totals for 19x1)

	Unrestricted	Restricted	Total	Year Ended June 30, 19x1 Totals
Sources of Working Capital:				
Excess (Deficiency) of Support and Revenue over Expenses before Capital Additions	$ (43,962.50)	—	$ (43,962.50)	$ (48,000.00)
Capital Additions	77,000.00	—	77,000.00	33,000.00
Excess (Deficiency) of Support and Revenue over Expenses after Capital Additions	$33,037.50	—	$ 33,037.50	$ (15,000.00)
Add Items Not Using Working Capital Depreciation	13,700.00	—	13,700.00	14,300.00
Working Capital Provided from Operations	$ 46,737.50	—	$ 46,737.50	$ (700.00)
Deferred Restricted Income	—	$12,000.00	$ 12,000.00	—
Total Sources of Working Capital	$ 46,737.50	$12,000.00	$ 58,737.50	$ (700.00)

Uses of Working Capital:

Purchases of Fixed Assets	$197,000.00	—	$197,000.00	$ 12,000.00
Reduction of Long-Term Debt	15,000.00	—	15,000.00	15,000.00
Deferred Restricted Income	—	12,000.00	12,000.00	—
Transfers between Funds	(190,000.00)	—	(190,000.00)	(15,000.00)
Uses of Working Capital	22,000.00	12,000.00	34,000.00	12,000.00
Increases (Decreases) in Working Capital	$ 24,737.50	—	$ 24,737.50	$ (12,700.00)
Changes in Working Capital Components: Increases (Decreases) in Current Assets				
Cash	$ 25,250.00	—	$ 25,250.00	$ (12,700.00)
Marketable Securities	500.00	—	500.00	—
	$ 25,750.00	—	$ 25,750.00	$ (12,700.00)
(Increases) Decreases in Current Liabilities: Current Portion of Long-Term Debt	—	—	—	—
Interest Payable	$ (1,012.50)	—	$ (1,012.50)	—
Increase (Decrease) in Working Capital	$ 24,737.50	—	$ 24,737.50	$ (12,700.00)

Fig. 9–3. Plant Fund's Statement of Changes in Financial Position

Under the uses of working capital, purchases of fixed assets are recorded. The Plant Fund is the only fund which records the purchases of fixed assets for the NFP organization. Recording these purchases in the Plant Fund does not mean that the Plant Fund uses any of these assets; it only means that the record of all fixed-asset purchases is maintained by the Plant Fund. Another use of working capital that would appear in the Plant Fund is the retirement of long-term debt. In the H. K. Fines Library, the reduction in long-term debt is shown as $15,000 for both fiscal periods. This $15,000 is the current portion of the long-term debt which is repaid each year.

The transfers from the Operating Fund are shown on the Statement of Changes in Financial Position as a deduction from the uses of working capital. Although transfers are a source, they are not included as one of the sources, but are shown as a deduction from the uses of working capital. For this reason, they are shown in the lower portion of the statement.

Also shown in the Statement of Changes in Financial Position in figure 9–3 is the restricted portion of the Plant Fund. The sources and uses of working capital in this section of the Plant Fund relate to the amounts obtained from income on the restricted investments. As the income earned on the $700,000 donation for the annex is restricted for the use of this construction project, it is shown as Deferred Restricted Income on the statement. The $12,000 in income is shown as both a source and a Use of Working Capital. Even though the increase in working capital in the total column is unaffected by this income, it needs to be recorded in the statement, because all sources and uses of working capital should be shown.

Some uses of working capital can be easily traced to the Balance Sheet in figure 9–2. For example, the change from June 30, 19x1, to June 30, 19x2, in the balance in Land, Buildings, and Equipment account is $183,300. This change is the difference between the assets that were purchased and added to the account balance, $197,000, and the depreciation expense recorded in the current year, $13,700, which is a reduction of the account's balance. Another example of this tracing procedure between the uses on the Statement of Changes in Financial Position and the Balance Sheet occurs in the reduction of long-term debt. A reduction in long-term debt of $15,000 is shown both on the Balance Sheet, where the decrease is from $330,000 in 19x1 to $315,000 in 19x2, and on the Statement of Changes in Financial Position. In the latter statement, the $15,000 payment is shown under Uses of Working Capital. A final example is the $190,000 transfer from the Operating Fund. The transfer is shown under Uses of Working Capital as a deduction, and on the SREF, transfers appear as the last item before the ending balance in the Fund Balance is determined.

This tracing process illustrates the interrelationship between the Statement of Changes in Financial Position and the other two financial statements. This relationship always exists between these three statements, and no set of financial records is complete without all three statements. Additional tracings can be made from Sources of Working Capital to the other financial statements, but they have not been made here.

The Notes to the Financial Statements for the H. K. Fines Library, as those notes relate to the Plant Fund, are presented in figure 9–4. When the notes for the H. K. Fines Library as a whole are considered, they should also include the notes presented in figures 6–4, 7–4, and 8–3, but the present emphasis is on the notes to the Plant Fund.

In note 1, the library's significant accounting policies as they relate to the Plant Fund are disclosed. The accounting procedures followed with fixed assets and depreciation are explained, as well as the library's policy with inexhaustible collections and books. It should be noted that when *unrestricted* fixed assets are sold, their proceeds are transferred to the Operating Fund; they are not added to the Cash balance in the Plant Fund. If these are sales of *restricted* assets, their proceeds increase the deferred amounts, a liability in the Plant Fund, to be used for plant acquisitions. The library's inexhaustible collection is not valued on the statements, but the portion of the collection that is exhaustible is included under the Equipment portion of the Land, Building, and Equipment account. Books that are used in the circulating library, which have not been valued on the statements, have a life of less than one year.

The information in note 2 about the Plant Fund's investments is similar to the disclosures that were made about the investments of other funds. The investment balances in this note are equal to the amounts shown in the Marketable Securities account of the unrestricted portion of the Plant Fund and the Investment account in the restricted portion of the Plant Fund. The Investment account in the restricted portion of the Plant Fund represents the donation for the annex which is invested in securities to earn the maximum return until it is used for construction. The note separates the investments in the Marketable Securities account from those in the Investment account. The note also provides disclosures about the market value of all these securities.

Note 1, Summary of Significant Accounting Policies

Fund Accounting

Plant Funds represent resources for plant acquisitions and funds expended for plant.

Plant Assets and Depreciation

Uses of operating funds for plant acquisition and principal debt service payments are accounted for as transfers to plant funds. Proceeds from the sale of plant assets, if unrestricted, are transferred to operating fund balances, or, if restricted, to deferred amounts restricted for plant acquisitions. Depreciation of buildings and equipment is provided over the estimated useful lives of the respective assets on a straight-line basis.

Inexhaustible Collections and Books

Because the values of the existing inexhaustible collections, including research books, are not readily determinable, the library has not capitalized them. Collections that are exhaustible are capitalized and included with equipment in the financial statements and are amortized over their estimated useful lives. Accessions and deac-cessions during 19x1 and 19x2 were not significant. Books used in the circulating library have not been capitalized because their estimated useful lives are less than one year.

Note 2, Investments

Investments are presented in the financial statements in the aggregate at the lower of cost (amortized, in the case of bonds) or fair market value.

	Cost	Market
Plant Fund—Unrestricted	$171,000	$188,300
Plant Fund—Restricted	712,000	750,000

Investments are composed of the following:

	Cost		Market	
	Unrestricted	Restricted	Unrestricted	Restricted
Corporate Stocks	$101,000	$412,000	$118,300	$450,000
U.S. Government Obligations	70,000	300,000	70,000	300,000
	$171,000	$712,000	$188,300	$750,000

Fig. 9–4. Notes to Plant Fund's Financial Statements

The determination of fair market value is determined by aggregating all current marketable securities. At June 30, 19x2, there was unrealized gain of $55,300 pertaining to the current portfolio. This portfolio had a cost on June 30, 19x1, of $870,500 and a market value of $915,400. The cost of the securities sold was based on a first-in, first-out method in both years.

Note 3, Plant Assets and Depreciation

A summary of plant assets follows:

Land	$1,000,000
Buildings	500,000
Equipment	129,000
	$1,629,000
Less: Accumulated Depreciation	79,000
	$1,550,000

Note 4, Long-Term Debt

A summary of long-term debt follows:

8% mortgage payable in semiannual installments of $3,500 for 15 years and a lump sum payment at the end of that period	$270,000
9% unsecured notes payable due in quarterly installments of $2,000	45,000
	$315,000

The 8% mortgage payable was incurred in 19x1. Building and land with a net book value of $285,000 as of June 30, 19x1, are pledged as collateral on the mortgage. No interest is to be accrued until January 1, 19x3, and at that time for only six months' interest. The first principal payment is made at that time also.

Note 5, Changes in Deferred Restricted Contributions

Balances at the beginning of year	$700,000
Additions:	
Investment Income	12,000
Balances at end of year	$712,000

Note 3 provides a listing of fixed assets, less the total of accumulated depreciation on these assets. The land is an inexhaustible asset, but it is listed here. Unlike the collection of books, which is also considered to be an inexhaustible asset, the value of the land is easily determinable and therefore a value is listed for the land. The accumulated depreciation in this note relates only to the exhaustible assets, which are the buildings and equipment. If the library's exhaustible collection is listed in the subsidiary accounts at a specific value, the value would be shown in this note as part of the cost of Equipment.

Note 4 provides disclosures about the amount of long-term debt, as well as the amount of the quarterly or semiannual payments on the principal of this debt. These payments do not include the interest payments on the debt. It is common for NFP organizations to incur debt that will be repaid in serial payments or installment payments. The amounts of these installations should be disclosed in the Notes to the Financial Statements. The amount of the annual installment payment is equal to $15,000, and is also equal to the current portion of the long-term debt payable on the Balance Sheet. Finally, it is equal to the amount of the transfer received from the Operating Fund in the period ending June 30, 19x1, on the SREF.

In addition to these disclosures, note 4 should provide disclosures about any asset that is used as collateral, as well as any unusual characteristics of the debt. The building to house the branch library and the land are used as collateral for the 8 percent mortgage debt of the H. K. Fines Library, and this fact is disclosed in note 4. In addition, it is disclosed that no interest is due on this mortgage until 19x3, as this is an unusual feature of any mortgage.

The final note, note 5, provides disclosures about the changes in the Deferred Restricted Contributions account during the current year. This account records the donation for the annex. The change in the account relates to the amount which was earned as investment income during the fiscal year. This income increases the balance in the deferred account because all income and gains earned on the donation must be used for the construction of the annex.

Summary

The recording of asset values is important for an NFP organization if that organization is to exercise responsibility for the public's support. This chapter has presented an overview of the Plant Fund and the concepts which are part of that fund, such as depreciation and an asset replacement policy. The Plant Fund is responsible for keeping track of the fixed assets of the NFP organization, the debt for the purchase of those assets, the repayment of that debt and interest on it, and the acquisition and retirement of assets. The financial statements for the Plant Fund which have been described in this chapter are the same basic three financial statements in the Operating Fund. The major difference with the Plant Fund's financial statements is the new accounts that have been introduced. Description of the Plant Fund is continued in the next chapter, where the typical journal entries for this fund are explored in more detail.

Exercise 9–3. The Financial Statements

1. Why is depreciation expense for the year a source of working capital on the Statement of Changes in Financial Position?
2. Describe the difference in the manner of handling exhaustible and inexhaustible collections on the financial statements.
3. Why is the value of land, an inexhaustible asset, recorded on the books, but the value of inexhaustible collections is not recorded?

10.

The Plant Fund with Journal Entries

The previous chapter introduced the Plant Fund and the accounting questions which surround it; this chapter will provide a more detailed look at typical transactions in the Plant Fund: the preparation of financial statements, based on the *dated* journal entries in this chapter and the financial statements in figures 9–1, 9–2, and 9–3. The financial statements in this chapter are presented in appendix A. In appendix B, another type of fund is introduced that is sometimes used in conjunction with the Plant Fund. The Plant Fund is the last major fund which is used by the NFP organization, but it is important in the functions it performs.

Typical Journal Entries for Plant Fund

The journal entries that are recorded for the Plant Fund are related to the acquisition of fixed assets, the recording of depreciation on those assets, disposing of fixed assets, the receipt of transfers from the Operating Fund, the incurrence and repayment of debt, the payment of interest on the debt, and the recording of investment income and gains or losses. The following situations illustrate the recording of journal entries for these types of transactions.

PURCHASING FIXED ASSETS

Three basic situations can develop with the acquistion of fixed assets in an NFP organization. First, the equipment or buildings can be purchased by the Operating Fund. Second, the fixed assets can be purchased by the Plant Fund with monies previously transferred from the Operating Fund. Third, they can be donated by parties outside the NFP organization. The accounting entries for each of these situations are considered in the following paragraphs.

If the fixed asset is purchased by the Operating Fund, the asset is recorded in the Plant Fund, and the Operating Fund simply records an increase in transfers. For example, if the Operating Fund has purchased a $15,000 word processor for the library, the entries to record this purchase in the Operating Fund and the Plant Fund are as follows.

Operating Fund

TRANSFER TO PLANT FUND	15,000	
CASH		15,000

Recording the transfer of cash to the Plant Fund

This entry records the purchase of the word processor by the Operating Fund. Although the asset is not recorded in the Operating Fund, the debit is made, instead, to the Transfer account. This account, a temporary account, is closed to the Fund Balance at the year-end, and it indicates that the Operating Fund has made a transfer to the Plant Fund, where the asset will be recorded with the following entry:

Plant Fund

EQUIPMENT	15,000	
Word Processor	15,000	
TRANSFER FROM OPERATING FUND		15,000

Recording the fixed asset purchased by the Operating Fund as a transfer in the Plant Fund

The word processor is debited to Equipment, a control account, and the specific subsidiary account, Word Processor. Some fixed assets will be combined into a group subsidiary account, such as a desk in the subsidiary account, Office Equipment, whereas more expensive fixed assets, such as the word processor, are maintained in a separate subsidiary account. The decision as to the proper way to classify an asset in the subsidiary accounts depends on the usage characteristics of the fixed asset. If similar fixed assets are to be written off over the same time period, it is easier to classify these assets together for depreciation purposes. The credit from recording the fixed asset in the Plant Fund is to the Transfer account and, eventually, to the Fund Balance. If this type of transaction occurs in the NFP organization and *it is significant,* a Note to the Financial Statements should disclose the nature of the transaction and the amount of the fixed assets transferred to the Plant Fund.

In many NFP organizations, the entry in the Operating Fund is made as a debit to an Expense account and no entry is made in the Plant Fund. With that type of entry, there is no control over the fixed assets, as they are not recorded anywhere in the books. In addition, the debit to the Expense account writes the asset off as an expense of that period, rather than through depreciation. This procedure should be used only with assets of insignificant monetary value.

Fixed assets also can be purchased by the Plant Fund with monies that had been previously contributed to the Plant Fund by the unrestricted portion of the Operating Fund. To illustrate this situation, assume that these transferred monies are available without restrictions or with only board restrictions. During the period ending June 30, 19x3, office furniture is purchased for $4,575 and a utility building is purchased for $25,000. Both purchases are recorded in the Plant Fund of the H. K. Fines Library with the following entry:

Plant Fund

Aug. 19	EQUIPMENT	4,575	
	Office Furniture		4,575
	CASH			4,575

Recording purchase of office furniture by Plant Fund

Sept. 28	BUILDINGS	25,000	
	Utility Building		25,000
	CASH			25,000

Recording purchase of utility building by Plant Fund

When the August 19 entry is contrasted with the previous entry in the Plant Fund, several similarities and differences are apparent. In both entries the control account is Equipment. Also, in both entries a subsidiary account is used, but there is a difference in the subsidiary accounts that should be noted. In the first entry, a specific account is maintained for the word processor, but in the second entry the purchase of office equipment is combined with other office equipment used in the library (i.e., office equipment such as desks and chairs are not maintained in separate accounts).

The major difference between the two entries relates to the credit side of the journal entry. The first entry records a credit to the Transfer account to show the asset was transferred from the Operating Fund, whereas the August 19 entry records a credit to the Cash account. When the Operating Fund purchases an asset and the asset is transferred to the Plant Fund, a transfer needs to be recorded. On the other hand, when the purchase is recorded directly in the accounts of the Plant Fund, only the Cash account is affected. The reason for this difference is that cash was previously transferred into the Plant Fund to purchase the assets and had at that time already increased the Transfer account. Therefore, it is not necessary to increase that account at the time the purchase is recorded in the Plant Fund. (The entry on September 28 for the purchase of the utility building is very similar to the August 19 entry, and is not discussed for that reason.)

Besides purchase, fixed assets can be acquired by donation to the NFP organization by an outside party. If this should occur, the donated assets are recorded at their fair market value,[1] which is generally considered the selling price of the donated asset at the time it is donated. The donor is usually aware of the fair market value, or if it is unknown, the asset can be appraised. As an example of this type of donation, assume that the H. K. Fines Library was given office equipment with a fair market value of $3,200. There are no restrictions on these donated assets, and the following entry is made in the Plant Fund accounts to record the donation:

Plant Fund

Sept. 5 EQUIPMENT	3,200	
Office Equipment	3,200	
SUPPORT—Gifts		3,200

Recording the fair market value of the office equipment donated to the organization

---

1. If the fair market value of a donated asset cannot be reasonably estimated, the donations are not recorded. If the donated item is passed through the organization to its subsidiary organizations, the donated items are not recorded as support. See American Institute of Certified Public Accountants, *Audits of Certain Nonprofit Organizations* (New York: AICPA, 1981), pp. 23–24.

There are several exceptions to this type of recognition given to a donated asset. First, if the donated asset is a work of art or similar type of donation, it may be difficult or impractical to determine its value. These types of assets are not capitalized—i.e., recorded—on the Balance Sheet. Although no value is shown for these assets on the Balance Sheet, they still should be catalogued in order for control to exist over them. In addition, a description of the policy followed by the NFP organization should be made in the Notes to the Financial Statements. (Of course, when cost information is available on a work of art, it should be disclosed.) Second, if there are donor restrictions on these contributed assets, they should be recognized as capital additions (rather than support) to the extent that they are expended during the year.

RECORDING DEPRECIATION ON FIXED ASSETS

The acquisition of fixed assets signifies the beginning of the period in which benefits from the asset are written off as depreciation expense. It is possible to have a Plant Fund without recording depreciation on the assets, but depreciation is recommended for the accounting systems of NFP organizations.

To illustrate the depreciation process, assume that a duplicating machine is purchased for $4,200 and the estimated life of the machine is 10 years. At the end of the 10-year period, it is assumed the asset will have a salvage value of $500. The method of depreciation that is used is the straight-line method. (The salvage value, the amount that is estimated to be obtainable from the asset when the asset is retired, should not be depreciated. When the salvage value of $500 is subtracted from the original cost, this is the cost of the asset that should be depreciated.) By dividing the depreciable cost of the machine ($3,700) by its estimated life of 10 years, the depreciation expense can be computed. In this case, it is $370 a year. The following entry to record recognition of depreciation on the machine is made at the end of the fiscal year as an adjusting entry:

DEPRECIATION EXPENSE	370		
Administration		370	
ACCUMULATED DEPRECIATION		370	
Office Equipment			370

Recording depreciation on office equipment

The debit to the Depreciation Expense account is posted to a control account in the general ledger. The debit to the Administration account will appear in the subsidiary ledger and on the SREF as part of the program expenses of Administration. The reason this expense appears as part of Administration's expenses is because the duplicating machine is used largely by Administration.[2] The Accumulated Depreciation account from the general ledger appears on the Balance Sheet as a deduction from the Land, Buildings, and Equipment account. A subsidiary account also records the posting from the credit to the Office Equipment account. The Accumulated Depreciation account in the general ledger maintains the total balance of all yearly depreciation charges of assets which have been written off. The depreciation expense for each year is added to the previous total in this account. The only time the balance in the Accumulated Depreciation account is reduced is when an asset is retired or sold. At those times, the depreciation associated with the asset must be written off the books. The Accumulated Depreciation account always carries a credit balance, but it is not listed with the liabilities or the Fund Balance section. Rather, it is deducted from the fixed-asset accounts because it is considered a "contra-asset" account.

Assume that the depreciation expense on the assets of the H. K. Fines Library for the year ending June 30, 19x3, is $13,700. The entry to record this depreciation expense in the accounts of the Plant Fund for the library follows:

Plant Fund

June 30	DEPRECIATION EXPENSE	13,700	
	Administration	11,700	
	Reference	1,200	
	Children's Library	500	
	Circulation	200	
	Regional History	100	
	ACCUMULATED DEPRECIATION 13,700		
	Buildings		7,700
	Equipment		6,000

Recording the depreciation on assets for the year ending June 30, 19x3

The June 30 entry for the depreciation expense for the H. K. Fines Library's Plant Fund is a more extensive depreciation entry than those previously described, but otherwise it is the same basic entry. The debits to the subsidiary accounts record the amount of deprecia-

2. The operating costs of Administration can be allocated to the other departments for internal decision making. This allocation procedure is explained on pages 397–400.

tion in each of the library's programs. This assignment is based on the fact that the assets being depreciated are specifically assigned to each of the five departments. In chapter 13 it will be shown how these costs can be allocated among the departments that provide a service to the patrons to determine a per unit cost of operations among these service departments. The credits are posted to the subsidiary accounts of each asset or group of assets (i.e., buildings and equipment) and to the control account Accumulated Depreciation. It would be possible to further subdivide the building and equipment credits to specific types of assets through use of a more detailed subsidiary ledger. This June 30 journal entry records all the depreciation expenses for the H. K. Fines Library for the period ending June 30, 19x3. The entry is recorded as an adjusting entry at the end of the year.

As previously stated, one of the decisions required in establishing a fixed-asset and depreciation policy is to determine how much depreciation to record on new asset purchases in their first full period of use. The H. K. Fines Library has established a policy that records half a year's depreciation on fixed assets purchased during the first half of the fiscal year, and it does not record any depreciation on fixed assets purchased in the latter half of the fiscal year (July 1 through June 30). The latter half of the fiscal year should begin on a specific date, such as January 1. This is a consistent policy which makes it easier to record depreciation on a fixed asset during its first partial year of use. If this procedure were not followed, it would be necessary to maintain depreciation schedules or subsidiary accounts based on the number of months the asset was used in the first year it was acquired. This would quickly become tedious if more than a few fixed assets were purchased during a year.

The H. K. Fines Library's purchase of shelving during the first half of the year illustrates this policy. On September 5, 19x3, the H. K. Fines Library purchased library shelving. The shelving cost $3,200, and the entry to record its purchase follows:

Plant Fund

Sept. 5	EQUIPMENT	3,200	
	Library Shelving		3,200
	CASH		3,200

Recording the purchase of library shelving for cash

This shelving has an estimated life of 10 years, with no salvage value at the end of its life. The yearly depreciation on this asset, using straight-line depreciation, is $320. As this fixed asset was purchased in the first half of the year, one-half year's depreciation is recorded. The entry to record the depreciation follows:

Plant Fund

June 30   DEPRECIATION EXPENSE   160
          Reference   160
          ACCUMULATED DEPRECIATION   160
          Library Shelving   160

Recording one-half year's depreciation on library shelving

The depreciation expense is included in the program expenses of the Reference Department because the shelving is used in that department. When the shelving was purchased, on September 5, its cost was recorded in a subsidiary account called Library Shelving. The depreciation recorded on the shelving is also recorded in that same subsidiary account. The balance in this account provides an easy way to determine the net book value of the fixed asset, which is the difference between the original cost of the asset and its accumulated depreciation.

DISPOSING OF FIXED ASSETS

Land, buildings, and equipment can be disposed of through the sale or retirement of those assets. When a sale occurs, the fixed asset can be sold for a gain or loss. This gain or loss occurs in relationship to the net asset value or book value of the item. For example, if an asset was purchased at a cost of $4,000 and it has accumulated depreciation of $1,700, its net asset value or book value is $2,300. If that asset is sold for less than $2,300, a loss is recognized, but if the asset is sold for more than $2,300, a gain is recorded in the books.

A question arises as to which fund this gain or loss on the sale of a fixed asset should be recognized. Should the gain or loss be recognized in the Plant Fund or the Operating Fund? The major purposes of the Plant Fund are to record the fixed assets held by the NFP organization, and any debt related to those assets, and to provide for replacement and acquisition of new assets, as well as the repayment of debt. The Operating Fund provides most of the resources for the Plant Fund to purchase assets and to repay debt principal and interest. Therefore, it may be better to recognize any gain or loss in the

Operating Fund. If the gain or loss is recognized in the Operating Fund, it would involve a transfer of the fixed asset to the Operating Fund from the Plant Fund at its net asset value, recognition of the gain or loss in the Operating Fund, and transfer of proceeds from the sale back to the Plant Fund. (It is assumed that these proceeds are not restricted by a party outside the NFP organization, and are available to the Plant Fund for the purchase of new assets.)

This procedure supports the position that the Operating Fund provides the majority of resources to the Plant Fund for the purchase of new fixed assets. Although these transfers support this position, it does not create a significant difference if the gains and losses are recognized in the Plant Fund rather than the Operating Fund. It *does* simplify the accounting procedures if recognition is made in the Plant Fund. Therefore, the H. K. Fines Library will recognize gains and losses in the Plant Fund. These gains and losses are recognized as nonoperating gains or losses on the SREF, rather than as part of revenue or support.

Assume that on January 1, 19x3, the H. K. Fines Library sells several office desks and chairs which had been in use for six and a half years. The office equipment originally cost $1,675, and at the time of its purchase it was estimated to have a salvage value of $300. The accumulated depreciation as of June 30, 19x2, was $825. The depreciation on the asset is brought up to date with the following entry:

Plant Fund

Jan. 1	DEPRECIATION EXPENSE	68.75	
	Administration		68.75
	ACCUMULATED DEPRECIATION	68.75	
	Office Equipment		68.75

Recording the depreciation on office equipment for the period from June 30, 19x2 to January 1, 19x3

The yearly depreciation on this fixed asset can be determined by dividing the accumulated depreciation on June 30, 19x2, by the number of years the asset has been in use—that is, six years, or one-half year less than on January 1, 19x3. This computation results in a yearly depreciation of $137.50, and half of this amount is the depreciation for the six-month period ending January 1, 19x3, as shown in the updating journal entry on that date.

At the time of the sale, the book value of the office equipment is equal to $781.25, which is determined by subtracting the accumulated depreciation ($825 + $68.75) from the original cost of the assets ($1,675). If the desks and chairs are sold for $835, a $53.75 gain results on the sale. This gain is the difference between the net asset value of the equipment ($781.25) and the selling price ($835). The entry to record the sale of the equipment follows:

Plant Fund

Jan. 1	CASH		835.00		
	ACCUMULATED DEPRECIATION		893.75		
		Office Equipment		893.75	
		EQUIPMENT			1,675.00
			Office Equipment		1,675.00
		GAIN ON SALE OF FIXED ASSETS		53.75	

Recording the sale of office equipment with the proceeds being unrestricted

The debit to the Cash account records the amount of cash received on the sale of the assets. The debit to the Accumulated Depreciation account records the reduction in the balance in this account and its subsidiary account, Office Equipment, from the disposal of the fixed asset. It is necessary to write off the accumulated depreciation associated with any asset that is sold or retired. The credit to the Equipment account and its subsidiary, Office Equipment, records the removal of the office equipment from the books of the library. The final credit to the Gain on Sale of Equipment account records any gains earned on the sale of the assets. The gain is recognized for the amount the assets are sold over their net asset value. In this case, that amount is $53.75.

All changes in the accounts are recorded on the Balance Sheet, except the credit to the Gain on Sale of Fixed Assets account. The balance in this account appears on the SREF. It is not part of support and revenue from operations of the organization; rather, it is placed in the lower portion of the statement, after Capital Additions but before the beginning Fund Balance from the previous year. The amount of the Gain is segregated from support and revenue from operations as it is a nonoperating item.

The amount of proceeds received from the fixed assets is transferred to the Operating Fund, if these amounts are unrestricted. If the proceeds are restricted by a third-party donor, they are part of the deferred restricted contributions, available only for specific fixed-asset purchases in the Plant Fund. In the present case, these proceeds are unrestricted, and therefore they are transferred to the Operating Fund, with the following entry:

Plant Fund

TRANSFER OUT TO OPERATING FUND	835
CASH	835

Recording the transfer of the proceeds from the sale of office equipment to the Operating Fund

Once the Operating Fund receives these monies, a decision can be made as to whether all the monies are going to be transferred back to the Plant Fund for the purchase of new assets, or whether only a portion of the proceeds will be transferred back. In the case of the H. K. Fines Library, all the proceeds are transferred back to the Plant Fund by the Operating Fund. Either all or a portion of the proceeds can be transferred back, depending on the situation. The entries to record the receipt of cash by the Operating Fund and the transfer back to the Plant Fund follow.

Operating Fund

CASH	835
TRANSFER IN FROM PLANT FUND	835

Recording receipt of cash transfer of proceeds from Plant Fund

TRANSFER OUT TO PLANT FUND	835
CASH	835

Recording transfer of proceeds from sale back to Plant Fund

Through these entries, the Operating Fund exercises its function of providing monies to the Plant Fund for the purchase of fixed assets. If the monies from the proceeds were retained in the Plant Fund, the Operating Fund would not be servicing the Plant Fund in this manner. Therefore, it is recommended that any unrestricted proceeds received by the Plant Fund from the sale of fixed assets be transferred to the Operating Fund. Once these monies are received by the Operating Fund, a decision can be made about the amount to return to the Plant Fund for the purchase of new fixed assets.

Once the monies are transferred back into the Plant Fund, the following entry is made in the Plant Fund:

Plant Fund

CASH	835	
TRANSFER IN FROM OPERATING FUND		835

Recording the receipt of the cash proceeds back into the Plant Fund from the Operating Fund

The result of these transfers is that the Plant Fund is allowed to keep the proceeds that were obtained from the sale of the fixed asset, but this decision was made from the point of view of the Operating Fund, which is responsible for the general operations of the organization. (The entries relating to these transfers have not been incorporated into the financial statements at the end of the chapter because the net effect of the transfers is zero.) The sale of the fixed asset on January 1 is recorded in the financial statements.

If the monies used originally to purchase the asset which was sold are restricted by a third-party donor, the proceeds from the sale may be restricted. In the case of restricted proceeds, the entries are slightly different. Restricted proceeds need to be recorded in the Deferred Restricted Contributions account. If the office equipment which was sold on January 1 is again sold, but this time the proceeds are restricted, the entry to record the sale on January 1 is again journalized in the same way, but an additional entry is needed. This additional entry records the cash proceeds of $835 as a liability in the Deferred Restricted Contributions account, as follows:

Plant Fund

FUND BALANCE	835	
DEFERRED RESTRICTED CONTRIBUTIONS		835

Recording the recognition of a deferred Restricted Contributions account for the amount of the proceeds received from the sale of the fixed asset

The increase in the balance of the Deferred Restricted Contributions account causes a reduction in the Fund Balance. In effect, this indicates that these monies are available only for the purchase of specific, donor-designated assets. This entry meets the objective of categorizing restricted proceeds as a liability.

The entries that have been illustrated with the sale of office equipment record the sale of fixed assets as a gain, but loss on a sale can occur. If the office equipment had been sold for a loss of $75, the entry to record the sale is very similar to the previous entry, except there is a debit to an account entitled Loss on Sale of Fixed Assets:

Plant Fund

CASH	706.25		
ACCUMULATED DEPRECIATION	893.75		
LOSS ON SALE OF FIXED ASSETS	75.00		
Office Equipment		893.75	
EQUIPMENT		1,675.00	
Office Equipment			1,675.00

Recording the loss of $75 in the sale of fixed assets

In recognizing the loss, it is obvious that the amount received for the fixed assets is less than the amount received when a gain was recognized. When a loss is recognized in the Plant Fund, the Operating Fund is likely to make a transfer of cash to the Plant Fund to reimburse it for the amount of loss incurred on the sale. (These types of transfers are discussed in the next group of transactions considered in the chapter.) Regardless of any later transfers from the Operating Fund, the Plant Fund needs to record a transfer of the proceeds to the Operating Fund for the $706.25 received from selling the fixed asset:

Plant Fund

TRANSFER OUT TO OPERATING FUND	706.25	
CASH		706.25

Recording the transfer of the proceeds from the sale of office equipment to the Operating Fund

Recognition of the transfer is recorded in the Operating Fund, as shown before.

The sale of a fixed asset is one way an asset can be removed from the books. The other way is through retirement of the asset after its useful life is completed or when it is no longer needed. When retirement of an asset occurs, the accumulated depreciation on the asset is written off the books, along with the original cost of the asset on the books. If any cash is received as a disposal value for the asset, this is recognized as a debit in the Cash account. A gain or loss can result if the asset is written off the books before the expiration of its originally estimated useful life. This gain or loss can be recognized on the retirement of a fixed asset if the amount received for the asset is more or less than the salvage value, respectively.

As an example of this type of situation, assume that an automobile used by the Lloyd Cloyd Library is completely depreciated. The automobile had an original cost of $5,600 and a net asset value of

$600, which coincidentally is equal to its original estimated salvage value. Upon retiring this asset, the NFP organization receives $450 in cash. As the amount received for the retired asset is less than its net asset value, a loss is recognized. The loss is equal to the difference between the amount received for the asset and its net asset value. This loss is equal to $150. Although the salvage value and the net asset value are equal for the automobile, this is only a coincidence, and the important factor in determining the existence of a gain or loss is the difference between the amount received for the asset and its net asset value. The entry to recognize retirement of the automobile is:

Plant Fund

LOSS ON RETIREMENT OF FIXED ASSETS	150		
CASH	450		
ACCUMULATED DEPRECIATION	5,000		
Automobile		5,000	
VEHICLES			5,600
Automobile			5,600

Recording the retirement of an automobile and the recognition of a loss on retirement

The subsidiary account in this entry is the Automobile account, and this account is written off in the journal entry with a credit of $5,600. The entry is similar to when a fixed asset is sold, but the loss account should indicate that the loss arose from the retirement of an asset, rather than the sale of one. The loss will appear in the nonoperating section of the SREF. The proceeds received from disposing of the fixed asset should be transferred to the Operating Fund. (This entry is not shown here.)

TRANSFERS FROM OPERATING FUND TO PLANT FUND

The Operating Fund makes various types of cash transfers to the Plant Fund. Some of these transfers may be required as part of the debt agreement under which the NFP organization obtained a loan, and other types of transfers may be a policy decision by the board to fund the replacement and acquisition of new assets. Transfers appear on the SREF below the Capital Additions section as part of the changes that occur in the Fund Balance. (See the H. K. Fines Library's SREF in figure 9–1 or figure 10A–1 in appendix A for examples of transfers on the SREF.) When a transfer is made, it is journalized in both the Operating Fund and the Plant Fund.

The Operating Fund in the H. K. Fines Library transferred $23,357.25 to the Plant Fund during the 19x3 fiscal year.[3] This transfer is composed of the amount of principal repayment on the debt ($15,000), and 60 percent of the yearly depreciation expense, or $8,357.25. Depreciation expense during the 19x3 fiscal year is $13,928.75. Although this funding policy will not pay for replacement of all the fixed assets, it is anticipated that the transferred monies can be invested to earn a return. Therefore, when it is necessary to replace specific assets, the Operating Fund will make only a minimum additional transfer to assist the Plant Fund to purchase the new asset. The entry to record the transfer from the Operating Fund to the Plant Fund for the H. K. Fines Library is shown in the following entry.

Operating Fund—Unrestricted

Dec. 31 TRANSFER TO PLANT FUND   23,357.25
             CASH   23,357.25

      Recording transfer from Operating Fund to Plant Fund. Principal $15,000 and depreciation expense $8,357.25

Plant Fund—Unrestricted

Dec. 31 CASH   23,357.25
             TRANSFER FROM OPERATING FUND   23,357.25

      Recording receipt of transfer from Operating Fund to Plant Fund

The transfers could be made at several times during the year, but in the illustration for the library the transfer is made only once during the year. The amounts which are transferred into the Plant Fund are from the unrestricted portion of the Operating Fund. If these transfers are restricted to specific uses by an outside party, they must be maintained in separate and restricted groups of accounts within the Plant Fund. In the case of the H. K. Fines Library, these restrictions are not present, and no separate accounting for the transfers is established in a restricted grouping of the Plant Fund.

---

3. If the amounts in the transfer for indebtedness repayment or for fixed-asset acquisition are significant by themselves, they should be separately disclosed.

PAYMENT ON DEBT

One of the responsibilities of the Plant Fund is to make periodic payments on the principal of the debt, and a second responsibility is to make payments on the interest on that debt. The debt issues are usually interest bearing, and the interest rate on the debt is stated for a yearly period. This means that a $10,000 note, payable at 14 percent interest, requires $1,400 in interest payments each year the loan is outstanding. This yearly interest payment is equal to $700 for each semiannual period, or 7 percent, and $350 for each quarterly period, or 3.5 percent. (The rate of interest on a debt is stated on a yearly basis, unless otherwise indicated.) The H. K. Fines Library has two debt issues: the first requires semiannual principal and interest payments, and the second requires quarterly principal and interest payments.

Footnote 4 in figure 9–4 discloses the amount of long-term debt in the Plant Fund at the beginning of the current year and the interest rate on that debt. The first debt security listed in note 4 is an 8 percent mortgage for $270,000 that is repayable in semiannual payments of $3,500 for the first 15 years. At the end of this 15-year period, the outstanding principal on the mortgage is required to be paid in its entirety. The first payment under the periodic repayment schedule is on January 1, 19x3, and the first interest payment is determined for the six-month period between July 1, 19x2, and January 1, 19x3.[4]

The interest on this mortgage is computed for each six-month period independently from the other six-month periods. These separate calculations are necessary because the interest in the two semiannual periods will be different, due to reduction in the principal of the loan by the $3,500 payment on the principal each January 1 and June 30. This payment reduces the principal owed for the six-month period from January 1 to June 30, 19x3, to $266,500 from the $270,000 owed on June 30, 19x2. The interest on this debt for the fiscal year ending June 30, 19x3, is $21,460, and it is calculated in figure 10–1.

It can be seen in figure 10–1 that the interest expense is first calculated for the period July 1, 19x2, to January 1, 19x3. Under the terms of the debt agreement, no interest expense was due on the debt prior to July 1, 19x2. In the calculation in figure 10–1, the outstand-

---

4. Although this is an unusual characteristic of a debt, it is presented in this fashion as an easier introduction to the computation of interest expense on debt.

1. Interest expense for first six-month period, ending Jan. 1, 19x3*

   a) $270,000 × .08 × ½ = $10,800.

2. Interest expense for second six-month period, ending July 1, 19x3, and recorded as adjusting entry on June 30, 19x3

   a) $270,000 − $3,500 = $266,500.

   b) $266,500 × .08 × ½ = $10,660.

* There was no interest expense accrued on the mortgage as of the end of the fiscal year ending June 30, 19x2.

FIG. 10–1.   Interest Expense on 8% Mortgage

ing principal of $270,000 is multiplied by the interest rate, 8 percent. This calculation determines the interest for a one-year period, but as the period under question is for half a year, the sum is multiplied by one-half, which represents the six-month period ending January 1. The recognition and payment of this interest expense is recorded in the following entry.

Jan. 1	INTEREST EXPENSE	10,800	
19x3	Administration		10,800
	CASH		10,800

Recording the payment of six months of interest on the 8% mortgage—July 1, 19x2 to January 1, 19x3

The interest expense is recorded as a program expense of Administration in the subsidiary ledger, and it will appear as part of that program's expense on the SREF.[5] At the same time that this interest payment is made, a payment is also made on the principal of the debt. Two semiannual payments of $3,500 are made on the principal. A distinction should be maintained between the payment on the principal of the debt and interest payments. Only interest payments are recorded as an expense of the period. The entry to record principal payments follows:

5. Again, the costs of Administration can be reallocated to other departments to determine the full costs of those programs. See pages 397–410.

Plant Fund

Jan. 1	LONG-TERM DEBT PAYABLE—Current	3,500	
19x3	CASH		3,500

Recording semiannual payment of debt's principal

June 30	LONG-TERM DEBT PAYABLE—Current	3,500	
19x3	CASH		3,500

Recording semiannual payment of debt's principal

The debit to the Long-Term Debt Payable—Current account reduces the balance in this account by $3,500 every six months. The "current" portion of long-term debt is that portion of the debt which appears in the current liabilities section of the Balance Sheet, rather than as part of the Long-Term Debt Payable account. It represents the debt which is to be repaid within the current fiscal year.

The next interest payment is made on July 1, 19x3. This payment is scheduled to be made one day after the end of the current fiscal year on June 30, 19x3. An adjusting entry is required on June 30 to recognize the interest owed on the debt as of that date. Computation of the amount of the interest payment is shown in figure 10–1 for June 30, 19x3. The principal has been reduced by the $3,500 payment on January 1; therefore, from that date only $266,500 is owed on the mortgage payable. The amount of interest expense on the outstanding debt is determined by multiplying the amount owed by the 8 percent interest rate. The result is divided in half to represent six months' interest expense from January 1 through June 30. The interest expense for this period is $10,660, and an adjusting entry is made to recognize the liability for this amount on June 30. The entry to record the adjusting entry follows:

June 30	INTEREST EXPENSE	10,660	
19x3	Administration		10,660
	INTEREST PAYABLE		10,660

Recording the interest expense owed as of June 30

The Interest Payable account appears under the current liabilities section of the Balance Sheet, and the interest expense will appear as part of Administration's program expenses. Although it may appear that there is only one day until this interest is paid, and therefore the June 30 entry can wait, this is not correct. If the adjusting entry is not made until the next day, it will not appear on the financial statements for the H. K. Fines Library as of June 30, 19x3, and the expenses and liabilities of the library will be understated for that period. To arrive at a true financial picture for the library, the expense and liability should be recorded in the current year.

To continue this illustration beyond the closing date of the financial statements on June 30, 19x3, assume that the interest expense is paid on July 1, 19x3, the following fiscal year. This cash payment requires that $10,660 be paid in cash for the interest on the mortgage. The entry on July 1 must consider the liability account Interest Payable, which was recorded on June 30, because once the cash payment is made, there is no longer any liability. The entry to record this cash payment follows:

| INTEREST PAYABLE | 10,660 | |
| CASH | | 10,660 |

Recording the payment of the interest expense and the reduction of the interest liability on July 1

The interest expense is recorded as an expense of the period ending June 30, 19x3, and not of the subsequent fiscal year. In the subsequent fiscal year, which begins July 1, the cash payment for the interest is recorded as a reduction of the interest payable. Under the accrual method of accounting, the interest expense is an expense of the period in which it is owed, and is not an expense of the period in which it is paid. The cash basis, which understates expenses and liabilities, would recognize the interest expense in the period ending June 30, 19x4.

The second debt security described in footnote 4 to the financial statements of the H. K. Fines Library is a $45,000 note, payable at 9 percent interest. This note is reduced by $2,000 payments each quarter; therefore, the amount owed, as well as the interest expense, is changed each quarter. The yearly expense on the note is $3,600, and determination of this interest expense is presented in figure 10–2, where it is seen that the amount of the principal is reduced by $2,000 each quarter. As the amount owed is reduced, so is the amount of interest which is paid in each quarter. The entries for

1. Interest expense for period ending July 1, 19x2, and recorded as adjusting entry on June 30, 19x2

   a) $45,000 × .09 × ¼ = $1,012.50

2. Interest expense for period ending Oct. 1, 19x2

   a) $43,000* × .09 × ¼ = $967.50

3. Interest expense for period ending Jan. 1, 19x3

   a) $41,000* × .09 × ¼ = $922.50

4. Interest expense for period ending Apr. 1, 19x3

   a) $39,000* × .09 × ¼ = $877.50

5. Interest expense for period ending July 1, 19x3, and recorded as adjusting entry on June 30, 19x3

   a) $37,000* × .09 × ¼ = $832.50

*A $2,000 principal payment is made each quarter, thereby reducing the outstanding debt by an equal amount.

The interest expense for the year is equal to $3,600. This is computed as follows: 967.50 + 922.50 + 877.50 + 832.50 = 3,600.

FIG. 10–2. Interest Expense on 9% Note Payable

payment of the principal and interest for the first three quarters are shown in the following:

July 1	LONG-TERM DEBT PAYABLE—Current	2,000.00	
	INTEREST PAYABLE	1,012.50	
	CASH		3,012.50

Recording interest payment and payment on principal

Oct. 1	LONG-TERM DEBT PAYABLE—Current	2,000.00	
	INTEREST EXPENSE	967.50	
	Administration		967.50
	CASH		2,967.50

Recording interest payment and payment on principal in 1st quarter

Jan. 1   LONG-TERM DEBT PAYABLE—Current   2,000.00
          INTEREST EXPENSE   922.50
          ·   Administration   922.50
                        CASH   2,922.50

Recording interest payment and payment on principal in 2d quarter

Apr. 1   LONG-TERM DEBT PAYABLE—Current   2,000.00
          INTEREST EXPENSE   877.50
                Administration   877.50
                        CASH   2,877.50

Recording interest payment and payment on principal in 3d quarter

The first entry on July 1 writes off the Interest Payable, which was recorded as an adjusting entry recognizing interest payable and interest expense in the previous year. The Interest Payable account appears on the Balance Sheet for the period ending June 30, 19x2 (figure 9–2), under current liabilities. Unlike the 8 percent mortgage, which allowed for a delay in initial principal and interest payments, the 9 percent debt did not have this clause in its payment schedule. As a result, the interest expense was accrued as an adjusting entry on June 30, 19x2. This adjusting entry was the same as the one prepared for the 8 percent mortgage on June 30, 19x3. All these adjusting entries for interest expense are similar.

The three entries on October 1, January 1, and April 1 record the quarterly reduction of the principal and the payment of interest. The difference between these entries and the one on July 1 is that the July 1 entry reduces the balance in the Interest Payable account to zero whereas the latter three entries recognize interest expense.

The next interest and principal payment date is July 1, and that occurs in the next fiscal year. Therefore, an adjusting entry is recorded for the amount of the interest owed as of June 30 so that the proper amount of interest expense is recorded in the correct fiscal period. The amount of interest expense owed for the fourth quarter of the year is $832.50, and its calculation is shown in figure 10–2. The entry to record the adjusting entry follows:

June 30   INTEREST EXPENSE   832.50
                Administration   832.50
                        INTEREST PAYABLE   832.50

Recording interest expense owed as of June 30

All debt outstanding at the end of the fiscal year requires an adjusting entry to record the amount of the interest expense owed but not yet paid out in cash. This entry is necessary in order to recognize the proper amount of interest expense in the current period.

The illustrations have provided examples where debt is repaid in serial installments over an extended period. This repayment schedule is typical of those incurred by an NFP organization, but it is also possible for an NFP organization to have a debt repayment schedule where the entire issue matures at the end of a specified time. The interest expense incurred on this type of debt is constant from year to year.

Another type of debt issue is one in which a note payable is discounted before the NFP organization receives the proceeds from the loan. This arrangement means that in order for an NFP organization to borrow $5,000, it must borrow *more* than $5,000, because the lending institution takes its interest from the amount that is part of the loan before any money is given to the NFP organization. For example, it may be necessary to negotiate a note payable for $5,300 in order to receive $5,000 in cash from a bank. If this should occur, the $300 is considered to be interest expense to the NFP organization. The following entry records this transaction.

CASH	5,000	
DISCOUNT ON NOTES PAYABLE	300	
NOTES PAYABLE		5,300

Recording the discounted note payable

The liability on the note is $5,300. The NFP organization received $5,000 from the lender, and it will be required to repay $5,300. The interest expense on the note should be recognized over the life of the note payable; therefore, the amount recorded as a discount needs to be written off to interest expense over the life of the note. If the note is for a six-month period (all months within the same fiscal period), the repayment of the note is recorded in the following fashion.

INTEREST EXPENSE	300	
NOTES PAYABLE	5,300	
DISCOUNT ON NOTES PAYABLE		300
CASH		5,300

Recording the repayment of the note payable and writing off the discount to interest expense

The note originated and was repaid in the same fiscal period, and there is no question about how much of the discount to recognize as interest expense. If the six-month term of the note should cover two fiscal periods, the interest expense has to be assigned to the correct periods. As an example, assume that the same note was issued on May 1, and the NFP organization's year-end is June 30. This requires an adjusting entry on June 30 that recognizes interest in the current fiscal year equal to the months of May and June, or two-sixths of the total interest expense of $300. The entry to record this adjusting entry on June 30 follows:

INTEREST EXPENSE   100
    DISCOUNT ON NOTES PAYABLE   100

Recording two-months interest expense in the current year with an adjusting entry on June 30

This recognition of interest expense is a necessary entry in any accounting system based on the accrual method. The remainder of the discount on the note payable is written off as interest expense when the note is repaid at the end of the six-month period.

The final entry for the H. K. Fines Library as it relates to the debt owed by the library is related to recognizing the current portion of the debt—the portion to be repaid within the next year. The installment payments that the library makes on its debt each year are equal to $15,000. This is the amount which should appear in the Long-Term Debt Payable—Current account at the end of each fiscal year. The entry to make the transfer of liabilities from the long-term portion to the current portion follows:

June 30   LONG-TERM DEBT PAYABLE   15,000
    LONG-TERM DEBT PAYABLE—Current   15,000

Recording the transfer of debt to be repaid within the next fiscal year in the current liabilities section of the Balance Sheet

This entry transfers $15,000 to the current liabilities section of the Balance Sheet. The transfer represents the amount of long-term debt that will have to be repaid during the current fiscal period. Although the subsidiary accounts are not shown, this entry is usually recorded with subsidiary accounts relating to each debt issue.

INCOME ON INVESTMENTS

The Plant Fund has invested monies it receives, and will not immediately use, for the replacement of fixed assets. These investments earn a return in the form of dividends or interest. The unrestricted portion of the Plant Fund had investment income during the current year of $23,000. This investment income is recorded in one consolidated entry on June 30:

Plant Fund—Unrestricted

June 30   CASH   23,000
                 CAPITAL ADDITIONS—Investment Income   23,000

       Recording the investment income on the unrestricted portion of the Plant
       Fund's investments

This type of investment income is recorded under the Capital Additions section of the SREF.[6] The restricted portion of the Plant Fund also earned income on its investments during the year equal to $13,700. This income is recorded with the following entry:

Plant Fund—Restricted

June 30   CASH   13,700
                 DEFERRED RESTRICTED CONTRIBUTIONS   13,700

       Recording the investment income on the restricted portion of the Plant
       Fund's investments

As the investment income is restricted by a third-party donor, it should appear as an increase in the liability account, Deferred Restricted Contributions, until it is expended.

GAINS AND LOSSES ON SALE OF INVESTMENTS

During the year, the Plant Fund sells portions of its investment portfolio for various reasons. These changes result in the recognition of gains and losses on the sale of investments. (Additional explanation of the recognition of gains and losses on the sale of investments is provided on pp. 219–22 with Endowment C.) For the H. K. Fines Library, assume that the unrestricted portion of the Plant Fund had realized gains on its investments of $6,890. The entry to record this net realized gain follows:

6. "Capital additions that are restricted for acquisition of plant assets should be treated as deferred capital support in the balance sheet until they are used for the indicated purpose. Once used, these amounts should be reported as capital additions in the statement of activity." American Institute of Certified Public Accountants, Statement of Position 78–10, *Accounting Principles and Reporting Practices for Certain Nonprofit Organizations* (New York: AICPA, 1979), par. 52. In the example, the credit of $23,000 is recorded as a credit to Capital Additions because these amounts have been spent on fixed assets during the year.

Plant Fund—Unrestricted

June 30 CASH	49,890	
GAIN ON SALE OF INVESTMENTS		6,890
MARKETABLE SECURITIES		43,000

Recording net realized gains on the sale of investments

This entry consolidates the effect of all gains and losses during the year. The Gain on the Sale of Investments account is transferred to the Capital Additions of the Plant Fund, and it is necessary to make another entry to record the transfer.[7] The entry to record the transfer follows:

Plant Fund—Unrestricted

June 30 GAIN ON SALE OF INVESTMENTS	6,890	
CAPITAL ADDITIONS—Net Realized Gains		6,890

Recording a capital addition equal to the net gains on investments

If the sale of investments occurs in the restricted portion of the Plant Fund, net gains or losses must also be recognized in that group of accounts. Assume that the sales of investments, $35,000 in this section of the Plant Fund, have resulted in a net loss of $10,100. This loss needs to be recorded in a manner similar to sales which resulted in net gains for the unrestricted portion of the Plant Fund. The entry to record the loss follows:

Plant Fund—Restricted

June 30 CASH	24,900	
LOSS ON SALE OF INVESTMENTS	10,100	
INVESTMENTS		35,000

Recording the net loss on the sale of investments in the restricted portion of the Plant Fund

The loss is recorded as a reduction in the Deferred Restricted Contributions account. It may require a legal interpretation as to whether the balance in this account can be reduced through a loss. It would be expected that since gains and income are recognized as

---

7. These amounts have also been expended on fixed assets during the current year, and they are considered to be increases in Capital Additions rather than deferred amounts.

increases in the deferred account, losses can decrease the balance in the account. The entry to record the transfer of the loss to the deferred account follows.

Plant Fund—Restricted

June 30	DEFERRED RESTRICTED CONTRIBUTIONS	10,100	
	LOSS ON SALE OF INVESTMENTS		10,100

> Recognizing a reduction in the deferred account equal to the net loss and writing off the loss

PURCHASES OF INVESTMENTS

Inasmuch as sales of investments occur in the Plant Fund, purchases of investments also occur. The unrestricted and restricted portions of the Plant Fund have purchased additional securities during the current year. These purchases are recorded in the following entries:

Plant Fund—Unrestricted

Feb. 15	MARKETABLE SECURITIES	10,000	
	CASH		10,000

> Recording purchase of investments by unrestricted portion of Plant Fund

Plant Fund—Restricted

Mar. 15	INVESTMENTS	37,000	
	CASH		37,000

> Recording purchase of investments by restricted portion of Plant Fund

Summary

This chapter has explained the use of the Plant Fund, the last major fund classification in the accounting system of an NFP organization. This fund's major responsibilities are the stewardship of the fixed assets of the organization, the repayment of debt that has been incurred to purchase fixed assets, and the payment of interest on the debt.

Many organizations do not keep track of their assets once they are purchased, but this policy is a mistake. An NFP organization has a responsibility to the public and its funding agencies to maintain its assets in a professional manner. If these assets are not recorded on the books, it is difficult to envision that they would be adequately maintained. A systemic funding policy should be instituted as part of the organization's asset replacement policy. The purpose of this funding policy is to avoid situations where no monies are available to purchase a new asset, or the purchase of a new asset can only be achieved through curtailments in other areas. The importance of following a policy of recording the fixed assets in the books of the organization and following a systematic plan to provide for the replacement of these assets cannot be stressed enough.

One aspect of asset accounting that could arise in an NFP organization has not been covered in the three funds considered up to this point. An NFP organization may become involved in construction of a fixed asset, such as a building or an addition to an existing building, and it is possible to handle this type of construction in the Plant Fund as it is likely that most of the monies that have been accumulated for the project are maintained in the accounts of the Plant Fund. It is also possible to keep track of the construction of a fixed asset in another fund, a fourth fund, called the Capital Projects Fund. The accounting entries that relate to this fund are explained in appendix B.

In some cases, this type of construction project is handled for the library by another governmental entity, such as a city government. If the need for new construction should arise, the decision will have to be made whether to record the construction project in the Plant Fund or the Capital Projects Fund. This alternative to the Plant Fund is presented in appendix B. For both funds, the journal entries are similar.

Exercise 10–1. Fixed-Asset Transactions (Do not use subsidiary accounts in preparing journal entries for the following problems)

1. The Martin County Library has sold a portion of its office equipment for $1,800. These assets were originally purchased with unrestricted monies by the Plant Fund. The original cost was $7,500, with no salvage value. At the present time, the accumulated depreciation on the assets is $6,000.

    a) Record the sale of the office equipment in the Plant Fund.
    b) Record the transfers in the Plant Fund and the Operating Fund.
    c) Assume that the Operating Fund transfers $500 back to the Plant Fund. Record the entries in the two funds.

2. On April 1, the Cheat River Library sold a duplicating machine that was purchased 10 years ago for $1,100 and had no salvage value. The

accumulated depreciation on this asset is $900. The bookkeeper knows that an updating entry for depreciation, up to the date of the sale, should be made, but the bookkeeper has forgotten how to record depreciation for a partial year of use. Record the journal entry for the bookkeeper.

3. The Carter Library has decided to retire fixed assets that have no selling value. These assets were purchased for $2,700 and they have a book value of $200. Record the entry in the Plant Fund for the retirement of the fixed assets.

4. A 10%, $12,000 serial debt is owed by the Willis Library on June 30, 19x7. The principal is being repaid in $2,000 installments every January 1 and July 1.

    a) Record the journal entry on January 1, 19x8, for the interest expense and principal payment.
    b) Record the adjusting journal entry on June 30, 19x8.
    c) Record the payment of interest and principal on July 1, 19x8.

5. A $5,700 discounted note payable was signed by the Able Library on March 31, 19x5, with the First National Bank. The note is for a period of 6 months, and it is discounted for $500 over the period.

    a) Journalize the entry to record the liability on March 31, 19x5.
    b) Record the interest expense on June 30, 19x5.
    c) Record the payment of the note when it matures on September 30, 19x5.

6. During the year ended June 30, 19x8, the Wicks Library had a $5,500 gain on the sale of $83,000 of security investments, at cost, from the restricted portion of the Plant Fund. Record the journal entry for the sale of the investments.

Appendix A Plant Fund Financial Statements

The financial statements for the H. K. Fines Library have been prepared for the fiscal year ending June 30, 19x3, using all the dated transactions occurring on pages 264–89, with the exception (as noted) relating to the transfer of proceeds from the sale of fixed assets. In addition, the financial statements prepared in figures 9–1 through 9–3, as well as the Notes to the Financial Statements in figure 9–4, were used in preparing the financial statements in appendix A. It is recommended that T accounts be opened for the accounts in the financial statements for the period ending June 30, 19x2, and the dated entries be posted to these T accounts. A trial balance of the balances in these T accounts should be taken before the financial statements are prepared.

H. K. FINES LIBRARY
Plant Fund
Statement of Support, Revenue, and Expenses and Changes in Fund Balances
Year Ended June 30, 19x3
(with Comparative Totals for 19x2)

	Unrestricted	Restricted	Total	Year Ended June 30, 19x2 Totals
Support and Revenue				
Gifts	$ 3,200.00	—	$ 3,200.00	—
Expenses (Note 4)				
Program Services:				
Reference	$ 1,360.00	—	$ 1,360.00	$ 2,500.00
Children's Library	500.00	—	500.00	1,200.00
Circulation	200.00	—	200.00	750.00
Regional History	100.00	—	100.00	500.00
Total Program Services	$ 2,160.00	—	$ 2,160.00	$ 4,950.00
Supporting Services:				
Administration	36,828.75	—	36,828.75	39,012.50
Total Expenses	$ 38,988.75	—	$ 38,988.75	$ 43,962.50
Excess (Deficiency) of Support and Revenue over Expenses	$ (35,788.75)	—	$ (35,788.75)	$ (43,962.50)
Prior-Year Expenses on Prior-Year Encumbrances	—	—	—	—

Excess (Deficiency) of Support and Revenue over Expenses before capital additions and nonoperating items	$ (35,788.75)	—	$ (35,788.75)	$ (43,962.50)
Capital Additions:				
Contributions	—	—	—	37,000.00
Investment Income, including net gains (Note 2)	29,890.00	—	29,890.00	40,000.00
Total Capital Additions	$ 29,890.00	—	$ 29,890.00	$ 77,000.00
Excess (Deficiency) of support and revenue over expenses after capital additions	$ (5,898.75)	—	$ (5,898.75)	$ 33,037.50
Nonoperating additions:				
Gain on Sale of Fixed Assets	53.75	—	53.75	—
Excess (Deficiency) of support and revenue over expenses after nonoperating items	$ (5,845.00)	—	$ (5,845.00)	$ 33,037.50
Fund balance at beginning of year	$1,421,787.50	—	$1,421,787.50	$1,198,750.00
Transfers—principal of indebtedness and acquisitions	23,357.25	—	23,357.25	190,000.00
Fund balance at end of year	$1,439,299.75	—	$1,439,299.75	$1,421,787.50

FIG. 10A–1. Financial Statement

H. K. FINES LIBRARY
Plant Fund
Balance Sheet
June 30, 19x3
(with Comparative Totals for 19x2)

Assets	Unrestricted	Restricted	Total	Year Ended June 30, 19x2 Totals
Current Assets				
Cash	$ 56,527.25	$ 1,600.00	$ 58,127.25	$ 31,800.00
Marketable Securities (Note 2)	138,000.00	—	138,000.00	171,000.00
Total Current Assets	194,527.25	$ 1,600.00	$ 196,127.25	$ 202,800.00
Investments (Note 2)	$ —	$714,000.00	$ 714,000.00	$ 712,000.00
Land, Buildings and Equipment at Cost, less Accumulated Depreciation of $51,700 and $40,335 respectively (Note 3)	1,571,265.00	—	1,571,265.00	1,550,000.00
Inexhaustible collections and books (Note 7)	—	—	—	—
Total Assets	$1,765,792.25	$715,600.00	$2,481,392.25	$2,464,800.00

Liabilities and Fund Balances

Current Liabilities				
Current portion of Long-term debt	$ 15,000.00	$ —	$ 15,000.00	$ 15,000.00
Interest Payable	11,492.50	—	11,492.50	1,012.50
Deferred Restricted Contributions (Note 5)	—	715,600.00	715,600.00	712,000.00
Total Current Liabilities	$ 26,492.50	$715,600.00	$ 741,492.50	$ 728,012.50
Long-Term Debt (Note 4)	$ 300,000.00	—	$ 300,000.00	$ 315,000.00
Total Liabilities	$ 326,492.50	$715,600.00	$1,042,092.50	$1,043,012.50
Fund Balance				
Undesignated	$1,439,299.75	—	$1,439,299.75	$1,421,787.50
Total Fund Balance	$1,439,299.75	$ —	$1,439,299.75	$1,421,787.50
Total Liabilities and Fund Balances	$1,765,792.25	$715,600.00	$2,481,392.20	$2,464,800.00

FIG. 10A–2. Financial Statement

H. K. FINES LIBRARY
Plant Fund
Statement of Changes in Financial Position
Year Ended June 30, 19x3
(with Comparative Totals for 19x3)

	Unrestricted	Restricted	Total	June 30, 19x2 Totals
Sources of Working Capital				
Excess (Deficiency) of support and revenue over expenses before capital additions	$ (35,735.00)[1]	—	$ (35,735.00)	$ (43,962.50)
Capital Additions	29,890.00	—	29,890.00	77,000.00
Excess (Deficiency) of support and revenue over expenses after capital additions	$ (5,845.00)	—	$ (5,845.00)	$ 33,037.50
Deduct: Gain on Sale of Fixed Assets	(53.75)	—	(53.75)	—
Add:				
Items not using working capital				
Depreciation	13,928.75	—	13,928.75	13,700.00
Loss on Sale of Investments	—	$ 10,100.00[2]	$ 10,100.00	—
Working Capital from Operations	$ 8,030.00	$ 10,100.00	$ 18,130.00	$ 46,737.50
Deferred Restricted Income	$ —	$ 3,600.00	$ 3,600.00	$ 12,000.00
Sale of Fixed Assets	835.00	—	835.00	—
Sale of Investments	—	24,900.00	24,900.00	—
Total Sources of Working Capital	$ 8,865.00	$ 38,600.00	$ 47,465.00	$ 58,737.50
Uses of Working Capital:				
Purchases of Fixed Assets	$ 35,975.00	—	$ 35,975.00	$197,000.00
Purchases of Investments	—	$ 37,000.00	37,000.00	—
Reduction of Long-Term Debt	15,000.00	—	15,000.00	15,000.00
Deferred Restricted Income	—	3,600.00	3,600.00	12,000.00
Transfers Between Funds	$ (23,357.25)	—	$ (23,357.25)	(190,000.00)

FIG. 10A–3. Financial Statement

Total Uses of Working Capital	$(27,617.75)	$(40,600.00)	$(68,217.75)	$(34,000.00)
Increases (Decreases) in Working Capital	$(18,752.75)	$ (2,000.00)	$(20,752.75)	$ 24,737.50
Changes in Working Capital Components:				
Increases (Decreases) in current assets:				
Cash	$ 24,727.25	$ 1,600.00	$ 26,627.25	$ 25,250.00
Marketable Securities	(33,000.00)	—	(33,000.00)	500.00
	$ (8,272.75)	$ 1,600.00	$ (6,672.75)	$ 25,750.00
(Increases) Decreases in current liabilities:				
Interest Payable	$(10,480.00)	—	$(10,480.00)	$ (1,012.50)
Deferred Restricted Contributions	—	$ (3,600.00)	$ (3,600.00)	—
Increase (Decrease) in Working Capital	$(18,752.75)	$ (2,000.00)	$(20,752.75)	$ 24,737.50

Notes to Statement Changes in Financial Position

[1]The Excess of $35,735 is recorded before capital additions but after nonoperating items of $53.75. This means that $53.75 was deducted from the $35,788.75 Excess shown on the SREF as "before capital additions and nonoperating items." (This adjustment is made in the Statement of Changes in Financial Position so that it will be easier to make the combined statement in chapter 11.)

[2]The loss of $10,100 from the sale of investments is shown under the restricted portion of the Statement of Changes in Financial Position. This is one manner of presenting this loss. The $10,100 loss does not represent an outflow of working capital from the Library; therefore, it must be shown as an increase in the sources of working capital. It would also be possible to show this as an increase in the Deferred Restricted Income under sources. If it were shown in this manner, the change in the Deferred Restricted Income would be $13,700. Under either method, the decrease in working capital for the restricted portion of the Plant Fund is $2,000.

Note 2, Investments

Investments are presented in the financial statements in the aggregate at the lower of cost (amortized, in the case of bonds) or fair market value.

	Cost	Market
Plant Fund—Unrestricted	$138,000	$167,000
Plant Fund—Restricted	714,000	735,000
	$852,000	$902,000

Investments are composed of the following:

	Cost		Market	
	Unrestricted	Restricted	Unrestricted	Restricted
Corporate Stocks	$ 68,000	$449,000	$ 97,000	$468,000
U.S. Government Obligations	70,000	265,000	70,000	267,000
	$138,000	$714,000	$167,000	$735,000

The determination of fair market value is calculated by aggregating all current marketable securities. At June 30, 19x3, there were unrealized gains of $50,000 pertaining to the current portfolio. This portfolio had a cost on June 30, 19x2, of $883,000 and a market value of $938,300. A net realized loss of $10,100 on the sale of marketable equity securities was included in the determination of the Excess (deficiency) of Support and Revenue over Expenses after Capital Additions for 19x3. The cost of the securities sold was based on a first-in, first-out method in both years.

Note 3, Plant Assets and Depreciation

A summary of plant assets follows:

Land	$1,000,000
Buildings	525,000
Equipment	138,300
	$1,663,300
Less: Accumulated Depreciation	(92,035)
	$1,571,265

FIG. 10A–4. Notes to the Financial Statements (These notes incorporate the necessary changes that have occurred during the 19x3 fiscal year only)

Note 4, Long-Term Debt

A summary of long-term debt follows:

8% mortgage payable in semiannual installments of $3,500 for 15 years and a lump-sum payment at the end of that period	$263,000
9% unsecured notes payable to a bank, due in quarterly installments of $2,000	37,000
	$300,000

The 8% mortgage payable was incurred in 19x1. Building and land with a net book value of $285,000 as of June 30, 19x1, are pledged as collateral on the mortgage. No interest is to be accrued until January 1, 19x3, and at that time for only six months' interest. The first principal payment is made at that time also.

Note 5, Changes in Deferred Restricted Contributions

Balance at beginning of year	$712,000
Additions:	
Investment income	13,700
	$725,700
Deductions:	
Loss on Sale of Investments	10,100
Balance at end of year	$715,600

FIG. 10A–4. (Continued)

June 30			
	TRANSFERS FROM OPERATING FUND	23,357.25	
	CAPITAL ADDITION—Investment Income	23,000.00	
	CAPITAL ADDITION—Net Realized Gains	6,890.00	
	SUPPORT—Gifts	3,200.00	
	MISCELLANEOUS REVENUE	53.75	
	EXPENSES		38,988.75
	FUND BALANCE		17,512.25

Recording closing entry for Plant Fund

FIG. 10A–5. Closing Entries for the Plant Fund (based on closing of temporary accounts on the SREF). Although these entries are made after the financial statements have been prepared, they are used to determine the proper balance in the Fund Balance at the end of the year.

Appendix B Capital Projects Fund

The purpose for establishing a capital projects fund is to account for the resources that are going to be used in construction of new facilities for the NFP organization. Initially, these resources consist of cash and temporary investments. The Capital Projects Fund records the utilization of these resources to construct a fixed asset such as a building. This construction project can be accounted for through the Plant Fund, but the establishment of a Capital Projects Fund serves the purpose of eliminating these accounting entries from the journals of the Plant Fund.

A Capital Projects Fund is closely related to a Plant Fund because once the project is completed, the cost of the fixed asset is transferred to the Plant Fund. Therefore, a characteristic of the Capital Projects Fund is that it is in existence only until the project is completed, and at that time any monies left in the fund are transferred to the Plant Fund or the Operating Fund. This type of transfer is referred to as a residual equity transfer. It is the transfer of the monies remaining in a fund after that fund has completed its functions.

The following entries are based on the assumption that the Plant Fund had restricted monies which were required to be used for building an annex to the library's main building. These monies are to be transferred to a Capital Projects Fund. Furthermore, it is assumed that the construction of the project is started and completed within one fiscal period. The first entry records the transfer of the restricted monies from the Plant Fund to the Capital Project Fund. For illustrative purposes, assume that the restricted monies have accumulated to a balance of $720,000.

Plant Fund—Restricted

TRANSFER TO CAPITAL PROJECTS FUND	720,000	
CASH		720,000

Transferring cash from restricted portion of Plant Fund to Capital Projects Fund

DEFERRED RESTRICTED CONTRIBUTIONS	720,000	
CAPITAL ADDITIONS—Contributions		720,000

Closing Deferred Restricted Contributions account to Capital Additions

The Transfer account and the Capital Additions account are later closed to the Fund Balance. This procedure assumes that the restricted portion of the Plant Fund is closed into the Capital Projects Fund. If the closing cannot be made in one entry, it may be necessary to close portions of the Plant Fund to the Capital Projects Fund as the latter fund expends money on the building. In that case, the entries shown for the Plant Fund are recorded for only the amount of expenses incurred. Finally, it should be noted that the deferred account is closed to the Capital Additions account, rather than a revenue account, when the deferred amounts have been restricted for plant acquisitions. This is the recommended procedure with donor-restricted contributions for plant acquisitions.*

* *Accounting Principles and Reporting Practices,* par. 52.

In the Capital Projects Fund, the following entry is made when the cash is received from the Plant Fund:

Capital Projects Fund

CASH	720,000	
FUND BALANCE		720,000

Recording the receipt of cash from the restricted portion of the Plant Fund

Both these entries, in the Plant Fund and the Capital Projects Fund, are made on the same date. The transfer could be made in the form of securities rather than cash. Once the monies are in the Capital Projects Fund, contracts will be signed for the building and construction of the facilities. These contracts are encumbered when they are signed. The following entry records an encumbrance which corresponds with the signing of a contract for $700,000:

ENCUMBRANCES	700,000	
RESERVE FOR ENCUMBRANCES		700,000

Recording the encumbrance on the contract

The next event which usually occurs in construction of a building is the billing from the contractor on the portion that is completed. Usually the contractor submits "progressive" billings on the contract, and does not wait until the building is completely finished to present a bill. In the present case, it is assumed that the contractor makes two billings. One is submitted when the building is half completed, and the last billing is made upon completion of the building. The first bill is for $355,000, and it is approved for payment. The following entry records the receipt and approval of the bill.

RESERVE FOR ENCUMBRANCES	355,000	
ENCUMBRANCES		355,000

Recording reversal of encumbrance

EXPENSES	355,000	
CONTRACTS PAYABLE		355,000

Recording approval of payment

In construction projects when payment is made on a billing, a portion of the payment is retained by the NFP organization until the project is entirely completed and has been approved as satisfactory. This retained portion usually amounts to about 5 to 10 percent. The H. K. Fines Library follows this policy in making all payments on the contract, and it retains 5 percent of each billing. Therefore, only $337,250 is paid on the contract; the rest remains in a liability account entitled Contracts Payable, owed to the contractor, until the contract is satisfactorily completed.

CONTRACTS PAYABLE	355,000	
CASH		337,250
CONTRACTS PAYABLE—Retained		17,750

Recording payment on contract and retained 5%

When the final billing on the contract is received, the construction project should be carefully checked to see that it meets the contract specifications. If the building meets the specifications, the outstanding amount owed on the contract is paid. The following entries record the approval and payment on the final billing on the contract which was for $360,000.

| RESERVE FOR ENCUMBRANCES | 345,000 | |
| ENCUMBRANCES | | 345,000 |

Reversing remainder in encumbrance accounts

| EXPENSES | 360,000 | |
| CONTRACTS PAYABLE | | 360,000 |

Recording approved billing on contract

The amount in the Contracts Payable account needs to be paid once the building is found to be satisfactory. The payment on the Contracts Payable and the retained percentage follow.

CONTRACTS PAYABLE	360,000	
CONTRACTS PAYABLE—Retained Percentage	17,750	
CASH		377,750

Recording the payment on the contract payable

At the same time that the building is approved, it should be recorded in the Plant Fund as a new fixed asset:

Plant Fund

| BUILDING | 715,000 | |
| FUND BALANCE | | 715,000 |

Recording the completed building in the Plant Fund

If the building will not be completed within the fiscal period it was started, an account called Construction in Progress is used in the Plant Fund to provide an indication of the construction which had been completed on the building. The Construction in Progress account is debited for the amount of approved billings from the contractor. Once the building is completed, this account is closed into a Building account. Both the Building account and the Construction in Progress account would be maintained in the Plant Fund.

The balances in the Expense account and the Cash account need to be closed once the project is completed. It is assumed that the monies in the Capital Projects Fund are transferred to the unrestricted portion of the Operating Fund if they are not used on the construction of the building. This transfer is called a "residual equity transfer," and it is made to the Operating Fund because it is assumed that the monies not used in the construction of the building are no longer restricted once the building is completed. These unrestricted monies can be used in the routine operations of the Operating Fund. The entries for the transfer and the closing of the accounts follow:

TRANSFER TO OPERATING FUND	5,000	
DUE TO OPERATING FUND		5,000

Recording amount of residual transfer to Operating Fund

FUND BALANCE	720,000	
TRANSFER TO OPERATING FUND		5,000
EXPENSES		715,000

Closing expenses and transfers to Fund Balance

DUE TO OPERATING FUND	5,000	
CASH		5,000

Recording transfer of cash to Operating Fund from Capital Projects Fund

Entries which correspond with the entries in the Capital Projects Fund should also be recorded in the Operating Fund. These entries in the Operating Fund recognize the amount which is initially due from the Capital Projects Fund and the receipt of the cash.

Operating Fund

DUE FROM CAPITAL PROJECTS FUND	5,000	
TRANSFERS FROM CAPITAL PROJECTS FUND		5,000

Recording amount due from Capital Projects Fund as a transfer

CASH	5,000	
DUE FROM CAPITAL PROJECTS FUND		5,000

Recording receipt of monies from Capital Projects Fund

When one fund is closed and its residual equity in the Fund Balance is transferred to another fund, the second fund should not recognize this transfer as a revenue item. The transfer should be recognized in a Transfer account which will later be closed to the Fund Balance of the fund which received the transfer. For this reason, the Operating Fund's journal entries recognized a credit to an account entitled Transfers from the Capital Projects Fund. Later, this account will be closed into the Operating Fund's Fund Balance.

These entries illustrate the type of transactions that can occur in a Capital Projects Fund. It is possible to record these entries in the Plant Fund, but as the construction of the building and its financing become more complex, it may be better to record these activities in a Capital Projects Fund.

The entries recorded in this appendix for the Capital Projects Fund have not been transferred into the financial statements of the H. K. Fines Library. They have provided an illustration of the Capital Projects Fund, but they will not be incorporated into the combined financial statements for the library.

11.

Combined Financial Statements and Review of Accounting Cycle

The purpose of this chapter is twofold. First, the chapter will focus on the culmination of the previous chapters' work in developing financial statements for the H. K. Fines Library with the preparation of combined financial statements for the library. Second, the chapter will refocus on the accounting cycle for an NFP organization, as was explained in chapter 2.

The combined financial statements illustrated in this chapter are part of the financial documents issued to the public to report on the financial condition of the library. The financial statements that have been prepared up to this time are largely for internal reporting purposes, and the detail in these individual fund financial statements is reduced prior to the issuance of combined statements to the public. This change is the major difference between the combined financial statements and the financial statements in earlier chapters, and it should be easy to trace the numerical amounts in the individual fund financial statements to the combined statements in this chapter.

The second portion of the chapter consists of a review of the accounting cycle. This review highlights aspects of the accounting cycle that would have been difficult to explain when the cycle was introduced in chapter 2. Several new special journals are introduced that will reduce the number of entries recorded in the general journal.

Combined Financial Statements

As the accounting for the Operating Fund, Endowment Fund, and the Plant Fund consists of separate, self-balancing sets of accounts, the financial statements for each of these funds was prepared separately in the previous chapters. Although these funds consist of separate, self-balancing account groups, they operate within the same organizational unit. Therefore, when financial statements for the organization as a whole are presented, they must be presented with combined financial statements for all three funds.

Note that the term *combined* financial statement is used and not *consolidated*. There is an important difference between these terms. "Combining" a statement simply involves adding amounts across account balances in the various funds. For example, if the liabilities in the Operating Fund are $110,000 and the liabilities in the Plant Fund are $114,000, a combined financial statement would show the total liabilities at $224,000. With a consolidated statement, the addition works differently. Assume that the Operating Fund owes $10,000 to the Plant Fund and, in turn, the Plant Fund has a receivable from the Operating Fund for an equal amount. Under a "consolidated" concept, the $10,000 is netted out from the receivables and liabilities of the respective funds before a consolidated financial statement is prepared. If the total liabilities in both funds were equal to $224,000, this netting process would leave a total in the consolidated liabilities of $214,000, which is $10,000 lower than under a combined statement. Also, $10,000 is deducted from the combined receivables balance.

Use of a consolidated statement is supported because an organization should not record monies owed to itself as liabilities in its financial statements, nor should that same amount be recognized as a receivable. In NFP accounting, the combined statement approach is supported because the funds in an NFP organization are a self-balancing set of accounts that, largely, are accounted for separately from one another. Obviously, differences will develop in the type of financial statements which are prepared, based on the combined or consolidated statement approach.

In preparing financial statements, NFP organizations use both the combined and the consolidated approaches. Between separate funds (i.e., Operating, Endowment, and Plant), the combined approach is used, but in the same fund group, the consolidated approach is used. The consolidated approach nets out any receivables and payables within a fund group, as between the separate endowments in the Endowment Fund of the H. K. Fines Library. This type of situation occurs where there is a subdivision of a major fund group, and with the H. K. Fines Library this occurs only within the Endowment Fund. If there are borrowings between restricted and unrestricted portions of the same fund, these amounts should be shown in the statements and not netted out against one another. This is a better policy because of the limited use to which monies of a restricted nature can be put and the importance of showing that the restricted amounts are properly used.

When there are interfund receivables and payables, these amounts are not netted against one another and eliminated from any totals in the combined financial statements for the organization. Therefore, in general, the combined approach is taken with interfund and restricted transactions, but the consolidated approach is used with intrafund transactions.

The combined financial statements represent the summation of all the accounting activities of the organization, from the source documents on up. A number of financial documents are prepared prior to the combined financial statements. As one moves down this list of statements from the combined financial statements, the amount of specific detail in each document becomes larger. The following list illustrates this change of detail, from the specific at the low end of the list to the least specific at the top.

1. Combined Financial Statements
   and Supplemental Schedules
2. Separate Fund Financial Statements
3. Special Reports
4. Trial Balances
5. Ledgers
6. Journals
7. Source Documents

The amount of detail in each of these documents influences who will be the potential user of the report or document. For example, the general public is not interested in the detailed information available in source documents, but the financial staff of the NFP organization is *very* interested in these documents. Source documents have a specific audience orientation, and so do the other reports and documents. Figure 11–1 presents a matrix of potential users of the documents and reports generated by an NFP organization. In figure 11–1 it can be seen that the general public concentrates on the combined financial statements and special schedules, whereas a governmental agency which provided monies to the NFP organization may be concerned with special reports on the way those monies were spent, as well as supporting copies of source documents. The audit opinion is not part of any sequence of specific-generalized information, but is included in the matrix to show the type of users who are interested in it.

	User					
Statement	General Public	Higher-Level Management	Financial Staff	Reporting for Government Grants	Donors	Creditors
Combined	*	*	*		*	
Separate Fund Financials		*	*			
Trial Balance			*			
Special Schedules	*	*	*	*	*	*
Journal Entries			*			
Source Documents			*	*		
Audit Opinion	*	*	*	*	*	*

*Financial documents of major interest.

FIG. 11–1. Matrix of Users' Interest in Financial Documents

This chapter culminates with the most generalized statement in the list by illustrating the combined financial statements for the H. K. Fines Library. The next chapter analyzes the combined financial statements and the data used to prepare those statements for future trends and levels of performance.

Preparing Combined Financial Statements

The combined financial statements for the H. K. Fines Library are presented in figures 11–2, 11–3, and 11–4. Figure 11–5 presents the Notes to the Financial Statements. These statements have been prepared in a form that could be issued to the general public as well as other users. It is expected that the audit opinion is also part of the financial package issued to users of the combined financial statements. The audit opinion is explained on pages 77–81, and an illustration of the type of audit opinion which would accompany the H. K. Fines Library's combined financial statements is presented as the first audit opinion on page 79.

The combined financial statements are the SREF, the Balance Sheet, and the Statement of Changes in Financial Position. A review of the combined statements in this chapter makes it apparent that some minor changes have been made in the previously prepared financial statements for the separate funds. Several additional journal entries were recorded in the Operating Fund. These entries occurred when the Endowment Fund and the Plant Fund were explained in chapters 8 and 10 respectively, but they had not been recorded when the Operating Fund was discussed in chapter 7. (See appendix to this chapter.) These are the only additional journal entries made to the combined statements. The other changes to these statements consisted of combining the balances in several accounts into one account balance. Finally, it should be remembered that all the closing entries which were shown in the appendixes to the chapters should only be made after the combined financial statements have been prepared. These closing entries were presented (in the appendixes to chapters 7, 8, and 10) to better illustrate the entire accounting sequence for the various funds.

COMBINED SREF

The combined SREF, presented in figure 11–2, is basically a summation of the SREFs for the Operating Fund, the Endowment Fund, and the Plant Fund. The first adjustment to the combined SREF which distinguishes it from the individual SREFs relates to the additional entries to the Operating Fund, made in chapters 8 and 10 and not previously recorded. These adjustments increase the amount of revenues and the amount in the Transfer account in the unrestricted portion of the Operating Fund.

H. K. FINES LIBRARY
Statement of Support, Revenue, and Expenses and Changes in Fund Balance
Year Ended June 30, 19x3
(with Comparative Totals for 19x2)

| | Operating | | | | | June 30, 19x2 |
	Unrestricted	Restricted	Plant	Endowment	Total	Totals
Support and Revenue						
Support						
Grants (Note 1)						
Governments	$160,000.00	$ 7,500.00	—	—	$ 167,500.00	$ 90,000.00
Other	—	—	—	—	—	3,500.00
Contributions and Bequests	2,300.00	2,850.00	$ 3,200.00	—	8,350.00	24,000.00
Total Support	$162,300.00	$10,350.00	$ 3,200.00	—	$ 175,850.00	$ 117,500.00
Revenue						
Book Fines and Sales	$ 5,500.00	—	—	—	$ 5,500.00	$ 2,100.00
Photocopying	8,000.00	—	—	—	8,000.00	3,785.00
Investment Income	2,500.00	$ 200.00	—	—	2,700.00	3,000.00
Revenue from Investments—Endowment	20,000.00	—	—	—	20,000.00	—
Total Revenue	$ 36,000.00	$ 200.00	—	—	$ 36,200.00	$ 8,885.00
Total Support and Revenue	$198,300.00	$10,550.00	$ 3,200.00	—	$ 212,050.00	$ 126,385.00

Expenses (Note 4)						
Program Services						
Reference	$ 38,017.00	$ 2,850.00	$ 1,360.00	—	$ 42,227.00	$ 35,500.00
Children's Library	36,278.00	—	500.00	—	36,778.00	18,500.00
Circulation	40,849.00	—	200.00	—	41,049.00	32,750.00
Regional History	13,939.00	—	100.00	—	14,039.00	14,200.00
Handicapped Services	—	7,500.00	—	—	7,500.00	—
Total Program Services	$129,083.00	$10,350.00	$ 2,160.00	—	$ 141,593.00	$ 100,950.00
Supporting Services Administration	$ 37,442.00	$ —	$ 36,828.75	—	$ 74,270.75	$ 63,012.50
Total Expenses	$166,525.00	$10,350.00	$ 38,988.75	—	$ 215,863.75	$ 163,962.50
Excess (Deficiency) of Support and Revenues over Expenses before Capital Additions and Nonoperating Items	$ 31,775.00	$ 200.00	$ (35,788.75)	—	$ (3,813.75)	$ (37,577.50)
Prior Year Expenses on Prior Year Encumbrances (Note 6)	11,900.00	—	—	—	11,900.00	5,700.00
Excess (Deficiency) of Support and Revenues over Expenses in Current Year before Capital Additions and Nonoperating Items	$ 43,675.00	$ 200.00	$ (35,788.75)	—	$ 8,086.25	$ (31,877.50)
Capital Additions:						
Contributions	—	—	—	—	—	$ 37,000.00
Investment Income including Net Gains (Note 2)	—	—	29,890.00	46,250.00	76,140.00	73,000.00
Total Capital Additions	—	—	$ 29,890.00	$ 46,250.00	$ 76,140.00	$ 110,000.00

FIG. 11–2. Combined Statement of Support, Revenue, and Expenses and Changes in Fund Balance for H. K. Fines Library

Continued

| | Operating | | | | | June 30, 19x2 |
	Unrestricted	Restricted	Plant	Endowment	Total	Totals
Excess (Deficiency) of Support and Revenue over Expenses after Capital Additions	$ 43,675.00	$ 200.00	$ (5,898.75)	$ 46,250.00	$ 84,226.25	$ 78,122.50
Nonoperating Additions: Gain on Sale of Fixed Assets	—	—	53.75	—	53.75	—
Excess (Deficiency) of Support and Revenue over Expenses after Nonoperating Items	$ 43,675.00	$ 200.00	$ (5,845.00)	$ 46,250.00	$ 84,280.00	$ 78,122.50
Fund Balances at Beginning of Year	$ 51,575.00	—	$1,421,787.50	$1,008,000.00	$2,481,362.50	$2,408,940.00
Transfers—Principal of Indebtedness and Acquisitions	$(23,157.25)	$ (200.00)	$ 23,357.25	—	—	—
Less: Prior-Year Expenses	(11,900.00)	—	—	—	(11,900.00)	(5,700.00)
Fund Balances at End of Year	$ 60,192.75	—	$1,439,299.75	$1,054,250.00	$2,553,742.50	$2,481,362.50

FIG. 11–2. (Continued)

The combined SREF for 19x3, like SREFs for individual funds for 19x3, presents the 19x2 totals for comparison. As comparative information, this is less useful than the information given in the SREFs for individual funds, because its aggregate character makes it harder to spot specific trends in the various funds. This is an argument in favor of preparing separate financial statements for each of the funds prior to preparing combined statements.

It should be noted that the important distinction between restricted and unrestricted accounts is maintained for the Operating Fund in the combined statement. This division is recognized in all financial statements prepared for an NFP organization. Finally, another aspect of this statement should be pointed out. The transfers between funds at the bottom of the SREF always net out to zero under the total columns. This result occurs because one fund's transfer "in" is another fund's transfer "out," with a net result equal to zero.

All the numbers on the combined SREF are traceable to the individual fund's statements. As noted, the Excess (deficiency) of Support and Revenues over Expenses before capital additions and nonoperating items is $20,000 higher for the unrestricted portion of the Operating Fund because the combined statement recognizes the income that the unrestricted Operating Fund received from the Endowment Fund. In addition, the transfer account in the unrestricted portion of the Operating Fund reflects the transfer to the Plant Fund from the Operating Fund, not previously recorded.

COMBINED BALANCE SHEET

This financial statement (figure 11–3) is largely an aggregation of the amounts shown on the fund's individual balance sheets. In the combined Balance Sheet, the restricted and unrestricted portions of the Operating Fund and Plant Fund are shown separately. This distinction should be maintained throughout the combined financial statements.

The major changes in the combined Balance Sheet from the individual fund's statements relate to the Operating Fund. The changes develop from journalizing the transfers of cash by the Operating Fund to the Plant Fund and the Cash received by the Operating Fund from the revenues earned through the Endowment Fund. These changes caused a net decrease of $3,357.25 in the Cash account and the undesignated Fund Balance in the unrestricted portion of the Operating Fund. The $8,900 revenue received by the restricted portion of

H. K. FINES LIBRARY
Balance Sheet
June 30, 19x3
(with Comparative Totals for 19x2)

Assets	Operating		Plant Fund		Endowment	Total	June 30, 19x2 Totals
	Unrestricted	Restricted	Unrestricted	Restricted			
Current Assets							
Cash	$14,892.75	$41,950.00	$ 56,527.25	$ 1,600.00	$ 31,250.00	$ 146,220.00	$ 103,500.00
Marketable Securities (Note 2)	25,000.00	—	138,000.00	—	—	163,000.00	171,000.00
Repurchase Premium Receivable	2,500.00	—	—	—	—	2,500.00	—
State Grant Receivable	—	—	—	—	—	—	16,000.00
Pledges Receivable, at Estimated Net Realizable Value	—	—	—	—	—	—	7,200.00
Prepaid Expenses and Other Current Assets	17,300.00	—	—	—	—	17,300.00	6,750.00
Total Current Assets	$59,692.75	$41,950.00	$ 194,527.25	$ 1,600.00	$ 31,250.00	$ 329,020.00	$ 304,450.00
Investments (Note 2)	$17,000.00	—	—	$714,000.00	$1,023,000.00	$1,754,000.00	$1,697,000.00
Land, Building, and Equipment—at Cost, less Accumulated Depreciation of $51,700 and $40,335 Respectively (Note 3)	—	—	$1,571,265.00	—	—	$1,571,265.00	$1,550,000.00
Inexhaustible Collections and Books (Note 1)	—	—	—	—	—	—	—
Total Assets	$76,692.75	$41,950.00	$1,765,792.25	$715,600.00	$1,054,250.00	$3,654,285.00	$3,551,450.00

Current Liabilities:							
Accounts Payable, Accrued Expenses, and Current Portion of Long-Term Debt	$16,500.00	$ 7,500.00	$ 26,492.50	—	—	$ 50,492.50	$ 28,387.50
Deferred Restricted Contributions (Note 5)	—	34,450.00	—	$715,600.00	—	$ 750,050.00	$ 726,700.00
Total Current Liabilities	$16,500.00	$41,950.00	$ 26,492.50	$715,600.00	—	$ 800,542.50	$ 755,087.50
Long-Term Debt (Note 4)	—	—	300,000.00	—	—	300,000.00	315,000.00
Total Liabilities	$16,500.00	$41,950.00	$ 326,492.50	$715,600.00	—	$1,100,542.50	$1,070,087.50
Fund Balance							
Unrestricted							
Designated by Board for							
Office Equipment	—	—	—	—	—	—	$ 4,945.00
Investments	$17,000.00	—	—	—	—	$ 17,000.00	$ 17,000.00
Undesignated	32,242.75	—	$1,439,299.75	—	—	$1,471,542.50	$1,432,967.50
Restricted	10,950.00	—	—	—	$1,054,250.00	$1,065,200.00	$1,026,450.00
Total Fund Balances	$60,192.75	—	$1,439,299.75	—	$1,054,250.00	$2,553,742.50	$2,481,362.50
Total Liabilities and Fund Balances	$76,692.75	$41,950.00	$1,765,792.25	$715,600.00	$1,054,250.00	$3,654,285.00	$3,551,450.00

Copyright © 1979 by the American Institute of Certified Public Accountants, Inc.

Fig. 11–3. Combined Balance Sheet for H. K. Fines Library

the Operating Fund from the Endowment Fund is incorporated into this Balance Sheet. This revenue change increased the Cash account by $8,900 and the Deferred Restricted Revenue account by an equal amount from the balances in the previously prepared Balance Sheet for the Operating Fund.

The only other changes relate to the combining of account balances in the combined Balance Sheet. For example, the Cash and Petty Cash accounts were combined into one total. Several "Due from" accounts were combined into the Prepaid Expenses and Other Current Assets account. The current liabilities have been combined into one account. The reason for combining these accounts is to eliminate unnecessary detail on the combined Balance Sheet. A difference exists between the amount of detail on financial statements for individual funds and the financial statements for reporting to the general public. The financial statements prepared for the general public should not be so abbreviated as to be misleading, but they do not have to contain all the detail on the individual financial statements for the various funds. These are the major changes on the combined Balance Sheet. The comparative columns for the two years allow comparisons to be made, but the detail in these comparative figures is not as great as on the individual balance sheets.

COMBINED STATEMENT OF CHANGES IN FINANCIAL POSITION

Figure 11–4 illustrates the Combined Statement of Changes in Financial Position for the H. K. Fines Library. The changes in this statement from the individual fund's statements are caused by the increase in revenues by the Operating Fund and the additional transfers out of the Operating Fund. The increase in the Transfer account under the unrestricted portion of the Operating Fund is caused by a $23,357.25 increase in transfers out of the Operating Fund, and the Excess in this same column is $20,000 larger than it was under the individual Operating Fund statement, due to the increase in revenues not previously recognized in the Operating Fund.

These changes also account for the $3,357.25 difference ($23,357.25 − $20,000) in the Cash account under Changes in Working Capital Components at the bottom of the statement. The net effect of the change is to cause a reduction in "Increase in working capital" in the unrestricted portion of the Operating Fund, from the $11,975 shown in chapter 7 to the $8,617.75 shown in figure 11–4.

The restricted portion of the Operating Fund was affected by an increase in Deferred Restricted Contributions of $8,900. This change is apparent when the combined statement is compared with the separately prepared Statement of Changes in Financial Position for the Operating Fund. In the Uses of Working Capital section, the Deferred Restricted Income also increased by $8,900. The net effect of these changes is zero. Under the Changes in Working Capital Components section, the Cash account and the liability account, Deferred Restricted Contributions, increased by $8,900. Again, the net effect of this change is zero. In other aspects, the Combined Statement of Changes in Financial Position is the same as the individual statements that appeared in the previous chapters.

It should be noted that the combined statement presents the changes in working capital for only the Operating Fund and the Plant Fund. A Statement of Changes in Financial Position was not prepared for the Endowment Fund, as it was not considered necessary for accurate financial reporting. A final aspect of this combined statement is that the "total" columns for June 30, 19x3, can be compared with the totals for June 30, 19x2, to highlight the changes in working capital that have occurred between the two years.

COMBINED NOTES TO FINANCIAL STATEMENTS

The combined Notes to the Financial Statements (figure 11–5) represent the comprehensive notes to the financial statements. The notes combine the notes from the other funds' statements in the same format that was illustrated in the previous five chapters and the appendixes to those chapters. The major change in these series of combined notes relates to "Note 2—Investments." The investments listed in this note are not subdivided into restricted and unrestricted portions in the same manner as were the notes to the Plant Fund. In this note, it would be possible to disclose information about the rate of return, exclusive of net gains and losses on investments, and the annual total return, based on market value. Any rates of return shown here should clearly indicate what they are based upon. The Combined Notes to the Financial Statements is basically an aggregation of the notes in the previous chapters, without significant changes.

H. K. FINES LIBRARY
Statement of Changes in Financial Position
Year Ended June 30, 19x3
(with Comparative Totals for 19x2)

	Operating		Plant			June 30, 19x2
	Unrestricted	Restricted	Unrestricted	Restricted	Total	Totals
Sources of Working Capital:						
Excess (Deficiency) of Support and Revenues over Expenses before Capital Additions	$ 31,775.00	$ 200.00	$(35,735.00)	—	$ (3,760.00)	$ (37,577.50)
Capital Additions	—	—	29,890.00	—	29,890.00	77,000.00
Excess (Deficiency) of Support and Revenues over Expenses after Capital Additions	$ 31,775.00	$ 200.00	$ (5,845.00)	—	$ 26,130.00	$ 39,422.50
Deduct: Gain on Sale of Fixed Investments Gain on Sale of Assets	—	—	$ (53.75)	—	$ (53.75)	$ (2,690.00)
Add: Items Not Using Working Capital Depreciation	—	—	13,928.75	—	13,928.75	13,700.00
Loss on Sale of Investments	—	—	—	$ 10,100.00	$ 10,100.00	—
Working Capital from Operations	$ 31,775.00	$ 200.00	$ 8,030.00	$ 10,100.00	$ 50,105.00	$ 50,432.50
Sale of Fixed Assets	—	—	$ 835.00	—	$ 835.00	—
Sale of Investments	—	—	—	$ 24,900.00	$ 24,900.00	$ 25,690.00
Deferred Restricted Contributions Received	—	$ 19,250.00	—	3,600.00	22,850.00	27,000.00
Total Sources of Working Capital	$ 31,775.00	$ 19,450.00	$ 8,865.00	$ 38,600.00	$ 98,690.00	$ 103,122.50
Uses of Working Capital:						
Purchases of Fixed Assets	—	—	$(35,975.00)	—	$ (35,975.00)	$ 197,000.00
Purchases of Investments	—	—	—	$(37,000.00)	(37,000.00)	—

Reduction of Long-Term Debt	—	—	(15,000.00)	—	(15,000.00)	15,000.00
Deferred Restricted Income	$(23,157.25)	$(19,250.00)	—	(3,600.00)	(22,850.00)	27,000.00
Transfers between Funds	—	(200.00)	23,357.25	—	—	—
Total Uses of Working Capital	$(23,157.25)	$(19,450.00)	$(27,617.75)	$(40,600.00)	$(110,825.00)	$(239,000.00)
Increases (Decreases) in Working Capital	$ 8,617.75	—	$(18,752.75)	$(2,000.00)	$(12,135.00)	$(135,877.50)
Changes in Working Capital Components						
Increase (Decrease) in Current Assets						
Cash	$(2,607.25)	$ 27,250.00	$ 24,727.25	$ 1,600.00	$ 50,970.00	$(143,540.00)
Petty Cash	500.00	—	—	—	500.00	—
Marketable Securities	25,000.00	—	(33,000.00)	—	(8,000.00)	500.00
Repurchase Premium Receivable	2,500.00	—	—	—	2,500.00	—
State Grant Receivable	(16,000.00)	—	—	—	(16,000.00)	8,900.00
Pledges Receivable	(7,200.00)	—	—	—	(7,200.00)	7,200.00
Due from Restricted Fund	7,500.00	—	—	—	7,500.00	—
Due from Estate of E. Parsons	2,300.00	—	—	—	2,300.00	—
Prepaid Expenses	750.00	—	—	—	750.00	(5,850.00)
(Increase) Decrease in Current Liabilities	$ 12,742.75	$ 27,250.00	$ (8,272.75)	$ 1,600.00	$ 33,320.00	$(132,790.00)
Accounts Payable	$ 10,375.00	—	—	—	$ 10,375.00	$ 2,625.00
Interest Payable	—	—	$(10,480.00)	—	(10,480.00)	(1,012.50)
Due to State Unemployment Fund	(3,000.00)	—	—	—	(3,000.00)	—
Due to Federal Government	(10,000.00)	—	—	—	(10,000.00)	—
Due to Unrestricted Fund	—	(7,500.00)	—	—	(7,500.00)	—
Deferred Restricted Contributions	—	(19,750.00)	—	(3,600.00)	(23,350.00)	(4,700.00)
Wages Payable	(1,500.00)	—	—	—	(1,500.00)	—
	$ (4,125.00)	$(27,250.00)	$(10,480.00)	$(3,600.00)	$(45,455.00)	$ (3,087.50)
Increase (Decrease) in Working Capital	$ 8,617.75	$ —	$(18,752.75)	$(2,000.00)	$(12,135.00)	$(135,877.50)

Copyright © 1979 by the American Institute of Certified Public Accountants, Inc.

FIG. 11–4. Combined Statement of Changes in Financial Position for H. K. Fines Library

Note 1, Summary of Significant Accounting Policies

The financial statements of the H. K. Fines Library have been prepared on the accrual basis. The significant accounting policies followed are described below to enhance the usefulness of the financial statements to the reader.

Fund Accounting

To ensure observance of limitations and restrictions placed on the use of resources available to the library, the accounts of the library are maintained in accordance with the principles of fund accounting. This is the procedure by which resources for various purposes are classified for accounting and reporting purposes into funds established according to their nature and purposes. Separate accounts are maintained for each fund; however, in the accompanying financial statements, funds that have similar characteristics have been combined into fund groups. Accordingly, all financial transactions have been recorded and reported by fund group.

The assets, liabilities, and fund balances of the library are reported in three self-balancing fund groups as follows:

Operating funds. These funds include unrestricted and restricted resources. They represent the portion of expendable funds that is available for support of library operations.

Plant funds. These funds represent resources restricted for plant acquisition and funds expended for plant.

Endowment funds. These funds are subject to restrictions or gift instruments requiring in perpetuity that the principal be invested and the income only be used.

Expendable Restricted Resources

Operating and plant funds restricted by the donor, grantor, or other outside party for particular operating purposes or for plant acquisition are deemed to be earned and reported as revenues of operating funds or as additions to plant funds, respectively, when the library has incurred expenditures in compliance with the specific restrictions. Such amounts received but not yet earned are reported as restricted deferred amounts.

Plant Assets and Depreciation

Uses of operating funds for plant acquisitions and principal debt service payments are accounted for as transfers to plant funds. Proceeds from the sale of plant assets, if unrestricted, are transferred to operating fund balances, or, if restricted, to deferred amounts restricted for plant acquisitions. Depreciation of buildings and equipment is provided over the estimated useful lives of the respective assets on a straight-line basis.

FIG. 11–5. Notes to Combined Financial Statements. These footnotes to the financial statements are based on the guidelines outlined in Statement of Position 78-10, *Accounting Principles and Reporting Practices for Certain Nonprofit Organization* (New York: AICPA, 1979).

Grants

The library records income from unrestricted grants in the period designated by the grantor.

Inexhaustible Collections and Books

Because the values of the existing inexhaustible collections, including research books, are not readily determinable, the library has not capitalized them. Collections that are exhaustible are capitalized and included with equipment in the financial statements and are amortized over their estimated useful lives. Accessions and deaccessions during 19x2 and 19x3 were not significant. Books used in the circulating library have not been capitalized because their estimated useful lives are less than one year.

Other Matters

All gains and losses arising from the sale, collection, or other disposition of investments and other noncash assets are accounted for in the fund that owned the assets. Ordinary income from investments, receivables, and the like is accounted for in the fund owning the assets, except for income derived from the investments of endowment funds, which is accounted for, if unrestricted, as revenue of the expendable operating fund or, if restricted, as deferred amounts until the terms of the restriction have been met.

Legally enforceable pledges less an allowance for uncollectible amounts are recorded as receivables in the year made. Pledges for support of current operations are recorded as operating fund support. Pledges for support of future operations and plant acquisitions are recorded as deferred amounts in the respective funds to which they apply.

Encumbrances represent obligations in the form of purchase orders, contracts, or other commitments which have been appropriated, but for which no liability has yet been incurred.

Note 2, Investments

Investments are presented in the financial statements in the aggregate at the lower of cost (amortized, in the case of bonds) or fair market value.

	Cost	Market
Operating Fund	$ 42,000	$ 46,500
Plant Fund:		
Unrestricted	138,000	167,000
Restricted	714,000	735,000
Endowment	1,023,000	1,079,000
	$1,917,000	$2,027,500

Continued

Investments are composed of the following:

	Cost	Market
Corporate stocks and bonds	$1,373,000	$1,460,500
U.S. Government Obligations	509,000	532,000
Municipal bonds	10,000	10,000
Repurchase Agreements	25,000	25,000
	$1,917,000	$2,027,500

The determination of fair market value is calculated by aggregating all current marketable securities. At June 30, 19x3, there was unrealized gain of $110,500 pertaining to the current portfolio. This portfolio had a cost on June 30, 19x2, of $1,868,000 and a market value of $1,956,000. A net realized gain of $29,750 and a net realized loss of $10,100 was included in the determination of Excess (deficiency) of Support and Revenue over Expenses after Capital Additions for 19x3. The cost of the securities sold was based on a first-in, first-out method in both years.

Note 3, Plant Assets and Depreciation

A summary of plant assets follows.

Land	$1,000,000
Buildings	525,000
Equipment	138,000
	$1,663,300
Less: Accumulated Depreciation	(92,035)
	$1,571,265

Note 4, Long-Term Debt

A summary of long-term debt follows.

8% mortgage payable in semiannual installments of $3,500 for 15 years and a balloon payment at the end of that period	$263,000
9% unsecured notes payable to a bank due in quarterly installments of $2,000	37,000
	$300,000

FIG. 11-5. (Continued)

Other Financial Information Issued in Conjunction with Combined Financial Statements

The three financial statements and Notes to the Financial Statements should be issued together. Included with these statements and notes

The 8% mortgage payable was incurred in 19x1. Building and land with a net book value of $285,000 as of June 30, 19x1, are pledged as collateral on the mortgage. No interest is to be accrued until January 1, 19x3, and at that time for only six months' interest. The first principal payment is made at that time also.

Note 5, Changes in Deferred Restricted Contributions

	Operating Funds	Plant Funds
Balances at beginning of year	$14,700	$712,000
Additions:		
Contributions and Bequests	20,000	
Investment Income	10,100	13,700
	$44,800	$725,700
Deductions:		
Funds expended during the year	(10,350)	—
Loss of Sale of Restricted Investments	—	(10,100)
Balance at end of year	$34,450	$715,600

Note 6, Current-Year Expenses on Prior-Year Encumbrances

The amount encumbered at the end of the 19x2 was $11,700. During the fiscal year ending June 30, 19x3, expenditures on these encumbrances totaled $11,900.

Note 7, Commitments and Contingencies

The library receives a substantial amount of its support from federal, state, and local governments. A significant reduction in the level of this support, if this were to occur, may have an effect on the library's programs and activities.

should be the audit opinion from the independent certified public accountant who examined the financial statements to see if they have been prepared under generally accepted accounting principles. (For additional information about the importance of an audit opinion, see pp. 77–81.) An example of an audit opinion which accompanies combined financial statements, prepared under generally accepted accounting principles, is illustrated on page 79.

The audit opinion covers the three financial statements and the notes to the financial statements. If other supplementary information is included in the financial report of the NFP organization, the audit opinion does not directly cover these supplemental schedules and reports. A written statement from the independent certified public accountant about the supplemental schedules should not be considered an audit opinion. An example of the type of statement which may be expressed by the independent certified public accountant on the supplemental information is illustrated in figure 11–6. When the first audit opinion on page 79 is compared with figure 11–6, it is apparent that the latter is not an audit opinion, although it provides assurances about the supplemental schedules.

To the Trustees of the   June 30, 19x4
NFP Library

Our examination was made for the purpose of forming an opinion on the basic financial statements taken as a whole. The following schedules are presented for the purpose of additional analysis and are not a required part of the basic financial statements. Such information has been subjected to the auditing procedures applied in the examination of the basic financial statements and in our opinion is fairly stated in all material respects in relation to the basic financial statements taken as a whole.

Certified Public Accountants

FIG. 11–6. Letter of Assurance on Supplemental Schedules from Independent Certified Public Accountants

The type of supplemental information which may be included as part of the financial report prepared by an NFP organization can include the following documents:

1. A schedule which compares actual with estimated revenues for the Operating Fund during the current year.
2. A schedule which compares actual expenses and encumbrances with budgeted appropriations in the Operating Fund to determine the differences that occurred during the current year.

The first supplemental schedule is a statement which compares actual revenues with the revenues which had been estimated at the beginning of the year to be collected from the various governments and other sources. This information can be important, because if predictions are not accurate, they can upset the spending plans of the organization. Inaccurate predictions may mean that adjustments are necessary to correct the methods that are used for predictive purposes. This type of statement relates specifically to the Operating Fund, rather than the Endowment or Plant Fund. A statement of this nature for the H. K. Fines Library is illustrated in figure 11–7 and is

H. K. FINES LIBRARY
Operating Fund
Statement of Comparison Between Budget Estimates
and Actual Revenue and Support
Year Ended June 30, 19x3
(with Comparative Totals for 19x2)

	19x3			19x2
	Budget Estimate	Actual Revenue	Actual Over (Under) Budget	Actual Revenue
Support and Revenues				
City of Fines	$ 78,000	$ 68,000	$ (10,000)	$60,000
Backlog County	66,000	66,000	—	30,000
State	26,000	26,000	—	—
Book Fines	2,500	2,700	200	1,500
Book Sales	3,000	2,800	(200)	600
Photocopying	8,000	8,000	—	3,785
Investment Income	—	2,500	2,500	3,000
Endowment Income	—	20,000	20,000	—
Miscellaneous	—	2,300	2,300	—
Transfers	—	200	200	—
Totals	$183,500	$198,500	$ 15,000	$98,885

Fig. 11–7. Statement of Comparison between Budget Estimates and Actual Revenue and Support

entitled Statement of Comparison between Budget Estimates and Actual Revenue and Support. The statement is simply a comparison between the amount of support and revenue which were actually collected from the various sources and the amounts estimated to be collected from these sources and recorded as Estimated Revenues in the journal at the beginning of the year. The information on revenues for preparation of the statement is quickly available in the Revenue ledger.

In the statement, the column entitled "Actual Over (Under) Budget" discloses the differences between the actual revenues and the estimated revenues. This column shows whether budgeted amounts have been over- or underestimated. The column entitled "19x2, Actual Revenue" provides the actual revenue from the previous year to compare with the actual revenues of the current year. In this manner, any trends in revenue collections over the two-year period become apparent.

In reviewing figure 11–7, it is apparent that budget estimates should have been made in the Operating Fund for investment income, endowment income, miscellaneous revenue, and transfers, as there are no balances in these accounts under the "Budget Estimate" column. When no budget estimates are provided under the account Estimated Revenues at the beginning of the year, there is underestimation of the revenues, with the result that spending plans are curtailed. Figure 11–7 makes it clear that the revenues received from the three governments have increased over the two-year period (the largest increase came from the county). In addition, there has been a significant increase in total revenues from the period ending June 30, 19x2, to June 30, 19x3.

Finally, in preparing the Statement of Comparison between Budget Estimates and Actual Revenue and Support the basis of accounting between the estimated revenues and actual revenues should be the same. The cash basis of accounting for estimated budget revenues should not be mixed with the accrual for recording the receipt of actual revenues. Without this consistency, no meaningful comparisons can be made.

Another type of supplemental schedule which can be developed as part of the financial report for distribution to the general public is a comparison between the actual expenses and encumbrances in the Operating Fund with the budget appropriations established at the beginning of the year. The purpose of this type of statement is to illustrate whether the appropriations under the finalized budget are actually used as guidelines within the organization. As these appropriations have been authorized by the board of the NFP organization, actual spending should not exceed the appropriations (except under special circumstances). In some cases, it may be impossible to comply with budget appropriations, but these should be considered extreme circumstances. If there are significant discrepancies between the appropriations and actual expenses and encumbrances, these differences should be further examined to determine the reason. A schedule of these differences is useful in highlighting how well the NFP organization is operating within its budget appropriations.

An example of this type of schedule is provided in figure 11–8 for the H. K. Fines Library. It is called the Statement of Comparison between Budget Appropriations and Actual Expenses and Encumbrances, and it separates the budgeted amounts and expenses and encumbrances according to programs. There may be other ways to separate these amounts, but the example is based on programs. The "actual encumbrances" in this statement are encumbrances that are still outstanding at the end of the 19x3 fiscal year.

The amounts shown under the "Actual Expenses and Encumbrances" column is equal to the amount on the SREF for the Operating Fund, except when those amounts include expenses for prior-year encumbrances. In those cases, these encumbrances have been deducted from the amount shown in the "Actual Expenses and Encumbrances" column. This column records only the expenses for the *current* fiscal year; therefore, any payments for prior-year encumbrances need to be deducted. The amounts under the "Budget Appropriation" column record the amount of the budget recognized at the beginning of the year in the Appropriations account and its subsidiary accounts. If there had been a large number of adjustments to the original appropriation, it would be possible to use budget columns with "before" and "after" adjustments.[1]

Under each program classification are a number of object expense classifications, such as supplies and automobile expense. Only a few of these object expenses and encumbrances were actually recorded in chapter 7;[2] the others have been added to the statement to illustrate

1. Although there were some minor adjustments to the original budget appropriation for the H. K. Fines Library, these were considered to be minor adjustments and no "before" and "after" columns were used.

2. The following expenses and encumbrances were included as part of the subsidiary accounts in chapter 7: Salary and Benefits (Payroll Expenses), Equipment Rental, Building Rental (Lease), and Miscellaneous. The following expenses and encumbrances were not included as subsidiary accounts in chapter 7: Supplies, Automobile Expense, Postage, Travel, Books, and Telephone. These object expenses could be added to the journal entries in chapter 7 by including additional subsidiary accounts in the entries. These additional subsidiary journal entries were not included in chapter 7 in order to keep the illustration as simple as possible.

H. K. FINES LIBRARY
Operating Fund
Statement of Comparison Between Budget Appropriations and Actual Expenses and Encumbrances
Year Ended June 30, 19x3

	Budget Appropriations	Actual Expenses & Encumbrances	Actual (Over) Under Budget	June 30, 19x2 Actual Expenses & Encumbrances
Administrative				
Supplies	$ 1,000	$ 1,200	$ (200)	$ 1,500
Automobile Expense	3,000	1,300	1,700	1,000
Postage	4,000	3,000	1,000	2,500
Salary and Benefits	27,000	28,300	(1,300)	16,250
Equipment Rental	400	42	358	450
Building Rental	7,000	5,500	1,500	—
Travel	2,000	1,200	800	2,000
Miscellaneous	600	350	250	300
	$ 45,000	$ 40,892	$ 4,108	$24,000
Reference				
Books	$ 5,700	$ 6,000	$ (300)	$ 5,000
Salary and Benefits	22,100	22,100	—	15,550
Telephone	1,750	1,000	750	1,250
Postage	2,325	1,000	1,325	1,500
Equipment Rentals	250	202	48	—
Travel	1,200	1,000	200	1,500
Miscellaneous	175	15	160	200
	$ 33,500	$ 31,317	$ 2,183	$25,000
Children's Library				
Books	$ 4,300	$ 4,500	$ (200)	$ 2,500
Postage	1,020	500	520	1,000

Salary and Benefits	31,000	30,600	400	9,150
Telephone	300	350	(50)	200
Equipment Rentals	200	178	22	—
Miscellaneous	180	150	30	150
	$ 37,000	$ 36,278	$ 722	$13,000
Circulation				
Records	$ 500	$ 400	$ 100	$ 300
Books	700	600	100	400
Salary and Benefits	28,000	25,400	2,600	18,550
Telephone	1,500	1,250	250	1,250
Periodicals	5,300	6,000	(700)	5,700
Equipment Rentals	400	189	211	—
Travel	2,000	1,750	250	—
Miscellaneous	100	60	40	100
	$ 38,500	$ 35,649	$ 2,851	$26,300
Regional History				
Books	$ 3,000	$ 3,200	$ (200)	$ 1,000
Salary and Benefits	9,800	9,800	—	9,000
Postage	500	400	100	200
Telephone	475	400	75	200
Equipment Rentals	125	89	36	200
Travel	—	—	—	—
Miscellaneous	100	50	50	500
	$ 14,000	$ 13,939	$ 61	$11,000
Totals	$168,000	$158,075	$ 9,925	$99,300

Fig. 11–8. Statement of Comparison between Budget Appropriations and Actual Expenses and Encumbrances

the type of object expenses and encumbrances that would normally appear in this type of schedule.

When the statement in figure 11−8 is reviewed, it can be seen that there are differences between the amount budgeted and the amount of expenses and encumbrances shown in the column entitled ''Actual (Over) Under Budget.'' These differences are both over and under the budgeted amounts. Although it may appear that only when the actual amounts are over the budgeted amounts an examination should be instituted, all significant differences should be reviewed to determine their cause. To be ''under budget'' is generally considered good, but if excessive amounts were approved initially, being ''under budget'' is not so significant. Therefore, if actual spending is significantly below the budgeted amounts, they should be investigated to determine why so much was initially allocated to this budget classification.

For example, in Circulation, Salary and Benefits expense was $2,600 under the budgeted amount. This difference could be explained by personnel leaving the library in the latter part of the fiscal year and not earning the salary which had been allocated. In any case, if this difference is considered significant, it should be investigated. For the same reason, it may be necessary to investigate why actual expenses and encumbrances are $1,300 over the budgeted amounts for Salary and Benefits in Administration.

These statements provide two examples of the type of supplemental schedules which can accompany an NFP organization's financial report. Another type of document that can accompany the financial report of the NFP organization is the ''transmittal letter,'' which is addressed to the general public and the board, and is written by the director of the NFP organization. The purpose of this letter is to highlight the financial environment the NFP organization is facing in the current year and in future years. The letter should point out that the responsibility for the financial statements rests with the management of the NFP organization, as the financial statements were prepared by the organization. In addition, it should be stated that the management of the NFP organization believes all necessary information and disclosures have been made to make the statements accurate and ensure maximum understanding for the reader. Also, the guidelines under which the statements have been prepared (i.e., generally accepted accounting principles) should be mentioned. If any environmental factors affect the NFP organization's operations, now or in the future, they should be mentioned. For example, if cutbacks in funding have occurred, they should be disclosed. The letter should be signed by the director of the NFP organization. An example of a

Ladies and Gentlemen:

Enclosed herein is the financial report of the H. K. Fines Library as of June 30, 19x3. The accuracy, completeness, and fairness of this report is the responsibility of the management of the H. K. Fines Library. Every effort has been made to ensure that the reports are accurately prepared and that all the necessary disclosures have been made to ensure the reader will understand the statements.

The accompanying reports, which have been prepared under generally accepted accounting principles, consist of two sections:

1. The financial statements, notes to the financial statements, and the auditor's opinion.
2. The supplemental financial schedules which highlight specific financial information about the Library's operations.

The Library is in sound financial condition as of the year ending June 30, 19x3, but there are several environmental factors affecting the Library which are of concern to its future functioning. In recent years, there have been cut-backs in the grants and funding available to the Library, especially from the Federal Government. During the fiscal year ending June 30, 19x3, the Library has been fortunate to receive an increase in support from the State and County. It is expected that this is only a temporary increase, and if past trends continue, the Library will be faced with making certain curtailments in its present level of services to the community. Every effort will be made to control costs prior to the curtailment of any of our programs.

A second factor affecting the Library's operations relates to the construction of a new annex. In order for construction to begin on the annex, certain variances from the city's building code need to be approved. At the present time, these changes are being considered by the city council, and the Library anticipates that these variances will be approved.

Efforts have been made over the past years to upgrade the financial reporting of the H. K. Fines Library in order to provide better financial information to the City Council and the citizens of the City of Fines and Backlog County. We hope that you will find the following financial statements useful in understanding your Library.

Respectfully submitted,

Sally Fines
Director

Fig. 11–9. Transmittal Letter

transmittal letter for the H. K. Fines Library is presented in figure 11–9.

These supplemental financial schedules and documents have been prepared to illustrate the schedules that can accompany the three major financial statements for an NFP organization. Depending on the specific conditions of the NFP organization, other types of supplemental schedules can be prepared which would provide disclosures about the restricted income generated from the endowments, along with the purposes for which it is to be used, or information about the fixed assets of the organization. The list of supplemental financial schedules is not limited to any three or four schedules, as their purpose is to provide additional information about the financial operations of the NFP organization. Obviously, those financial conditions vary from one organization to another.

The report which is issued to the public about the financial operations of the NFP organization is illustrated in figure 11–10, where it can be seen that the transmittal letter relates to all the financial statements and schedules in the financial report; and it is included in the first section of the financial report issued to the public. The major financial statements are included in the second section o the financial report. Included with these financial statements are Notes to the Financial Statements and the audit opinion. The supplemental financial schedules follow the main financial statements. The types of supplemental schedules in the third section can vary. The ones included in this illustration are the Statement of Comparison between Budget Estimates and Actual Revenue and Support and the Statement of Comparison between Budget Appropriations and Actual Expenses and Encumbrances.

Exercise 11–1. Combined Statements and Supplemental Schedules

1. Explain the difference between the consolidated and combined financial statements. For an NFP organization, which method is more likely to be used?

2. Last year was the first year the Henry Mooreville Library had its financial statements prepared on an accrual basis. Prior to this time, a cash-based accounting system was used. Several older members of the Library Board objected to this "new" method of accounting when the financial statements were issued last year. Although the director and the bookkeeper made extensive efforts to explain the accrual method of accounting and its advantages, they are worried that this debate will again be a serious problem when the financial statements are presented to the board this year. Can you suggest any type of supplemental schedule which might help to satisfy the members of the board who object to use of the accrual method?

Transmittal Letter

Basic
Financial
Documents:

SREF

Balance
Sheet

Statement of Changes
in Financial Position

Notes to the Financial
Statements

Audit
Opinion

Supplemental
Schedules:

Statement of Comparison between
Budget Appropriations and Actual
Expenses and Encumbrances

Statement of Comparison between
Budget Estimates and Actual
Revenue and Support

Fig. 11–10. Components of an NFP Organization's Financial Report

Review of Accounting Cycle

In chapter 2 the accounting cycle for an NFP organization was outlined in an eight-step procedure. These eight steps are continually repeated to generate the financial statements which were prepared in the earlier sections of this chapter. Each of these steps is reviewed in this section of chapter 11 in order to highlight certain aspects of the process, as well as to indicate the chapters in which each of these steps was previously explained. Before entries are journalized, the transactions must be carefully analyzed. Step 1 outlines this procedure.

1. *Analyzing Transactions.* This process involves analysis of the source documents such as invoices and purchase orders to determine the proper accounts to debit and credit. This procedure also involves the accounting analysis of budgets established by the governing board, which has fiscal responsibility over the NFP organization. (See chapters 4, 5, 7, 8, and 10.)

Skill in analyzing source documents for the type of debit and credit entry develops as more experience with this process is gained. The type of documents that are received by any organization is somewhat repetitive, so that this analysis requires familiarity with the documents to be performed effectively, rather than extensive training.

CASH DISBURSEMENTS JOURNAL

Date	Description	Check Number	Cash Credit	BUDGETARY Encumbrances (Un) Code No.	Amt.
May 1	Vendor Co.	1406	2500 –	2041	2500 –
May 3	ABC Supply	1407	3000 –	2042	3000 –
May 4	Plant Fund	1408	2000 –		
May 5	ABC Supply	1409	1100 –	2042	1100 –
May 6	Parsons Estate	1410	300 –		
May 9	Payroll	1411	5100 –	2044	5100 –

FIG. 11–11. Cash Disbursements Journal

2. *Journalizing Transactions*. These procedures involve the recording of debits and credits in the general journal and subsidiary
journals. Journalizing transactions occurs after the source documents
have been analyzed. The journalization of a transaction is its entry
point into the accounting system. (See chapters 4, 5, 7, 8, and 10.)

A large portion of the material in this text has been devoted to the
journalizing of transactions in the general journal. Depending on the
frequency of transactions, it may be possible to develop special journals which reduce the work of the journalizing process. It is possible
to use a special journal for cash disbursements, cash receipts, and
purchases. The Cash Disbursements journal records every cash payment made by the NFP organization, and the Cash Receipts journal
records all cash flowing into the organization. The Purchases journal
would record all approved purchases made by the organization. Examples of the Cash Disbursements and Cash Receipts journals are
presented in figures 11–11 and 11–12, respectively.

In recording transactions in figure 11–11, supporting information
is provided about the cash payment. Once the purchased items have
been received and the invoice is approved for payment, the check is
written. The "Date" column records the date the check is written.
The "Description" column provides a space for the name of the

CASH RECEIPTS JOURNAL

		1	2	3	4	5	6	7
Date	Description	Cash Debit	Revenues/Support		Deferred Restricted Contributions		MISCELLANEOUS CREDITS	
			Code #	Amt. (Cr.)	Code #	Amt. (Cr.)	Code #	Amt.

FIG. 11–12. Cash Receipts Journal

company or the fund receiving the payment. The "Cash" column records the amount of the check, and the payment is also recorded as a debit to an expense.[3] As figure 11–11 is only an example of a Cash Disbursements journal, only two expenses, Personnel and Supplies, are listed in the journal. The amounts recorded as expenses are also listed under the "Total Expenses" column. If budgetary accounts are used, encumbrances need to be reversed when the payment is made, and the reversal is shown under the columns "Encumbrances (Un)" and "Encumbrances (R)." (These two columns represent unrestricted and restricted encumbrances.) No separate column is established for the account Reserve for Encumbrances because encumbrances and reserve for encumbrances have equal balances. Therefore, the "Encumbrances" columns can provide all the information about the reserve for encumbrances. The "Miscellaneous Debits" column records debits that do not "fit" under the other columns. (Additional descriptions about use of this journal are provided shortly.)

The second special journal that is illustrated is the Cash Receipts journal in figure 11–12, which records all the inflows of cash to the organization. Again, there are "Date" and "Description" columns. The former records when the cash was received, and the latter names the source of the cash receipt. The "Cash" column is for all debit entries to the Cash account, and the other columns are for the credit portion of the entry which generated the cash inflow. For example, typical credits are for revenue and support, such as library fines, book sales, or grants. The "Deferred Restricted Contributions" column records cash inflows that are restricted as to use. The "Miscellaneous Credits" column records credits which do not belong in other columns.

These two journals illustrate the meaning of "special" journals. The advantages of special journals become apparent when the posting process is considered.

3. *Posting.* The posting process involves transferring entries from the journals to the accounts in the ledgers. The ledgers are a listing of all the accounts with their balances. This procedure may occur less frequently than the journalizing process. (See chapter 2.)

The posting process is a mechanical operation which transfers the amounts already entered in the journal into the ledgers, where the

---

3. The expenses in the Cash Disbursements Journal are classified on an object basis rather than a program basis. Prior financial statements classified expenses according to a program basis. It is possible to switch from one method to the other, depending on the needs of the user of the financial information.

balances in each account can be summarized and totaled. Posting is usually done on a monthly basis so that monthly financial data can be summarized. Throughout the explanations of the Operating Fund, Endowment Fund, and the Plant Fund, the posting process was implicit. Preparation of the financial statements in the appendixes required that T accounts be posted to in order to generate the proper account balances. It is important that the posting process be accurately done; otherwise, errors can appear in the financial statements.

As indicated, the special journals make the posting process easier by reducing the number of postings to frequently used accounts, like Cash. With a general journal, each cash payment recorded in the journal is separately posted, but with the special journal, only the totals to the "Cash" columns are posted to the general ledger. This short-cut makes the posting process much easier. The special journal is useful where there are repetitive-type entries for payment of cash, receipt of cash, or the recording of purchase orders.

As is apparent in figure 11–11, all dates, names of recipients of cash, check numbers, and cash credit are recorded for each entry in the journal. After this information is recorded, use of the other columns varies. Six entries in the Cash Disbursements journal illustrate the way to use this journal. It should be noted that if these entries had been made in a general journal, they would require six separate postings. With use of the special journal, if these six entries were the only ones made during the month, one posting to the Cash account in the general ledger is required for the total of the six entries in the "Cash" column. This posting can be made once at the end of the month.

Under the "Budgetary" columns, reversals to unrestricted and restricted encumbrances are posted as a total to the Encumbrance and Reserve for Encumbrance control accounts in the general ledger. The "Code No." column indicates that the amounts in the "Encumbrances" columns are also individually posted to the object expense accounts in the Appropriation-Expense ledger.[4]

The Cash Disbursements journal in figure 11–11 has been organized so that the expenses are classified on an object basis, that is, salary, travel, etc. To develop expense information on a program basis, each expense has a code number, related to each program in

---

4. When the control accounts Encumbrances and Reserve for Encumbrances are reversed after the totals from the Cash Disbursements Journal are posted, the subsidiary accounts that are related to these control accounts also need to be reversed. The reversal of the subsidiary accounts can be done by posting the amounts recorded in the "Encumbrances" column separately or by recording the reversal of the subsidiaries in a Purchases Journal where the amounts were originally encumbered.

the library, so that postings from the expense columns can be made (on an individual basis) to program expenses and (in total) to object expenses. For example, in the "Expenses—Personnel" column, the "10" recorded under "Code No." represents a posting to the Reference Department, and the total in the "Personnel" column will be posted to the Personnel account in the Appropriation-Expense ledger. The postings of totals occur at the end of the month and the individual postings occur at various times during the month or at the end of the month, depending on the number of items recorded.

As stated, the Cash Disbursements journal uses an object-of-expense approach. The total in the "Cash" column is posted as a total to the general ledger. The totals in the "Encumbrances" columns are posted to control accounts in the general ledger. Individual amounts in the "Encumbrances" columns are posted to the Appropriation-Expense ledger to the amounts previously encumbered. The totals of each expense column are posted to the Appropriation-Expense ledger as a debit in an object expense account. Individual expense amounts are posted to a program expense account in another subsidiary ledger. The total for the "Total Expenses" column is posted to the control account Expenses in the general ledger so that the total of all the expenses in the Appropriation-Expense ledger and the program expenses are equal to the control account balance in the general ledger. The "Total Expenses" column is not posted to individual accounts. The "Miscellaneous Debits" column is not posted as a total; instead, all amounts recorded in this column are posted individually. In figure 11–11, the $2,000 entry in this column is posted as an individual entry to account number 5011 in the general ledger.

The posting process for the Cash Receipts journal in figure 11–12 is very similar to the posting process for the Cash Disbursements journal. The total for the "Cash" column is posted, as a total, to the Cash account in the general ledger once a month. The "Revenues/Support" column records all revenues and support received by the NFP organization. The total in this column is posted to the general ledger account Revenue and Support, which is a control account over the Revenue ledger. Amounts recorded in this column are individually posted to the Revenue ledger. The column title "Code No." records the account number in the Revenue ledger to which the amount is posted. The "Deferred Restricted Contributions" column is posted as a total to the control account in the general ledger. Individually, the amounts in this column are posted to the subsidiary accounts in the restricted portion of the Operating Fund which records these liabilities. The "Miscellaneous Credits" column is individually posted to the specific accounts recorded under the "Code

No." column. The total in this column is not posted to any account.

The posting process is performed on a monthly basis so that monthly financial schedules can be prepared. At quarterly and yearly periods, more comprehensive financial statements are prepared from the postings to the account balances. As part of these year-end procedures, adjusting entries are recorded in the general journal. After these entries are recorded, they too are posted to the ledger accounts to ensure that the financial statements contain accurate and timely information.

4. *Adjusting Entries and Posting.* Certain types of accounting activities are recorded as adjustments at the end of the fiscal year. These adjustments can be "catch-up" adjustments or they can be necessary to correct for missing or inaccurately recorded journal entries. (See chapters 3, 7, 8, and 10.)

The adjusting entries in the chapters have included adjustments for interest expenses, depreciation, wages payable, and reserve for supplies. The adjusting entries must be recorded and posted to the ledgers in order for the financial statements (which are based on the balances in the ledger accounts) to be accurate.

The adjusting entries that were illustrated in the chapters were largely "catch-up" entries for bringing depreciation or interest expense up to date. Adjusting entries can also be recorded for corrections to transactions that were incorrectly recorded during the year. These types of corrections may be brought to the attention of the management of the NFP organization during an audit. Once all the journal entries are posted to the general ledger, it is time to prepare a trial balance.[5]

5. *Preparing the Trial Balance.* The trial balance is a summation of all the balances in the accounts (contained in the ledger) to ensure that the debits are equal to the credits. The trial balance must be prepared prior to preparation of the financial statements to make certain that the accounts are in balance. (Chapter 11.)

Errors can arise in the ledger accounts through faulty postings of debits and credits. The preparation of a trial balance and the equality of the debits and credits in that trial balance help to ensure that this type of error has been eliminated. Preparation of a trial balance consists simply of adding up the balances in the general ledger to be certain that the debits and credits are equal.

---

5. A trial balance can be prepared before the adjusting entries are made, as well as after the adjusting entries have been posted.

As an illustration of this procedure, assume that the accounts in figure 11–13 comprise the Operating Fund accounts in the general ledger of the Hatfield Library on June 30, 19x5. Although the number of accounts shown is not extensive, the procedure to prepare a trial balance for a more extensive ledger is the same. In figure 11–14, a trial balance is prepared for the Hatfield Library.

It is assumed that the trial balance in figure 11–14 is prepared just prior to preparation of the financial statements at the June 30 year-end and before any closing entries have been made. As can be seen in figure 11–14, both the debit and credit totals are equal to $413,700. This equality does not mean that all journal entries have been correctly recorded, because the wrong account could have been debited or credited, and there would still be equality among debits and credits in the trial balance.

Although this type of error may exist in the trial balance, the equality of the debits and credits in the trial balance provides assurances that *other* types of errors have been eliminated. A trial balance is a useful statement to complete before preparing the financial statements. Figure 11–14 shows the trial balance as a formal document, but it does not have to be prepared in this manner. A simple adding-machine tape will serve as a trial balance if it shows the debits and credits are equal. This tape should be dated and signed by the person who prepared it, and it should be retained in the organization's records. Regardless of the form of the trial balance, once a trial balance is prepared, the financial statements can be completed.

6. *Preparing the Financial Statements.* The monthly schedules and year-end financial statements provide the governing board and the management of the NFP organization an indication of performance levels during the time period under consideration. These reports are important for decision making. (See chapters 3, 6, 8, 9, and 11.)

The financial statements are prepared to determine how the NFP organization performed during the fiscal year. A review of these statements determines whether there was an excess or a deficiency, whether the Fund Balance increased or decreased, and the sources and uses of working capital.

The amount of detail that appears in a financial statement revolves around the materiality of the items. For example, the Land, Building, and Equipment account in the Plant Fund's Balance Sheet could have been separated into three accounts, but such separation was not assumed to add to the financial presentation. These accounts (i.e., Land, Building, and Equipment) are usually separated in the ledger

BOOK FINES Account No. 400	Debit	Credit
Date		4500 —
Jun 30 Balance		

GRANTS Account No. 401	Debit	Credit
Date		93000 —
Jun 30 Balance		

MISCELLANEOUS REVENUES Account No. 402	Debit	Credit
Date		4200 —
Jun 30 Balance		

BOOKS Account No. 500	Debit	Credit
Date	26000 —	
Jun 30 Balance		

SALARIES Account No. 501	Debit	Credit
Date	53000 —	
Jun 30 Balance		

PERIODICALS Account No. 502	Debit	Credit
Date	9700 —	
Jun 30 Balance		

SUPPLIES Account No. 503	Debit	Credit
Date	13000 —	
Jun 30 Balance		

ESTIMATED REVENUES Account No. 600	Debit	Credit
Date	100000 —	
Jun 30 Balance		

RESERVE FOR ENCUMBRANCES Account No. 601	Debit	Credit
Date		97000 —
Jun 30 Balance		

ENCUMBRANCES Account No. 602	Debit	Credit
Date	97000 —	
Jun 30 Balance		

APPROPRIATIONS Account No. 603	Debit	Credit
Date		100000 —
Jun 30 Balance		

FIG. 11–13. Summarized General Ledger Accounts for Hatfield Library

accounts, but combined into one account in the Balance Sheet. Another example of this type of difference occurs when the numbers on the financial statements are rounded off to the nearest dollar. Rounding is not a material change, and leaving cents on the financial statements conveys a sense of excessive accuracy as many of these numbers are estimations. The financial statements that were prepared in chapter 9, the appendix of chapter 10, and this chapter did not round dollar amounts to the nearest dollar. The reason for including cents in the dollar amounts was so that the account balances could be traced from the journal entry to the financial statement with minimum confusion. It is acceptable to round all financial figures to the nearest dollar in financial statements for an NFP organization.

The financial statements prepared in the text present various levels of accounting detail. The financial statements in chapter 11 represent an overall financial picture of the organization, with all the funds combined. These financial statements can be issued to the general public. The financial statements prepared in chapters before chapter 11 present more detail on specific funds than is necessary for issuance to the general public. For example, rather than three endowment

Hatfield Library
Operating Fund
Trial Balance June 30, 19x5

Account No.	Account	Debits	Credits
100	Cash	$ 1,500	
110	Marketable Securities	17,000	
111	Investments	25,000	
120	Fixed Assets	71,500	
200	Deferred Restricted Contributions		$ 23,000
201	Accounts Payable		7,000
202	Wages Payable		12,000
203	Long-Term Debt Payable		50,000
300	Fund Balance		23,000
400	Book Fines		4,500
401	Grants		93,000
402	Miscellaneous Revenues		4,200
500	Books	26,000	
501	Salaries	53,000	
502	Periodicals	9,700	
503	Supplies	13,000	
600	Estimated Revenues	100,000	
601	Reserve for Encumbrances		97,000
602	Encumbrances	97,000	
603	Appropriations		100,000
Totals		$413,700	$413,700

FIG. 11-14. Trial Balance for Hatfield Library on June 30, 19x5

funds in the combined financial statements, only one endowment fund is used. The more detail on a financial statement, the more likely it should be used for internal decision making, rather than for issuance to the public.

Additionally, it should be noted that the financial statements prepared for the general public do not have to be the same as those that are prepared for internal decision making. The financial statements that have been prepared in the previous chapters have followed the recommendations of the AICPA. Those prepared for *internal* decision making should also be based on an accrual method, but they can deviate from recommended guidelines for reporting to the general public.

For example, recommended procedures call for expenditures to be divided on a program basis, but for internal decision-making purposes, it may be more useful to have this information presented on the basis of library objectives or on a community classification, such as a city versus county basis. As will be explained in chapter 13, direct costs are costs directly related to the activities of a program or department, and they contrast with indirect costs, which are allocated to a program or department. It may be useful to have financial statements which highlight the effect of direct costs separately from indirect costs on programs. In this way, those costs that are more easily controllable by a program director become apparent. These examples of deviations from recommended methods may present information in a way that will reveal trends that are not apparent in financial statements prepared under recommended procedures.

An NFP organization may prepare two sets of financial statements: one set for the general public and another set for internal purposes. The set prepared for internal use highlights financial aspects important for decision making, and they can be "tailor made" for a particular administrator. (It should be noted that statements prepared for internal decision making should only be used within the NFP organization, and should not be distributed to the public as they are likely to be misunderstood.)

7. *Journalizing and Posting the Closing Entries.* The balances in certain accounts need to be closed at the end of the fiscal year because they are temporary accounts that relate only to a specific time period. These accounts are the expense accounts, revenue accounts, and the budgetary accounts. (See chapters 5, 7, 8, and 10.)

The closing entries were recorded in the appendixes to the previous chapters. They are used to close the temporary accounts in each fund as that fund was explained. Although the closing entries were journalized and posted after the various funds were explained, the temporary accounts were still used in the combined SREF for the H. K. Fines Library in this chapter. This is a deviation from the eight-step procedure, because once the closing entries are posted to the ledger, all the temporary accounts have zero balances and they cannot be used to prepare financial statements. Therefore, if the steps were followed in the proper sequence, the financial statements in chapter 11 should have been prepared before any closing entries had been made. To illustrate the accounting associated with each fund, the steps were not followed in order. It was believed that presenting the closing entries with the specific fund under study more clearly illustrated the accounting procedures for that fund. Once the closing entries have been journalized and posted, the final trial balance is prepared.

8. *Preparing a Final Closing Trial Balance*. This is a year-end trial balance that is the final step in the fund accounting cycle, and it is prepared after the final closing entries have been posted to the ledger accounts. The purpose of this trial balance is to ascertain that the debits and credits in the accounts that have not been closed are in balance. (Chapter 11.)

The trial balance acts as a check on the posting process to assure that the accounts are in balance. The examples in figures 11−13 and 11−14 are of a trial balance after the initial posting process. In step 8, the trial balance is used to provide assurances that the accounts are in balance after the closing entries have been posted and prior to beginning the journalizing process for the new fiscal year. As an example of the preparation of this post-closing trial balance, assume that all the temporary accounts in figure 11−13 have been closed. It is assumed that the appropriations in the Hatfield Library are lapsing appropriations, and all appropriations that are not expended at the end of the year are returned to the granting agency. Under these conditions, no outstanding encumbrances will exist after the closing entries. (See pp.111−14 for an explanation of lapsing appropriations.)

The accounts that are left with balances are shown in figure 11−15.[6] The trial balance in figure 11−16 is based on the ledger accounts in figure 11−15. This trial balance proves the equality of the debits and credits in the accounts, and because it is prepared after the closing entries have been posted, it is called a "post-closing" trial

---

6. Usually the difference between revenue and support and expenses is closed to the Fund Balance. In the case of the Hatfield Library, there is no difference between the revenue and

CASH			Debit	Credit
Date		Account No. 100		
Jun 30	Balance		1 500 —	

MARKETABLE SECURITIES			Debit	Credit
Date		Account No. 110		
Jun 30	Balance		17000 —	

INVESTMENTS			Debit	Credit
Date		Account No. 111		
Jun 30	Balance		25000 —	

FIXED ASSETS			Debit	Credit
Date		Account No. 120		
Jun 30	Balance		71500 —	

DEFERRED RESTRICTED CONTRIBUTIONS			Debit	Credit
Date		Account No. 200		
Jun 30	Balance			23000 —

ACCOUNTS PAYABLE			Debit	Credit
Date		Account No. 201		
Jun 30	Balance			7000 —

WAGES PAYABLE			Debit	Credit
Date		Account No. 202		
Jun 30	Balance			12000 —

LONG-TERM DEBT PAYABLE			Debit	Credit
Date		Account No. 203		
Jun 30	Balance			50000 —

FUND BALANCE			Debit	Credit
Date		Account No. 300		
Jun 30	Balance			23000 —

FIG. 11–15. Summarized General Ledger Accounts for Hatfield Library after Temporary Accounts Have Been Closed

balance. The trial balance procedure is not complicated, but it is important because of the assurances it provides.

Summary

This chapter illustrates the combined financial statements for the H. K. Fines Library. These combined financial statements are based on the financial statements that had been prepared for each of the funds in the library, and they are similar to those financial state-

---

support and expenses; so the balance in the Fund Balance remains unchanged after the closing entries are posted.

Hatfield Library
Operating Fund
Post-Closing Trial Balance
June 30, 19x5

Account No.	Account	Debits	Credits
100	Cash	$ 1,500	
110	Marketable Securities	17,000	
111	Investments	25,000	
120	Fixed Assets	71,500	
200	Deferred Restricted Contributions		$ 23,000
201	Accounts Payable		7,000
202	Wages Payable		12,000
203	Long-Term Debt Payable		50,000
300	Fund Balance		23,000
	Totals	$115,000	$115,000

FIG. 11–16. Post-closing Trial Balance for Hatfield Library

ments. The financial statements, Notes to the Financial Statements, and auditor's opinion are the main financial documents of an NFP organization. In addition to these statements, the NFP organization may want to highlight certain aspects of its financial operations with supplemental schedules. The types of supplemental schedules vary with the needs of the specific organization. A transmittal letter should be written by the director of the NFP organization to introduce the organization's financial report and to provide additional descriptions about the activities of the organization. Together, these documents comprise the financial report which is presented to the general public.

The second part of the chapter reviews the accounting cycle. It highlights the eight steps in the accounting cycle, and it outlines the importance of the trial balance in the accounting cycle. Finally, it provides examples of special journals that can be used in an accounting system to reduce the number of entries in the general journal, as well as simplify the posting process from the journal to the general ledger.

Exercise 11–2. Special Journals and the Trial Balance

1. Describe the major purpose of the special journals.
2. Earlier, the bookkeeper for Bright Mountain Library had correctly prepared the trial balance after the adjusting entries had been journalized and posted. Now the financial statements for the year ended June 30, 19x4, are completed and the closing entries have been journalized but not posted. The bookkeeper wants you to prepare the post-closing trial balance from the trial balance that was prepared after posting the adjustment entries. The trial balance you are to use is presented below, and it is called the Adjusted Trial Balance.

Bright Mountain Library
Operating Fund
Adjusted Trial Balance
June 30, 19x4

	Debits	Credits
Cash	$ 15,000	
Due from the Federal Government	75,000	
Due from the State	35,000	
Accounts Payable		$ 46,000
Long-Term Debt Payable		68,000
Fund Balance		14,200
Book Fines		4,800
Book Sales		6,000
Support		586,000
Books	125,000	
Salaries and Benefits	320,000	
Maintenance	80,000	
Utilities	75,000	
Reserve for Encumbrances		70,000
Encumbrances	70,000	
Estimated Revenues	600,000	
Appropriations		600,000
	$1,395,000	$1,395,000

Additional information: Assume that at the end of the 19x4 fiscal year, the outstanding encumbrances are equal to $12,000.

Appendix

Four journal entries have been recorded after the Operating Fund was explained in Chapters 6 and 7 that affect the accounts in the Operating Fund. These transactions have been incorporated into the combined financial statements and are recorded below.

Plant Fund [Chap. 10]

1. Operating Fund—Unrestricted

| Dec. 31 | TRANSFER TO PLANT FUND | 23,357.25 | |
| | CASH | | 23,357.25 |

Recording transfer of cash from Operating Fund to Plant Fund

Endowment Fund [Chap. 8]

1. *Operating Fund—Unrestricted*

June 1	DUE FROM ENDOWMENT C	20,000	
	REVENUE FROM		
	INVESTMENT—Endowments		20,000

Recording amount due from Endowment C. Revenue in Endowment C is made available to unrestricted portion of Operating Fund

| June 30 | CASH | 20,000 | |
| | DUE FROM ENDOWMENT C | | 20,000 |

Recording receipt of cash from Endowment C

2. *Operating Fund—Restricted*

| June 30 | CASH | 8,900 | |
| | DEFERRED RESTRICTED CONTRIBUTIONS | | 8,900 |

Recognition of investment income from Endowment A in restricted portion of Operating Fund

Part 3.

An Evaluation of Financial Results

Part 3 (chapters 12 and 13) analyzes the financial statements to determine trends that they may highlight. In addition, these two chapters provide the administrator with examples of financial decision-making techniques.

12.

Ratio Analysis

Financial statements prepared under GAAP represent an accepted method of accounting that is widely understood. This common foundation provides a basis for further analysis of these statements, and this analysis provides the NFP organization with information about its financial and performance trends. The points of financial interest for NFP organizations are slightly different than for profit-oriented corporations. The major interest groups in a profit-oriented corporation, especially the stockholders, create this difference in financial orientation. For example, the groups interested in the financial performance of a corporation are the management, the stockholders, the creditors, and governmental agencies. The stockholders, a very influential group, are interested in high returns in the form of dividends and stock appreciation. This concern for dividends and stock appreciation translates into high earnings. The managers of these firms are aware of the effect of poor financial performance on their careers, and they, too, are concerned with high rates of return. The other two interest groups are concerned with different aspects of the corporation's performance. The creditors of a corporation are interested in the corporation's long-term earning power, so that it can repay its borrowings. The governmental agencies are interested in various regulatory aspects of the corporation.

In an NFP organization, it is significant that no stockholder group is present. Although the interests of creditors and governmental agencies are unchanged, the "elimination" of stockholders is one of the important factors that changes the orientation of management from return on investment toward provision of services. The concern of management is related to the overall financial ability of the NFP organization to continue to meet its program goals and provide services.

It is important that the service orientation of an NFP organization be understood prior to analyzing its financial statements. Financial analysis of the NFP organization is not oriented toward rate-of-return considerations. The NFP organization is concerned with the viability of its programs, and this concern is related to questions about its cash position, its Fund Balance, and the sources from which it receives support. Financial analysis can have several approaches. When one analyzes the financial reports of NFP organizations, it is important that financial analysis take into account the central question of the NFP organization's ability to continue its programs. The analysis in chapter 12 is directed toward the organization's ability to provide services to the public.

Financial Ratio Analysis

"Ratio analysis" can be related to financial ratios or performance ratios. "Financial ratios" involve the analysis of financial data, largely from the financial statements, to determine trends; "performance ratios" are related to evaluating the efficiency of program performances. They are concerned with evaluations of the activities of personnel in the organization to determine how efficiently they are performing their functions. Performance ratios can be computed by using financial data, level-of-output information, or a mixture of both.

In this section, financial ratios will be evaluated; then, in a later section, performance ratios will be analyzed. A first consideration with financial ratios is the method of accounting that is used. When financial ratios are computed, it is assumed they are based on an accrual system of accounting. If an organization is using the cash basis, the computation of these ratios will not have much significance. If only cash-based financial statements are available, they need to be converted to the accrual basis before any of these ratios can be interpreted.

For ratios to have meaning, they must be compared over a historical period to determine trends or between similar-size organizations (at the same period) to determine deviations. A historical comparison can investigate ratio trends within one organization over consecutive time periods. The primary purpose of this analysis is to determine how ratios have changed over the specified period and whether improvement or deterioration has occurred in these ratios. As indicated, a second type of comparison is made among similar-size organizations at the same time period. (The basis for "similar size" could be the dollars in the budget appropriation.) The primary purpose of this type of comparison is to determine how similar NFP organizations are performing at the same point in time. This would allow an organization to determine if it is seriously out of alignment in a particular financial area. At the present time, there is no set of financial ratio data for different-size libraries that would provide information among various-size libraries for comparison. Therefore, it is necessary to make comparisons within a particular library to determine historical trends. This necessitates development of ratios over more than a one-year period for comparative data to be available.

Many of the financial ratios that are explained in this section are directed at the organization as a whole rather than any specific fund. Several types of ratios are used to measure the financial flexibility of the NFP organization. For example, two NFP organizations may receive the same amount of revenue and support, and both could have approximately the same expenses, yet one of these organizations would be able to have a flexible response to the changing requirements of its patrons whereas the other organization could not respond or is very slow to respond. The reason for this difference can be attributed to the type of administration in the two organizations, but it can also be related to the financial structures of the two organizations.

For one organization to respond to the changing needs of its users, there must be sufficient funds for it to add or change programs. It is possible to apply financial ratio analysis to determine if any of the inaction is related to an organization's financial structure. In order for monies to be available for new programs, discretionary spending choices must be available for the administration to make. Yet, in some cases, expenditures of the NFP organization may be heavily weighted toward mandated expenditures, which may be necessary under grant programs or other restricted conditions under which monies have been received.

In figure 12–1, ratio 1 can be used to measure the financial flexibility of an NFP organization. As the percentage of mandated expenses and transfers becomes a larger percent of total revenue and support, the organization is less able to respond to the needs of its patrons with new

1. Percentage of Mandated Expenses and Transfers $= \dfrac{\text{Mandated Expenses and Transfers}}{\text{Total Revenues and Support}}$

2. Discretionary Fund Balance Changes $= \dfrac{\text{Current Year Board Designated and Undesignated Fund Balance}}{\text{Prior Year's Board Designated and Undesignated Fund Balance}}$

3. Fund Balance Ratio $= \dfrac{\text{Board Designated and Undesignated Fund Balance}}{\text{Total Assets}}$

4. Spending Ratio $= \dfrac{\text{Total Revenue and Support}}{\text{Total Expenses and Mandatory Transfers}}$

5. Excess/Deficiency Ratio (Operating Fund) $= \dfrac{\text{Operating Fund Excess (Deficiency)}}{\text{Total Revenue and Support}}$

6. Governmental Support $= \dfrac{\text{Revenue and Support from Governmental Support}}{\text{Total Revenue and Support}}$

7. Rate of Return on Investments $= \dfrac{\text{Investment Income}}{\text{Average Cost}}$

8. Debt Ratio = $\dfrac{\text{Long-Term Debt}}{\text{Total Assets}}$

9. Fund Balance Coverage Ratio = $\dfrac{\text{Expendable Fund Balance*}}{\text{Plant Debt Whose Related Assets Are Invested in Plant Assets Only}}$

10. Operating Debt Ratio = $\dfrac{\text{Debt Applied to Operating Programs}}{\text{Debt Incurred in Current Year}}$

11. Plant Aging Ratio** = $\dfrac{\text{Accumulated Depreciation}}{\text{Gross Plant Assets}}$

12. Cash Turnover = $\dfrac{\text{Expenses and Mandatory Transfers}}{\text{Average Monthly Cash Balance}}$

*The restricted and unrestricted fund balances in the Operating Fund, Plant Fund, and Quasi- Endowment Fund.
**This ratio excludes equipment.

FIG. 12–1. Financial Ratios

programs or special activities. If this ratio is computed for two organizations, and for one it is 50 percent and for the other it is 89 percent, it is obvious that it would be hard for the second organization to respond to additional needs of its patrons with new spending or through curtailment of old programs. An organization that has 89 percent of its programs mandated cannot respond very quickly to new needs. Ratio 1, the "Percent of Mandated Expenses and Transfers," indicates the financial flexibility of NFP organizations.

"Mandated transfers," referred to in several financial ratios in figure 12–1 (besides ratio 1), needs to be explained. Mandated transfers are those transfers which are required to go outside the organization to another organization.[1] If the ratio were computed for one fund, it would be any required transfers made outside the specific fund. In both cases, there would have to be a more compelling requirement for the transfer than as a requirement of the board of the NFP organization.[2] Any transfers made under the action of a board is considered a discretionary and not a mandatory transfer.

Another ratio of financial flexibility relates to "discretionary" balances in the organization's Fund Balance. A discretionary Fund Balance is any portion of the Fund Balance which has been designated for a specific purpose by the board and any portion of the Fund Balance which is undesignated. The discretionary balance in the Fund Balances can be used for new programs and capital expenditures. Therefore, increases in discretionary portions of Fund Balance totals are an indication of increases in financial flexibility. Ratios 2 and 3 in figure 12–1 are directed at detecting changes in the unrestricted fund balances. Ratio 2, "Discretionary Fund Balance Changes," is directed at determining the change in the Fund Balance available for discretionary expenditures from one year to the next. In ratio 2, the discretionary portion of the Fund Balance for the current year is divided by the discretionary portions of the Fund Balance total in the previous year.

If the result of the computation in ratio 2 is more than 100 percent, it indicates that there has been an increase in the Fund Balance available for discretionary spending. If the result is less than 100 percent, it means that the discretionary portion of the Fund Balances

---

1. These mandated transfers may be made to organizations outside the entity receiving the initial transfer or to an organization that is a subsidiary organization associated with (but outside) the organization initially receiving the transfer.

2. This type of mandated transfer might be received by the Plant Fund from the Operating Fund. This mandated transfer could be legally required under a debt agreement.

has decreased from the previous year and the financial flexibility of the organization is also likely to have decreased. Continual decrease in the discretionary portion of the Fund Balance indicates the limitations in the organization's ability to respond to the needs of its patrons within a reasonable period of time. Another check on this trend is the relationship between the discretionary portion of the Fund Balance and total assets. If there is a continual decrease in the discretionary portion of the Fund Balance as a percentage of total assets, it would be expected that the financial flexibility of the organization would also tend to decrease. Ratio 3, the "Fund Balance Ratio," measures this relationship by dividing the total assets of the NFP organization into the discretionary portion of the Fund Balance. A continual decrease in the Fund Balance ratio from year to year provides an indication that the organization's financial flexibility is also decreasing.

These first three ratios are directed at analyzing the financial flexibility in an NFP organization and its ability to respond to new program and activity needs. The ability of an NFP organization to respond to legitimate needs of its patrons within a reasonable time period is an indication of the financial flexibility of that organization.

The next three ratios are concerned with analyzing trends in the revenue and support received by the NFP organization. These ratios are specifically directed at determining how well the expenditures of the current year stayed within the revenue and support received in the current year. They are also directed at determining the level of governmental support to the organization. Ratio 4, called the "Spending Ratio," shows whether the organization's expenses stayed within the revenues received in the current year. All revenue and support is divided by total expenses and mandatory transfers. The numerator in this ratio does not include capital additions received during the year, but only revenue and support. Transfers that are not mandatory are not included in the denominator of the ratio. If the ratio is equal to 1, it means the organization broke even in terms of the relationship between revenue and support and expenses and mandatory transfers. If the ratio is greater than 1, there was a surplus, and if the ratio is less than 1, a deficiency developed during the year. In the latter case, the organization could draw on a previous year's surplus, available in the Fund Balance, to finance its operations during the year. This type of deficit financing can exist on only a short-term basis, as sources of surplus will eventually cease to be available.

The fifth ratio relates the excess or deficiency in the Operating Fund to the total revenue and support received by that fund during the current fiscal year. This ratio is called the "Excess-Deficiency Ratio" and is specifically related to the *unrestricted* portion of that fund. The Operating Fund records receipt of the majority of support and revenue, and this ratio shows the relationship between the excess or the deficiency and the total revenue and support in the Operating Fund. The "excess" is the amount of revenues and support that remains after current-year expenses have been deducted. Any prior-year expenses, deducted to compute the excess or deficiency, should be added back to the excess before the ratio is computed. Capital additions should not be included in the ratio as part of the revenue and support, and mandatory transfers should be deducted from the excess or added to the deficiency. This ratio shows a relationship between an adjusted excess and revenue and support that would high-light problems more quickly than the relationship between the unad-justed data on the SREF. If there is a deficiency, the Excess-Deficiency Ratio will be equal to a negative number, and the major significance of a negative number is that a deficiency exists. This ratio provides a means of determining whether the Operating Fund's operations were financed from current-year revenues and support. When the ratio is viewed over a several-year period, it also provides a means to determine if the Operating Fund is tending toward continual deficiencies.

Another concern—beyond whether the organization is operating within the finances it receives in a year—is the sources of support. Ratio 6 investigates the percentage of revenue and support received from intergovernmental sources. Revenue received from intergovernmental sources includes all the monies received from the federal, state, city, and county governments, regardless of the form in which it is granted. The major source of revenue and support for many NFP organizations is other governments, and if this source of monies should decrease, it can have major impacts on the program services offered. For this reason, decreases in the percent of revenue and support received should be further analyzed to determine the specific source which has been reduced. Ratio 6, "Governmental Support Rate," is directed at determining the amount of revenue and support received from intergovernmental sources as a percentage of all revenue and support. Review of this ratio over a period of several years should provide a clear indication of the trend in this source of revenue and support, as well as the rate at which it is changing.

It is possible to determine the percentage contributions of other sources to the total revenue and support of the organization. Although this will not be done here, another revenue source that will be analyzed is the percent of return on investments held by the organization. It would be possible to determine the amount of return on the investments as a percentage of the total return and support, but a more widely used measure is the rate of return based on the cost of investments. Ratio 7, "Rate of Return on Investments," investigates this relationship by dividing the investment income (without gains and losses) by the average cost of investments during the year. The average cost of investments is found by adding the beginning and ending investment cost values and dividing the total by 2. The rate of return on investments is based on a cost valuation, and this is a common way to determine the rate of return.[3] From this information it can be determined whether the organization is earning an adequate rate of return on its investments for the amount of risk it is willing to accept. If it appears that the rate of return is low, this may indicate that a change in portfolio management is needed.

Ratios 5, 6, and 7 analyze various aspects of the revenue and support received by the organization. Continued levels of support to the organization are important to its long-term survival. Another factor that also affects its existence is long-term constraints on the use of support and revenue. Earlier, it was seen that the financial flexibility of the organization can be affected if large amounts of its financial activities are mandated through the conditions under which support is received. Another facet of financial flexibility is the level of debt within the organization. The level of debt impacts on the financial flexibility of the organization, but it goes beyond these effects to seriously affect the continued functioning of the organization. The next three ratios are concerned with the level of debt within the NFP organization.

Although many NFP organizations do not have a high level of debt, the amount of long-term debt held by an organization could seriously impede its activities. Curtailment could occur when decreases in revenues and support required that the remaining inflows be applied to the payment of debt principal and its interest. If these payments are not made, it could result in default on the debt, with the entire principal becoming due at once. The "Debt Ratio," ratio 8, determines the level of debt as a percentage of total assets in the organization. The information needed to compute the ratio can be collected from the NFP organization's Balance Sheet. The higher the percentage of debt, the more difficult it is for an NFP organization to

3. Either a cost or market valuation can be used to determine the rate of return. This choice determines the denominator in the rate-of-return calculation. As an example of these valuations, see footnote 2 for the H. K. Fines Library.

finance its normal operations when there are cutbacks in the inflow of its regular sources of revenue and support. The more uncertainty in the regular inflows of revenue and support to the organization, the more important it is to maintain a lower level of debt.

As previously stated, the debt incurred by an NFP organization can have an effect on its long-term existence. Ratio 9, the "Fund Balance Coverage Ratio," analyzes the relationship between the debt incurred by the NFP organization to purchase its plant facilities, and its expendable fund balances. [4] The expendable Fund Balance consists of fund balances in the Operating Fund, quasi endowments, and the Plant Fund. The restricted and unrestricted portions of these fund balances are included in this computation because, in many cases, restricted fund balances are used to finance the purchase of plant assets. Only debt which has been used to purchase plant assets is divided into the expendable Fund Balance. A ratio of 1 to 1 means there are just enough expendable fund balances to finance the debt, whereas a ratio lower than 1 to 1 indicates that the debt could not be covered by the expendable fund balances. If the organization does not have a 1 to 1 coverage ratio, it is likely that current revenues are being used to repay the debt because of this priority commitment to debt payments. In addition, the ratio shows how the NFP organization's operations would be affected if its debt burden had to be immediately repaid. Furthermore, if the ratio is not 1 to 1, it indicates that the level of debt needs to be closely watched.

Another ratio that analyzes the debt area is ratio 10, which establishes a relationship between the amount of debt incurred in the current year and the amount of dollars applied to current operating programs. This ratio is called the "Operating Debt Ratio." Generally, if debt is incurred and it is not used to finance plant facilities, it is likely used for current operations. This debt is generally short term, but it could also be long-term debt.

If an NFP organization is experiencing financial difficulty in operating its programs, it may turn to short-term debt to finance these operations. If the Operating Debt Ratio is computed, this practice will become apparent. The Operating Debt Ratio should be close to zero; [5]

---

4. See Peat, Marwick, Mitchell & Co., *Ratio Analysis in Higher Education* (New York: Peat, Marwick, Mitchell & Co., 1980), p. 1.

5. If there is no short-term debt incurred in the current year, this ratio does not need to be computed. If it *is* computed, the denominator will be zero and the computation does not make sense, because you cannot logically divide by zero. This is a pertinent point with all ratios. Another point with the Operating Debt Ratio is that it would be possible for the borrowing to occur at the end of one fiscal year and not be used until the following fiscal year. In the second

if it is not, it indicates that debt is being used to finance current operations. If an NFP organization is in the position of making up revenue shortfalls through borrowings, it is not likely to be sustainable in the long run. Current operations should not be financed through debt issues.Eventually, the growing debt burden (to make up revenue shortfalls) will drain monies from other operations and even raise questions about the long-term existence of the NFP organization.

The next two financial ratios investigate two separate areas. The first ratio, ratio 11, is concerned with determining the age of the plant assets used by the NFP organization. The second and last ratio, ratio 12, is directed at determining how efficiently the cash of the organization is handled.

The "Plant Aging Ratio," ratio 11, analyzes the amount of accumulated depreciation which has been recorded, compared with the gross plant assets. The objective of this ratio is to provide indications about the age of the physical plant. As the amount of the accumulated depreciation increases, it indicates an aging physical plant, which is likely to require replacement. Note that accumulated depreciation on equipment is not included in this ratio; unlike equipment replacement, an aging physical plant can indicate a major financial burden for the NFP organization, especially if it has not established a funding policy.[6] The older the plant facilities, the closer the Plant Aging Ratio approaches 1. If the ratio were equal to 1, it would mean the plant assets were completely depreciated. A ratio of 1 would indicate that these assets have to be replaced very soon. It would also indicate that the maintenance costs of operating these aged assets are rapidly rising.

The last ratio, "Cash Turnover Ratio," attempts to determine the level of average monthly cash balances that are maintained in relation to the amount of yearly expenses and mandatory transfers. A high turnover ratio indicates that minimum cash balances are maintained in relationship to expenses and mandatory transfers. Excessive cash balances reduce the amount of earnings that can be achieved from investing this cash into short-term investments. (The average monthly cash balance is computed by determining the cash balance at the end of each month and finding the average of this total.) The Cash Turn-

---

year, no short-term debt was borrowed; so that the denominator is zero, but the short-term debt borrowed at the end of the first year is used for financing operations. The ratio provides an indication of financial activities, but it can be circumvented with year-end, short-term borrowings.

6. For information about a funding policy, see page 277, Transfers from Operating Fund to the Plant Fund.

over Ratio should be checked to determine if minimum cash balances are maintained—those balances that are minimum to meet the payment needs of the organization. This level of cash needs to be balanced against cash shortages, because no organization wants to reach the point where it can no longer pay its current liabilities, as they become due, because its cash balance is too small. A point has to be set between cash balances that are too low and those that are unnecessarily high.

The majority of the financial ratios highlighted here are directed at the viability of the NFP organization. Once these ratios are computed, they need to be compared (over several years) to produce trends and provide indications about changes, if any, in the NFP organization. These ratios are important because although an organization may continue to exist, it may exist only with a curtailed level of activities. Reduced program activities may occur because of cutbacks in resources, but also because of subtle changes in financial structure which become apparent only when financial ratios are computed over a several-year period. It is important that these changes be recognized. Financial ratios are important for analyzing the continued viability of an organization, but other types of ratios are useful in providing information about how efficiently the organization is operating. These ratios are called "performance" ratios.

Exercise 12–1. Financial Ratio Analysis

1. Compute all twelve financial ratios in figure 12–1 for the H. K. Fines Library, based on the combined financial statements and notes to the financial statements in figures 11–2, –3, –4, and –5 for the period ending June 30, 19x3.

    Additional information:
    a) There are no mandatory transfers.
    b) Twenty-five percent of all expenses is mandated.
    c) The balance in the expendable Fund Balance in the quasi endowment is $150,000.

2. A series of financial ratios has been calculated for the Sandra Treble Library for the year ending June 30, 19x8. The results of the computation are shown below, and they need to be interpreted. You are to (a) interpret the results of the computations to the library's administration and (b) determine if additional information would help you understand the implications of these ratios.

Sandra Treble Library: Ratio Analysis Results

	Ratio	Results
(1)	Percentage of Mandated Expenses and Transfers	70%
(2)	Discretionary Fund Balance	102%
(3)	Fund Balance Ratio	10%
(4)	Spending Ratio	1.2%
(5)	Excess/Deficiency Ratio (Operating Fund)	1%
(6)	Governmental Support	79%
(7)	Rate of Return on Investments	11%
(8)	Debt Ratio	3%
(9)	Fund Balance Coverage	5 times
(10)	Operating Debt Ratio	0
(11)	Plant Aging Ratio	75%
(12)	Cash Turnover	25 times

3. Financial ratio information for the Sandra Treble Library (question 2) has been collected for the June 30, 19x6 and 19x7 fiscal years, as well as for the 19x8 year-end. With this new data, reanalyze the financial situation facing the Treble Library in the year ahead.

Sandra Treble Library: Three-Year Ratio Analysis Results

	Ratio	Results		
		19x6	19x7	19x8
(1)	Percentage of Mandated Expenses and Transfers	75%	73%	70%
(2)	Discretionary Fund Balance	70%	65%	102%
(3)	Fund Balance Ratio	9%	8.2%	10%
(4)	Spending Ratio	.88	.98	1.2
(5)	Excess/Deficiency Ratio	−3%	.05%	1%
(6)	Governmental Support	87%	80%	79%
(7)	Rate of Return on Investments	4%	12%	11%
(8)	Debt Ratio	1%	2%	3%
(9)	Fund Balance Coverage	8	6	5
(10)	Operating Debt Ratio	0	0	0
(11)	Plant Aging Ratio	75%	72%	75%
(12)	Cash Turnover	10	18	25

4. In chapter 12 it was stated that the computation of financial ratios, based on financial statements prepared under the cash basis rather than the accrual basis, lacked any meaning. Describe the changes that would

occur in the following ratios if they were based on a cash system rather than an accrual method of accounting.

a)   Debt Ratio
b)   Fund Balance Coverage Ratio
c)   Operating Debt Ratio
d)   Plant Aging Ratio
e)   Rate of Return on Investments
f)   Spending Ratio

Performance Analysis

Although financial ratios have common meaning across various types of NFP organizations, performance ratios are more specifically related to a definite type of NFP organization. The reason for the singularity of performance ratios is that a specific activity is measured and that activity may not be common among all NFP organizations. There can be a higher level of conformity among NFP organizations' financial statements, upon which the financial ratios are based, than the activities performed within those organizations. As the types of performance measures developed for NFP organizations will vary, this section will consider the two general types of performance ratios that can be used, and implementation and use of a system of performance evaluation.[7]

Performance analysis, as it is considered here, relates to the evaluation of the performance of departments, programs, and the individuals who are responsible for the functioning of those programs or departments. There are two general types of performance ratios: measures of efficiency or productivity and measures of effectiveness. These two aspects of performance must be considered together (whenever possible) for a complete performance evaluation. Prior to considering these two types of performance measures, another question should be answered: Why use performance ratios?

There are a number of reasons for developing performance ratios within an NFP organization. The major reason is to develop some form of feedback to the administration and the public about performance levels within the organization. Feedback is important if the

7. For information on developing performance measures for libraries, see Douglas Zweizig and Eleanor Jo Rodger, *Output Measures for Public Libraries: A Manual of Standardized Procedures* (Chicago: American Library Association, 1982).

administrators within an NFP organization are to have an impact on the activities that are performed within the organization. Through use of these measurement procedures, it can be determined whether performance is improving or deteriorating. Performance ratios can be used to determine whether services are being provided to the public at a satisfactory rate. If performance measures are established at specific levels of performance, it is easy to determine whether these objectives have been met. In effect, performance measures allow for better control over the activities of the organization, and they provide a way to measure services provided to the patrons of an NFP organization.

As previously stated, performance ratios are directed at either the efficiency or effectiveness of a function. When the efficiency of an operation is considered, an attempt is made to determine the relationship between the resources used and the results obtained from using those resources. In many cases, this type of measure is concerned with cost per unit output.[8] When there is a decrease in cost per unit of output, it is generally considered favorable from an efficiency or productivity viewpoint. In figure 12–2, two performance ratios illustrate the type of performance ratios that can be directed at efficiency measures. The first ratio, "Cost per Item," puts a per unit cost on each item put into the library's collection. This measure is computed by dividing the total program costs by the number of accessions during the year.[9] This is a measure of how much it costs to operate the entire library, and it indicates the cost of new material acquired for the library.[10] If it were clear that some of the yearly costs of operations in the library are not part of normal operations, they should be excluded from total program costs. An example of this type of cost might be a special grant for remodeling the building.

An NFP organization would normally establish goals, in terms of a performance measure, based partially on past performance and partially on the needs of the organization which are assumed to be reachable within the current year. Such a goal might be to reduce the per unit cost of items added to a library's collection during the year by 5 percent. Of course, if the performance measure is a broad one, like the cost per unit of items added to the entire library, nonachievement of this goal leaves the administration of the library in a quandary. This situation arises because it is difficult to determine what

---

8. An example of an efficiency measure related to a factor other than cost per unit information might be a tally of the number of overtime hours used.

9. Program costs are assumed to be "full" costs, which are explained on pages 397–98, 405.

10. Accessions are not all book accessions. It would be acceptable to count accessions other than books as equal to a specified number of books.

actions need to be taken to improve such a broad per unit cost measure. Therefore, it is always better to have a per unit cost measure established by programs or departments, rather than on an entire-library basis. If cost objectives of a particular program or department are not satisfactory, it is easier to determine where to take corrective actions.

Another illustrative efficiency measure that could possibly be used to determine an NFP organization's cost of operation in one area is its maintenance cost per square foot. Ratio 2, the "Maintenance Cost Ratio," measures this cost by dividing the number of square feet in the organization's physical facilities into total maintenance costs for the fiscal year. Again, a goal can be established to reduce the cost per square foot of maintenance expenses by a specific percentage.

Both ratios in figure 12–2 are concerned with the efficiency of an NFP organization, but other areas of performance evaluation are concerned with the effectiveness of the organization. Effectiveness measures are concerned with how well a service is provided or how well an activity meets its established objectives. This type of measure may be concerned with reducing the time it takes to perform a task, rather than per unit cost information. Another measure of effectiveness within an NFP organization is whether costs stay within budget guidelines. To determine whether budget guidelines are being followed, variances from budget appropriations should be investigated with a schedule such as a Statement of Comparison between Budget Appropriations and Actual Expenses and Encumbrances (as illustrated in figure 11–8). This type of schedule can be prepared on a monthly basis if an allotment system is used. As a performance objective, this determines whether an NFP organization's administration is effective in controlling its costs of operation. Many other measures of effectiveness can be developed.[11]

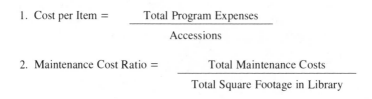

1. Cost per Item = $\dfrac{\text{Total Program Expenses}}{\text{Accessions}}$

2. Maintenance Cost Ratio = $\dfrac{\text{Total Maintenance Costs}}{\text{Total Square Footage in Library}}$

Fig. 12–2. Two Efficiency Measures

11. Zweizig and Rodger, *Output Measures.*

It should be remembered that there is another side to the effectiveness and efficiency measures that needs to be considered if these measures are used. Although they indicate how well a task is performed, they cannot measure the satisfaction of patrons with the service being received. It is conceivable that a task could be performed with more efficiency and more effectively, and at the same time could generate less satisfaction among patrons who receive the service. These performance measures should not be used without evaluating the effect on the people who are receiving the service. Of course, it is more difficult to gauge the effect on patrons' satisfaction, but it should not be assumed that increases in efficiency and effectiveness automatically guarantee increases in satisfaction among patrons.

Another concern with performance measures is their successful implementation. The following five steps are useful in implementing and using performance measures for an NFP organization.

1. Providing Top Management Commitment
2. Developing Performance Measures
3. Collecting Data on Performance Levels
4. Analyzing Performance Data for Implications to Decision Making
5. Taking Action

These five steps (tailored to a particular NFP organization) should be used in the development and use of a performance system. The first step is expression of a strong commitment from top-level administration for the implementation and use of performance measures. There needs to be a commitment through actions on the part of high-level administration for the establishment of performance measures and objectives. It should be clear that additional time and effort will be needed to implement and use the system; therefore, top-level administration should be supportive of this need for time.

The second step relates to development of the performance measures themselves, which can be done by a committee or by the administration of an NFP organization. Whatever method is chosen, it should be clear that the people who are going to be evaluated should make a contribution to the development of these measures. This participation is important for a commitment to performance measures to exist among the individuals who will attempt to achieve them. It is important that these performance measures be considered fair, and one way to achieve this is through input in forming them from those groups which are to be evaluated.

A number of considerations need to be focused upon in development of performance standards that are tailored to an NFP organization. First, the service centers which are going to be evaluated need
to be determined—those programs or departments that provide services to the patrons. Usually this is fairly simple, and is based on the
organizational structure within the NFP organization. When service
activities are intermingled between two organizational units, this step
takes more planning. Once the service centers within an NFP organization are classified, the second step is to identify the type of services provided by these units. These services are considered workload measures, and they provide administrators a good idea of the
service being provided by these centers.[12] After the service activities
are identified, efficiency and effectiveness measures are developed to
evaluate the success with which these services are being provided to
the public. Finally, a set of achievable objectives for the current year
is established around the performance measures which have been
developed for the service center. (Each of these steps will be described in more detail in the following paragraphs.)

As stated, after the service centers are located within an NFP
organization, the services provided by these centers must be identified. The type of service activities relates to factors such as the
number of questions asked, the number of miles of street to be
cleaned, the number of meals prepared, or the number of patron
visits. The service activity will vary from one NFP organization to
another, depending on the major function of the organization. Before
any performance measures are computed, data on the amount of
service activities that occurred in a service center should be disclosed
for analysis.

Once the service center's activities have been defined, efficiency
and effectiveness measures are developed to evaluate the service
center's functions. As previously stated, the efficiency measures usually (but not always) relate to cost per unit information. Examples of
these types of measures are cost per item added to a collection, cost
per meal served, number of man-hours per patron, or cost per theater
ticket sold. Effectiveness measures determine how well functions are
being performed. Performance measures of this nature relate to aver-

---

12. In some cases, demand figures are developed for the service center prior to identifying
the specific services provided. An example of demand data would be the number of handicapped people requesting a particular service.

age response time to questions or calls, capacity levels at theater performances, percentage of users satisfied with service, variances between approved and actual budget figures, or the level of collections from pledges in a fund drive.

In developing performance measures, several behavioral implications should be considered. First, if the performance measure is not seen as clearly relating to the service function that is being performed, it is not likely to have much influence on the actions of the persons performing the service. The measures should be clearly and uniquely related to the type of service activities that are being performed in a service center. This will make it clear to the individuals being evaluated that their efforts are leading to better performance evaluations. Another behavioral effect can arise if these measures are imposed on a group of workers by higher-level administration without providing them with input into the development of the performance measure. Under these conditions, there is likely to be dissatisfaction with these performance measures. The people being evaluated by performance indicators should have some input into their development so that there is more of a feeling of responsibility to meet the performance goals which will be set.

Another facet of behavior which should be considered when any type of performance analysis is used to evaluate programs or personnel is changes in behavior because of the use of one or a limited number of performance ratios. Some types of favorable behavioral changes are expected when performance measures are adopted, but the imposition of a performance measure may also create dysfunctional behavioral changes. These changes are most apparent when only one performance measure is used to evaluate personnel. For example, consider the changes that would occur in teaching behavior if a college or university's only criterion for tenure was high ratings on teacher evaluations completed by the students. Obviously, the changes that would occur in the teacher's classroom behavior are not likely to be the behavior changes that the university initially wanted to encourage. Performance measures can be a powerful tool in encouraging behavior change if they are accepted and properly used, but care needs to be exercised that the type of behavior changes are the ones that were initially contemplated.

The third step, as previously listed, in implementation of performance measures is collection of data. The reporting system within the NFP organization should already lend itself to the collection of data for the development of performance measures. If possible, the use of performance measures should require development of only a minimum number of new forms to collect performance information. In addition, the personnel who are involved with the collection of the data should clearly understand how it is to be collected and how the ratios are to be computed.

Once the data are collected, they need to be analyzed for implications to decision making. This is the fourth step in the list of five. This analysis should determine whether the objectives which were established for performance areas are being accomplished. For example, if organizational changes or physical changes have been made in order to better service the patrons of the NFP organization, the performance measures should be analyzed to determine if these changes have actually improved service. The performance measures for the various programs or departments in the NFP organization should be presented in a manner that makes them easy to analyze. This presentation should include information on a prior period, whether monthly or quarterly, so that comparisons can be made with the current period. In addition, the objectives for a particular service area should be clearly stated on the evaluation forms, along with information on service activity for the service center. This type of presentation makes it easy to compare information for decision-making purposes. The analysis of performance results should help management determine whether recent changes are having the anticipated effect on the organization, whether there are areas where the servicing of patrons is becoming difficult, whether there are areas in the NFP organization where performance needs to be improved, as well as whether the organization is meeting its performance objectives.

Examples of these types of forms are shown in figures 12–3, 12–4, and 12–5. These reports are from the annual budget documents in the cities of Abilene, Texas; Thunder Bay, Ontario; and St. Paul, Minnesota. These reports are presented in a fashion that is particularly pertinent for administrators to make decisions about performance. In all three reports, the objectives for each department are clearly set forth so that they can be compared with actual results. The three reports were selected because they represent three different types of NFP organizations for which performance measures have been developed. Without an adequate presentation of performance information, it is difficult for administrators to analyze the results of a program's or department's operations. The three reports provide examples of the type of document which would aid the administrator in decision making.

```
ANNUAL BUDGET
CITY OF ABILENE
ACTIVITY PERFORMANCE INDICATORS
```

DEPARTMENT Community Services 700	DIVISION Maxwell Golf Course 7030	ACTIVITY 0722 Club House Operations	FUND General 100

ACTIVITY DESCRIPTION   To collect fees, supervise play and provide quality club house services.

OBJECTIVES

1. To increase percentage of expenditures covered by revenue by 20%
2. To reduce club house cost by 5% during the next year

INDICATORS OF PERFORMANCE

MEASUREMENT	last FY	current FY	next FY
DEMAND			
Number of senior citizen memberships	100	100	100
Number of days open	365	365	365
Number of tournaments	7	8	8
Number of potential rounds of golf	60,000	60,000	60,000
WORKLOAD			
Number of greens fees collected	22,679	27,029	35,038
Number of membership fees collected	86	100	100
Number of driving range participants	0	5,000	15,000
PRODUCTIVITY			
Revenue from greens fees	$75,522	$79,600	$166,000
Revenue from memberships	$8,400	$10,000	$10,000
Other revenue	$21,979	$26,000	$30,000
Total revenue	$105,901	$115,600	$206,000
Cost per round played		$3.12	
EFFECTIVENESS			
Percent of total expenditures covered by revenue	47%	44%	69%
Percent of club house cost vs. total cost	30%	28%	25%

FIG. 12–3. City of Abilene, Texas, Performance Indicators (Source: 1981 Annual Budget for City of Abilene)

The City of Thunder Bay

1980 PERFORMANCE MEASUREMENT PROJECT

DATE December 31, 1980

PAGE 2

DEPARTMENT	PROGRAM AREA	SIGNATURE
Library	Technical Services	Grover Burgis – Chief Librarian

PROGRAM DESCRIPTION

To process acquisition through order of all information forms, invoicing, cancellations, and maintain periodical and book inventory and to catalogue, classify and process all books and audio-visual material.

COLLECTION FREQUENCY CODE

1 Annual   4 Monthly
2 Bi-annual   5 Weekly
3 Quarterly   6 Daily

	PERFORMANCE MEASUREMENTS	SOURCE AND HOW COLLECTED	HOW ANALYSED OPTIONS	COLL. FREQ. CODE
DEMAND/WORKLOAD	Orders sent per month	internal records	Manual	1
	Order received/invoiced	"	"	1
	Number of serial titles handled	"	"	1
	Number of serials handled	"	"	1
	Number of books, A/V items, etc. catalogued	"	"	1
EFFICIENCY	Items catalogued per month	internal records	Manual	1
	Turnaround time per item	"	"	1
	Gross cost per item catalogued	approved budget, internal records		1
EFFECTIVENESS	Percentage of items process with "X" working days	internal records	Manual	1
	Percentage of items catalogued without major error	"	"	1

FIG. 12–4. City of Thunder Bay, Ontario, Performance Indicators (Source: 1980 Performance Measurement Manual and Catalogue for City of Thunder Bay)

ACTIVITY PROGRAM DATA

ACTIVITY TITLE	ACTIVITY NUMBER	DEPARTMENT	DIVISION
Conservatory	03120	Community Services	Parks & Recreation

Objectives

By being open every day of the year the conservatory can provide to all visitors, resident and non-resident, an attractive & educational display of horticultural materials. Seasonal plants are produced in the 7 growing houses and are displayed with the permanent plant collection. Outdoor plants are also produced and are used in over 125 beds in the park and in the downtown areas. By maintaining and encouraging cooperation with schools, commerical growers and organizations, tour groups, horticultural clubs, interested individuals and the parks and rec. dept. we intend to continue to promote St. Paul as one of the Midwest's most unique public facilities. Although greatly reduced, guided tours and limited classes will continue to be offered. Horticultural information continues to be requested and where possible the staff supplies answers from personal knowledge and from available sources.

Program Performance Data

	1978 Actual	1978 Actual	1980 Authorized	1980 Estimated	1981 Estimated
Propagation cuttings	300,000	300,000	300,000	300,000	300,000
seeding	125,000	125,000	125,000	125,000	125,000
bulbs	7,900	7,900	8,800	9,100	9,000
Hours open	1,917	1,735	1,735	1,735	1,735
Shrubs forced	450	450	450	450	425
No. of flower beds	120	137	137	130	130
Guided tours	77	68		55	70
Workshops	15	8		10	10
attendance	400	150		200	200
Question (phone) attendance	600	700		700	700
Visitor attendance	825,000	850,000		850,000	900,000
cost per visit (exclude heat)	.18	.20		.18	.19
Average total cost per day	463.50	471.30		441.90	492.00
Labor cost per week	2,751.00	2,565.00		2,609.00	2,936.00
Flower Bed Costs Labor 3 mo.	120 @	137 @		130 @	130 @
	275.00	224.00		240.00	271.00
Materials	16.50	15.00		14.50	16.00
Heating costs (70% of total)	33,807.00	25,758.00		33,460.00	38,500.00
Av. year around heating cost per visit	.04	.03		.039	.042

Budget Summary

	1978 Actual	1979 Actual	1980 Authorized	1981 Proposed	1981 Authorized
Salaries	128,822	134,125	145,538	152,808	152,808
Other	27,593	19,002	25,647	25,190	25,190
Total	156,415	153,127	171,185	177,998	177,998
Personnel	8.5	7.5	7.5	8.0	8.0

Comments

1981 based on addition of one halftime gardener, because of lost CETA help. Without addition, flower beds will be reduced to 105, Spring and Fall shows will reduce in size, and possibly reduce summer hours to the same as winter.

Addition of maintenance of new Japanese Garden will also put strain on conservatory staff.

FIG. 12–5. City of St. Paul, Minnesota, Performance Indicators (Source: 1981 Budget: General Fund and Debt Service Funds for City of Saint Paul)

Once performance indicators are presented in report form, the fifth and last step in implementing and using a performance system is taking corrective actions when performance does not meet the objectives, or providing the proper incentives for good performance. The implementation of a performance system is, in effect, the implementation of a feedback system, and one important reason for having a feedback system is to take the appropriate actions when feedback is received. The type of corrective actions will vary with the type of performance measure and the ability of the NFP organization to make changes when they are considered necessary. It should not be thought that all variances from objectives will require corrective actions. Before any actions are taken, the magnitude of the variance from the objective needs to be considered, as well as the alternatives for corrective action available to the organization. When the need for rewards for good performance arises, they should be provided in a way that makes it clear that efficiency and effectiveness are being recognized. An example of such a reward is merit pay for outstanding performance.

Once a performance measurement system is implemented, problems can still arise. (Several of these problems have already been alluded to in the discussion of performance measures.) A problem can arise if only one performance measure is used to evaluate activities. Individuals will exhibit dysfunctional behavior to meet the requirements of this one performance measure. Examples of this type of behavior abound in all organizations. For example, assume response time is used as the most important performance measure for a service center. As a result, the response time may decrease, but this lower response time may be achieved by a relatively large percentage decrease in *satisfactory* response. To overcome this problem, response time should be interrelated to other measures, such as counting the number of questions or calls being answered with the idea that if the number of calls is decreasing, it is because of unsatisfactory responses. Therefore, it is not good practice to use just one performance measure in one service center, as the personnel will concentrate only on that performance measure, to the possible detriment of the overall organization's functions.

The problem of less satisfactory performance, while at the same time improving the performance ratio, is a problem for any performance measure. There may be improvements in performance, as measured by the performance measure, when at the same time patrons recognize a decrease in the level of services received. A method that can be used to evaluate this problem is to survey the patrons of the NFP organization to determine how they perceive the delivery of services. The administration of any survey should coincide closely with the time period in which the performance measures are computed; otherwise, it will be difficult to relate the perceived changes by patrons to the performance measures.

Another problem with the use of performance measures is the difficulty that may develop in collecting performance information. Any performance ratio which requires the tabulation of additional information (outside that information already collected by the organization) should be closely scrutinized for its importance. Such a ratio may be investigating a portion of the workload, which is not a significant activity (otherwise, information about it would already be easily available). Usually the information upon which the performance measures are based is already collected in some form. Any performance measures which require the tabulation of additional information should be of especially significant value to the organization to require this additional work.

Many efficiency ratios are based on per unit cost information. As will be explained in chapter 13, some costs are directly related to the functions of a program and some are allocated or assigned to the program. These allocated or assigned costs are indirect overhead costs that are important to the functioning of the organization as a whole, but they do not directly contribute to the service function which is being evaluated by the cost per unit performance measure. In addition, these costs are assigned on some basis that is outside the control of the person who is responsible for the particular service center. Therefore, in cost per unit performance evaluations it is not a good idea to include indirect or allocated costs as part of the cost data of a performance measure for a specific department or program. In chapter 13 these costs are used to determine the full costs of operations, but they should not be used to evaluate specific service centers. The purpose of these full cost data is important from an overall organizational viewpoint, but not in evaluation of a specific service center within an NFP organization.

Another consideration which is necessary when using per unit cost information is the effect of inflation on the cost measure. There may be an increase in per unit costs that does not reflect decreases in efficiency, but is simply attributable to the effects of increased inflation. Therefore, at times when inflation is considered serious, per unit cost information should be adjusted for the effects of inflation.

A last consideration in the use of performance measures that may create a problem is the timeliness of the information. Evaluations of performance measures should occur on at least a monthly basis.

Therefore, without timely information on performance measures, the collected information will be too late for effective or meaningful actions to be taken. The information used to compute the ratios must be timely enough for action to be taken on a *current* problem, not on an old one which has changed since the information was collected. Additionally, praise for good performance levels should be given as closely as possible to the actual performance.

Unlike financial ratios, which can be generated largely from reviewing the data in the accounts and on the financial statements, performance ratios require a commitment on the part of administrators to establish performance objectives within the NFP organization. Once these objectives are established, information must be collected to determine if these objectives are being met. If these performance measures are accepted and the objectives are not achieved, it also means that lower evaluations may be necessary for those who are not performing at the accepted levels. Although it is sometimes felt that the services provided by an NFP organization are unquantifiable, they *can* be quantified if consideration and thought is put into the process of determining the evaluation measures.

Summary

Financial ratio analysis is concerned with the continued viability of the NFP organization, and the ratios that were presented are directed at this area. Financial ratios are useful for bringing to light financial trends that might otherwise go unnoticed. Another area of ratio analysis is concerned with the use of performance ratios to measure the efficiency and effectiveness of operations. This latter group of ratios tries to answer questions as to whether the various programs are achieving their goals and how efficiently and effectively these goals are being achieved. The type of performance measure developed for an NFP organization will vary with the type of goals established for its programs. Financial ratios are more all encompassing for all types of NFP organizations because this group of ratios is based on financial statements that have common characteristics.

With both financial ratios and performance ratios, it is difficult to make comparisons between NFP organizations, as is commonly done with profit-oriented corporations. Comparisons need to be done *within* the NFP organization, from one year to the next. These ratios can be a useful tool for managerial planning and decision making if used in this manner.

Exercise 12–2. Performance Ratio Analysis

1. In recent years, the Harry Malone Library has been experiencing a decrease in governmental support. The director of the library has been aware of this trend and an attempt has been made to make up for the decrease with campaigns for pledges of financial support from the public. The total amount of pledges received has varied a great deal from year to year, and a large number of pledges have remained uncollected at year-end.

    a) Are there any performance measures which might be used so that the amount of variances in year-to-year pledges is apparent and more control is exercised over this variation?

    b) Suggest a performance measure that might be used to reduce the amount of uncollected pledges.

    c) Can you think of any type of financial ratio which would help to determine whether the pledges are substituting for the funds lost from governmental sources?

2. The Moreland County Library has been experiencing an increase in the cost of repairs and maintenance to its building in recent years. In order to monitor the performance of the Custodial Department, which is responsible for the repairs and maintenance of the library, a performance measure was introduced. This performance ratio divided the number of square feet in the library into the costs of repairs and maintenance; this ratio was computed from data over the past three years. A goal was set in the current year to reduce the cost per square foot to one-half of its average over the last three years. The director emphasized to the Custodial Department the need to cut costs by achieving this goal, and the severe consequences if it was not attained. At the end of the current year, the goal had been achieved. The director was very happy with the results, and was about to explain to the board the success the library had achieved with reducing repair and maintenance costs, when the pipes from the lavatory above the boardroom burst and quickly ended the meeting. The director was embarrassed and decided never to use performance evaluation again. Comment on this situation and suggest ways to avoid problems such as this one when performance measures are used.

3. The difference between budget appropriations and actual expenses is considered a performance measure at the Whittfield Library. The Circulation Department at the Whittfield Library had been managed by Mrs. Beth Wilson for twenty years. During that period, Mrs. Wilson never exceeded her budgeted appropriations. Mrs. Wilson retired at the begin-

ning of the current fiscal year, and the Circulation Department was headed by Mr. Thomas Jones during the current fiscal year just ended. The Circulation Department's budgeted appropriations have just been compared with its total expenses in the current year, and the results show that expenses exceeded budgeted amounts by $1,000. Within the department, there were both positive and negative variances from budgeted amounts. The director of the library has just told Mr. Jones, "When Mrs. Wilson was in charge, the budgeted amounts were *always* under expenses!" Should Mr. Jones be reprimanded for excessive spending? Why do you think Mrs. Wilson's expenses were never over the budgeted amounts?

13.

Exercising Accounting Control

Once the financial statements have been prepared, they can be analyzed with financial ratios, but there are some other factors which need to be taken into consideration. These factors are control considerations. The financial statements provide a basis for some control measures that can be determined, but, like performance ratios, other information usually needs to be collected before these evaluations can be made. This chapter deals with three areas of control: cash, budgetary, and cost control. Each of these areas is separately considered and specific recommendations are used to demonstrate controls in these areas. With cash control, the major concern is having enough cash available to pay current liabilities as they become due. This is the focus of the cash control section in the chapter. Two ratios are introduced that assist in determining the relationship between cash and the amount of current liabilities owed. In order to have budgetary control, the expenses and encumbrances of an NFP organization must remain within appropriation guidelines. The budgetary control measures suggested in this chapter assist in this process. The last section of the chapter will demonstrate a way of calculating the full costs of programs through cost allocation. In this manner, per unit cost information is used to determine whether the costs of operations are becoming excessive.

Cash Control

Although the emphasis in the previous chapters has been on the accrual basis of accounting, the cash basis is useful in analyzing the organization's cash flow. The analysis of cash is made to ensure that there is enough cash available to pay projected expenses. When an NFP organization does not have enough cash on hand to pay its current liabilities as they become due, because its cash inflows are lower than its cash outflows, it is still a viable organization but the organization is having a "liquidity crisis." This situation occurs when cash inflows cannot keep up with cash outflows, and it is a temporary situation. If the organization were no longer viable—that is, if it were bankrupt—there would be no chance of a return to a normal cash position, but with a liquidity crisis, the organization is not bankrupt; it is temporarily short of monies. To avoid this situation, the NFP organization needs to study its future cash inflows and outflows. It also needs to be aware of the relationship between its current liabilities and those current assets that are used to pay off its current liabilities as they become due. If an NFP organization cannot pay its current liabilities, it may be experiencing a liquidity crisis, and this is likely to be a symptom of more difficult times ahead. This is a cash problem that questions the organization's viability. Is the organization going to be able to continue to provide its services without curtailment?

The concept of liquidity has been described, but prior to beginning any cash analysis, the term "quick assets" needs to be explained. This term refers to the most liquid of the current assets. (The "liquidity" of an asset determines how quickly it can be converted into cash.) Obviously, the most liquid asset is cash itself. Other examples of liquid assets are marketable securities (i.e., short-term investments). Short-term investments can be readily converted into cash through their sale. Therefore, quick assets are current assets that are cash or current assets that can be quickly converted into cash.

Inventories, such as supplies inventory, can also be converted into cash, but it is a much slower conversion process than with securities; therefore, inventories are not considered to be quick assets. For the same reason, prepaid assets, such as insurance or lease prepayments, are not considered quick assets. With profit-oriented corporations, accounts and notes receivable are considered quick assets because they can be easily sold or discounted.[1] With an NFP organization, the receivables it holds must be reviewed to ensure that they are legally acceptable for discounting. (It is doubtful whether intrafund or interfund accounts receivable can be discounted.) If receivables are not legally enforceable, they are not included in the determination of the quick assets. For this same reason, any receivables which are uncollectible should not be included in any quick-asset total. The amount of receivables included in the quick assets should be the net receivables arrived at after deducting the uncollectible accounts and those legally uncollectible intrafund or interfund receivables.[2]

The reason for separating current assets into quick assets is to determine the liquidity of an organization's assets. Determination of the amount of quick assets is important because comparison between these assets and current liability totals shows how easy—or difficult—it is for the organization to pay its current liabilities with its most liquid current assets.[3] In this analysis, the assumption is made that current liabilities will be paid with current assets, and the most liquid of the current assets will be used first. The comparison can be formalized into a ratio called the "acid-test ratio," which is measured by dividing the current liabilities into the quick assets. The equation for the ratio follows:

$$\text{Acid-Test Ratio} = \frac{\text{Quick Assets (Cash + Marketable Securities + Net Receivables)}}{\text{Current Liabilities}}$$

If this ratio is equal to 1, it means that each dollar of current liabilities is covered by 1 dollar of quick assets, and the current liabilities can be paid off completely with quick assets. If the ratio is less than 1, it means that the NFP organization could not pay off its current liabilities with its most liquid assets, and in order to pay off these liabilities other assets would have to be sold. If the ratio is less than 1, it does not mean there is an immediate problem, but it may mean that this is an area that should be watched for potential difficulties. This ratio is an indicator of the immediate relationship between

1. "Discounting" refers to the process of receiving money for a note receivable before it is due. The amount of money received is less than the face value of the note, and therefore it has been "discounted."

2. Intrafund receivables and payables can arise with a fund when subdivisions of that fund exist. For example, the Endowment Fund within the H. K. Fines Library was subdivided into separate endowments, and it would be possible to have intrafund receivables and payables within this one fund.

3. Any payables which correspond with intrafund or interfund receivables should be eliminated from the current liability totals.

quick assets and current liabilities. For better indications as to its significance, the ratio should be compared over a definite time period to determine the trend of the ratio. If the ratio has been declining over a period of time, it provides an indication that the NFP organization may soon begin to experience difficulties in paying its liabilities.

Another way of looking at this same relationship is with a "cash availability schedule,"[4] which should be prepared on a monthly basis. Figure 13–1 illustrates a cash availability schedule, whose purpose is the same as the acid-test ratio, that is, to determine the organization's ability to pay its current liabilities with its most liquid assets. The cash availability schedule presents this information in terms of total dollars rather than as a ratio. The information is also presented on a comparative basis so that the liquidity of the NFP organization can be compared with a similar period last year. This comparison provides an indication as to whether the Cash Excess (Deficiency) is better or worse than in a comparable period in the previous year. This year-to-date comparison provides information as to whether there is a monthly period each year when this relationship tends to deteriorate.

Figure 13–1 has been developed for the Operating Fund of the Edwards Library and not for the library as a whole. As a result, the receivables and payables to other funds are included in the schedule. If the schedule had been developed for the entire library, these inter-fund receivables and payables would be eliminated from the schedule if they could not be legally enforced. In figure 13–1 it can be seen that the Cash Deficiency has increased from June 30, 19x4, to June 30, 19x5, by $11,400. This is an indication that the Operating Fund of the Edwards Library may have difficulty meeting its payments in the future.

The relationship between the quick assets and the current liabilities provides the most stringent test of the liquidity of an NFP organization. Another ratio that can also be used to evaluate this relationship is "current ratio," which measures the dollar-for-dollar relationship between current liabilities and current assets. This ratio widens the type of assets that can be used to pay current liabilities to *all* current assets rather than the most liquid assets.[5] When this relationship is equal to 1, it means that the current liabilities can be paid with the

---

4. Joint Financial Management Improvement Program, *Managers—Are You Looking for More Meaningful Financial Reports?* (Washington, D.C.: U.S. Government Printing Office, 1980), p. 25.

5. Although the ratio widens the type of assets included, intrafund and interfund receivables and payables must be legally enforceable to be included in the computation.

Edwards Library
Operating Fund
Cash Availability Schedule
June 30, 19x5
(with Comparative Totals for 19x4)

	June 30, 19x5	June 30, 19x4
Cash	$ 17,000	$31,000
Marketable Securities	15,000	24,000
Due from Endowment Fund	30,000	—
Due from Restricted Fund	7,500	5,500
Total Quick Assets	$ 69,500	$60,500
Accounts Payable	$ 17,500	$15,500
Due to Plant Fund	15,000	—
Long-Term Debt Payable Current Portion	20,000	20,000
Accrued Payables	22,500	20,100
Other Payables	7,500	6,500
Cash Required	$ 82,500	$62,100
Cash Excess (Deficiency)	$ (13,000)	$ (1,600)

FIG. 13–1. Cash Availability Schedule for Edwards Library

available current assets. If the ratio is equal to less than 1, it means that if the current liabilities were due, they could not all be paid with the amount of current assets available. In that type of situation, long-term assets, such as plant facilities, might have to be sold to pay the current liabilities. The equation for this ratio follows:

$$\text{Current Ratio} = \frac{\text{All Current Assets}}{\text{Current Liabilities}}$$

All current assets are included in this calculation; so it is not considered as stringent a test of the relationship as the acid-test ratio. The additional assets in the computation are inventories and prepaid assets. The value which can be obtained for these assets is usually lower than the value at which they are listed on the balance sheet; therefore; it is important that the acid-test ratio also be computed any time the current ratio is calculated. For the current ratio to have meaning, it should be compared with equivalent periods in previous years.

These ratios and schedules of liquidity are important evaluation tools which provide indications as to whether the NFP organization can continue to provide a full level of programs to the public. Once the NFP organization cannot meet its payments on its current liabilities, it will soon have to curtail its operations. To prevent this, other techniques are available to recognize the potentiality of this problem.

One way to help control the relationship between payments and cash resources is to prepare a "cash budget." Unlike the cash availability schedule, which determines the difference between quick assets and current liabilities, the cash budget shows the actual outflows and inflows of cash expected to arise in the organization. The cash budget is a *projection* of cash behavior in the organization. The purpose of the cash budget, which is prepared for a monthly, quarterly, and yearly period, is to show when the organization will have excess cash available or will have to raise cash to support its expenditure plans. When excess cash is available, the most efficient organization is one which can keep this excess cash invested in temporary, interest-bearing investments. If the cash budget shows that cash will be needed by the organization in the near future, arrangements can be made to sell short-term investments or to borrow the needed cash. In both cases, the cash budget allows the cash requirements to be determined ahead of time, so that the NFP organization will not find itself in a situation where it temporarily has no cash to make necessary payments. Although a cash shortage may not be considered a problem, because there is always plenty of cash available, the high availability of cash may be a symptom of another problem: inefficient management of cash resources. Cash should not be allowed to remain idle or be kept in low-yielding savings accounts.

A cash budget is illustrated in figure 13–2 for the Operating Fund of the Mary Sloan Library. This cash budget represents the quarterly period, January 1 through March 31, 19x8, for the Sloan Library. The cash budget is divided into two basic sections. The top section records the inflows of cash and the bottom section records the out-

Mary Sloan Library
Unrestricted Operating Fund
Cash Budget
For the Months of January, February, and March

	January	February	March
Cash In			
Beginning Cash Balance	$ 5,000	$ 5,000	$ 5,000
Book Fines	150	100	70
User's Fees	180	180	180
Book Sales	800	—	—
Interest and Dividends	12,000	—	—
Totals	$18,130	$ 5,280	$ 5,250
Cash Out			
Installment Payment	$ 3,500	$ —	$ —
Book Purchases	7,000	5,000	7,300
Rental	750	750	750
Payroll	10,000	10,000	10,000
Payments on Accounts Payable	1,400	1,400	1,400
Repairs on Bookmobile	—	—	1,250
Totals	$22,650	$ 17,150	$ 20,700
Cash Balance (Deficit) at End of Month	$ (4,520)	$ (11,870)	$ (15,450)
Required Cash Balance	5,000	5,000	5,000
Increase (Decrease) in Securities	$ (9,520)	$ (16,870)	$ (20,450)

FIG. 13–2. Cash Budget for Mary Sloan Library Operating Fund (Unrestricted Portion)

flows. In the top section, it can be seen that the beginning balance in the Cash account is the first source of cash. The NFP organization wants to have an ending balance in the Cash account equal to $5,000 at the end of each month; therefore, each beginning cash balance is shown at $5,000.[6] The other sources of cash are book fines, user's fees, book sales, and the receipt of dividends and interest on short-term investments. These sources are some examples of cash inflows to the library, but they should not be considered all inclusive. The total cash available for January is shown as $18,130, the actual cash received during the month. The cash inflow is the amount of cash expected to be received each month.

The lower section of the cash budget deals with the outflows of cash from the library. These outflows are equal to $22,650, and they are composed of installment payments on the mortgage, book purchases, rentals, payroll, payments on accounts payable, and payments for repairs on the bookmobile. These outflows are $4,520 more than the cash inflows for the month of January. This difference is called the "Cash Balance (Deficit) at the end of the month." In addition to this deficit for January, a beginning cash balance of $5,000 is required for February, and there are two ways to get a positive cash balance of $5,000 in February. One way is to borrow the needed cash on a short-term basis and the other way is to sell marketable securities. In either case, a total of $9,520 in cash is needed during January.

The Sloan Library receives its payments of support from various governmental agencies at the beginning of the fiscal year. These cash payments are not allocated to the library but received in total at the beginning of the year. The library invests these amounts in temporary investments, and they are available for use during the year. To make up for the $4,520 deficit and the required $5,000 beginning cash balance, $9,520 of investments will have to be sold in January. It is assumed that the sale is made, and the cash balance for February is equal to $5,000. The sale of the marketable securities is recorded in the last row of the cash budget. If there were a cash increase during the month, it would be recorded here also.

The months of February and March in the quarterly cash budget for the Sloan Library show that the amount of each monthly deficit is increasing; so additional marketable securities will have to be sold to finance the monthly operations of the library. These sales will equal $16,870 and $20,450 in February and March, respectively. At the beginning of each year, the library should prepare a yearly cash budget in order to determine if it will have enough marketable securities to finance its operations through the year. When a cash budget of this type is prepared, certain cash payments will have to be estimated

6. The ending balance for one month is the next month's beginning balance.

from the payment schedules of previous years. Again, it should be noted that the cash budget records when the cash is actually paid out and when it is actually received, rather than when any amount is owed.

Adjustments to the cash budget should be made if the NFP organization receives its monies for operations on an allotment basis. Under an allotment basis, monies are periodically (perhaps quarterly) tranferred to the organization for operational purposes. In this situation, the cash budget should be established to determine if the organization has sufficient monies to operate through the allotment period.

These are some of the techniques that can be used in cash control with an NFP organization to ensure that potential problems are foreseen. Other methods that can be used in an NFP organization to ensure that, once the monies are available they are used properly by the organization, are considered as part of the budgetary control for an NFP organization.

Exercise 13–1. Cash Control

1. The current assets and current liabilities of the Elizabeth Yuhasz Library are presented below. The director of the library is interested in knowing whether the library is likely to have future difficulties in paying its current liabilities. You have been selected to investigate this situation. Compute the following:

   a) Current Ratio
   b) Acid-Test Ratio
   c) A cash availability schedule
   d) From the analyses in a, b, and c, write a short analysis of the library's ability to pay its current liabilities.

Elizabeth Yuhasz Library
Partial Balance Sheet
Oct. 1, 19x9

Cash	$15,000	Accounts Payable	$ 28,000
Marketable Securities	25,000	Due to Plant Fund	5,700
State Grant Receivable	17,500	Current Portion of	
Due from Operating		Long-Term Debt	35,000
Fund	5,700	Long-Term Debt	150,000
Inventories	3,500		
Equipment, net of			
depreciation	37,000		

2. The Helen Cloyd Library has had problems in the past year in planning its cash requirements. During the year, this has led to periods when it was questionable whether liabilities could be paid. To help overcome this problem, the library has decided to establish a cash budget for the first quarter of its fiscal year. The following information has been collected to help you in developing the budget. Prepare a cash budget for the months of July, August, and September, based on the following information.

    a) Collection of intergovernmental revenues of $200,000 for the year is expected to be received on July 1. Of this amount, all except $10,000 of cash is expected to be immediately invested.

    b) A $5,000 installment payment on long-term debt will be made in July.

    c) The payroll is $17,500 per month and various miscellaneous payments are $1,000 per month.

    d) A policy was started on August 1 that the cash balance at the beginning of each month is to be $10,000.

    e) The beginning cash balance on July 1 is $12,000.

    f) Book purchases are expected to average $7,500 in July and $6,000 in August and September.

    g) Roof repairs are expected to cost $11,000, and they will be paid in August.

    h) Dividends and interest are expected to be equal to 1% of the monthly beginning balance invested in securities. This amount should be rounded to the nearest dollar.

    i) The June 30 ending balance, invested in securities in the last year, was $3,000.

    j) Book fines are expected to be $300 in July and $200 in August and September.

Budgetary Control

If budgetary control measures are to be important, it is necessary to operate the NFP organizations within the budget guidelines which have been established by the board of directors at the beginning of the year. If a department or program administrator does not stay within the established budget guidelines, this should be negatively reflected in any evaluations of performance, if these guidelines are to have meaning. In order to help the adminstrator stay within budget guidelines, the accounting system should produce reports which provide guidance in showing how close expenses are to exceeding budget limits.

At the beginning of the fiscal year an appropriation is made to the various programs or departments in an NFP organization. During the year, accounting reports should be prepared which show the level of expenditures at the program or department level. This report should show how close the expenditures have been to date to the initial amount which was appropriated. In addition, it should show the amount of outstanding encumbrances, the unencumbered balance, the percentage of the appropriation spent, the amount spent in the current month, and the percentage amount spent as of a comparative period in the previous year.

An example of a report of this nature is presented in figure 13–3 for the Nora J. Helena Library. The report is called an Operating Report. Although the Operating Report in figure 13–3 illustrates only Administration and Circulation, this report usually is presented with each of the library's programs listed on it; the objective is to assist in the control of budget expenditures. The report itself is organized around object classifications such as salaries, automobile, telephone and postage, printing, etc. Each of these object classifications is listed under a program classification, and the program heading serves as a total for all the object classifications under that program. The column totals at the bottom of the report provide a summation for the entire organization.[7]

Reviewing figure 13–3, it can be seen how convenient it is to determine the level of budget spending. In the first column, the names of the programs and object expenses are listed. The second column records the account numbers for the object expenses and program accounts. The third column records the amount of the original budget appropriation. The fourth column is a summation of the expenses to the end of the current month. The fifth column records the amount of outstanding encumbrances as of the end of the current month. When the amounts in columns 4 and 5, expenses and encumbrances respectively, are deducted from the original appropriation, the unencumbered balance in column 6 is computed. The total appropriation in column 3 is divided into total expenses and encumbrances to determine the percentage spent in column 7. The dollars spent during the month are presented in column 8. Finally, column 9 shows the percentage of the appropriation spent as of this same date in the prior year. This information allows the reader to compare column 9

7. It should be noted that these costs are all "direct" costs, which are explained on page 397.

Nora J. Helena Library
Operating Report
For Month Ended March 31, 19x3

(1) Description	(2) Account Code	(3) Appropriation Amount	(4) Expenses Year-to-Date	(5) Encumbrances Year-to-Date	(6) Unencumbered Balance	(7) % Spent	(8) Month-Date Expenses	(9) % Spent Prior Year-to-Date
Administration	7,000	78,000	59,000	1,600	17,400	77.69	7,370	70.18
Salaries	7,001	60,000	45,000	—	15,000	75.00	5,000	75.00
Automobile	7,002	2,000	1,700	—	300	85.00	200	60.15
Telephone & Postage	7,003	3,000	1,800	—	1,200	60.00	500	50.00
Printing	7,004	7,000	5,700	1,100	200	97.14	700	85.23
Supplies	7,005	6,000	4,800	500	700	88.33	970	80.00
Circulation	8,000	65,000	48,000	2,450	14,550	77.62	7,570	81.07
Salaries	8,001	42,240	31,680	—	10,560	75.00	3,520	75.00
Books	8,006	15,000	10,500	2,300	2,200	85.33	3,100	83.14
Telephone & Postage	8,003	2,000	1,700	—	300	85.00	300	81.15
Printing	8,004	2,300	2,000	150	150	93.48	200	80.00
Supplies	8,005	3,460	2,120	—	1,340	61.27	450	76.13
Totals		250,000	169,000	41,000	40,000	84.0	25,000	90.15

Fig. 13–3. Operating Report for Nora J. Helena Library

with column 7 to determine if spending activity is ahead or behind the activity of the previous year. The totals at the bottom of the report show the total results for the entire library through March 31, 19x7.

This report is a very useful tool for the administrator who is trying to ensure that the budget is maintained within appropriation guidelines. For example, the "% Spent" column clearly shows the amount of spending on each object expense and in each program to the end of the current month. If any of these amounts have exceeded budgeted amounts, the percentage spent will exceed 100. The column also indicates to the program administrator whether sufficient monies are available to complete the year without overspending the budget. At the end of the year, this column again quickly shows whether the level of spending for the year exceeded 100 percent in any program or object classification.

Similar information is available from the "Unencumbered Balance" column, except this column shows the dollar amount that is still available for spending by the library in the remainder of the year. The totals at the bottom of this column show the total unencumbered balance for the library as a whole. This may be important, depending on the appropriation level recognized by the board. For example, if the board appropriated monies to the various programs but not specifically to object expenses in each program, then a positive total at the bottom of this column may mean that total expenses and outstanding encumbrances have not exceeded the budgeted amounts. On the other hand, if the board appropriated monies specifically to each object expense, a positive total at the bottom of this column is not as important, because there could be a positive total even though specific object expenses could exceed budgeted amounts. This is an example of differences in control levels which can be exercised by the library's board. With specific control, the object expenses are budgeted and any amounts spent in excess of this appropriation exceed the budget limits. If program levels only are budgeted, reallocations can be made between object expenses within programs as long as the total program appropriation is not exceeded.

The "Encumbrance Year-to-Date" column allows the reader of the report to know the amount of outstanding encumbrances at the end of any month. The total of this column should correspond with the balance in the Reserve for Encumbrances account on the Balance Sheet. If the library has a policy that there should be no outstanding encumbrances at the end of the year, this column should not have a balance at that time. If a balance *does* exist in this column, there is a discrepancy from organizational policy.

As previously stated, the "% Spent"—Prior Year-to-Date" column can be compared with the "% Spent" column to determine the percentage changes in spending from the previous year. When this comparison is made in figure 13–3 for Administration, it can be seen that spending for the current year, 19x7, is ahead of the previous year by approximately 7.5 percent. This may or may not be significant, depending on the amount of unencumbered monies remaining. When the individual object expenses under Administration are reviewed, it is apparent where the additional spending occurred. Automobile, telephone and postage, printing, and supply expenses all exceeded percentage spending from the previous year. When such a trend is apparent, the amounts remaining in each object expense should be checked to ensure that enough of the appropriation is left to complete the year without running short of monies. In addition, if this increase in spending is considered significant, the reasons for the increase should be investigated. When Circulation is reviewed, it can be seen that although several object expenses are more than last year, the overall spending of the appropriation is lower this year to date.

The "Month-Date Expense" column shows the spending during the past month. In order to make any sort of comparison in this column, the Operating Report from the previous month, February, has to be compared with the Operating Report in figure 13–3. The main purpose of this column is to provide disclosures about monthly spending. The "Expenses Year-to-Date" column is included in the report for the same reason: to provide disclosures about total spending to date. These two columns are not included in the report for comparison purposes.

The accounting information for the Operating Report can be easily collected if the accounts are correctly coded. As indicated in chapters 2 and 11, it is possible to collect information about object expenses if the ledger accounts are properly coded. This type of coding requires that a more extensive system of subsidiary accounts be used to collect information, but these accounts can all be maintained in a manual system. When a computerized system is in use, the information is very easy to collect.

When a coding system is considered, it is necessary to set up a system where expenses can be classified according to programs, object expense subdivisions, and special programs. Figure 13–4 illustrates a four-digit coding system for the Expense accounts. The object expenses are represented by two digits, 01, 02, 03, etc. This object coding system divides the expenses into the following classifications:

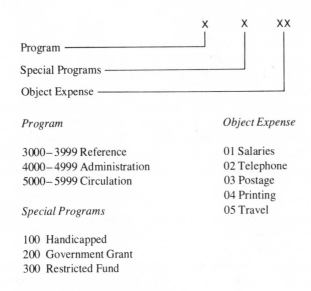

X   X   XX

Program ————————————————⌐
Special Programs ——————————————⌐
Object Expense ——————————————————⌐

Program	Object Expense

Program

3000–3999 Reference
4000–4999 Administration
5000–5999 Circulation

Special Programs

100 Handicapped
200 Government Grant
300 Restricted Fund

Object Expense

01 Salaries
02 Telephone
03 Postage
04 Printing
05 Travel

FIG. 13–4. Account Code Numbers

salaries (01), telephone (02), postage (03), printing (04), and travel (05). The object coding could be extended to 99 object expenses.

The next level of coding relates to special programs, such as programs for the handicapped, a special government grant on which expenses need to be separated, and a restricted grant. The coding is 100 for handicapped expenses, 200 for the government grant, and 300 for the restricted grant.

The final level of coding relates to the program level which appears in the financial statements in the previous chapters. In figure 13–4 it can be seen that 3000 to 3999 represents the Reference Department, 4000 to 4999 represents Administration, and Circulation is represented by the coding sequence 5000 to 5999.

With this coding system, it is possible to classify expenses for the program level on the financial statements, and the object level for more detailed schedules prepared for internal cost control. It is also possible to accumulate expenses on special programs, such as the program for the handicapped, to determine their cost. For example, asssume that an expense is coded 3001, which means it is a salary expense for the Reference Department. If the expense had been coded 3101, it would be a salary expense incurred through the Reference Department, which is related to the program for the handicapped run by the library. As another example, assume an expense code is 4205. This is an Administrative expense, related to a specific government grant, and it involves travel related to that grant. The system described here uses a four-digit code, but it is possible to have coding systems that use up to fourteen or sixteen digits.

Although it was not stated, the accounts listed in figure 13–3 were also coded. Administration was represented by a 7000 to 7999 coding and Circulation included the accounts from 8000 to 8999. The object expenses were coded on a 01, 02 system. These coding numbers were listed in the second column of the Operating Report in figure 13–3.

The expense coding system illustrated in figure 13–4 was for only one fund. It would be possible to expand this four-digit coding system by one digit to represent the three funds normally found in an NFP organization. For example, number 1 in front of the four-digit code can represent the Operating Fund, and a 2 or 3 can represent the Endowment and Plant Fund, respectively. This code change would allow expenses to be classified on a fund basis. For example, the code 1–3001 would be an Operating Fund salary expense in the Reference Department.

The advantages of an account coding system are obvious. A coding system allows for the collection of expenses in various types of groups for the specific type of report that is being prepared. For example, salary expenses can be aggregated on a program basis, according to some special program such as that for the handicapped; on a fund basis; or for the organization as a whole. These aggregations of expenses are a great help in determining if expenses are becoming too large in any one area. They also provide an easy way of tracing the changes in expenses in a fund or program over a several-year period to determine the trend of expenses.

This coding system has been specifically related to the expenses of an NFP organization, but with the same type of coding system it would be possible to record revenues according to funds and other divisions.

Exercise 13–2. Budgetary Control

Outline the type of Operating Report that would be useful in the NFP organization for which you work. Specify the column headings and the programs which should be included in this report.

Cost Allocation

In the combined financial statements presented in chapter 11, expenses were classified according to program functions, such as Reference, Circulation, Children's Library, and Regional History. It is assumed that these four programs are also the major departments within the H. K. Fines Library. Also included in the expense classification scheme was Administration, but unlike the other departments, Administration is considered a support function rather than a program function. Administration provides service to all the library's programs. The identification of a service function focuses on the difference between support structure and program structure in the library. Largely due to Administration's support function, its operating expenses cannot be directly traced to the various programs in the library. In order to determine the full costs of the program activities, the costs of Administration have to be allocated to the various programs in the library in some logical fashion. This section deals with the allocation of costs of support departments to program activities. The costs of these support functions are called "indirect costs."

Indirect costs are those costs that cannot be directly traced to the program activities of a library. In addition, these costs benefit more than one program in the library. For example, the activities performed in Administration benefit all the programs of the library. Other examples of indirect costs incurred through support services are costs incurred in maintenance and custodial services, the costs of the accounting department, depreciation on physical facilities used by all personnel, and the costs incurred in the operation of a technical services department. These expenses cannot be traced directly to any specific program because they provide support to all the activities of the library.

Before any allocation of indirect costs to program functions, all programs should be clearly defined so that there is no confusion between programs and support services. A program can generally be recognized because it is directly responsible for interacting with the public in one specific area. A program could be related to handicapped services but not the accounting function, under this definition.

Indirect costs are defined as those costs incurred in the library's support functions; other costs, incurred in the program areas of the library, are called "direct costs." An example of a direct cost is the salary paid to the head of the Circulation Department, as that cost can be seen as directly benefiting a program. A direct cost can be directly traced to a program, and its benefits to that program can be clearly outlined. The direct costs and the allocated indirect costs to each program together comprise the full costs of a program.

A program activity would have difficulty performing its functions without the support of the various activities of administration, technical services, accounting, and building maintenance. Program activities cannot occur without supporting services. With this in mind, it is clear that the costs of a program are not made up only of direct costs of that program but also the costs of support services it receives. Still, the question may be asked, Why assign these indirect costs to the library's programs? The answer is that in order to have some concept about the costs of a program to the public, the full cost of those programs must be determined, and the only way to determine full costs is to allocate indirect costs. This allocation provides answers to questions about which program is the most expensive for the library to conduct. The allocation procedure can determine whether the cost of providing program activities is increasing and, if it is, which program's costs are increasing most rapidly. If it is necessary to cut a program back, this procedure can determine the amount of cost savings that will arise from the cutback. The answers to these questions can be based on objective information with a cost allocation procedure.

A cost allocation procedure attempts to find some way to allocate the costs of services to programs. Although it is not possible to find a direct relationship between the indirect costs of services and programs, an allocation procedure should be based on some sort of logical relationship between these two areas. Figure 13–5 illustrates the allocation bases that can be used to allocate the expenses of the service area to programs. The first column in figure 13–5 lists five indirect cost "pools." A first step in the cost allocation procedure is

Indirect Cost Pool	*Allocation Base*
Depreciation—Building	Direct Expenses or Area Usage
Maintenance and Custodial	Square Footage of Space
Accounting Department	Direct Expenses
Administration	Number of Full-Time Equivalent Employees
Technical Services	Books Cataloged to Programs

Fig. 13–5. Allocation Bases for Some Typical Cost Pools

to divide the services' expenses into cost pools. The cost pools are used to accumulate the indirect costs of similar activities before they are assigned to the various program activities.

The second column in figure 13–5 lists the allocation bases that are used to allocate the costs in the cost pools. For example, the building depreciation expenses are allocated to the programs based on the percentage of direct expenses in each program. This is one allocation that can be used; another method of depreciation allocation could be based on the square footage used in each program area. The depreciation expense on equipment used in a specific program is not considered to be an allocated expense but, rather, a direct cost of that program. Only when equipment is used by all program areas should an allocation procedure be established for the depreciation on this particular piece of equipment.

The maintenance and custodial expenses are allocated to the programs on the square footage used by each program. The relationship between the cost of maintenance and custodial services and the square footage is fairly well accepted. (The underlying assumption is that it takes more time to maintain larger areas.) The costs of accounting services which are largely payroll expenses are allocated to each program on the direct expenses in each program. (This allocation assumes that more time is involved in record keeping for programs wth more direct expenses.) Another way of allocating these expenses could be based on the number of full-time-equivalent (FTE) employees.[8] This method is used to allocate the administrative costs to the various programs. It is assumed that more administration time is devoted to programs which have larger numbers of FTE employees. Finally, the method used to allocate the costs of technical services department is based on the number of books cataloged for each program.

The method that is used to allocate the costs of the service departments to the programs of the library should be based on some method in which the information is already collected or easily available. The method should not require the collection of information not already available in the system. For example, it would be possible to allocate the costs of the accounting department based on the number of docu-

8. The term ''full-time-equivalent employees'' is important when there are part-time employees working for the NFP organization. For example, when two part-time employees are working for the organization, they are the equivalent of one full-time employee for cost allocation purposes. All part-time employees' working hours must be summed to determine their contribution in terms of full-time equivalents.

ments processed for each program, but the additional work involved in collecting this information is not justified.

The allocation of these costs may be reflected on the combined financial statements, or this information may only be prepared for internal cost analysis. In preparing the financial statements, some or all the service costs may be allocated to the programs of an NFP organization. If all the service costs are allocated, no service department costs will be disclosed on the financial statements. In the SREF for the H. K. Fines Library in figure 11–2, Administration costs were disclosed as a separate cost item. In this financial statement, these indirect costs had not been allocated to the five programs of the library. It is not necessary to allocate the costs of services to the programs for financial reporting purposes, but, in order to determine the full cost of programs, these costs should be allocated to the programs in reports prepared for cost analysis within the organization or, sometimes, to show the full cost of grant programs.

Several methods can be used to allocate the indirect costs to programs.[9] The method that is illustrated here, called the "step-down" method of cost allocation, begins by allocating one service department's expenses to all other service departments and programs. This procedure continues, with reallocation through each of the other service departments and programs, until all service costs have been allocated to the programs. With this method, it is important to realize that all indirect costs are allocated forward to departments and programs that have not received a cost allocation from a service department. This process continues until all the costs in all service departments have been completely reallocated to programs. Indirect costs are never allocated back to a service department, which has already assigned its costs to another service department.

The step-down allocation is illustrated here for the Harriet Fairchild Library. The first step in this cost allocation procedure is to determine the allocation bases in each department and program. For example, the number of square feet (an allocation base) in each program area needs to be determined. The information on the allocation bases for the Fairchild Library is recorded in figure 13–6, where the amount of direct expenses, square footage, number of FTE employees, and number of books cataloged is shown for the four programs and four service departments in the library.

---

9. These methods are the direct allocation method, the step-down method, and a cost-allocation method using simultaneous equations. For an explanation of these methods, refer to a textbook on cost accounting.

| | Service Departments | | | | Programs | | | | |
	Maintenance & Custodial	Accounting	Administration	Technical Services	Circulation	Reference	Children's Library	Regional History	Totals
Direct Expenses	$12,000	$18,000	$26,000	$22,000	$ 57,000	$32,000	$25,000	$18,000	$210,000 /$180,000
Square Footage	—	1,750	2,600	3,000	117,000	30,000	57,000	5,000	216,350
No. of FTE Employees	5	3	6	5	6	3	4	2	20
Books Cataloged	—	—	—	—	60,000	13,000	20,000	8,000	101,000

Total Depreciation Expenses = $89,000

Fig. 13–6. Allocation Bases for Fairchild Library

The second step in this cost allocation process is to determine the order in which the service costs are to be assigned. The order of allocation is important because a different pattern will result in a different total cost for each program. In the Fairchild Library, the following order of cost allocation and basis of allocation was selected:

1. Depreciation; direct expense base
2. Maintenance and Custodial; square footage base
3. Accounting; direct expense base
4. Administration; number of FTE employees base
5. Technical Services; number of books cataloged base

Generally, the order of cost allocation varies from one organization to another. In this instance, the reason for selecting depreciation expense as the first cost to be allocated is because it relates to all other activities; and operating costs (the allocation base) for the service departments and programs are readily available. The reason for picking technical services last is because if it were chosen first, some of its costs would have to be allocated to service departments lower on the allocation list where little relationship existed, such as maintenance and custodial services.

Once the order of allocation is chosen and the basis for allocating the costs has been determined, the allocation process can begin. It distributes costs by using a simple percentage of the total allocation base. The percentages are computed from the "Total" column in figure 13–6, and the amounts in this column are computed by adding across each of the four rows. The percentage allocation to each service department and program is shown in figure 13–7, where the first column is the "Base," which represents the denominator in determining the percentages of cost allocated. The "Base" is taken from the "Total" column summations in figure 13–6.

It should be noticed that although the service costs are allocated forward, they are never allocated backward. The process of forward allocation is apparent when the costs in the Accounting Department are allocated. Accounting expenses are allocated forward to Administration, Technical Services, Circulation, Reference, Children's Library, and Regional History, using the same base (operating expenses) as was used to allocate depreciation expense. Unlike the depreciation expense, the dollar amount of that operating expense allocation base is equal to $180,000, rather than $210,000. A base of $180,000 is used because accounting expenses must be allocated forward. Therefore, the Maintenance and Custodial Department as well as the Accounting Department receive no allocation of account-

Service	Base	Maintenance & Custodial	Accounting	Administration	Technical Services	Circulation	Reference	Children's Library	Regional History
Depreciation	$210,000	.057*	.086	.124	.105	.271	.152	.119	.086
Maintenance & Custodial	216,350		.008**	.012	.014	.541	.139	.263	.023
Accounting	180,000	—	—	.144†	.122	.317	.178	.139	.10
Administration	20	—	—	—	.25‡	.30	.15	.20	.10
Technical Services	101,000	—	—	—	—	.594§	.129	.198	.079

$* \dfrac{12,000}{210,000}$ $** \dfrac{1,750}{216,350}$ $† \dfrac{2,600}{180,000}$ $‡ \dfrac{5}{20}$ $§ \dfrac{60,000}{101,000}$

FIG. 13–7.   Percentage Allocations for Fairchild Library

ing expenses. When the direct operating expenses of these two departments, $30,000,[10] is eliminated from the total operating expenses, the base becomes $180,000. By dividing $180,000 into the remaining direct operating expenses for each department and program, the percentages in figure 13–7 for the distribution of accounting expenses (in the third row) are determined.

The process of forward allocation can also be seen when the number of FTE employees is used as an allocation base for distributing the costs of Administration to Technical Services, Circulation, Reference, Children's Library, and Regional History. Although the number of FTE employees in the Fairchild Library is equal to 34, the number of FTE employees in the departments to which the costs are going to be allocated are equal only to 20; therefore, the base must also be equal to 20. The percentages in the fourth row of figure 13–7 are based on 20 employees, divided into the number of employees in each department and program to which the costs of Administration are allocated.

The first allocated expense, depreciation expense, is based on the direct operating expenses in each service department and program. The "Base" for operating expenses is equal to the total of all direct operating expenses in the library, or $210,000.[11] The percentage figures for the service departments and programs are computed by dividing this "Base" into the operating expenses for each department and program. In this manner, 5.7 percent of the depreciation expense is allocated to the Maintenance and Custodial Department and 8.6 percent of the depreciation expense is allocated to the Accounting Department. The same procedure is followed for each of the other departments and programs to determine their cost percentages.

This procedure will result in an initial allocation, with a subsequent reallocation, until all service department costs are allocated to the programs. Allocation of the actual expenses is shown in figure 13–8, where it can be seen that depreciation expenses are allocated once, across all departments and programs, and then reallocated four times. Reallocation is apparent in the Maintenance and Custodial Department. Depreciation expense of $5,703 is first allocated to the Maintenance and Custodial Department; it is then reallocated to all the other departments and programs when the $17,073 total in the Maintenance and Custodial Department costs is allocated. This process continues until all dollar amounts in the service departments have been allo-

10. The $30,000 is composed of $12,000 in Maintenance and Custodial and $18,000 in Accounting expenses.
11. Also see the "Total" column in figure 13–6.

cated to the direct costs in the program departments. Once this allocation procedure is completed, the amounts accumulated in each program are the full cost of its operation.

The allocation procedure in figure 13–8 is based on the percentages that were computed in figure 13–7. For example, in order to
assign depreciation expenses to the various departments and programs
in the library, the percentages based on operating expenses in figure
13–7 are multiplied by the total depreciation expenses of $89,000.
This multiplication results in the costs allocated to the other departments and programs in the library. At the time of the cost distribution, the column containing depreciation expenses is reduced to a
zero balance.

The allocation of Administration costs is another example of this
process. In order to assign the costs in Administration to the other
departments and programs in the Fairchild Library, we need to know
the percentage breakdowns on the number of employees in the departments and programs (to the right of "Administration" in figure
13–7). The percentages shown in figure 13–7 (25%, 30%, 15%,
20%, and 10%) are multiplied by the total costs in Administration
($40,954.72) to determine the amount of these costs to allocate to the
respective departments and programs.[12] Once these amounts are computed, the $40,954.72 is deducted from the total direct and allocated
costs in Administration. This deduction reduces the costs in Administration to zero. At the same time, the allocation is made to the other
departments and programs.

In the same manner, the total costs in Technical Services are assigned to the programs based on the percentages of books cataloged
in figure 13–7. These percentages are equal to 59.4, 12.9, 19.8, and
7.9 percent. Multiplication of these percentages by the $44,969.15
total cost in Technical Services results in the amounts allocated to
each of the programs.[13] The cost total in Technical Services is reduced to zero when the costs of this department are allocated to the
remaining programs.

The objective of the cost allocation procedure in figure 13–8 is to
determine the full costs of each of the four programs in the Fairchild
Library. The full costs are shown in figure 13–8 under each of the
programs. The full costs for Circulation are $137,529.20, and it is
composed of $57,000 of direct costs (i.e., costs charged directly to

12. It can be seen in figure 13–8 that the amount allocated to Technical Services is
$10,238.68, which is equal to 25% of $40,954.72.
13. Of the total costs in Technical Services ($44,469.15), $10,238.68 had just been allocated
from Administration.

| | Service Departments | | | | | | | Programs | | |
	Depreciation	Maintenance & Custodial	Accounting	Administration	Technical Services	Circulation	Reference	Children's Library	Regional History	Totals
	$89,000.00*	$12,000.00	$18,000.00	$26,000.00	$22,000.00	$57,000.00	$32,000.00	$25,000.00	$18,000.00	$89,000.00
1.	(89,000.00)	5,073.00	7,654.00	11,036.00	9,345.00	24,119.00	13,528.00	10,591.00	7,654.00	$89,000.00
		$17,073.00								
2.		(17,073.00)	136.58	204.88	239.02	9,236.49	2,373.15	4,490.20	392.68	17,073.00
			$25,790.58							
3.			(25,790.58)	3,713.84	3,146.45	8,175.61	4,590.72	3,584.89	2,579.06	25,790.58**
				$40,954.72						
4.				(40,954.72)	10,238.68	12,286.42	6,143.21	8,190.94	4,095.47	40,954.72
					$44,969.15					
5.					(44,969.15)	26,711.68	5,801.02	8,903.89	3,552.56	44,969.15
Full Cost of Programs						$137,529.20	$64,436.10	$60,760.92	$36,273.77	

Per Unit Data

No. of books checked out (100,000)	$1.38	—	—	—
No. of reference *questions* answered (400,000)	—	$ .16	—	—
No. of children's books checked out (150,000)	—	—	$ .41	—
No. of regional history books checked out (18,000)	—	—	—	$2.02
No. of persons checking out books (Cir. 60,000; Child's 30,000; Reg. Hist. 15,000)	2.29	—	2.02	2.42

*Given in figure 13–6.

**Due to rounding differences.

Fig. 13–8. Cost Allocations to Programs of Fairchild Library

this program) and $80,529.20 of costs allocated from the various service departments. This makes the Circulation Department twice as expensive to operate as any of the other programs. This difference is not as apparent when the direct costs of operation are compared across programs.

The full costs of programs should be viewed from a per unit perspective. For example, a per unit cost for checked-out books can be determined. This per unit figure provides some indication of the cost of providing these services to the public. In addition, it provides a comparison between the three programs as to the cost per unit of services provided. Whenever per unit costs are computed, care should be exercised in their interpretation. For example, in figure 13–8 the Children's Library has the lowest per unit check-out cost in any of the three programs where these per unit data have been calculated, but when books are checked out of this collection, usually a large number are checked out by each person. This effect may influence the manner in which this per unit data should be interpreted. Although the same number of people may use the collection in the Children's Library as in Circulation and Regional History, the larger number of books checked out by each person may unfavorably (and unjustifiably) influence the per unit figures against the other two collections.

If the per unit figures are changed to the number of patrons checking books out from the three collections, the unit costs are much closer, as can be seen in the last row in figure 13–8. The costs for Circulation, Children's Library, and Regional History are $2.29, $2.02, and $2.42, respectively. These unit costs, clearly, are not out of line with one another. The disparity when per unit information was based on the number of books checked out disappears. The point is not that there should be no disparity existing between per unit costs, but that the underlying reasons for any difference should be investigated before conclusions can be drawn about per unit costs.

Per unit cost information can be very useful in making decisions about the operations of a program. In making comparisons between per unit costs, decisions can be made as to whether the costs of operating one program are out of line with the other programs. If this appears to be the case, analysis can focus on determining the reasons for this apparent difference, with the objective of lowering these high costs. The full costs of these programs and the unit costs are likely to lead to conclusions as to which programs, from a cost perspective, should be providing the maximum level of benefits to the patrons of a library.

Cost allocation procedures provide information about the full costs of operating programs in an NFP organization, as well as unit cost information. The process of determining indirect costs for allocation can also provide information about the cost of eliminating a program or department. The costs that can be eliminated when a program or department is dropped are the direct costs that are associated with that department. It may be assumed that these costs are shown as incurred by the program or department on the financial statements, but this assumption should *not* be made as the costs shown on the financial statements may or may not include the indirect costs of operating that program. If indirect costs are included in the program expenses on the financial statement, it cannot be assumed that elimination of the program will eliminate all costs associated with the program (as shown on the financial statements). This may lead to the statement, ''I thought we were going to save more!'' Indirect costs are allocated costs, and they need to be examined separately from direct costs in a program to determine if the elimination of a program will have any effect on them. If the Regional History Department (figure 13–8) were eliminated, the direct costs that would be saved would be $18,000 in unallocated costs. The allocated costs, $18,273.77, are not likely to be affected by elimination of the department because these costs relate to service departments which are expected to continue functioning in the same manner. As these allocated costs remain, they will be reallocated to the remaining three programs, which means that the costs of $18,273.77 would now be allocated among Circulation, Reference, and Children's Library. Through development of a cost schedule, as in figure 13–8, it is possible to determine very clearly the costs that can be saved by eliminating or cutting back a particular program. This information cannot be assumed to be available from the amounts shown under program expenses on a financial statement.

Other considerations besides cost concerns always need to be taken into account when decisions about cutbacks in programs have to be faced. There may be a particular need for a program in an NFP organization that overrides cost considerations, but per unit and full cost data can provide administrators with additional information for making a decision. Whether cost considerations are of primary or secondary importance to an administrator, they should be considered in making these kinds of decisions.

The development of full cost reports requires planning. Summarization of accounting data for financial reporting purposes is usually different from summarization for internal cost reporting. The accounts have to be coded in such a fashion to make it easy to generate this information for both purposes. Furthermore, the functions of staff may have to be analyzed to determine if job responsibilities are divided between programs. In such cases, the salaries of these individuals will be assigned to programs as a direct cost in the same proportion as their job is divided between programs.

Summary

The development of financial statements is important as they demonstrate to the public the fiscal responsibility of an organization. Financial statements cannot provide all the answers to all the questions, especially in relation to internal operations. This chapter is concerned with illustrating reports and schedules that can provide additional information about internal operations. Specifically, it is concerned with control measures for cash, budgets, and cost allocation procedures. The schedules prepared in the chapter are directed at controlling budgetary expenditures and monitoring the availability of cash in the organization. In addition, with the use of cost schedules, administrators should be able to get a clearer idea of the full costs of a program. The topics covered in the chapter are directed at the internal operations of the organization.

Exercise 13–3. Cost Allocation

1. The Sherman Hanks County Library is attempting to determine the full cost of its programs for the year ended June 30, 19x1. Three programs have been identified in the library, and there are three service departments. The service departments are Administration, Custodial, and Technical Services. It has been decided that service department costs will be allocated to the programs, using the step-down method. Information about the costs in each department and program follows. Administration costs are to be allocated first and Technical Services last.

Program or Department	Cost of Operations	Allocation Base	No. of Employees	Square Feet	Cataloged Books
Program 1	$60,000	—	4	4,000	11,000
Program 2	18,000	—	2	1,500	3,000
Program 3	65,000	—	4	3,500	7,000
Administration	60,000	No. of employees	3	1,500	—
Custodial	16,000	Square feet	2	—	—
Technical Services	23,000	No. of books cataloged	2	800	—

Determine the full costs of each of the three programs. Allocation of Administration cost is based on the number of employees, Custodial cost allocation is based on square footage, and Technical Services costs are allocated on the number of books cataloged for each program.

2. Using the full costs of the three programs determined in question 1, answer the following questions.

   a) What is the per unit cost of the books cataloged in the programs?

   b) Assume that the numbers of patrons checking books out of the collections in the three programs during the fiscal year ended June 30, 19x1, are as follows:

   > Program 1 — 12,000
   > Program 2 — 15,000
   > Program 3 — 16,000

   What is the per unit cost of patrons using the collection in the three programs?

   c) What do the different per unit results in (a) and (b) indicate about the programs?

   d) Which of these per unit measures would be more useful to the library in determining whether its objectives are being met?

3. Using the data in figures 13–6 and 13–7 for the Fairchild Library, assign the costs in the service departments to the programs, based on the following order (rather than the order in the chapter).

   > Depreciation
   > Administration
   > Maintenance and Custodial
   > Accounting
   > Technical Services

   a) What is the total cost of each program?

   b) Do the differences in program costs in question 3 and the costs shown in the chapter mean that cost allocation is inaccurate and should not be used?

Appendix

Answers to Exercises

Chapter 2.

Exercise 2–1

1. A = L + FB

    = $35,000 + $40,000

    = $75,000

2. FB = A – L

    = $45,000 – $45,000

    = Zero. The Fund Balance has a zero balance.

3. L = A – FB

    = $55,000 – $15,000

    = $40,000

4. FB = A − L

    = $15,000 − $17,500

    = −$2,500. The Fund Balance has a deficit. There have been more expenditures than there have been inflows of resources.

5. FB = A − L

    = $25,000 − $15,000

    = $10,000. The Fund Balance should be equal to $10,000. The bookkeeper has made a $2,000 mistake. The bookkeeper will have to check the books to find the error if the books are going to balance.

Exercise 2–2

1. Asset (DR); Asset (CR). Two asset accounts are affected.
    Equipment (DR); Cash (CR).

2. Asset (DR); Liability (CR).
    Equipment (DR); Accounts Payable (CR).

3. Asset (DR); Liability (CR).
    Cash (DR); Deferred Restricted Contributions (CR).

4. Asset (DR); Liability (CR).
    Cash (DR); Loans Payable (CR).

Exercise 2–3

1. a) No. It creates a liability.
    b) No. This transaction is like a refund from a previous expenditure.
    c) Yes. User's Fee Revenues.
    d) Yes. Interest Revenues.

2. a) This is an expense.
    b) This is not an expense but the purchase of an asset.
    c) This is not an expense but the purchase of an asset.
    d) This is usually not immediately an expense. It appears on the books as a prepaid asset or an asset that had been paid for ahead of its use. Once it is used, it turns into an expense.

Exercise 2–4 (Names of Expense and Revenue accounts can vary from those shown)

1. Asset (DR); Revenue (CR).
    Cash (DR); Theatrical Revenues (CR).

2. Asset (DR); Revenue (CR).
   Cash (DR); Investment Revenue (CR).

3. Expenses (DR); Asset (CR).
   Xerox Rental Expense (DR); Cash (CR).

4. Expenses (DR); Liabilities (CR).
   Book Expenses (DR); Accounts Payable (CR).

   Although it may appear that books should be recorded as an asset, if these books are part of the circulating collections they only have an expected life of one year, and they are an expense. If the book purchases have an expected life of over one year, they should be recognized as an asset when they are purchased.

Exercise 2–5

1. a) Journalizing requires that entries be made in the *General Journal*.
   b) Posting requires the use of the *General Journal* and the *General Ledger*.

2. June 5	Office Supplies Inventory	$725	
	Accounts Payable		$725
	Purchased office supplies		
June 7	Cash	85	
	Deposits Payable		85
	Patrons' deposits		
June 11	Delivery Expenses	7	
	Cash		7
	UPS delivery charge		
June 16	Deposits Payable	50	
	Cash		50
	A portion of deposits is returned		
June 27	Cash	75	
	Fines Revenue		75
	Total fines collected for month		
June 27	Salary Expenses	7,500	
	Cash		7,500
	Employees' salaries for month		
June 27	Accounts Payable	725	
	Cash		725
	Paid for office supplies received on June 5		

3. a) T accounts must be established for the following accounts:

Cash

Date	P/R	Amt.	Date	P/R	Amt.
June 5	5	$1,200	June 1	5	$250
			4	5	750
			6	5	50

Accounts Payable

Date	P/R	Amt.	Date	P/R	Amt.
June 1	5	$250	In a "normal" situation, there would be a credit balance in this account		

Salaries Payable

Date	P/R	Amt.	Date	P/R	Amt.
June 4	5	$750	In a "normal" situation, there would be a credit balance in this account		

Interest Revenue

Date	P/R	Amt.	Date	P/R	Amt.
			June 5	5	$1,200

Miscellaneous Expenses

Date	P/R	Amt.	Date	P/R	Amt.
June 6	5	$50			

b) The balance in the Cash account is $150. This is the different between the debit of $1,200 and the total credits of $1,050 ($250 + $750 + $50 = $1,050).

See page 19 for a definition of the term "balance."

4. The General Ledger.

5. The posting reference, which is the account number, had not been transferred to the General Journal. Without this cross-reference, it is very difficult to trace transactions from the General Journal to the General Ledger.

6. It is possible to trace an entry from the General Journal to the General Ledger because the account number of an account to which a debit or credit journal entry is posted into is written into the post reference column in the General Journal. This allows for a reference to the proper account to the General Ledger.

   The same process works in reverse for the process of tracing an entry from the General Ledger to the General Journal. The cross-reference key in the General Ledger is the page number of the General Journal and the date of the entry in the General Journal. Both the page number and the date are transferred to the General Ledger in posting process, and they allow for tracing entries back to the General Journal.

7. See figure 2–20.

Chapter 3.

Exercise 3–1

1. a) No. Entries are made only when cash flows into or out of the organization.
   b) Yes.
   c) Yes.

2. a) No. There is no cash inflow.
   b) Yes.
   c) Yes, if expected to be collected within 60 days; otherwise no.

3. a) No. There is no cash outflow.
   b) Yes.
   c) No. This is one of the exceptions to the accrual method.

4. a) An expenditure.
   b) A prepaid asset.
   c) An expenditure, as there is no recognition of this type of prepaid item.

5. The purchases method recognizes the expenditure for inventory items when they are purchased whereas the consumption method recognizes the expenditure when the inventory item is actually used. Under the second method, the expenditure is recognized at a later period.

Exercise 3–2

1. Journal entries for:

Question 2

    a) *Cash:*   No entry

b) *Accrual:*	PLEDGES RECEIVABLE	22,500
	PLEDGE REVENUE	22,500

The pledges receivable are recorded for only the amount that is estimated to be collectible. In some cases, an uncollectible account is established for the $2,500 estimated to be uncollectible.

c) *Modified Accrual:*

	PLEDGES RECEIVABLE	22,500
	PLEDGE REVENUE	22,500

Question 3

    a) *Cash:*   No entry

b) *Accrual:* June 30	INTEREST EXPENSE	7,000
	INTEREST PAYABLE	7,000

    c) *Modified Accrual:*   No entry

Question 4

a) *Cash:*	INSURANCE EXPENDITURE	250
	CASH	250
b) *Accrual:*	PREPAID ASSETS	250
	CASH	250
c) *Modified Accrual:*	INSURANCE EXPENDITURE	250
	CASH	250

2. In all three accounting methods the entry is the same.

May 1	SUPPLIES EXPENSE OR EXPENDITURES	750
	CASH	750

3. The entries follow:

Accrual and Modified Accrual

May 1	INVENTORY OF SUPPLIES	750
	CASH	750

Cash: The cash method only recognizes inflows and outflows of cash, and it does not use a consumption method.

May 1	SUPPLIES EXPENSE	750
	CASH	750

Exercise 3–3

1. The Balance Sheet is a financial statement which provides a list and a dollar balance for assets, liabilities, reserves of the fund balance as well as the Fund Balance account. The Balance Sheet shows the balances in these accounts as of a specific date.

2. a) As compared with the accrual-based balance sheet the cash-based statement does not list any liabilities.
   b) The cash-based accounting system does not recognize any reserves in the fund balance.
   c) No prepaid assets are recognized on the cash-based balance sheet usually.

3. In the case of Receipts over Expenditures, a cash-based statement is being used. When the Excess is described as Support and Revenue over Expenses, it is the terminology used on an accrual-based financial statement. In both cases, the result of operations is positive. For example, in the case of an accrual statement the support and revenues are more than expenses.

4. The major difference between these terms is that in the Excess of Support and Revenue over Expenses the operations show a positive net Excess; i.e., support and revenue total to more than expenses. In the Excess of Expenses over Support and Revenue a negative net Excess exists; i.e., expenses are more than the total of support and revenue.

5. The major difficulty in using a cash-based balance sheet in making financial decisions is that no liabilities are listed. This makes it appear that all the cash is available for spending when this is usually not the case. In using a cash-based Statement of Receipts and Expenditures, the difficulty is that the expenditures are not assigned to the periods in which they are incurred and the revenues are not assigned to the periods in which they are earned. The overall result of all this is a rather unclear financial picture for any NFP organization using a cash-based system on its financial statements.

Exercise 3–4

	Balance Sheet Prepared Under:		
	Cash Basis	Accrual Basis	Modified-Accrual Basis
Cash	X	X	X
Interest Income Receivable		X	X
Prepaid Insurance		X	
Reserve in Fund Balance		X	X
Accounts Payable		X	X

Exercise 3–5

Outer Banks Pirate Museum
Balance Sheet
June 30, 19x5

Assets		Liabilities	
Cash	$75,000	Salaries Payable	$ 3,700
Inventory of Supplies	500	Deferred Restricted	
Grant Receivable	12,500	Contributions—Grants	12,500
		Total Liabilities	$16,200
		Fund Balance	
		Unrestricted	$71,300[1]
		Restricted:	
		Reserve for Inventory	
		of Supplies	500
		Total Liabilities &	
Total Assets	$88,000	Fund Balance	$88,000

Chapter 4.

Exercise 4–1

a) ESTIMATED REVENUES   110,000

        APPROPRIATIONS   101,100

        FUND BALANCE   8,900[2]

b) ESTIMATED REVENUES   110,000

    Investment Income   75,000

    Federal Awards   25,000

    Fund-raising Campaign   10,000

    APPROPRIATIONS   101,100

        Personnel   75,000

        Administrative Supplies   4,500

        Craft Supplies   5,200

        Utilities   10,100

        Staff Development   1,100

        Publicity   1,200

        Repairs & Maintenance   4,000

    FUND BALANCE   8,900

---

1. When the entire amount of estimated revenues is not entirely used for appropriations, the balance is credited to the Fund Balance.

2. The unrestricted fund balance is determined as follows: ($75,000 − $3,700). Under the accrual method, expenses have increased by the $3,700 because of the recognition of salaries owed to employees which caused the balance in the Fund Balance to decrease.

c) Without some type of departmental expense information, it is very difficult to control the level of expenses. The major reason is that responsibility for overexpending cannot be traced to a single department or individual. The accounting system must provide sufficient information to assign this responsibility. This information can be developed with account numbers being assigned to the expense accounts in each department.

	Debits	Credits
d) ESTIMATED REVENUES 110,000		
Investment Income	75,000	
Federal Awards	25,000	
Fund-raising Campaign	10,000	
APPROPRIATIONS 101,100		
Craft Education	50,550	
Personnel		37,500
Administrative Supplies		2,250
Craft Supplies		2,600
Utilities		5,050
Staff Development		550
Publicity		600
Repairs & Maintenance		2,000
EXHIBITS	50,550	
Personnel		37,500
Administrative Supplies		2,250
Craft Supplies		2,600
Utilities		5,050
Staff Development		550
Publicity		600
Repairs & Maintenance		2,000
FUND BALANCE	8,900	

Exercise 4-2

1. From a quick review of the account, it is obvious that the bookkeeper made many mistakes in recording the transactions, and it will be necessary to review all the accounts in the library's accounting system. The corrected Craft Supplies account is shown below. The $300 transfer to the Regional History Collection is a transfer that can be taken out of the Craft Supplies account. In fact, it may be necessary to make other transfers from one account to another during the library's fiscal year. The transfer should be shown as a reduction of the year's appropriation because it is not an expense of the Craft Supplies account.

The returned supplies on August 1 should be considered a reduction of a previous expense and therefore an increase in the unencumbered balance. The bookkeeper incorrectly recorded all invoice entries in the accounts as no check was made between the original purchase order and the final invoice. All accounts in the system need to be reviewed because of the bookkeeper's mistakes.

APPROPRIATION-EXPENDITURE LEDGER
Account No.: 72-734
Account Title: Craft Supplies
Appropriation: $975

Year: 19x8 - 19x9
Fund: General

Date	Description	P.R.e.f.	Purchase Order Number	ENCUMBRANCES			Expense	Unencumbered Balance
				Issued	Liquidated	Outstanding Balance		
July 1	Budget Approp							975
July 15	Craft Supplies		15	185		185		790
July 25	Invoice Rec.		15		185	—	200	775
Aug. 1	Ret Damaged Craft Supplies -$25		15			—	(25)	800
Sept. 5	$300 Transferred to Regional History					—		500 -300
Sept. 9	Craft Supplies		25	225		225		275
Oct. 3	Invoice Rec.		25		225	—	250	250

2. A number of solutions are acceptable for this problem, as long as the personnel salaries are recorded at the proper amounts and the total estimated revenues are computed correctly. The amount of investment income is not given, but it can be calculated. The amount appropriated for the various expenditures can be summed to $206,400. The amount of the credit to Fund Balance is $6,600; therefore, the amount of the Estimated Revenues must equal $213,000. Once the Estimated Revenues is determined, the earned revenues are totaled to $94,200 and subtracted from the Estimated Revenues, leaving the amount estimated to be earned in investment income of $118,800.

The dollar amounts that are allocated to appropriations other than personnel salaries can vary from one answer to the other. The major purpose of this exercise is to develop an understanding of the relationships between Estimated Revenues, Appropriations, and the Fund Balance, as well as attempting to set up a budget and the initial budget entry for a specific organization.

	Debits		Credits
ESTIMATED REVENUES	213,000		
Investment Income	118,800		
Tuition Fees—Craft Ed.	57,000		
Ticket Revenues—Plays	25,000		
Ticket Revenues—Bus Trips	12,200		
APPROPRIATIONS		206,400	
Bookkeeping		7,500	
Personnel			6,700
Supplies			800
Administration—Director		50,800	
Personnel			41,000
Publicity			2,200
Telephone			2,100
Staff Development			800
Professional Fees			4,700
Trip Coordination		5,500	
Personnel			4,000
Reservation Deposits			1,000
Supplies			500
Children's Activities		56,500	
Personnel			32,500
Set Production Labor			11,000
Set Production Supplies			9,000
Costumes			4,000
Art Exhibits		22,100	
Personnel			15,100
Showing Rentals			7,000
Crafts Education		64,000	
Personnel			6,500
Supplies			2,500
Faculty Salaries			55,000
FUND BALANCE		6,600	

Chapter 5.

Exercise 5-1

a) June 30

	FUND BALANCE	2,500	
	APPROPRIATIONS	120,000	
	RESERVE FOR ENCUMBRANCES	5,000	
	EXPENSES		122,500
	ENCUMBRANCES		5,000

In this case, the Fund Balance is reduced because expenses are more than appropriations.

June 30

	FUND BALANCE	2,000	
	REVENUES	118,000	
	ESTIMATED REVENUES		120,000

Again, the Fund Balance is reduced. This time it is reduced because all the estimated revenues did not materialize through collections.

b) June 30

	FUND BALANCE	7,500	
	APPROPRIATIONS	115,000	
	EXPENSES		122,500

In this entry, the Reserve for Encumbrances and Encumbrances are not closed because they are nonlapsing.

June 30

	FUND BALANCE	2,000	
	REVENUES	118,000	
	ESTIMATED REVENUES		120,000

c) The accounts payable would not be equal to the Encumbrances because encumbrances only become accounts payable after the sales invoice is received and approved for payment. At that point, the original encumbrance is reversed out of the accounts and an account payable may be recognized. Any equality is only a chance occurrence.

d) Lapsing

Herchal Public Library
Balance Sheet
June 30, 19x8

Assets		Liabilities & Fund Balance	
Cash	$ 15,000	Liabilities	
Grants Receivable	18,000	Accounts Payable	$ 25,700
Inventory	2,200		
Investments	125,000	Fund Balance[1]	132,300
		Reserve for Inventory	2,200
		Total Liabilities	
Total Assets	$160,200	& Fund Balance	$160,200

1. The beginning balance in the Fund Balance needs to be adjusted for the total of

Nonlapsing

Herchal Public Library
Balance Sheet
June 30, 19x8

Assets

Cash	$ 15,000
Grants Receivable	18,000
Inventory	2,200
Investments	125,000
Total Assets	$160,200

Liabilities, Appropriations, & Fund Balance

Liabilities		
Accounts Payable		$ 25,700
Appropriations	$5,000	
Less: Encumbrances	5,000	—
Fund Balance		
Unreserved*		$127,300
Reserved for: Encumbrances		5,000
Inventory		2,200
Total Fund Balance		$134,500
Total Liabilities, Appropriations, &		
Fund Balance		$160,200

*Beginning Balance in Fund Balance	$136,800
Loss: Adjustment to Fund Balance	
for debits in closing entries[1]	9,500
End of Fiscal Year Balance in Fund Balance	$127,300

---

the debit entries in the closing entries in (a). In a lapsing appropriation, the unexpended appropriation ($5,000), which is currently part of the Fund Balance, will be returned to the agency that granted the spending authority.

Beginning Balance in Fund Balance	$136,800
Less: Adjustment	4,500
End of Fiscal Year Balance in Fund Balance	$132,300

1. The beginning balance in the Fund Balance is adjusted for the total of the debit entries in the closing journal entry in (b).

e) The similarities between the two statements is that the total assets and total liabilities and fund balance amounts are equal at $160,200. The differences relate to the recording of the outstanding Appropriations, Reserve for Encumbrances, and the Encumbrances.

The Encumbrance cannot be considered an asset because it does not provide a future benefit. Therefore, it is not listed with the assets. Instead, it is shown as a reduction of an outstanding appropriation. The effect of the encumbrance once it is reversed and the invoice is paid is a decrease of the appropriation. The appropriation and the encumbrance cancel one another.

The Reserve for Encumbrances account is a reserve of the Fund Balance, indicating the entire Fund Balance is not available for spending. This reserve account performs the same function as a Reserve for the Inventory of Supplies. Notice the total of the Fund Balance is the same in the lapsing and nonlapsing statements. In addition, the amount available for spending is equal in both cases.

f) The difference is equal to (120,000 − 118,000) $2,000. This amount is probably not a significant difference if it is spread over all the revenue sources, but if it is related to only one revenue source, it may be a significant difference. In that case, a reevaluation of this one revenue source may be necessary so that projections will be more accurate in the future.

Exercise 5–2

1. a)	July 1	ENCUMBRANCES, 19x1	12,700	
	19x1	ENCUMBRANCES (old)		12,700
		RESERVE FOR ENCUMBRANCES (old)	12,700	
		RESERVE FOR ENCUMBRANCES, 19x1		12,700
		APPROPRIATIONS (old)	12,700	
		APPROPRIATIONS, 19x1		12,700

The new accounts opened on July 1 are Encumbrances, 19x1; Reserve for Encumbrances, 19x1; and Appropriations, 19x1. The purpose of this procedure is to ensure that these encumbrances and appropriations are associated with the proper year—the period ending June 30, 19x1.

b)	July 15	RESERVE FOR ENCUMBRANCES, 19x1	12,700	
	19x1	ENCUMBRANCES, 19x1		12,700
		EXPENSES, 19x1	13,200	
		CASH		13,200

c)	June 30	FUND BALANCE	500	
	19x2	APPROPRIATIONS, 19x1	12,700	
		EXPENSES, 19x1		13,200
2. a)	July 21	RESERVE FOR ENCUMBRANCES, 19x1	7,100	
	19x1	ENCUMBRANCES, 19x1		7,100
		Reversing the encumbrances		
		EXPENSES, 19x1	7,100	
		CASH		7,100
		Recognizing the expense		

b) At the cutoff date, August 31, the remaining outstanding encumbrances for which no invoices have been received ($400) are canceled.

	Aug. 31	RESERVE FOR ENCUMBRANCES, 19x1	400	
	19x1	ENCUMBRANCES, 19x1		400
		Reversing the encumbrances		
		APPROPRIATIONS, 19x1	400	
		FUND BALANCE		400
		Closing Appropriation account to Fund Balance		
c)	June 30	APPROPRIATIONS, 19x1	7,100	
	19x2	EXPENSES, 19x1		7,100
		Closing entries		
3. a)	July 1	RESERVE FOR ENCUMBRANCES (old)	7,300	
	19x2	RESERVE FOR ENCUMBRANCES, 19x2		7,300
		ENCUMBRANCES, 19x2	7,300	
		ENCUMBRANCES (old)		7,300
		APPROPRIATIONS (old)	7,300	
		APPROPRIATIONS, 19x2		7,300
b)	July 16	RESERVE FOR ENCUMBRANCES, 19x2	1,250	
	19x2	ENCUMBRANCES, 19x2		1,250
		Reversing the encumbrances		
		EXPENSES, 19x2	1,200	
		CASH		1,200
		Recognizing the expense		
	July 31	RESERVE FOR ENCUMBRANCES, 19x2	525	
	19x2	ENCUMBRANCES, 19x2		525
		Reversing the encumbrances		

b) July 31   APPROPRIATIONS, 19x2   525
   19x2   FUND BALANCE   525
            Closing unused appropriation to Fund Balance

   Aug. 10   RESERVE FOR ENCUMBRANCES, 19x2   5,175
   19x2   ENCUMBRANCES, 19x2   5,175
            Reversing the encumbrances

            EXPENSES, 19x2   5,500
               CASH   5,500
            Recognizing the expense

   Aug. 31   RESERVE FOR ENCUMBRANCES, 19x2   350
   19x2   ENCUMBRANCES, 19x2   350
            Canceling amount remaining in encumbrances account

            APPROPRIATIONS, 19x2   350
               FUND BALANCE   350
            Closing balance of unfilled encumbrances
            on Aug. 31 into Fund Balance

c) June 30   FUND BALANCE   275
   19x3   APPROPRIATIONS, 19x2   6,425
               EXPENSES, 19x2   6,700
            Closing expenses for 19x2 to Appropriations
            account and Fund Balance

Chapter 6.

Exercise 6– 1

1. The Operating Fund involves the accounting for the daily operations of the organization. The general transactions of the organization should be handled through the Operating Fund.

2. The terms "restricted" and "unrestricted" as they relate to the Fund Balance mean that the restricted portion of the Fund Balance is unavailable for reappropriation by the board of an NFP organization whereas any portion of the Fund Balance which is part of the unrestricted portion can be reappropriated by the board for new spending purposes. The restricted portion of the Fund Balance is restricted for use because it is a reserve that is not available for spending.

The account group classification for "restricted" and "unrestricted" is based on whether the donor-received contributions have restrictions on their use. If contributions are received with restrictions, it is necessary to segregate these assets into a restricted account group. If the contributions and support received by the organization have no restrictions on them and they can be used in any of the daily operations of the organization, they are listed as unrestricted assets.

The difference in the use of these terms is largely one of degree. Both relate to restrictions in the use of resources, but the restriction in the Fund Balance is a total restriction.

3. a) The Statement of Support, Revenue, and Expenses and Changes in Fund Balances.
   b) The Balance Sheet.
   c) The Statement of Changes in Financial Position.

4. The distinction between revenue and support items occurs in how they are generated. Revenue is generated through the earnings of the NFP organization. Earnings are received in return for providing something of value. Examples of revenues are book fines, membership dues, or various types of service revenues. Support is received through contributions to the organization. These contributions can be either solicited or unsolicited by the organization. In either case, they are provided without any expectation of something being received in return for the contribution. Typical examples of contributions are grants, gifts, and bequests.

5. Discretionary board restrictions in the Fund Balance relate to the unrestricted portion of the Fund Balance. A board restriction of the Fund Balance is a reserve of a portion of the Fund Balance for a specific purpose. Once this restriction has been made by the board, this portion of the Fund Balance is called "designated." The board may establish this portion of the Fund Balance for some future purchase of assets. In any case, it is a discretionary reservation which means the board can take this portion of the Fund Balance on or off reserve as they see fit.

6. The major purpose of the restricted account group in the Operating Fund is to separate those donor-designated contributions of monies that can only be used for specific purposes from those other assets that can be used in any of the daily operations of the organization. The reason for this separation is to enable the organization to clearly show that the donors' contributions are being used for their designated purposes.

7. The Statement of Changes in Financial Position provides information about the sources and uses of resources in the organization. The other financial statements do not provide any information of this type.

8. Working capital is equal to the difference between current assets and current liabilities. Under the Statement of Changes in Financial Position presented in chapter 6, this is the way the changes in sources and uses of resources is defined.

9. The investment should be listed on the balance sheet at $12,000. In addition, a loss should be recognized for $3,000 on the investments. This is considered an adjusting entry, and it is recorded at the end of the fiscal year.

10. Unrealized gains and losses arise in relationship to any securities that are valued using the lower of cost (amortized cost) or market value, or the market value method of valuation. Unrealized gains and losses are recorded as the difference between the market price of a security and its initial cost. In this sense, they are unrealized, as the gain or loss did not arise in a sale to a party outside the organization.

Under the lower of cost (amortized cost) or market value method, all unrealized losses and unrealized gains must be aggregated into two separate totals in the notes to the financial statements. If the total of all market changes from cost results in an unrealized loss, this total should be recognized in the SREF along with realized gains and losses. If the total of all market changes from cost results in an unrealized gain, they are only recognized in the SREF to the extent that this gain is a recovery of a previous loss.

Under the market value of valuation, the unrealized losses and unrealized gains are all recognized in the period in which they occur, without any consideration of previous recoveries. If they are considered unrestricted, they appear on the SREF before the excess of revenue and support over expenses before capital additions. If they are restricted, they are reported as additions or deductions from capital additions. Again, the total of unrealized gains and losses should be separately disclosed in the notes to the financial statements.

11. The following entries should be made.

19x4

June 30   UNREALIZED LOSS ON SECURITIES[1]   400
               ALLOWANCE FOR UNREALIZED
               LOSS ON SECURITIES   400
               Recording unrealized loss (in aggregate) as of balance sheet date

Sept. 15   CASH   450
               LOSS ON SALE OF INVESTMENT[2]   450
               MARKETABLE SECURITIES   900
               Recording realized loss on sale of investments

19x5

June 30   ALLOWANCE FOR UNREALIZED
               LOSS ON SECURITIES   350
               RECOVERY OF UNREALIZED
               LOSS ON SECURITIES[3]   350
               Recording recovery of unrealized loss

1.	Market	Cost	Unrealized Gain (Loss)
Texas Oil Co.	$1,600	$1,500	$ 100
Mushroom Cloud Energy, Inc.	400	900	(500)
Unrealized Loss			($ 400)

2.

Cost of Investment	$900
Investment sold for	450
Realized Loss	$450

A realized loss on the investment is recognized when the investment is sold to a party outside the organization. No consideration should be given to the entry made on June 30, 19x4, because that entry relates to the entire portfolio, not to one security.

3.	Market	Cost	
Texas Oil Co.	$1,750	$1,500	$ 250
Air & Space Technology, Inc.	750	1,050	(300)
Unrealized Loss			(50)

There has been a recovery in the portfolio equal to $350 ($400 − $50), and this is recorded as a reduction in the valuation account. The Recovery Account is recorded on the SREF.

12. Investments

Marketable equity securities are carried at the lower of cost or market at the balance sheet date; that determination is made by aggregating all current marketable equity securities. Marketable equity securities included in current assets had a market value of $2,000 and $2,500 on June 30, 19x4 and 19x5, respectively. The cost of the securities was $2,400 and $2,550 in the years ending June 30, 19x4 and 19x5, respectively.

At June 30, 19x5, there was a gross unrealized gain of $250 and a gross unrealized loss of $300.

A net realized loss of $450 on the sale of marketable equity securities was included in the determination of the Excess of Support and Revenue over Expenses for 19x5. The cost of the securities sold was based on the first-in, first-out method. A reduction of $350 in the valuation allowance for net unrealized losses was included in the Excess of Support and Revenue over Expenses during 19x5. The valuation allowance was established in 19x4 by a charge against support and revenue of $400.

13. Both events (a) and (b) represent potential liabilities to the organizations and as such are considered contingencies. There are three different ways that contingencies can be handled. They can be (1) ignored in the financial statements; (2) disclosed in the footnotes; and (3) disclosed in the footnotes and journalized in the ledgers.

A journal entry is required if it is very likely that the event will occur. There are two types of journal entries which can be made. The first type would reserve a portion of the Fund Balance for the potential liability which might occur. The second type recognizes a loss as a debit entry and establishes a liability with a credit entry. In terms of a lawsuit, this latter entry would not be made unless the court had already decided the amount of the damage settlement against the organization. To recognize a loss and a liability prior to the damage award being settled is to admit guilt in the case; therefore, this entry would only be made after the amount of the damage settlement had been determined.

A reserve of the Fund Balance would not likely be considered an admission of guilt, and if it appeared that the organization would lose its case, this type of entry would be acceptable. When the possibility of a loss is disclosed in the footnotes, the range of the loss, if it is estimable, should be disclosed.

To summarize, an entry should be made if it is likely that the organization will lose its court case. Disclosure should be made if there is a reasonable possibility of a potential obligation occurring out of the litigation. If the suit is a nuisance suit and there are not likely to be any damages awarded, disclosure does not have to be made in the footnotes. The disclosure in the footnotes should disclose the circumstances of the case, and, if estimable, the possible loss or a range of loss.

a) The event of a loss of $75,000 is likely for the Pole Town Library. Therefore, disclosure should be made, and a journal entry recorded. As the case has not been settled, it is likely that the entry to reserve a portion of the Fund Balance would be appropriate. This entry follows:

FUND BALANCE—UNDESIGNATED	75,000	
FUND BALANCE—DESIGNATED BY BOARD		75,000
Reserving portion of Fund Balance for potential		
contingency in lawsuit		

In addition to the entry, the circumstances of the case should be disclosed in the footnotes in the following manner.

Litigation: During October 19x5, a civil action was filed against the Library by the estate of the late Mr. _____ alleging the violation of an agreement whereby $75,000 was contributed to the Library. The suit asks for the return of the $75,000.

The Library has engaged its attorney to vigorously contest this action. The Board, after taking into consideration information furnished by counsel, has established a reserve in the Fund Balance.

b) The potential of a $125,000 loss for the Mason-Dixon Library is unlikely in this lawsuit, and if any loss occurs, it is likely to be in the range of $1,000 to $3,000. As the occurrence of a loss is unlikely, no journalization is necessary. Disclosure is necessary, but the amount of any settlement is so small it will not be disclosed. The footnote follows:

Litigation: During October, 19x5, a civil action was filed against the Library by a patron alleging that negligence on the part of the Library resulted in injury to the plaintiff. The suit asks for damages of $125,000.

The Library has engaged its attorney to vigorously contest this action and has denied the allegations set forth therein. The Board, after taking into consideration information furnished by counsel, is of the opinion that the outcome of this matter will not materially affect the financial position or operations of the Library.

Exercise 6-2

Kellogg Library
Operating Fund
Statement of Changes in Financial Position
Year Ended June 30, 19x8

	Unrestricted	Restricted
Sources of Working Capital:		
Excess of Support and		
Revenue over Expenses	$17,200	—
Working Capital provided		
from Operations	$17,200	—
Deduct: Realized Gain on Sale of		
Investments	(2,100)	—
Add: Unrealized loss on investments	5,700	—
	$20,800	
Sale of Investments (including		
gain of $2,100)	22,100	—
Deferred Restricted Contributions		
Received		$11,000
Total Sources of Working Capital	$42,900	$11,000
Uses of Working Capital:		
Deferred Restricted Contribution		
Recognized as Support	—	$11,000
Total Uses of Working Capital	—	$11,000
Increase in Working Capital	$42,900	—
Changes in Working Capital Components:		
Increase (Decrease) in current		
assets:		
Cash	$ 7,000	$ 5,000
State Grant Receivable	30,500	—
Inventories	400	—
	$37,900	$ 5,000
(Increase) Decrease in current liabilities:		
Accounts Payable	$ 5,000	—
Deferred Restricted Contributions	—	$(5,000)
Increase in Working Capital	$42,900	—

Chapter 7

Exercise 7–1

1. a) June 30   RESERVE FOR ENCUMBRANCES   15,200
                 ENCUMBRANCES   15,200
                 Reversal of prior-year encumbrances

                 EXPENSES—Prior Year   14,700
                 ACCOUNTS PAYABLE   14,700
                 Recognizing expenses from prior year

                 ACCOUNTS PAYABLE   14,700
                 CASH   14,700
                 Paying accounts payable

                 APPROPRIATIONS   15,200
                 CASH   14,700
                 FUND BALANCE   500
                 Closing Appropriations and Expenses—Prior Year accounts

   b) Either of the following entries is acceptable:
      June 30   PAYROLL EXPENSE   17,000
                 WAGES PAYABLE   17,000
                 Recording the payroll

      June 30   PAYROLL EXPENSES   17,000.00
                 DUE TO FEDERAL GOVT., Income Taxes   7,250.00
                 DUE TO FEDERAL GOVT., FICA   1,190.00
                 DUE TO MEDICAL PLAN   473.20
                 WAGES PAYABLE   8,086.80
                 Recording payroll

                 PAYROLL EXPENSE   1,663.20
                 DUE TO FEDERAL GOVT., FICA   1,190.00
                 DUE TO MEDICAL PLAN   473.20
                 Recording employer's payroll expenses

   c) June 30   EXPENSES   315
                 CASH SHORTAGE   10
                 CASH   325
                 Replenishing Petty Cash Fund and recognizing shortage in fund[1]

   d) June 30   PREPAID RENT   1,500
                 RENT EXPENSE   1,500
                 Recognizing unused rent as prepaid asset[2]

                 FUND BALANCE   1,500
                 RESERVE FOR LEASES   1,500
                 Recording reservation of portion of Fund Balance

---

1. The shortage should be recognized as a Miscellaneous Expense of the period.
2. The original entry for the rent expense was:

e) June 30   PLEDGES RECEIVABLE   7,500
                 PLEDGE REVENUE   7,125
                 ESTIMATED UNCOLLECTIBLE PLEDGES   375
                 Recognizing pledges receivable, revenues, and
                 estimated uncollectible pledges

                 ESTIMATED UNCOLLECTIBLE PLEDGES   120
                 PLEDGES RECEIVABLE   120
                 Writing off uncollectible pledges

f) June 30   FUND BALANCE—Undesignated   9,000
                 FUND BALANCE—Designated   9,000
                 Recording transfer from undesignated to
                 designated portion of Fund Balance

Exercise 7-2

1. May 1   CASH   6,000
                 DEFERRED RESTRICTED
                     CONTRIBUTIONS   6,000
                     Harold Miner Fund   6,000
                 Establishing the Harold Miner Fund

   June 15[1]   EXPENSES—Restricted   1,700
                 Harold Miner Fund   1,700
                     CASH   1,700
                 Recognizing expenditure for book purchases

                 DEFERRED RESTRICTED
                     CONTRIBUTIONS   1,700
                 CONTRIBUTIONS—Support   1,700
                 Recognizing increase in support and
                 reduction in liabilities

2. *Unrestricted Account Group:*

   June 10   EXPENSES   500
                 Regional History   500
                     CASH   500
                 Recognizing expenses made in anticipation of federal grant

   June 30   DUE FROM RESTRICTED GROUP   500
                 EXPENSES   500
                     Regional History   500
                 Recognizing amount due unrestricted account
                 group from restricted account group

                 RENT EXPENSE   3,600
                     CASH   3,600

1. The encumbrance entry is omitted, but it could have been included.

Restricted Account Group:

June 30	EXPENSES	500	
	Federal Grant	500	
	DUE TO UNRESTRICTED GROUP		500

Recognition of expenses paid by unrestricted
account group in restricted account group accounts

Chapter 8.

Exercise 8–1

1. a) Capital additions are increases in the Fund Balance of an endowment. Capital additions can arise from three main sources. These sources are gifts, net realized gains, or net investment income. If these amounts are contributing to increases in the principal of an endowment, they should not be recognized as revenues or as other types of income because they are permanently restricted for use once they become part of the endowment's principal, whereas revenues are not restricted in this manner.

b) The total-return concept has developed as a definition of the return earned on an endowment. Under the total-return concept, the return is considered to be the net realized gains of the endowment as well as the investment income. In some cases, even the unrealized gains and losses are part of the total return. Without adopting the total-return concept, the return on an endowment is considered to be the investment income earned only.

c) Quasi endowments are established by the NFP organization itself, rather than by an outside donor. As the NFP organization has established the endowment, the endowment can operate as a discretionary endowment. This type of endowment can be established and closed at the discretion of the board.

d) The spending rate is established as part of the total-return concept. It is the percentage of the total return that is available for spending. It is a rate that is established by the board.

e) An investment pool is formed by a group of endowments when they merge their assets into one endowment fund. The group shares the income and the net realized gains in the investment pool. The main advantages of this type of arrangement arise from sharing the risk of investing, increases in the efficiency of investment decisions, and the possibility of lower commission charges.

Exercise 8–2

1. *Cross Endowment*[1]

---

1. These entries record the transfer of cash between the two funds and the recognition of a capital addition in the endowment.

June 30	GAIN ON SALE OF INVESTMENTS	27,000	
	CAPITAL ADDITIONS— Net Realized Gain		27,000

Recognizing capital addition equal to net gains on the investments

June 30	DUE TO OPERATING FUND—Restricted	30,000	
	CASH		30,000

Recording transfer of cash to Operating Fund

Operating Fund—Restricted

June 30	CASH	30,000	
	DEFERRED RESTRICTED REVENUE		30,000

Recognizing liability on cash received from Cross Endowment

2. *Lord Harold Endowment*

Oct. 1	CASH	6,000	
	DUE TO OPERATING FUND—Unrestricted		6,000

Recording net income received by endowment

Oct. 1	CASH	35,000	
	GAIN ON SALE OF INVESTMENTS		5,000
	INVESTMENTS		30,000

Recording realized gains on sale of investments

Oct. 1	GAIN ON SALE OF INVESTMENTS	5,000	
	DUE TO OPERATING FUND—Unrestricted	6,000	
	CASH		11,000

Forwarding cash to Operating Fund and writing off
liability and gain

Operating Fund—Unrestricted

Oct. 1	CASH	11,000	
	REVENUE FROM INVESTMENTS—		
	Endowments		11,000

Recording receipt of cash from endowment[2]

3. *Ross Endowment*

July 1	INVESTMENT INCOME (or Due		
	to Operating Fund)	18,000	
	TRANSFERS TO OPERATING FUND	7,000	
	CASH		25,000

Forwarding cash to Operating Fund equal to spending rate of 10%[3]

---

2. A "Due from" account had not been recognized in the accounts of Operating Fund prior to Oct. 1 because all the information became available on that date.

3. The amount available to Operating Fund is determined by multiplying the total cost value of the securities, $250,000, by the spending rate of 10%. This computation makes $25,000 available to the Operating Fund. Of this amount, $18,000 is

Operating Fund—Unrestricted

July 1	CASH	25,000	
	TRANSFERS FROM ENDOWMENT		7,000
	REVENUE FROM ENDOWMENTS		18,000

Recording receipt of cash from Operating Fund

Exercise 8–3

1. a)

	Shares	Computation
Endowment X	1,467	$110,000/75$
Endowment Y	960	$(15,000 + 57,000)/75$
Total	2,427	

b) $\$17,000 + \$20,000 = \$37,000/2,427 = \$15.245$ per share

Endowment X $1,467 \times \$15.245 = \$22,364.42$
Endowment Y $960 \times 15.245 = \underline{\$14,635.20}$
$\$36,999.62$[1]

2. a)

FUND BALANCE—Endowment A	50,000[2]	
RESERVE FOR REALIZED GAINS AND LOSSES	9,000	
CASH		59,000

Recording withdrawal from investment pool by Endowment A

b)

FUND BALANCE—Endowment A[3]	1,500	
FUND BALANCE—Endowment B	2,000	
FUND BALANCE—Endowment C	3,000	
FUND BALANCE—Endowment D	2,500	
RESERVE FOR REALIZED GAINS AND LOSSES		9,000

Closing Reserve account to endowments' fund balances which remain in investment pool

c) Endowment A: $\$125,000 - \$50,000 - \$1,500 = \$73,500$
Endowment B: $78,000 - 2,000 = 76,000$
Endowment C: $48,000 - 3,000 = 45,000$
Endowment D: $67,000 - 2,500 = 64,500$

---

available in net income, and the rest comes from realized gains of $2,000 and unrealized gains of $5,000. The realized gains and unrealized gains account for the transfer to Operating Fund.

1. This amount does not add up to $37,000 because of rounding.
2. $200/500 = 40\% \times \$125,000 = \$50,000$.
3. These amounts are calculated as follows:

Endowment A: 300 shares $\times \$5 = \$1,500$
Endowment B: 400 shares $\times \$5 = \$2,000$
Endowment C: 600 shares $\times \$5 = \$3,000$
Endowment D: 500 shares $\times \$5 = \$2,500$ $\dfrac{\$9,000 \text{ Difference}}{1,800 \text{ Shares}} = \$5$ per share
  Total Shares 1,800

3. Unrealized gains and losses are automatically recorded when market value is used to value a security because the change from one market value to another *is* the unrealized gain or loss.

Chapter 9.

Exercise 9–1

1. a) Truck Cost $12,500
      Less: Salvage Value   2,500 $10,000= $2,000 yearly
      Depreciable Cost $10,000   5 years depr. expense

   b) Office Equipment $ 3,000
      Less: Salvage Value   250 $ 2,750= $275 yearly
      Depreciable Cost $ 2,750   10 years depr. expense

   c) ExhaustibleCollection[1] $90,000
      Less: Salvage Value   — $90,000= $22,500 yearly
      Depreciable Cost $90,000   4 years depr. expense

2. DEPRECIATION EXPENSE   24,775
      ACCUMULATED DEPRECIATION—Equipment   24,775
         Accumulated Depreciation—Truck   2,000
         Accumulated Depreciation—Office Equipment   275
         Accumulated Depreciation—Exhaustible Collection   22,500
      Recording depreciation expense for the year[2]

Exercise 9–2

1. a) Auto $6,000
      Less: Salvage Value   1,500 $\dfrac{\$4,500}{5 \text{ years}} = \$1,500 \times 1/2 = \$750$
      Depreciable Cost $4,500

   Only one-half of a year's depreciation is recorded on an asset during the first year it is placed in service.

---

1. If the exhaustible collection has a life of more than one year, it is written off through depreciation charges. If the life of the collection is less than one year, it is written off as an expense of the current period.

2. It is possible to record this journal entry as shown or to record the entry for each asset separately. The accumulated depreciation is recorded in the Equipment control account and in each of the subsidiary accounts.

Book Value:

      $6,000

Less: <u>750</u>

      $5,250

DEPRECIATION EXPENSE	750	
ACCUMULATED DEPRECIATION—Equipment		750

Recording depreciation expense for first year on auto

b) This asset requires retroactive adjustment.

Building	$60,000
Less: Salvage Value	—
Depreciable Cost	$60,000

$\dfrac{\$60,000}{60 \text{ years}} = \$1,000$ yearly depreciation $\times$ 34.5 years[1] = $34,500.

The accumulated depreciation on the building should be equal to $34,500 after the depreciation is recorded for 1985.

Book Value:

Cost	$60,000
Less: Retroactive adjustment to accumulated depreciation	<u>34,500</u>
Book Value after the depreciation is recorded for 1985	<u>25,500</u>

FUND BALANCE	33,500	
ACCUMULATED DEPRECIATION—Buildings		33,500

Recording retroactive adjustment to Accumulated Depreciation account for 33½ years of unrecorded depreciation

DEPRECIATION EXPENSE	1,000	
ACCUMULATED DEPRECIATION—Buildings		1,000

Recording current year's depreciation expense on building

c) No depreciation is recorded because this item is expensed in the current period by the library. The amount that is acceptable as an expense depends on the overall size of the library. In a small library, a $400 purchase is a significant purchase, but in a larger library a $1,000 purchase is an insignificant purchase. Therefore, the dollar cutoff depends on the specific library under consideration.

d) These library user cards are issued to patrons who are authorized to use the library. There is a question as to whether these cards should be recorded as an

---

1. In its first year of use, 1950, one-half year of depreciation is recorded.

asset and written off as depreciation or whether they should be an expense of the current period. The answer to the question should be based on whether the cards provide a future benefit to the library. An asset provides this type of benefit. As the cards' use do provide a future benefit, they should be recorded as an asset and written off over the two-year life of the cards. From a practical viewpoint, they would probably be written off as an expense when they are purchased. The entry to record the depreciation expense for the first year follows:

DEPRECIATION EXPENSE   300
    ACCUMULATED DEPRECIATION—Equipment   300

Recording half a year's depreciation on user cards. One-half year's depreciation is recorded because this is the first year cards have been in service

Book Value = Cost − Accumulated Depreciation
    $900   = $1,200 − $300

2. The entry to record the replacement of the roof, which is a betterment, requires that the Accumulated Depreciation—Building account be debited. The entry follows.

July 1, 1987   ACCUMULATED DEPRECIATION—Buildings 75,000
                        CASH   75,000
                Recording payment of $75,000 for replacement of roof

The building originally has a life of 55 years. The depreciation for June 30, 1988, has not been recorded, and at the present time the building has been in use for 25 years. It has a remaining life of 30 years. The roof replacement extended the life of the building by 10 years, which extended the remaining life of the building to 40 years.

The accumulated depreciation on June 30, 1987, was equal to $55,000. This is determined as follows:

a) $\dfrac{\$121,000}{55 \text{ years}} = \$2,200$ yearly depreciation

b) $2,200 × 25 years = $55,000 accumulated depreciation

The net book value of the building is $66,000 ($121,000 − $55,000). Once the effect of the $75,000 debit to the Accumulated Depreciation account is taken into consideration, the value of the building increases to $141,000 ($66,000 + $75,000). This asset value is written off over the remaining life of the building (40 years). The computation follows:

c) $\dfrac{\$141,000}{40 \text{ years}} = \$3,525$ yearly depreciation after the effect of the roof replacement is taken into consideration

The entry to record the depreciation on June 30, 1987 and 1988, follows.

June 30, 1987	DEPRECIATION EXPENSE	2,200	
	ACCUMULATED DEPRECIATION—		
	Buildings		2,200
	Recording depreciation based on asset value of		
	$121,000 and life of 55 years		

June 30, 1988	DEPRECIATION EXPENSE	3,525	
	ACCUMULATED DEPRECIATION—		
	Buildings		3,525
	Recording depreciation based on asset value of		
	$141,000 and life of 40 years		

3. The director is correct in wanting to establish an asset replacement policy by setting aside monies for the purchase of fixed assets. Depreciation and a replacement policy are mutually exclusive events, and there is no assurance that monies will be available for the purchase of new fixed assets, even though depreciation has been recorded in the books.

4. a) Building purchase price $52,000
   Closing costs   1,200
   Renovating old
      building   17,000
      $70,200   Total cost on books

b) Land purchase price $19,500
   Closing costs   600
   Title search   120
   Demolishing old building[1]   2,500
      $22,720   Total cost on books

c) Microcomputer
      purchase price $4,600
   5% sales tax   230
   Freight   125
      $4,955   Total cost on books

   Software Package
      purchase price $1,100
   5% sales tax   55
   Implementation cost   525
      $1,680   Total cost on books

---

1. The cost of demolishing an old building on land purchased for an intended use without the old building is a cost the purchaser has accepted as part of the cost of the land.

5. The library's building has a remaining life of 25 years and the loading dock can only have a value as long as the building exists; therefore, the dock is written off over 25 years rather than 30 years. The loading dock is not a betterment of the building because it does not extend the life of the building. The entry to record the depreciation at the end of its first year of use records a complete year's charge for depreciation.

DEPRECIATION EXPENSE	180	
ACCUMULATED DEPRECIATION—Equipment		180

Recording depreciation expense on loading dock for a full year[1]

Exercise 9–3

1. Depreciation is a source of working capital on the Statement of Changes in Financial Position because although it is recorded as an expense, it is not an outflow of resources from the organization like other cash expenses. The amount recognized as depreciation expense remains in the organization and it becomes a source of working capital.

2. It is difficult to determine an accurate value for inexhaustible collections. They may be items that are priceless, and for this reason they are not recorded at any value on the Balance Sheet. Exhaustible collections that have a life of over one year are recorded as part of the Equipment account and depreciated like the other assets in that account.

3. Land is an inexhaustible asset, like some types of inexhaustible collections. Unlike inexhaustible collections, the value of land is easily determinable. Therefore, the value of the land is recorded on the books, but the value of the inexhaustible collection is not recorded, mainly because its value is so difficult to determine.

Chapter 10.

Exercise 10–1

1. a) *Plant Fund*

CASH	1,800	
ACCUMULATED DEPRECIATION	6,000	
EQUIPMENT		7,500
GAIN ON SALE OF FIXED ASSETS		300

Recording sale of office equipment for a gain of $300 with unrestricted proceeds

---

1. A 25-year life is equal to a write-off of 4% a year: $4,500 × .04 = $180.

b) *Plant Fund*

TRANSFER OUT TO OPERATING FUND	1,800	
CASH		1,800

Recording transfer of proceeds from sale of office equipment
to Operating Fund

Operating Fund

CASH	1,800	
TRANSFER IN FROM PLANT FUND		1,800

Recording receipt of cash transfer of proceeds from Plant Fund

c) *Operating Fund*

TRANSFER OUT TO PLANT FUND	500	
CASH		500

Recording transfer of proceeds of $500 from sale back to Plant Fund

Plant Fund

CASH	500	
TRANSFER IN FROM OPERATING FUND		500

Recording receipt of $500 cash transfer back into Plant Fund
from Operating Fund

2. Computation:

a) $\dfrac{\$900 \text{ Accumulated Depreciation to Date}}{10 \text{ (Number of Years Required to Accumulate Depreciation)}} = \$90$ yearly depreciation

b) $90 yearly depreciation $\times\ 9\,/\,12 = \$67.50$.

The calculation for the nine months for which depreciation has to be computed.

DEPRECIATION EXPENSE	67.50	
ACCUMULATED DEPRECIATION		67.50

Updating depreciation for nine-month period from June of
previous calendar year to Apr. 1

3.

LOSS ON RETIREMENT OF FIXED ASSETS	200	
ACCUMULATED DEPRECIATION	2,500[1]	
EQUIPMENT		2,700

Recording retirement of a fixed asset with book value of $200

---

1. Accumulated depreciation is difference between asset's original cost ($2,700)
and its net asset value or book value of $200.

4. a) Computation:

$10,000 principal[2] × 10 interest rate = $1,000 yearly interest

$$\frac{\$1,000 \text{ yearly interest}}{2} = \$500 \text{ interest in first six-month period,}$$
ending Jan. 1, 19x8

Jan. 1 19x8	INTEREST EXPENSE	500	
	CASH		500
	Recording payment of interest expense on serial debt		

Jan. 1 19x8	LONG-TERM DEBT PAYABLE—Current	2,000	
	CASH		2,000
	Recording payment of $2,000 on principal		

b) Computation:

$8,000 principal[3] × .10 interest rate = $800 yearly interest

$$\frac{\$800 \text{ yearly interest}}{2} = \$400 \text{ interest in second six-month period,}$$
ending July 1, 19x8

June 30 19x8	INTEREST EXPENSE	400	
	INTEREST PAYABLE		400
	Recording adjusting entry for interest expense at end of year		

c)

July 1 19x8	INTEREST PAYABLE	400	
	CASH		400
	Recording payment of interest and reduction of liability interest payable at beginning of next fiscal year		

July 1 19x8	LONG-TERM DEBT PAYABLE—Current	2,000	
	CASH		2,000
	Recording payment of $2,000 on principal		

5. a)

Mar. 31 19x5	CASH	5,200	
	DISCOUNT ON NOTES PAYABLE	500	
	Notes Payable		5,700
	Recording discount and notes payable		

b) Computation:

The interest expense which will be recorded on this note is $500. The $500 interest expense is for a six-month period; therefore, for the period from

---

2. $10,000 is used to compute the interest expense rather than the $12,000 which is owed as of June 30, 19x7, because a $2,000 serial payment is made on July 1, 19x7 (not shown).

3. $8,000 is used to compute the interest expense, rather than $10,000, because of $2,000 serial payment made on Jan. 1.

March 31 to June 30, a three-month period, half the interest expense or $250 should be recorded.

	June 30	INTEREST EXPENSE	250	
	19x5	DISCOUNT ON NOTES PAYABLE		250
		Recording interest expense as adjusting entry on June 30 for half the discount on the notes		
c)	Sept. 30	NOTES PAYABLE	5,700	
	19x5	INTEREST EXPENSE	250	
		DISCOUNT ON NOTES PAYABLE		250
		CASH		5,700
		Recording payment of the note and write-off of remainder of discount as interest expense		

6.	CASH	88,500	
	INVESTMENTS		83,000
	GAIN ON SALE OF INVESTMENTS		5,500
	Recording sale of investments at gain of $5,500		
	GAIN ON SALE OF INVESTMENTS	5,500	
	DEFERRED RESTRICTED CONTRIBUTIONS		5,500
	Recording transfer of gain to deferred restricted account[4]		

Chapter 11.

Exercise 11–1

1. A consolidated financial statement eliminates all interrelated liabilities, receivables, or other similar interrelated accounts that exist between two or more separate organizational or accounting groups within one organization. This method views the whole organization as being of primary importance, and its parts of secondary importance. The combined approach modifies this view. It regards the parts to be of equal importance with the overall organization. When combined financial statements are prepared, they do not eliminate the interrelated accounts. The balances in these interrelated accounts are simply totaled to arrive at the totals for the combined financial statements.

An NFP organization uses the combined approach more than the consolidated approach. When separate subdivisions of a specific fund exist, the consolidated approach may be used to eliminate interrelated receivables and payables.

2. There may be an easy solution to this problem. A supplemental schedule can be developed which shows the *cash* disbursements and receipts. This schedule would

---

4. This assumes that the gain on the sale of investments is required to become part of the restricted portion of the Plant Fund.

satisfy the board members because financial statements prepared on a cash basis generally consist mainly of this type of inflow-outflow information. This supplemental schedule should clearly be marked as "cash based." If possible, it should only be issued to the board, and it should not be issued as part of the financial report issued to the general public. It would be possible to prepare this schedule on a program or object basis, or in fact any acceptable basis. The supplemental schedules provide a flexible means for additional financial information to be included with the financial reports.

Exercise 11-2

1. Simply stated, the major purpose of the special journals is to provide an easier way of recording journal entries rather than in the general journal. When certain types of entries tend to repeat themselves, it is advisable to establish a special journal to record these entries.

2. Once the closing entries have been made, the temporary accounts no longer have balances in them. These temporary accounts are composed of revenues, support, expenses, and the budgetary accounts, except those encumbrances that are still outstanding at the end of the fiscal year.

Bright Mountain Library
Operating Fund
Post-Closing Trial Balance
June 30, 19x4

	Debit	Credit
Cash	$ 15,000	$
Due from the Federal Government	75,000	
Due from the State	35,000	
Accounts Payable		46,000
Long-Term Debt Payable		68,000
Fund Balance[1]		(1,000)
Reserve for Encumbrances		12,000
Encumbrances	12,000	
Appropriations		12,000
	$137,000	$137,000

1. Computation of the balance in the Fund Balance account:

Beginning Balance	$ 14,200
Add: Revenue and Support	596,800
Deduct: Expenses	(600,000)
Balance	$ 11,000
Deduct: Reserve for Encumbrances	(12,000)
Balance at Year-End (Deficit)	$ (1,000)

Chapter 12.

Exercise 12–1

1. (1) Percentage of Mandated Expenses and Transfers:

$$\frac{(.25 \times \$215,863.75) + 0}{\$212,050} = 25.45\%$$

(2) Discretionary Fund Balance:

$$\frac{\$17,000 + \$1,471,542.50}{\$4,945 + \$17,000 + \$1,432,967.50} = 102.3\%$$

(3) Fund Balance Ratio: $\dfrac{\$1,488,542.50}{\$3,654,285} = 40.7\%$

(4) Spending Ratio: $\dfrac{\$212,050}{\$215,863.75 + 0} = .982$

(5) Excess/Deficiency Ratio (Operating Fund):

$$\frac{\$43,675}{\$198,300} = 22\% \text{ (Unusually high)}$$

(6) Governmental Support: $\dfrac{\$167,500}{\$212,050} = 78.9\%$

(7) Rate of Return on Investments:

$$\frac{\$2,700 + \$20,000}{(1,868,000 + 1,917,000)/2} = 1.2\% \text{ (Very low)}$$

(8) Debt Ratio: $\dfrac{\$300,000}{\$3,654,285} = 8.2\%$

(9) Fund Balance Coverage:

$$\frac{\$60,192.75 + \$1,439.299.75 + \$150,000}{\$263,000} = 6.27 \text{ times}$$

(10) Operating Debt Ratio: As no debt was incurred in the current period, this ratio was not computed.

(11) Plant Aging Ratio: $\dfrac{\$51,700}{\$525,000} = 9.8\%$

(12) Cash Turnover: $\dfrac{\$215,863.75 + 0}{(\$146,220 + \$103,500)1^1/2} = 1.73 \text{ times (Very low)}$

The $1,000 deficit can be shown as a debit in the trial balance or as a deduction in the credit column of the trial balance. Both methods are acceptable, but in either case there will be a debit balance of $1,000 in the Fund Balance account in the ledger.

1. Cash data are reported only on a yearly basis by the Fines Library.

2. a) (1) A large percentage of the library's expenses and transfers are mandated. This affects the library's ability to respond to changes by financially supporting the change. (2) There has been an increase from the previous year in the amount of discretionary fund balances available. This allows the library to have surplus resources available for spending. (3) It is difficult to interpret anything from this ratio without additional information. (4) The library's expenses and mandatory transfers are less than its revenue and support. This effect is likely to be responsible for the increase in the discretionary Fund Balance. (5) This ratio relates to the Operating Fund, and it shows that the Operating Fund had an Excess during the 19x8 fiscal year equal to 1% of total revenue and support. It would be useful to have more information on this ratio from previous years so that additional conclusions could be made. (6) The amount of governmental support is the largest portion of the revenue and support received by the library. (7) The rate of return on investments is equal to 11%. These are short-term investments and their rate of return should be at least close to other types of short-term investments such as U.S. Treasury Bills. (8) The debt ratio is low as a percentage of total assets. (9) The debt is adequately covered by the expendable Fund Balance. The debt could be paid off by the expendable Fund Balance if necessary. (10) The Operating Debt Ratio is zero. This means that none of the debt incurred in the current year is being used to finance current operations. (11) A 75% Plant Aging Ratio indicates that the plant facilities of the library are relatively old, and if a funding policy is not in effect, a potential financial burden is likely to develop soon for the library. (12) Comparative data from previous years need to be available to interpret this ratio.

b) In this analysis, it would be helpful to have financial data from the previous two years so that a three-year comparison of the ratios could be made. In addition, it would be helpful to have some performance information, i.e., rate of returns, on short-term investments.

3. (1) The percentage of mandated expenses and transfers over the three-year period has been decreasing as a percentage of total revenue and support. (6) This decrease in mandated expenses and transfers is probably related to the decreased level of governmental support over the same three-year period. (8) It is interesting to note that the level of debt has also slowly been increasing over the period, although it still appears to be very low. (10) Also, none of it is being used for operating expenses, as can be seen in the Operating Debt Ratio. (9) There has been a decrease in the expendable Fund Balance coverage over the debt incurred to purchase plant assets. This may be the reason for the increase in the debt ratio over the three-year period. (11) The purchase of plant assets may also be the reason for the decrease in the Plant Aging Ratio from 19x6 to 19x7.

(12) The cash turnover ratio has increased over the three-year period, indicating that the library is attempting to maintain the minimum cash balance on hand. (7) This may allow the organization to keep more of its cash invested. This fact by

itself may not increase the Rate of Return on Investments, but it may affect the type of investments that are made, as well as reducing commission costs. At any rate, the return on investments has more than doubled over the three-year period.

(2) The discretionary part of the Fund Balance had decreased along with the (3) dollar amount of Fund Balance as a percentage of total assets. This trend reversed itself in 19x8, when both these percentages increased. Both these ratios may be affected by (4) the Spending Ratio and (5) the Excess/Deficiency Ratio. These ratios both showed deterioration in 19x6 and 19x7, meaning that the library was having difficulties keeping its expenses and transfers within its revenue and support limits. In 19x6, there was a negative Excess/Deficiency Ratio, which shows more was spent by the Operating Fund than was received.

The library appears to be in sound financial condition at the present time. The debt level is low, although it is slowly growing. Expenses and transfers appear to have become more limited in relationship to current-year revenue and support in 19x8 than in the previous two years. There are no major financial recommendations for the library. As long as the debt level remains at the current low level, it does not require monitoring. If that level should increase, a new evaluation would be required. The library has a high level of government support, but this is an operating condition of many NFP organizations. The percentages of mandated expenses and transfers have been decreasing, along with governmental support, and in 19x8 the library is still able to keep expenses and transfers within revenue and support inflows. This is an indication of an attempt at fiscal responsibility within the library. It cannot be determined whether this has been achieved with a curtailment in programs, but with 70% mandated expenses and transfer, there is not much room for curtailments.

4. a, b, and c) These ratios do not make any sense under a cash basis as no liabilities are recorded under cash accounting. Therefore, any numerator or denominator in a ratio having liabilities in it would have a zero balance. The zero balance would result in a nonsensical answer.

   d) Accumulated depreciation is not computed under a cash system. This results in answers that do not make any sense. No significance should be placed on the ratio under a cash system.

   e) In a cash system, the amount of investment income is recognized as the cash flows into the organization rather than when it is actually earned, as occurs in accrual accounting. The rate of return under a cash system is very likely to be different than under accrual-based accounting. It is uncertain as to whether this rate difference will be higher or lower in a cash system as compared to an accrual basis.

   f) The ratio is affected by the difference in the timing of revenue, support, and expense recognition between the cash and accrual methods. The effect on the ratio is uncertain.

Exercise 12-2

1. The answers to this question will vary a great deal.

   a) One performance measure would be the following:

   $$\% \text{ of increase or decrease} = 1 - \frac{\text{Current Year's Pledges Received}}{\text{Last Year's Pledges Received}}$$

   This measure would determine the amount of percentage increase or decrease in pledge collections from the previous year. To attempt to have better control over these changes, a goal should be established to increase the pledges collected on a percentage basis from one year to the next.

   b) The percentage of uncollectible pledges could be determined based on the total pledges made. A goal could be established to reduce this percentage from previous years. In an attempt to measure the effectiveness of collection efforts, the relationship between the amount of late pledges collected and collection efforts, i.e., letters, telephone calls, etc., should be evaluated.

   c) The expenses for the year could be divided into the revenue and support received from governmental sources. The total expenses also could be divided into the pledges collected. These measures show the contribution toward expenses by both sources of revenue and support. It would be hoped that as the percentage of governmental support toward expenses decreased the percentage contributed by pledges would increase. In this manner, the ratios will show whether the decrease in governmental support is being replaced through the pledges received.

2. Behavioral problems can develop from the use of performance measures when only one measure is used. Usually personnel whose activities are going to be evaluated are going to try to achieve the goals set under the performance measure regardless of the detrimental consequences for the organization. In this manner, the individual's goals may be achieved, but at the same time, the organization's goals will not be reached. In the case of the Custodial Department, the goal of cost reduction was met, to the overall detriment of the organization. Repair and maintenance costs were reduced to the point where the structure of the building was damaged. If the only goal is to cut costs, the Custodial Department only has to stop using materials and supplies. If the goal is to cut costs and maintain the building, other performance measures have to be instituted, such as the number of man-hours on repair, cost per repair project, and the number of repair jobs completed. Using one performance measure will always distort the behavior of evaluated personnel, especially when a great deal of emphasis is placed on that measure.

3. Several factors need to be considered before any action is taken against Mr. Jones. First, the question should be answered as to why Mrs. Wilson never exceeded her budget. To begin with, the budget may have been excessive, and the resources allocated to Circulation were more than was needed. Therefore, the budget adopted by Mr. Jones in his first year as department head was more

realistic than those under Mrs. Wilson. Perhaps Mrs. Wilson had neglected certain types of repairs that had to be corrected by Mr. Jones in his first year as head of Circulation. Before any action is taken, these questions should be answered. It may be that the budget recommended by Mr. Jones and adopted by the board was a more honest budget than the ones recommended and adopted under Mrs. Wilson. Mrs. Wilson's actual spending may never have exceeded her budget because the amounts she managed to get budgeted were more than she needed in the first place.

Chapter 13.

Exercise 13–1

1. a) Current Ratio $= \dfrac{\$15,000 + \$25,000 + \$17,500 + \$3,500}{\$28,000 + \$35,000}$

$= \dfrac{\$61,000}{\$63,000}$

$= .968$

b) Acid-Test Ratio $= \dfrac{\$15,000 + \$25,000 + \$17,500}{\$28,000 + \$35,000}$

$= \dfrac{\$57,500}{\$63,000}$

$= .913$

c) Cash Availability Schedule

Cash	$15,000
Marketable Securities	25,000
State Grant Receivable	17,500
Total Quick Assets	$57,500
Accounts Payable	$28,000
Current Portion of L-T Debt	35,000
Cash Required	$63,000
Cash Deficiency	$(5,500)

d) The library is unable to repay its current liabilities with current assets at the present time. Under the more stringent requirements of the quick asset evaluation in the cash availability schedule, the library is $5,500 short of being able to repay its current liabilities. At the present time, the weak current ratio and acid-test ratio need to be monitored to ensure that they do not deteriorate any further.

2.

Helen Cloyd Library
Cash Budget
For the months of July, August, and September

Cash In	July	Aug.	Sept.
Beginning Cash Balance	$ 12,000	$ 10,000	$ 10,000
Collection of Intergovernmental Receivables	200,000	—	—
Book Fines	300	200	200
Interest and Dividends*	1,930	1,762	1,427
Totals	$214,230	$ 11,962	$ 11,627
Cash Out			
Investments	$190,000	$ —	$ —
Installment Payment	5,000	—	—
Payroll	17,500	17,500	17,500
Miscellaneous Payments	1,000	1,000	1,000
Book Purchases	7,500	6,000	6,000
Roof Repairs	—	11,000	—
Totals	$221,000	$ 35,500	$ 24,500
Cash Balance (Deficit) at end of month	$ (6,770)	$(23,538)	$(12,873)
Required Cash Balance	10,000	10,000	10,000
Increase (Decrease) in Securities	$(16,770)	$(33,538)	$(22,873)

*Interest and Dividends:

July

		Aug.	
June 30, ending balance	$ 3,000	July 1, beginning bal.	$193,000
Investment on July 1	190,000	Less: July decrease	16,770
	$193,000	Aug. beg. balance	$176,230
	× .01		×.01
Interest in July	1,930.00		$1,762.30
		Rounded to	$1,762.00

Sept.

Aug. 1, beginning balance	$176,230
Less: August decrease	33,538
Sept. beg. balance	$142,692 ×.01 = $1,426.92 rounded to $1,427

Exercise 13–2

Answers are specific to your organization.

Exercise 13–3

1. Step 1) Base Distribution

	Administration	Custodial	Technical Services	Programs			Total
				1	2	3	
No. of Employees	—	2	2	4	2	4	14
Square Footage	—	—	800	4,000	1,500	3,500	9,800
Books Cataloged	—	—	—	11,000	3,000	7,000	21,000

Step 2) Percentage Distribution

Service	Base	Custodial	Technical Services	Programs		
				1	2	3
Administration	14	.1428	.1428	.28571	.1428	.28571
Custodial	9,800	—	.082	.408	.153	.357
Technical Services	21,000	—	—	.524	.143	.333

Step 3) Cost Allocation

	Administration	Custodial	Technical Services	1	2	3	Total
	$60,000	$16,000	$23,000.00	$ 60,000.00	$18,000.00	$ 65,000.00	
1.	(60,000)	8,568	8,568.00	17,142.00	8,568.00	17,142.00	$59,988.00[1]
		$24,568					
2.		(24,568)	2,014.58	10,023.74	3,758.90	8,770.78	24,568.00
			$33,582.58				
3.			(33,582.58)	17,597.27	4,802.31	11,183.00	33,582.58
				$104,763.01	$35,129.21	$102,095.78	

1. The difference is due to rounding the percentages in step 2.

2. a)

	1	2	3
Program Costs	$104,763.01	$35,129.21	$102,095.78
Books Cataloged	11,000	3,000	7,000
Cost per Book Cataloged	$9.52	$11.71	$14.59

b)

	1	2	3
No. of Patrons	12,000	15,000	16,000
Cost per Patron	$8.73	$2.34	$6.38

c) The results in part (a) indicate that program 3 has the highest costs per book cataloged and program 1 has the lowest costs. In part (b), the results indicated that program 1 has the highest costs and program 2 has the lowest cost per patron using the collections. The difference is due to the per unit measure chosen.

d) The results in parts (a) and (b) illustrate that care has to be taken in choosing a per unit variable as the per unit measures can provide very different views of the functioning of the programs. It is important to choose a per unit variable that is concerned with the objectives of the organization. In this case, one objective of the library is to encourage patron use; therefore, the second per unit measure based on the number of patrons using each of the collections in the three programs is a better measure upon which to base the per unit costs.

3. a) Step 1

Service	Base	Administration	Maintenance & Custodial	Accounting	Technical Services	Circulation	Reference	Children's Library	Regional History
Depreciation	$210,000	.124	.057	.086	.105	.271	.152	.119	.086
Administration	28[1]	—	.179	.107	.179	.214	.107	.143	.071
Maintenance & Custodial	213,750[2]	—	—	.0082	.014	.5474	.14	.2667	.0234
Accounting	$154,000[3]	—	—	—	.143	.37	.208	.162	.117
Technical Services	101,000	—	—	—	—	.595	.129	.198	.079

1. Includes all employees except those in Administration.
2. Includes all square footage except those in Administration.
3. Excludes Maintenance and Custodial, Accounting, and Administration.

3. a) Step 2

	Depreciation	Administration	Maintenance & Custodial	Accounting	Technical Services	Circulation	Reference	Children's Library	Regional History	Total
	$89,000.00	$26,000.00	$12,000.00	$18,000.00	$22,000.00	$ 57,000.00	$32,000.00	$25,000.00	$18,000.00	$89,000.00
1	(89,000.00)	11,036.00	5,073.00	7,654.00	9,345.00	24,119.00	13,528.00	10,591.00	7,654.00	$89,000.00
		$37,036.00	$23,702.44							
2.		(37,036.00)	6,629.44	3,962.85	6,629.44	7,925.70	3,962.85	5,296.15	2,629.56	37,035.99[1]
3.			(23,702.44)	194.36	331.83	12,974.72	3,318.34	6,321.44	554.64	23,695.33[1]
				$29,811.21						
4.				(29,811.21)	4,263.00	11,030.15	6,200.73	4,829.42	3,487.91	29,811.21
					$42,569.27					
5.					(42,569.27)	25,328.72	5,491.44	8,428.72	3,362.97	42,611.85[1]
Full costs of program						$138,378.29	$64,501.36	$60,466.73	$35,689.08	

1. The difference is due to rounding the percentages in step 1.

3. b) All cost allocation methods are somewhat inaccurate. The differences are not usually very significant when per unit calculations are made. This does not mean that the methods are useless. The important point is to have comparative dollar information about the programs in the organization. When a logical method of cost allocation is chosen, these comparative differences should tend to exist regardless of the order in which the service costs are "stepped down."

Index

Compiled by Mary Jane Anderson